Shopsmith Inc.
3931 Image Drive
Dayton, Ohio 45414-2591

Dear Woodworking Friend,

We hope you enjoy your book, and we'd like to thank you for your interest in Shopsmith. You may already know that Shopsmith is synonymous with Woodworking and the remarkable MARK V woodworking system. But the truth is, you don't have to own a MARK V to take advantage of all that Shopsmith offers.

We do more than sell woodworking equipment — we provide a complete **system** that includes most everything you need to get the most out of woodworking, including project plans, hand tools, hardwoods, finishing products and the instruction you need to develop and expand your woodworking skills. We're your Total Woodworking Company.

From our humble beginning, we have grown and established ourselves as the leader in home woodworking. We have a growing network of more than 40 retail stores conveniently located across the U.S. and Canada. And we're opening more. Our stores are unique in the woodworking industry. They educate woodworkers of all abilities through regularly scheduled classes and seminars taught by our own expert instructors. Plus, our other educational resources — such as books and video training tapes — provide a complete woodworking education. We also keep you abreast of the latest innovations and techniques of interest to woodworking enthusiasts.

In addition to our outstanding educational programs, we also offer our customers the most comprehensive warranty offered by any power tool manufacturer — The Shopsmith Gold Medal Buyer Protection Plan. And our FREE Service Hotline is always just a toll-free phone call away, should you ever have questions or need assistance. Our Customer Services Representatives and store personnel undergo extensive training on woodworking and Shopsmith equipment, so they can provide the answers to your questions.

If you have any questions about woodworking or Shopsmith equipment, please call our toll-free number (1-800-543-7586). We can also direct you to the store nearest you.

All this and more — it's just part of the Shopsmith commitment. So come join the Shopsmith family of woodworkers and find out how fun, safe and rewarding woodworking can be.

Sincerely,

John R. Folkerth

John R. Folkerth
Chairman, Shopsmith, Inc.

Popular Science

WOODWORKING PROJECTS

1989 Yearbook

Collected and Written by Nick Engler

Published by **Popular Science Books**
Danbury, CT

Published by

Popular Science Books
Grolier Book Clubs, Inc.
Sherman Turnpike
Danbury, CT 06816

Special Thanks to:
The Studebaker Family, Tipp City, OH
Wertz Hardware, West Milton, OH
The Connecticut Cane and Reed Company, Manchester, CT
Deborah Morgan-Lamar and Gregory Lamar, Elmira, NY
Shopsmith, Inc., Dayton, OH
The Workshops of David T. Smith, Morrow, OH
Wood-Mizer Products, Indianapolis, IN

Designed by Linda Watts, Bookworks, Inc.

ISSN: 1040-8002
ISBN: 1-55654-047-7

Manufactured in the United States of America

Preface

Those of you who have enjoyed previous editions of the *Popular Science Woodworking Projects Yearbooks* know that I usually start out with an upbeat introduction, previewing the plans in the book, then finishing up with some good advice to check our measurements before you start to build. That's always the conventional way to begin a woodworking book; plans and measurements are basic to woodworking. But this year, let's talk about something even more basic. Let's talk about the wood that is starting to disappear from this planet.

Please don't think of this as yet another doom-and-gloom lecture from a born-again environmentalist. I'm just a woodworker who prizes his lumber. Like many woodworkers that I know, I've noticed that it's becoming more difficult to find specific types of lumber. The wood is not just expensive to purchase, it's also getting *hard to find.* The reason for this increasing scarcity is complex, more complex than I have room to explain completely. But I'll give you a general picture. There are several factors at work:

Greenhouse effect — As you've heard many times, the global climate is warming due to increased amounts of carbon dioxide in the atmosphere. This is the by-product of burning fossil fuels for nearly 200 years. The speed with which the climate is warming is having an adverse effect on many trees. Trees can normally survive shifts in climate by adapting or moving. Antarctica, for example, used to be covered with trees. The temperature dropped and the trees moved north to warmer parts. But this happened over millions of years. The greenhouse effect may change the climate over a few decades. Trees cannot adapt to the heat or move to cooler regions that quickly. Entire forests are in danger, and there may be mass extinctions of many wood species.

Acid rain — It is not clear how acid rain effects trees. One prevalent theory is that the increased acidity from air pollution releases harmful minerals in the soil that, in turn, destroy the trees' immune system. This makes the trees more susceptible to disease, pests, droughts, and changes in the environment. Whatever the specifics, most botanists agree there is a correlation between acid rain and tree kills. The West Germans think that acid rain is destroying the vast Black Forest. Since the late 1940's, over 70 percent of these German trees have died. Now, the same thing is happening to the hardwood forests of the eastern United States and Canada.

Overuse — During this century, for the first time in the history of the planet, we have used more wood than we have grown. Trees are remarkably useful beings, and we find more uses for them with each new technological advance. Vast rain forests in South America have been stripped bare and the wood sent to industrial nations to be turned into paper, building materials, and other products. Some botanists calculate that we would have to replant an area somewhere on this planet equivalent to the size of Texas with trees, just so that once again our forests would grow as fast as we are *presently* cutting them down. But as our population and industrialization increases, so does the rate with which we are using up the trees. Soon, we may have to replant areas equivalent in size to Alaska, then Siberia, then...

At this point, many of us are tempted to say, "What can one person do?" and throw up our hands. I used to do that, but I can't any more. My mind changed when several local lumberyards began to experience shortages of ordinary woods that I love to work with. Recently, for example, I was unable to find any 8/4 oak for several weeks — and I live a stone's throw from an area that used to boast of the largest oak forest on the continent.

If you think about it, there are *two* important things that one person can do: First, you can become *informed.* As I said, this is just the broad-brush; the problem is very complicated. Detailed information is available from various media, but you have to watch, listen, read — and think. Only when you have enough information can you decide how to solve the problem. This information also helps you accept the changes and sacrifices that have to be made to affect a solution.

Second, you can *support* solutions that are consistent with your informed decisions. Legislators, political action committees, and various organizations are constantly proposing new courses of environmental action. You can help expedite those proposals that make sense to you with your votes, donations, and time.

This may seem too obvious and too little, given the magnitude of the problem. But it can be enough, provided other like-minded woodworkers and tree-users join the brigade. No one of us can replant a Texas-sized forest. But if we each take responsibility for a few trees — in other words, do just a little — then the task becomes possible.

Nick Engler

Contributors

Phil Baird ◆ Phil wanted to go into education, and woodworking seemed like a good thing to teach. So he got some formal workshop training along with his teaching certificate. Today, he teaches industrial arts to Junior high school students in the Warren County, Ohio, school system. He has built his own home — and much of the furniture in it — outside of Rochester, Ohio.

Larry Callahan ◆ Larry learned woodworking from his father, and soon found that he could build things better than he could buy them. To this day, he builds much of his own furniture, cabinets, built-ins, and improvements on his home in West Milton, Ohio. He does this not to save money, but because it's the only way to get exactly what he wants. Not surprisingly, he's chosen an exacting line of work. He helps to build, test, and maintain new electronic circuits for the Air Force.

Nick Engler ◆ For many years, Nick made traditional American musical instruments — banjos, dulcimers, and autoharps. Later, he founded the woodworking magazine, *HANDS ON!*, and helped to publish over 100 project plans, how-to manuals, and a syndicated newspaper column for woodworkers. Today, he is a contributing editor to *American Woodworker* magazine and has written ten books on woodworking and woodworking projects.

Mary Jane Favorite ◆ Mary Jane grew up around woodworkers and woodworking. Some of her earliest memories are of turning spindles and bowls with her grandfather in his workshop. Today she designs and helps to build furniture and wooden accessories for many different publications. Her woodworking illustrations are often featured in *American Woodworker* magazine. She has co-authored one how-to book, *50 Storage Projects for the Home,* and is currently working on two more.

W.R. Goehring ◆ For over fifteen years, Rick has been creating furniture in the countryside outside of Gambier, Ohio. His designs are derived from Shaker, Moravian, Amish, and other American country woodworking traditions. "I'm drawn to straightforward pieces," he says. "I like to work with designs that are familiar and accessible." He is active in the Ohio Arts Council and Ohio Historical Society, and his work has been featured in *Crafts of America.*

Jim McCann ◆ Jim has been woodworking ever since he was a little shaver (pun intended). His father taught him the basics, and he finished his education at Eastern Kentucky University. He spent time as a craftsman and a designer on the staff at *HANDS ON!* magazine. He now works in the engineering laboratory at Shopsmith, Inc., designing and testing new woodworking tools.

David T. Smith ◆ David is the proprietor and master craftsman of *The Workshops of David T. Smith,* an organization of prolific woodworkers and potters who make museum-quality reproductions of American country artifacts just outside of Morrow, Ohio. There are over a dozen craftsmen at *The Workshops.* But despite the number of workers, each piece is hand-built by just one craftsman, in a manner similar to the large furniture shops of Philadelphia and Newport in the 1700's. David is currently working on a book of his collected designs, *American Country Furniture.*

David Wakefield ◆ David is a native of Australia and the son of Oliver Wakefield, a famous English comedian. His family traveled extensively, but David eventually came to rest in Athens, Ohio. He operates *Howling Wolf Woodworks,* manufacturing moving wooden toys. He has published a book of his toy designs, *Animated Toys,* and is working on a second book of toy dinosaurs.

Contents

Projects

Techniques

PROJECTS

Text, photography, and woodworking by Jim McCann.

Queen Anne Tables

This classic set of living room tables features some ingenious new joinery.

These elegant tables will be the focal point of your living room! There are three different pieces — a side table, a corner table, and a coffee table. Each piece is designed and built in the traditional "Queen Anne" style, with cabriole legs and shaped aprons.

Some of the joinery, however, is not quite so traditional. The drawers are joined with something I like to call a "beaver tail joint." This new joint, although time-consuming, is fairly easy to make. It requires no special tools; beaver tails can be made with ordinary workshop equipment. Like dovetails, they are both functional and decorative, but they require less handwork to achieve a proper fit.

The tables themselves, like the beaver tails, are also time-consuming to make. They are not a weekend project, nor are they a project for an inexperienced woodworker. To make the project less imposing, you may want to build one table at a time so that you can give yourself a little rest between each piece. If you make all the tables at once, however, you can mass-produce many of the parts.

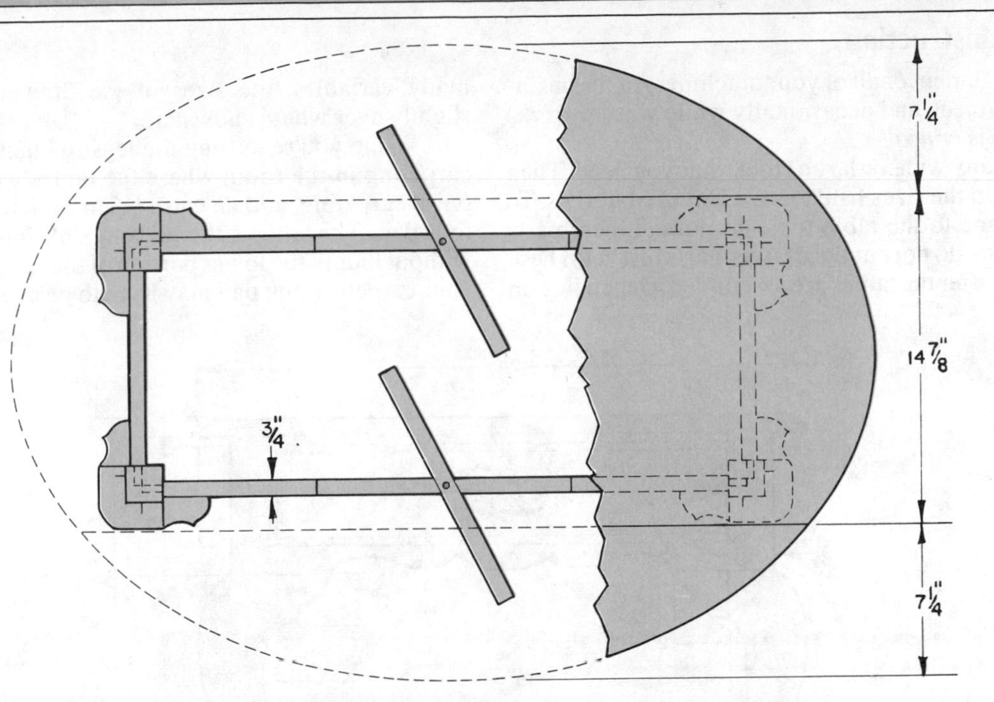

TOP VIEW

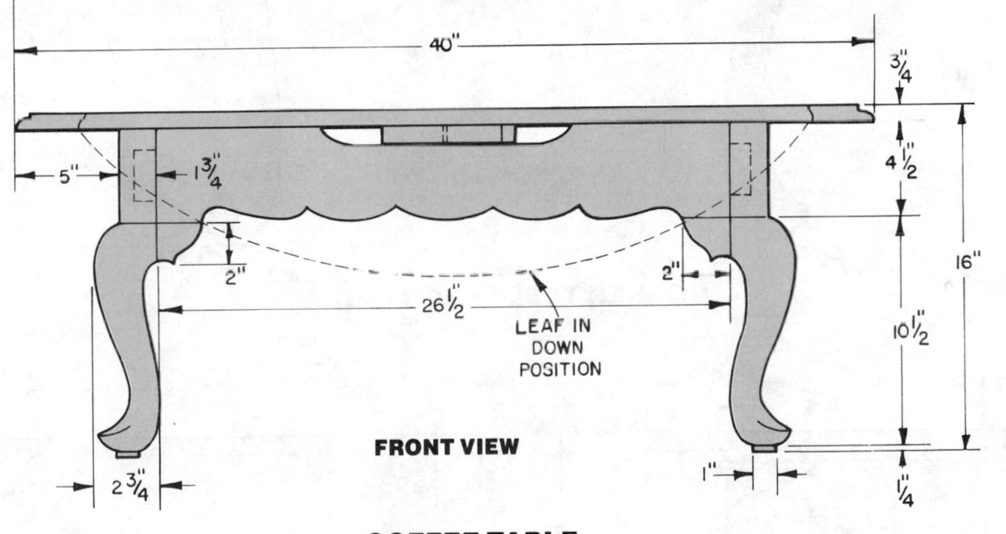

FRONT VIEW

COFFEE TABLE

Materials

Regardless of how long you intend to draw this project out, buy all the lumber at the same time. This way, all the stock will match. You will need four quarters (1″) and twelve quarters (3″) cabinet-grade hardwood, preferably cherry, maple, mahogany, or walnut. Queen Anne furniture was traditionally built from mahogany.

Purchase approximately 30 board feet of four quarters stock and 35 board feet of twelve quarters stock. Surface the four quarters stock to ¾″ thick, and cut the twelve quarters stock into 3″ x 3″ square blocks to make the legs. You'll also need about 4 board feet of utility lumber (such as poplar) surfaced to ½″ thick, 2 board feet of maple surfaced to ¾″ thick, one quarter sheet of ¼″ plywood, and 1½′ of ¼″-diameter hardwood dowel. Besides the lumber, buy hinges, drawer pulls, top retainers, and wood screws that are listed in the Bill of Materials.

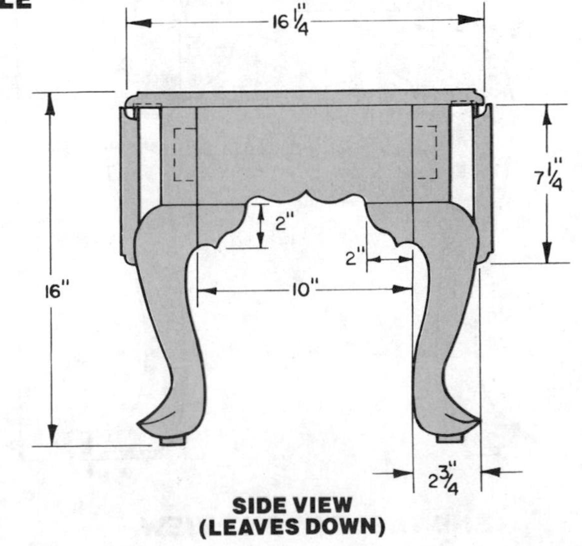

SIDE VIEW
(LEAVES DOWN)

Starting Construction

Check the alignment of all of your machinery at the beginning of this project, and occasionally while you are working. Precision is *critical!*

Glue up any wide or large stock that you need. Then cut the stock to the sizes listed in the Bill of Materials. To prevent damage to the table tops, do not cut these parts until later. Also, do not cut the drawer parts just yet. These must be sized after the tables are assembled. Depending on many variables, the sizes of the drawers may change slightly over what I show here.

While you're cutting the legs to length, consider the carpeting in the room where the tables will be used. For plush carpeting, add an extra 1/4" to each leg to extend the foot pad. This allows the pads to sink into the carpeting without hiding the lower portion of the foot. Depending on your carpeting, the pad may have to be even thicker.

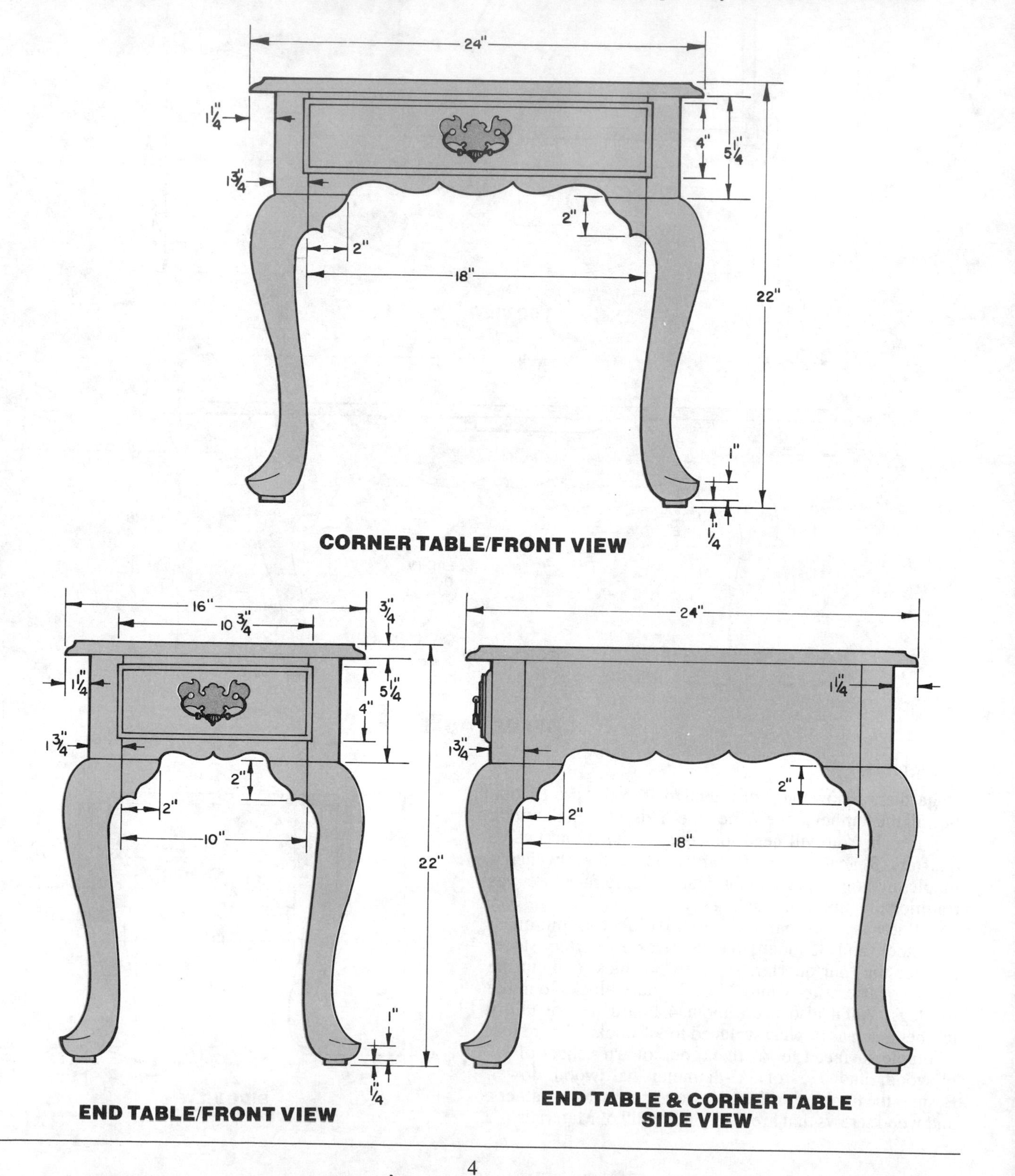

CORNER TABLE/FRONT VIEW

END TABLE/FRONT VIEW

END TABLE & CORNER TABLE SIDE VIEW

Cutting the Patterns

Enlarge the patterns for the legs, ears, and skirts, then trace these onto plywood or hardboard stock. Cut out the patterns with a bandsaw or scroll saw. Sand the edges of the templates smooth, but be careful to leave the corners and profiles sharp.

Note that the leg pattern is made in two pieces. This is because the pattern must be drawn on the inside of the leg on two surfaces.

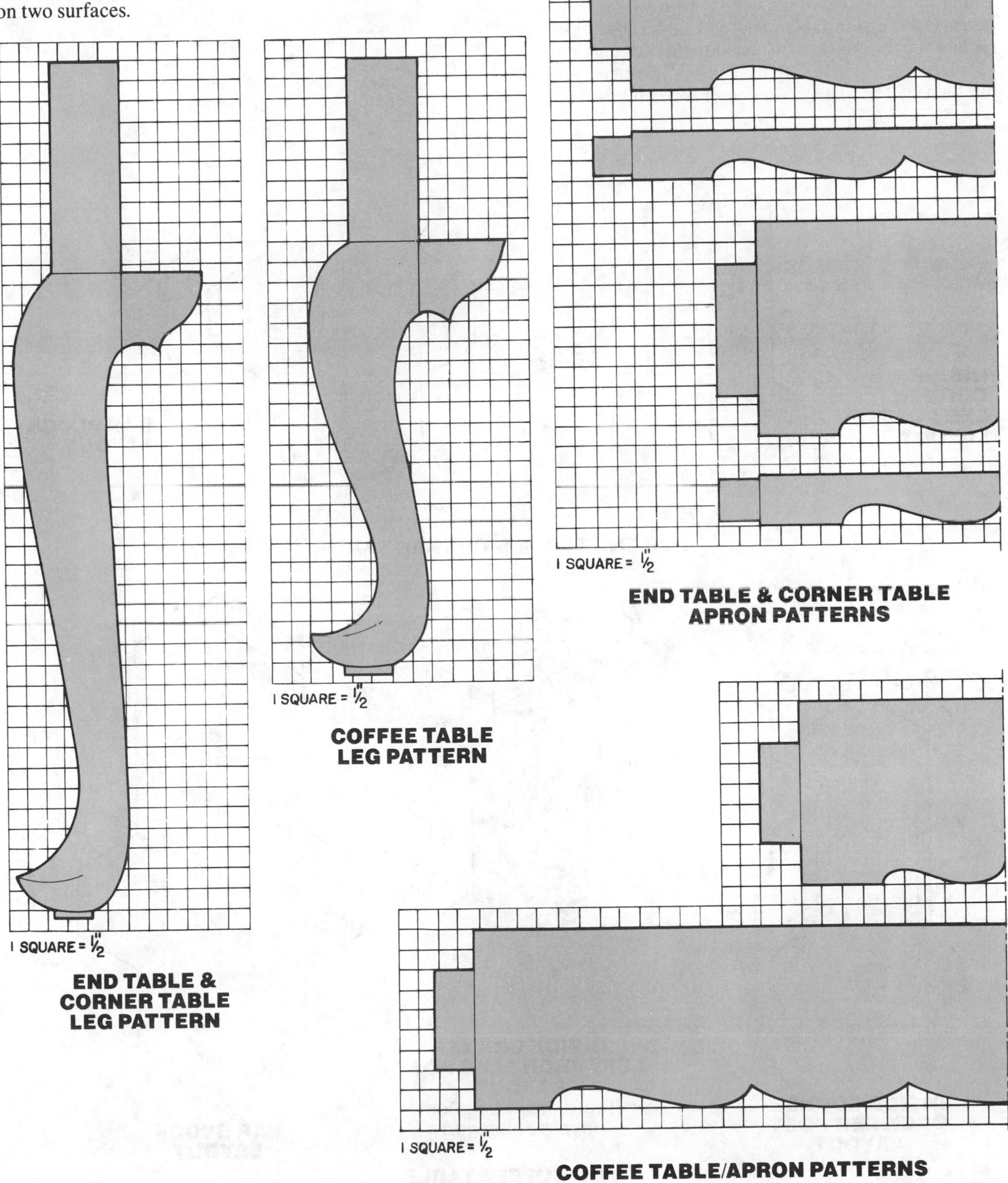

END TABLE & CORNER TABLE LEG PATTERN

COFFEE TABLE LEG PATTERN

END TABLE & CORNER TABLE APRON PATTERNS

COFFEE TABLE/APRON PATTERNS

Making the Leg Joinery

Find and mark the sapwood sides of all the leg stock. Use this to determine the inside corners of the legs. (You want the heartwood, which looks better, to face out.) Mark the reference lines on all four sides of each leg. These lines help you to accurately position the templates. Lay out the mortises and the sockets on the sides and top ends of the legs. Note that each leg is different from the others. Right and left legs, for example, will be mirror images of each other. On the side tables and end tables, the front legs require sockets for the rails, but not the back legs.

Drill the sockets first, using a 1¼″-diameter Forstner bit, then switch to a 7/16″-diameter wood bit for the mortises. To make these mortises, drill a series of holes to make long slots. (See Figure 1.) Square up the sides and ends of the slots with a hand chisel.

After you have cut all the joinery in the legs, glue the ear blocks to the leg stock, as shown in the *Leg and Ear Stock Layout* drawing. Be sure to align the reference lines on the legs stock and the ear blocks precisely.

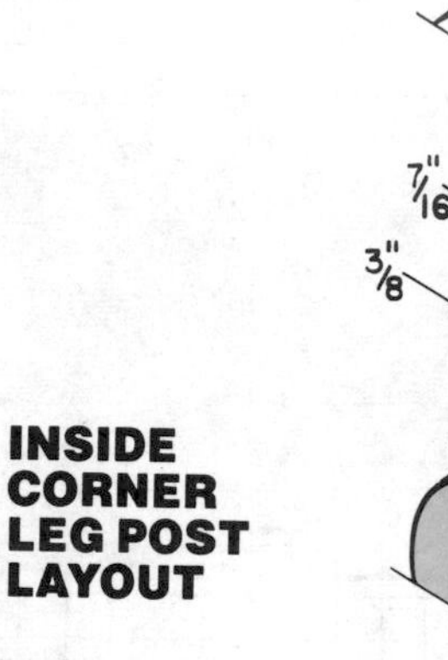

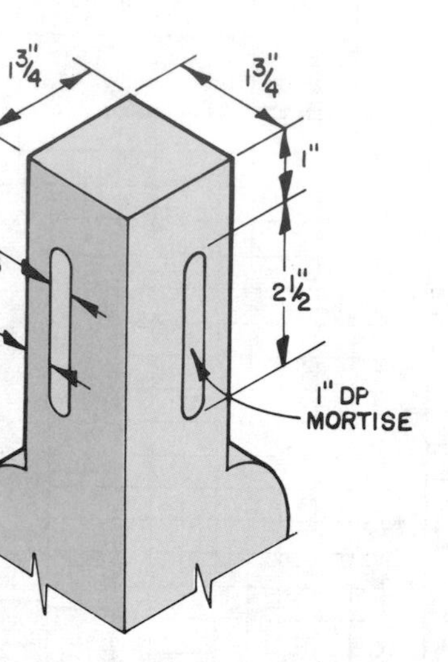

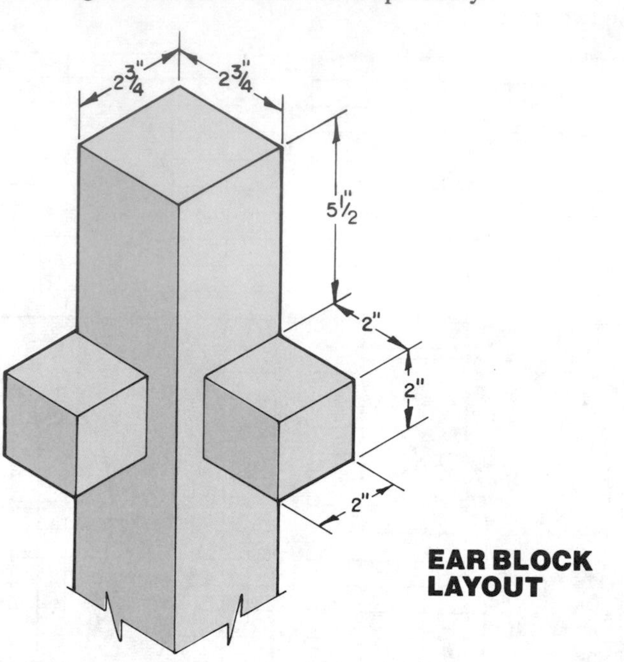

FOR END TABLE & CORNER TABLE

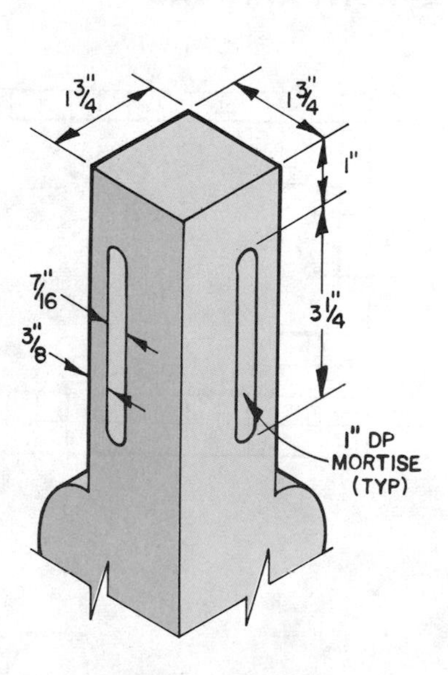

INSIDE CORNER BACK LEG POST LAYOUT

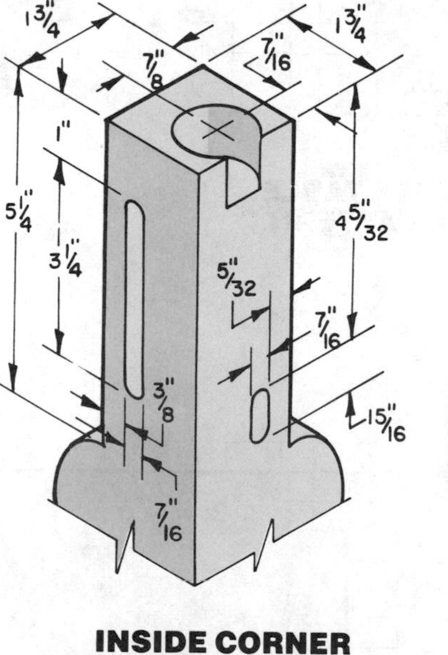

INSIDE CORNER LEFT FRONT LEG POST LAYOUT (Right Front Leg Post is mirror image.)

EAR BLOCK LAYOUT

FOR COFFEE TABLE

Cutting the Cabriole Legs

If you've made cabriole legs from a previous project, then you understand how to make a compound cut on your bandsaw: Cut the design in one face, tape the waste back to the workpiece, and cut the second face. However, these legs aren't quite that simple. Because all the legs have "ears," the process is more involved.

Trace the leg and ear patterns on the two *inside* faces of each workpiece, making sure that the back edge of the leg pattern is flush with the inside corner. (See Figure 2.) Use your reference lines to make sure that the templates are positioned properly before you trace each pattern.

Using the bandsaw, cut the faces of the leg post down to the knee (where the cabriole curve begins). Adjust the upper blade guide of your bandsaw so that it clears the ear block, and cut the waste free of the posts. (See Figure 3.) One ear should lie flat on the bandsaw table, while the other sticks up. Cut the knee and the ear, saving the scrap. Lower the blade guide to clear the leg stock only, and cut the rest of the leg shape. (See Figure 4.) Once again, save the scrap.

Tape the scrap back onto the workpiece to make the stock reasonably square again, and turn the stock 90°, so that the other ear now lies on the table. (See Figure 5.) Repeat the sequence of cuts. When you remove all the stock, you'll have a rough cabriole leg with ears. Repeat these steps for all of the legs.

Sculpting the Legs

Remove the saw marks from the legs with sanders. Small (1″-diameter) drum sanders make short work of sanding the tight curves underneath the ears.

Divide the legs into quarters, vertically. Mark the lines on the faces of the leg and foot. (See Figure 6.) Use these

Figure 1. Cut the joinery in the legs before you cut the shapes of the legs. To make a mortise with your drill press, drill a series of holes. Then square up the ends and the faces of the resulting slot with a hand chisel.

Figure 2. Glue the ear blocks to the legs, and trace the patterns onto the *inside* faces of the stock.

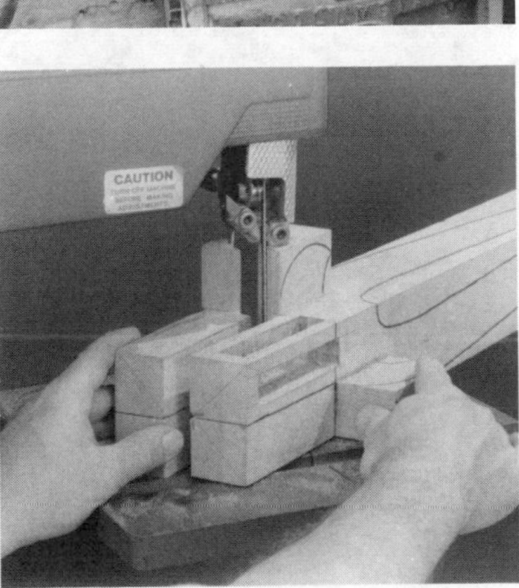

Figure 3. Cut the posts, then adjust the height of the upper blade guide so that it clears the ears. Cut the waste free from the posts. Then cut the shape of the ear. Save the waste.

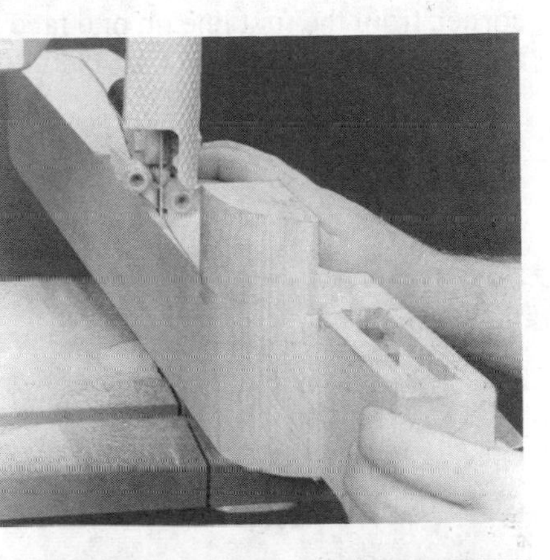

Figure 4. Readjust the blade guide and cut the remainder of the leg. Once again, save the scrap.

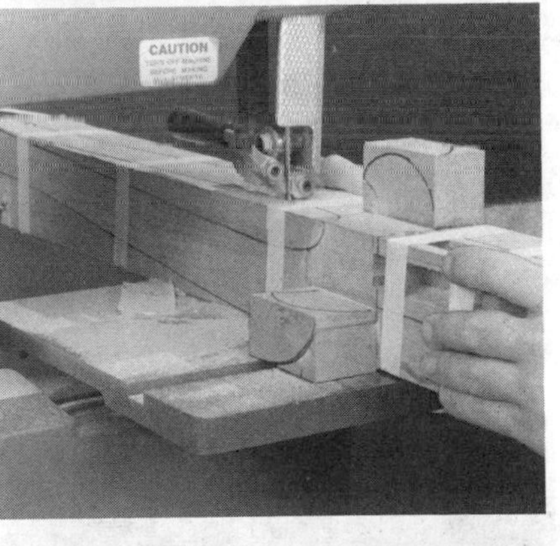

Figure 5. Tape the waste back to the leg stock, turn the work-piece 90°, and cut the other face.

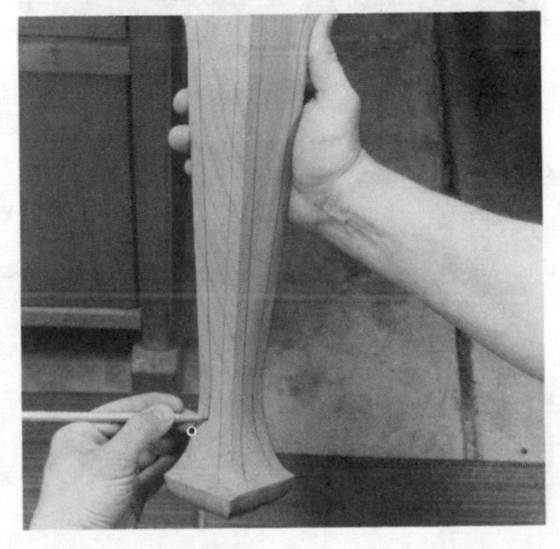

Figure 6. Divide the faces of the leg and foot into quarters, and mark the lines on the stock.

lines as references to evenly round the workpiece. As you work, use masking tape to cover nearby corners and other areas of the wood that you don't want to mar. (See Figure 7.)

Mount the leg in a vise, foot facing up. Mark a circle on the bottom of the foot to delineate the pad. With a backsaw, saw off the three outside corners of the foot, cutting from the first guideline on one face to the first guideline on an adjacent face. (See Figure 8.) Still using the backsaw, cut across the corners of the pad, forming an octagon. Undercut the corners to remove the waste.

Using the edge of a rectangular, double-cut file, round the pad, following the pattern lines. With a cabinet rasp, round the three cut corners of the foot to make a circular shape. (See Figure 9.)

Mount the leg in a bar clamp and secure the clamp to your workbench with bench dogs and hand screw clamps. (This will serve as a fixture to hold the leg while you sculpt it.) Use the cabinet rasp to chamfer the leg stock at each corner, from the first line on one face to the first line on an adjacent face. (See Figure 10.) Continue working, gradually rounding over the surfaces, a corner at a time. Use the reference lines to help keep your curves as "fair" as possible — even, all the way around the leg. Widen the flat on the top of the foot, blending it into the curves of the legs. (See Figure 11.) Continue rasping and scraping, removing a little stock at a time, until the leg is contoured as shown in the lead photograph. Repeat this process for each leg.

Smoothing the Legs

Using a pneumatic sander (if you have one), or 60# sandpaper (if you don't), sand away the rasp marks on the legs. Start at each knee and work down to the foot, always sanding with the grain. Switch to progressively finer sandpaper or sanding sleeves to make the legs as smooth as possible.

Remove the saw marks from the leg posts with a block plane. This plane must be *very* sharp, since you are cutting nearly straight across the grain. (See Figure 12.) Hand sand or scrape the legs to remove any sanding marks left by the machine sanders.

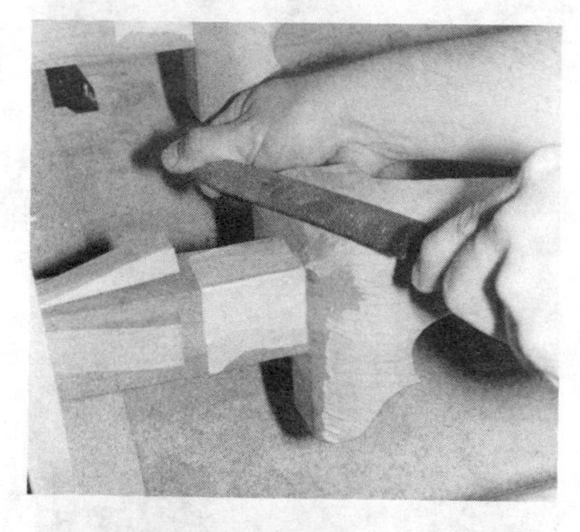

Figure 7. While you're sculpting the legs, use masking tape to protect parts that you don't want to cut or damage.

Figure 8. Using a back saw, cut off the three outside corners of the foot.

Figure 9. Round the sawn corners of the foot.

Figure 10. Chamfer the corners of the stock between the lines.

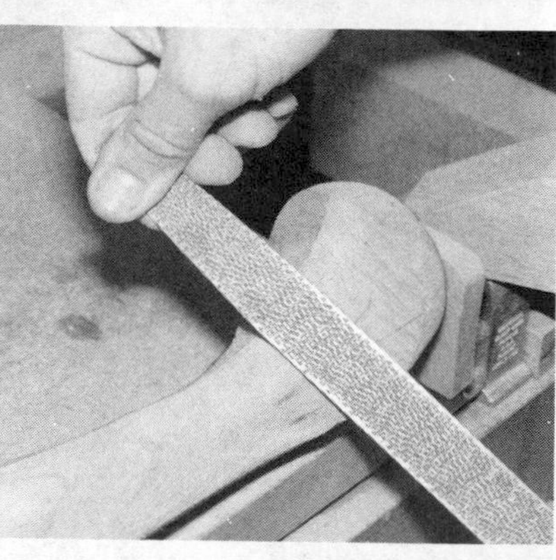

Figure 11. Feather the top of the foot to flatten it and blend the other surfaces of the leg with it.

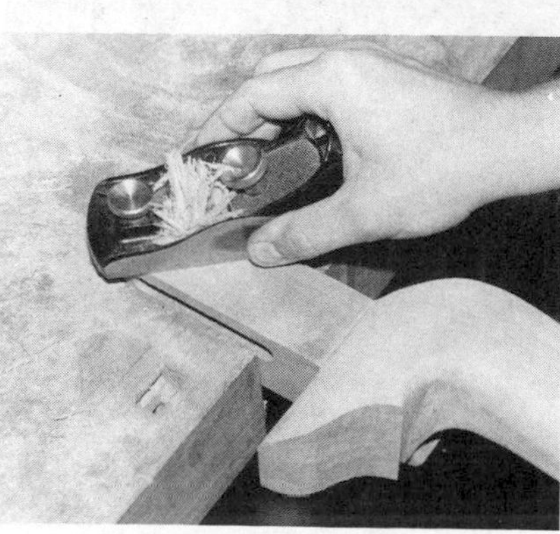

Figure 12. Smooth the leg post with a block plane.

Making the Aprons

Cut the tenons in the aprons *before* you cut the shapes of the aprons. Start by making a trial tenon in a block of scrap wood to test your table saw setup. When you're satisfied the setup is correct, cut the tenons in the good stock.

Hand fit the tenons in their respective mortises, shaving the tenons down with a sharp chisel. Chamfer the corners of the tenons to make room for glue.

Stack together and align the bottom edges of all similar aprons. Hold them together in a stack with masking tape. Lay out the pattern for each apron on the top piece in each stack, then pad-saw the shape of the apron on a bandsaw. Also, cut out the drop leaf support from the side aprons of the coffee table. Sand the sawn contours before un-taping the stacks.

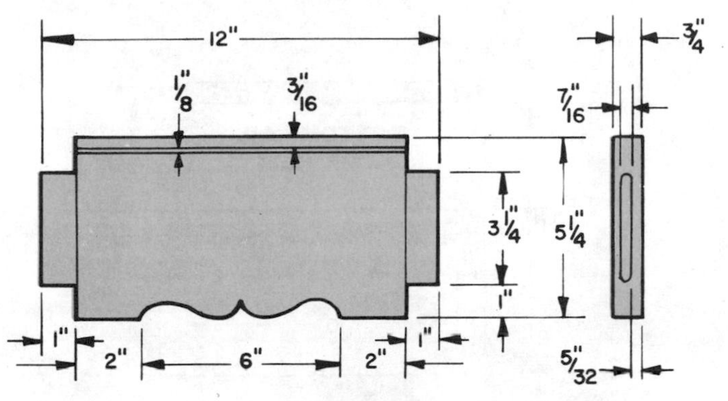

END TABLE
END APRON LAYOUT

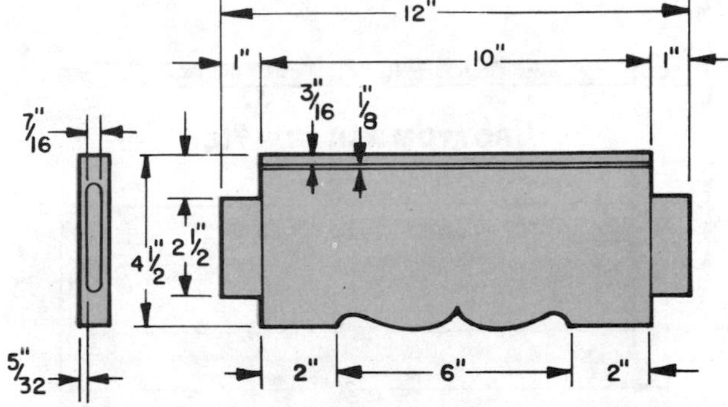

COFFEE TABLE
END APRON & TENON LAYOUT

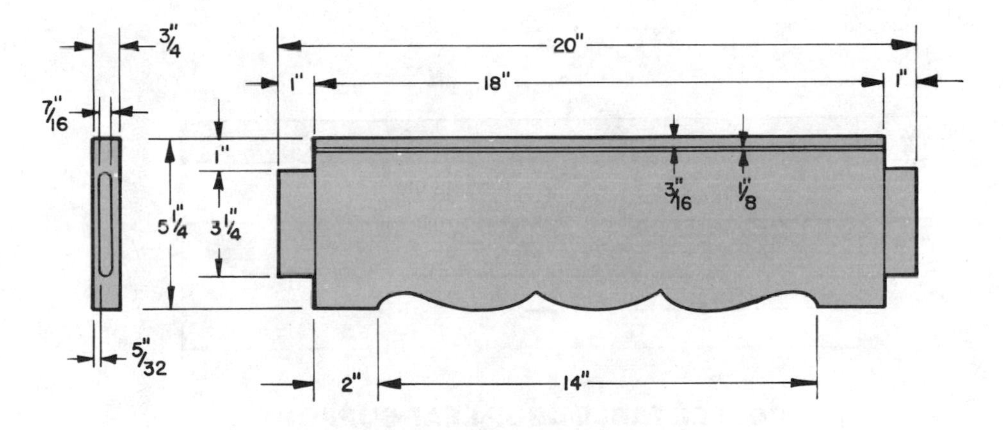

CORNER TABLE/END APRON LAYOUT
END TABLE & CORNER TABLE/SIDE APRON LAYOUT

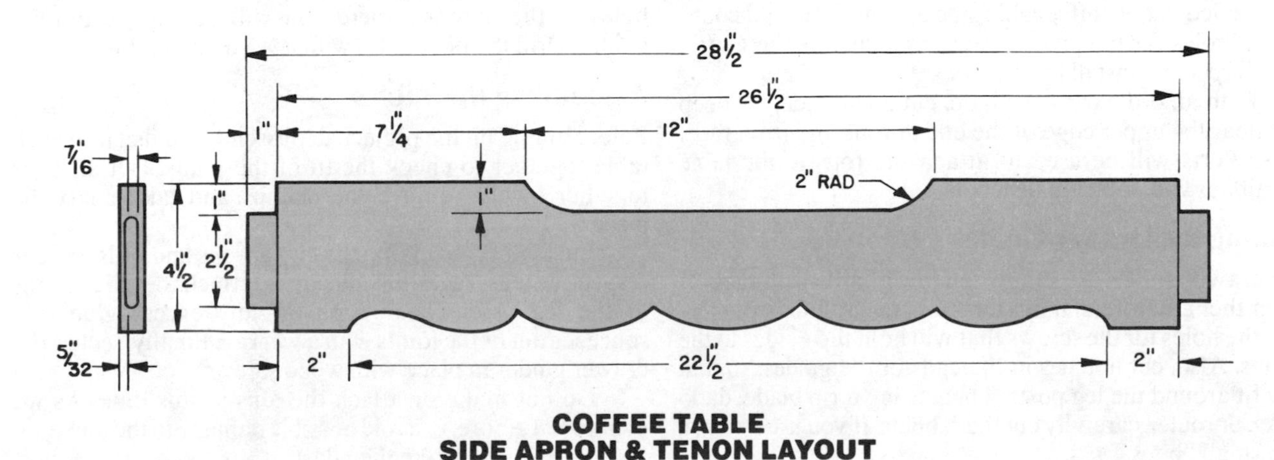

COFFEE TABLE
SIDE APRON & TENON LAYOUT

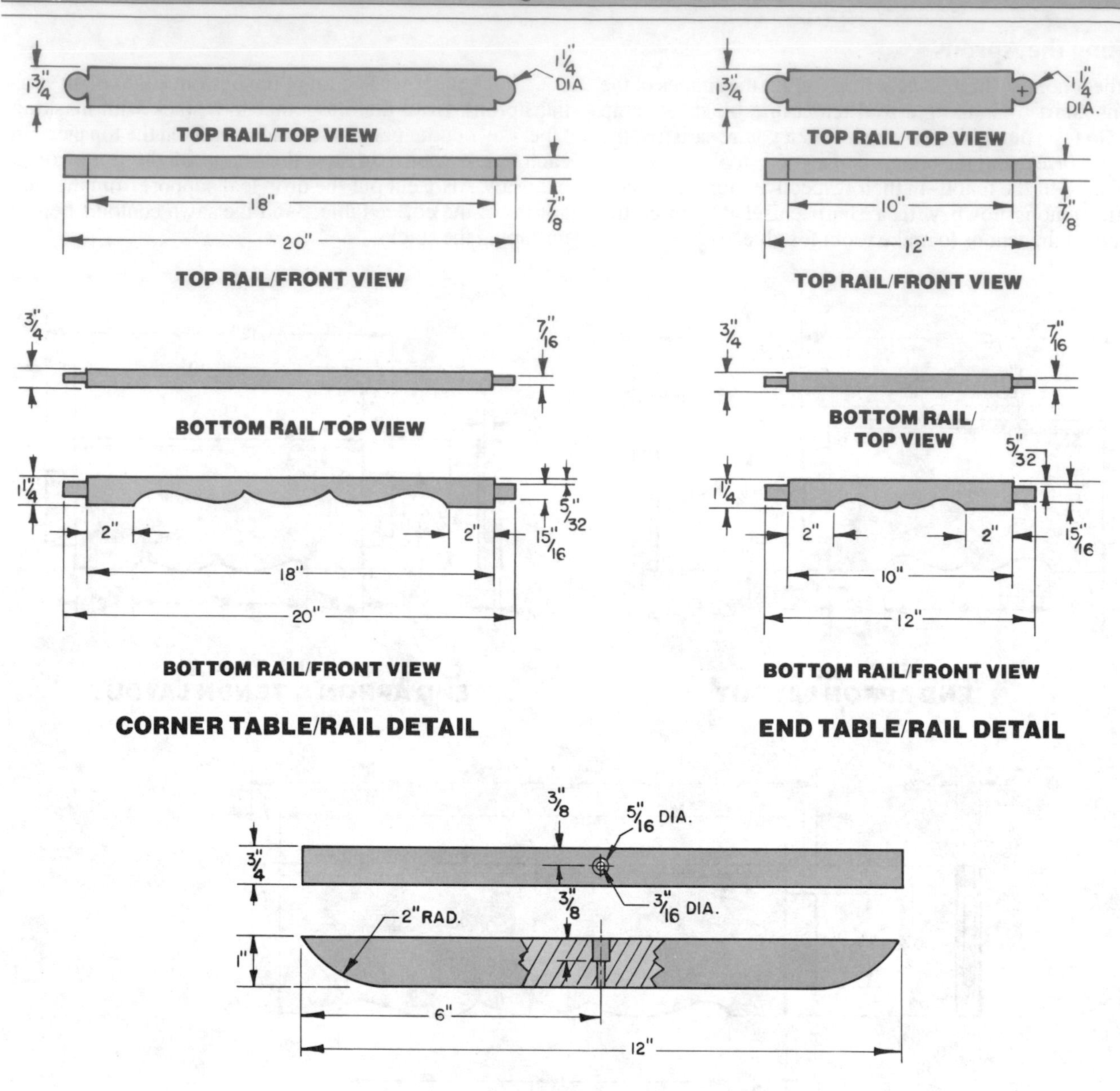

COFFEE TABLE/DROP LEAF SUPPORT

Tape the drop leaf supports back into the recesses that you created in the coffee table side aprons. Drill and countersink holes for the pivot screws, as shown in the *Coffee Table/Top View.* Install the screws.

With an ordinary saw blade, cut a ⅛"-wide, ¼" deep kerf near the upper edge of the end aprons and front rails. These kerfs will be used to attach the tops to the table assemblies with tabletop fasteners.

Making the Drawer Guides

The drawer guides are simply narrow boards with rabbets cut in them. Before making the rabbets, drill and counterbore the holes for the screws that will hold the guides to the aprons. Also, cut notches in the ends of the guides, so that they fit around the leg posts. Then, using a rip blade, dado cutter, or router, carefully cut the rabbets. If you use a router, take small "bites."

With a punch or an awl, mark the positions of the pilot holes in the aprons, where you will attach the drawer guides. Drill the pilot holes with a ⅛"-diameter bit.

Assembling the Tables

Before gluing up the project, dry assemble and clamp each table together to check the fit of the joints. If it all goes together nicely, remove the clamps and take apart the pieces.

First, glue and clamp the end aprons and rails to their respective legs. After the glue dries, attach the side aprons to the leg assemblies. Wipe off any excess glue that squeezes out of the joints with a wet rag. Finally, secure the drawer guides in place with wood screws.

Do not make or attach the tops at this time. As we mentioned before, to avoid possible damage to the tops, you want to wait and make them last.

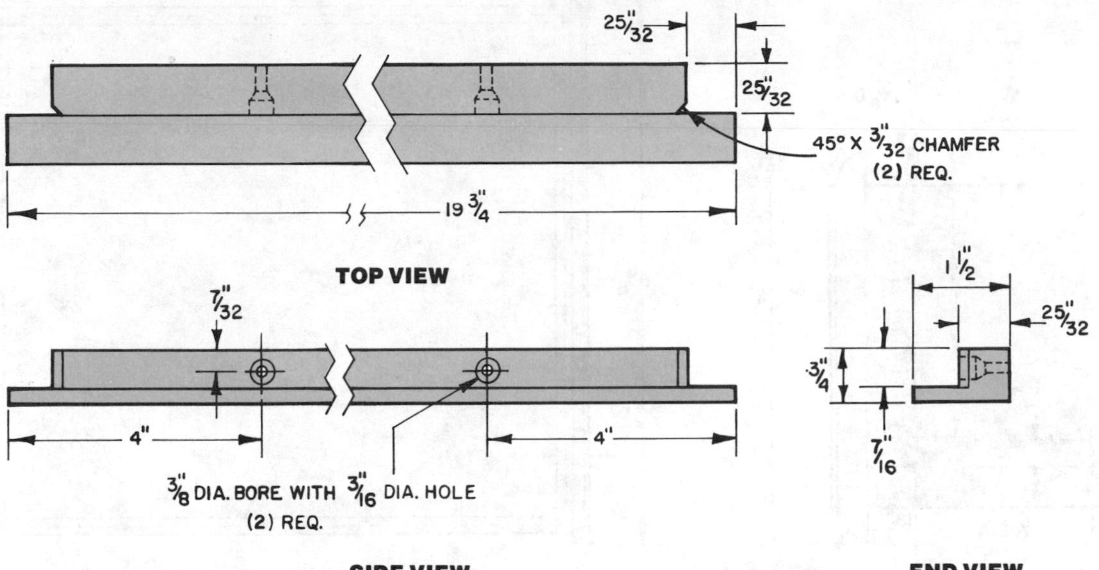

END TABLE & CORNER TABLE/DRAWER GLIDE

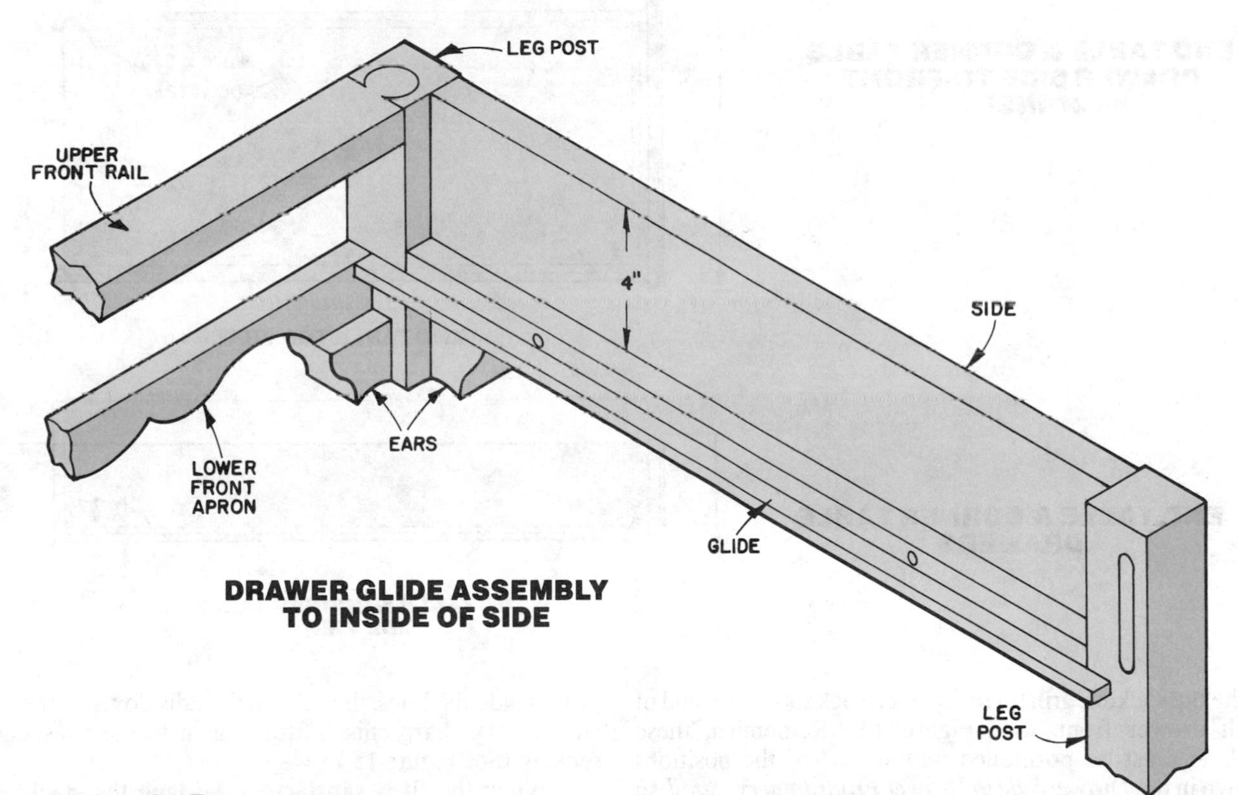

DRAWER GLIDE ASSEMBLY
TO INSIDE OF SIDE

Constructing the Drawers

Measure the drawer opening to double-check the sizes of the drawers against the Bill of Materials. If necessary, make adjustments in the sizes of the drawer parts. Remember, the drawer fronts are larger than the drawer openings so that you can cut a rabbet all the way around each front and create a lip. Also, plan to leave 1/16″ of space between the sides and top edges of the drawer and the drawer opening, so that the drawer will slide freely.

When you have re-figured the sizes of the drawer parts, cut the stock you need. Using a router or shaper, cut a rabbet all the way around the inside edge of the drawer fronts. Don't use the dado cutter for this particular cut. You want the rabbet to be as smooth as possible, much smoother than the dado cutter will cut.

Lay out the beaver tail joinery on a piece of scrap stock. This scrap must be exactly the same thickness and width as the drawer fronts. (The length isn't critical.) Using your drill press or horizontal boring machine and a 5/8″ brad-point bit, make the sockets in the test piece. When you're satisfied that your machinery is properly set up to

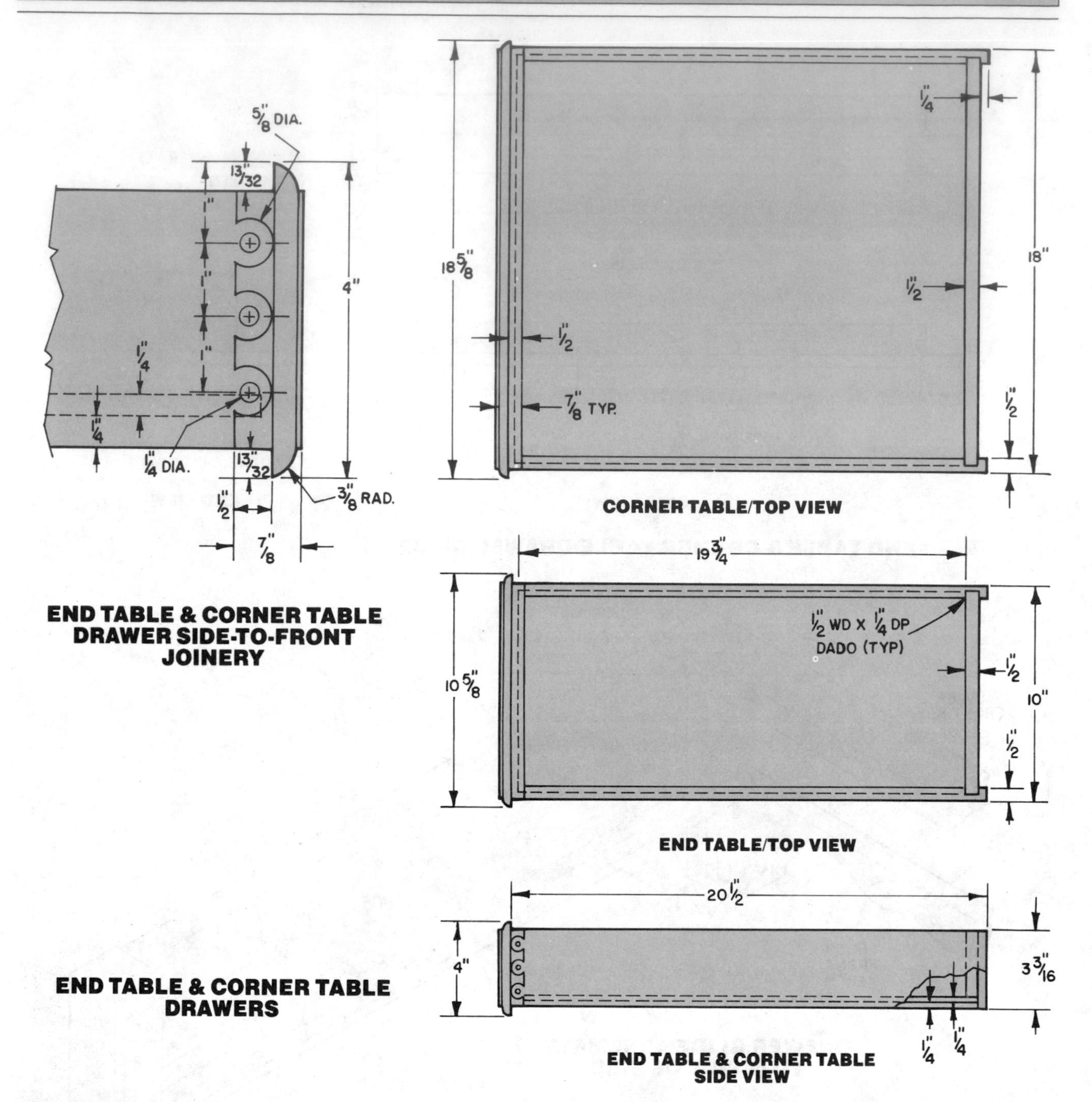

make the sockets, drill three ½″-deep sockets in each end of each drawer front. (See Figure 13.) Remember, these sockets must be positioned within 1/64″ of the positions shown in the *Drawer Side to Drawer Front Joinery Detail*, so that the beaver tails will fit properly.

Tip ◆ Do not change your drilling or boring setup just yet. You'll need it again to make the holes for the pins.

Stack the drawer sides so that the top edges and ends are flush, and tape the stack together. Use the drawer front as a template to trace the shapes and positions of the beaver tails onto a drawer side. (See Figure 14.) Cut out the shapes of the beaver tails on the bandsaw, using a ⅛″ blade. Stay just outside the lines, then shave the tails down to the lines with a very sharp chisel, fitting them to their respective sockets. (See Figure 15.)

When the fit is satisfactory, un-tape the stack. Dry assemble the sides to the drawer fronts. Then, using the same drilling setup you used to make the sockets, drill ¼″-diameter dowel holes in the center of each beaver tail. (See Figure 16.) Use these to pin the sides to the drawer fronts.

Cut the remainder of the drawer joinery with a dado cutter or a router. Make a ½″-wide, ¼″-deep dado in the sides to hold the drawer backs, and ¼″-wide, ¼″-deep grooves in the backs, sides, and fronts to hold the drawer bottoms. Dry assemble the drawers to test the fit of the joints, but do not glue them up just yet. Wait until you've completely assembled the tables.

Making the Tops

Finally, it's time to make the table tops. Glue up the wide stock that you need and cut them to size. Don't cut the oval shape of the coffee table top yet.

Using a router or a shaper, make a rule joint in the edges of the coffee table top and drop-leaves, where the parts meet. Mortise and mount the drop leaf hinges to the underside of the top and leaves. Test the action of the leaves to be sure that you properly positioned the hinges.

Clamp the top-and-leaves assembly to your workbench so that the leaves are up, flush to the table top. Lay out the oval shape, as shown in the *Coffee Table/Top View.*

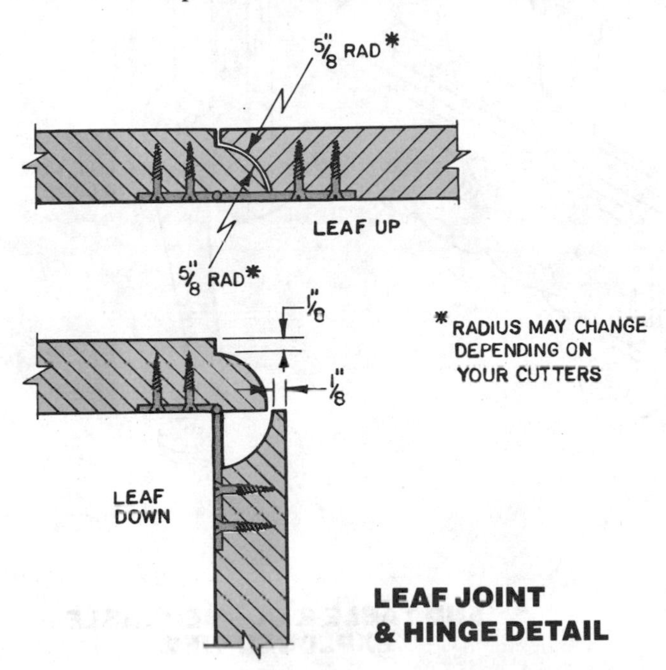

Remove the hinges, and cut out the shape of the parts on a bandsaw. Smooth the edges of the parts with a sander.

Install the hinges again and make sure that the curve of the oval is "fair," especially where the top and the leaves meet. If necessary, do a little more work on the edges with a sander. Then cut a decorative edge all around the oval with a router. Also, shape the edges of the corner table top and end table top.

Final Assembly and Finishing

Turn the table tops upside down on your workbench and carefully position the leg-and-apron assemblies on top of them. Mark the position for the top retainers and drill pilot screws. Install the retainers, securing the tops to the tables.

Glue the parts of the drawers together, and put the dowel pins in the beaver tails. Wipe away any excess glue with a wet rag. After the glue dries, install the drawer pulls.

Remove the tops from the tables. Also remove any hardware, including retainers, hinges, and pulls. Sand and scrape the surfaces until they are as smooth as you can make them, then apply a finish.

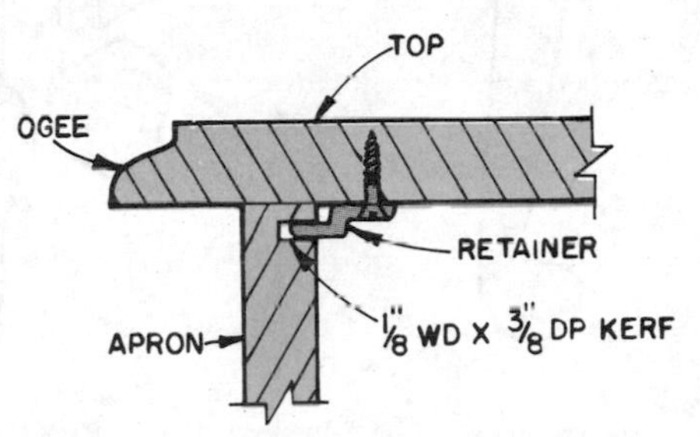

Figure 13. Drill the beaver tail sockets in the drawer front with a 5/8"-diameter bit.

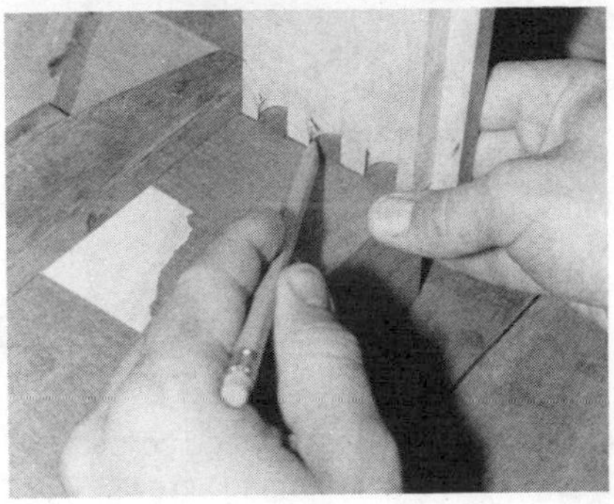

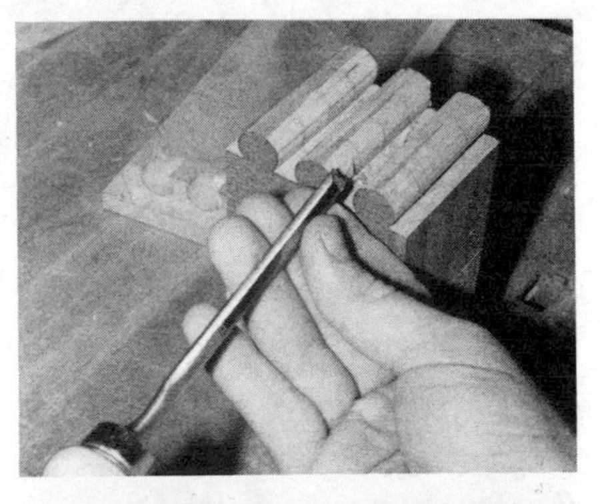

Figure 15. After you saw them to their rough shapes, use a chisel to shave all the beaver tails, fitting them to the sockets.

Figure 14. Use the sockets you have just made in the drawer front to trace the shapes of the beaver tails on the drawer sides.

Figure 16. In the center of each beaver tail, drill a 1/4"-diameter hole for a dowel pin.

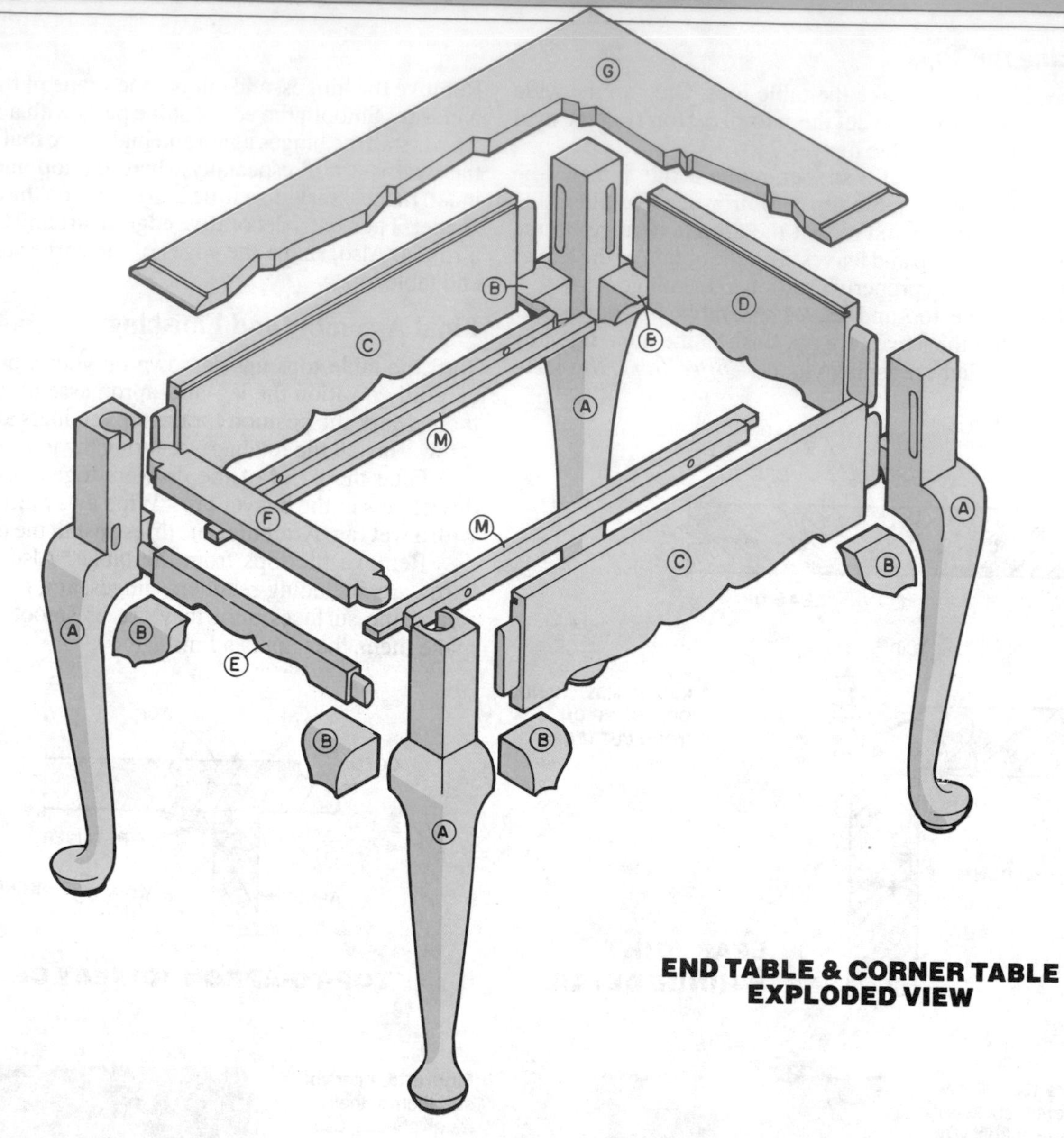

END TABLE & CORNER TABLE EXPLODED VIEW

BILL OF MATERIALS — End Table

Finished Dimensions in Inches

	Part	Dimensions
A.	Legs (4)	2¾ x 2¾ x 21¼
B.	Ears (8)	2 x 2 x 2
C.	Side aprons (2)	¾ x 5¼ x 20
D.	Rear apron	¾ x 5¼ x 12
E.	Front apron	¾ x 1¼ x 12
F.	Front rail	⅞ x 1¾ x 12
G.	Top	¾ x 16 x 24
H.	Drawer front	⅞ x 4 x 10⅝
J.	Drawer sides (2)	½ x 3³⁄₁₆ x 20½
K.	Drawer back	½ x 2¹¹⁄₁₆ x 9½
L.	Drawer bottom	¼ x 9½ x 19¾
M.	Drawer glides	¾ x 1½ x 19¾
N.	Beaver tail dowel pins	¼ dia. x 1

HARDWARE

Top retainers with screws (4)
#10 x 1¼″ Roundhead wood screws (4)
Drawer pull and mounting screws

BILL OF MATERIALS — Corner Table

Finished Dimensions in Inches

	Part	Dimensions
A.	Legs (4)	2¾ x 2¾ x 21¼
B.	Ears (8)	2 x 2 x 2
C.	Side aprons (2)	¾ x 5¼ x 20
D.	Rear apron	¾ x 5¼ x 20
E.	Front apron	¾ x 1¼ x 20
F.	Front rail	⅞ x 1¾ x 20
G.	Top	¾ x 24 x 24
H.	Drawer front	⅞ x 4 x 18⅝
J.	Drawer sides (2)	½ x 3³⁄₁₆ x 20½
K.	Drawer back	½ x 2¹¹⁄₁₆ x 17½
L.	Drawer bottom	¼ x 17½ x 19¾
M.	Drawer glides	¾ x 1½ x 19¾
N.	Beaver tail dowel pins	¼ dia. x 1

HARDWARE

Top retainers with screws (4)
#10 x 1¼″ Roundhead wood screws (4)
Drawer pull and mounting screws

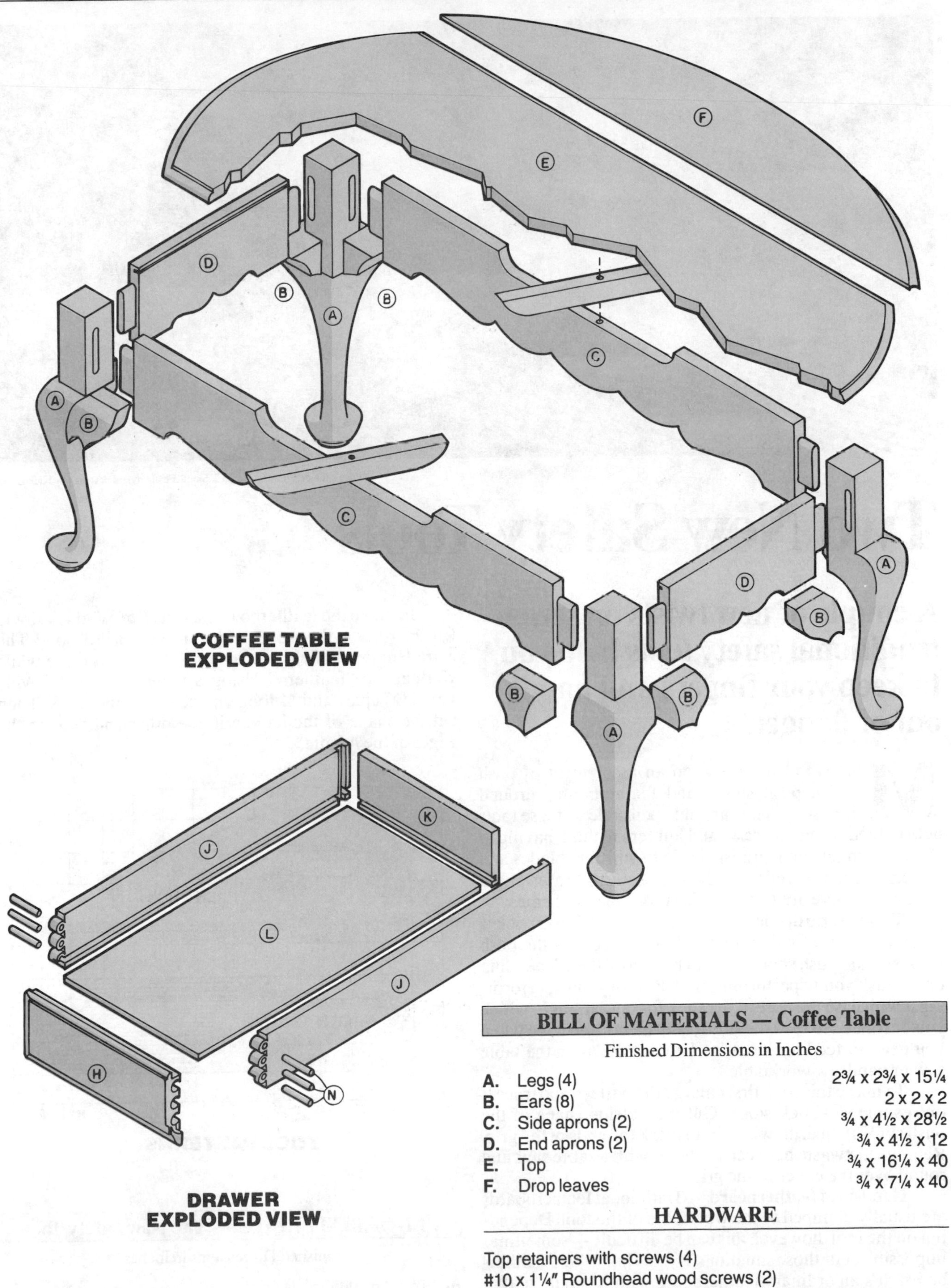

BILL OF MATERIALS — Coffee Table

Finished Dimensions in Inches

	Part	Dimensions
A.	Legs (4)	2¾ x 2¾ x 15¼
B.	Ears (8)	2 x 2 x 2
C.	Side aprons (2)	¾ x 4½ x 28½
D.	End aprons (2)	¾ x 4½ x 12
E.	Top	¾ x 16¼ x 40
F.	Drop leaves	¾ x 7¼ x 40

HARDWARE

Top retainers with screws (4)
#10 x 1¼″ Roundhead wood screws (2)
1½″ x 3″ Drop leaf hinges and mounting screws (2 pair)

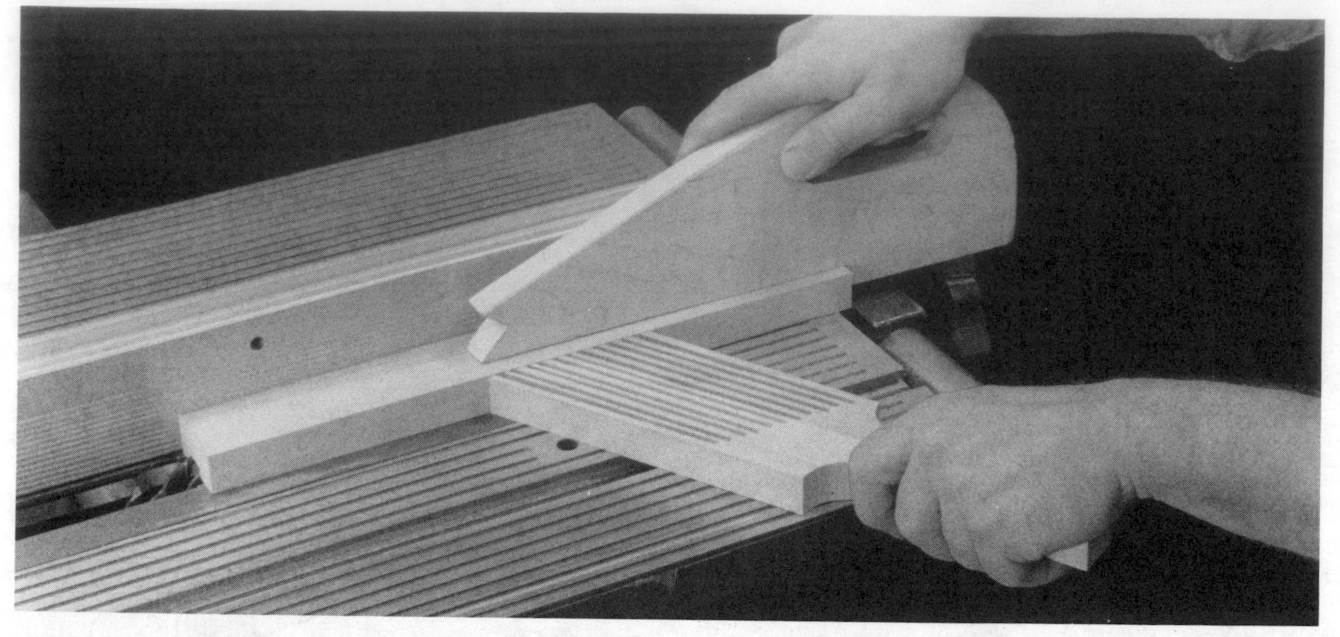

Push stick designed by David T. Smith. Featherboard designed by Nick Engler.

Two New Safety Tools

A couple of new twists on some traditional safety tools help you to keep your fingers and hands out of danger.

Most woodworkers keep an assortment of push sticks, push shoes, and featherboards around their shop. They are indispensable — these tools help to feed wood into saws and jointers without having to put your fingers dangerously close to whirling blades and cutters. To make your woodworking a little safer and a little easier, here are two new variations on old themes:

Two-way push stick — The two-position push stick is a combination of two traditional safety tools — the push stick and the push shoe. You can use it as either, depending on the task you're performing and the tool you're performing it with. Use the nose of the stick for operations in which you only need to feed the stock, and the bottom edge when you need to feed the stock *and* hold it down on the table saw or bandsaw worktable.

To make this tool, first enlarge the pattern and trace it onto some ¾"-thick stock. Cut the outside shape of the push stick, then drill two holes to mark the ends of the grip. Remove the waste between the holes with a sabre saw, and round over the edges of the grip.

Hand-held featherboard — Traditional featherboards are usually clamped to the worktable of the tool. Depending on the tool, however, this can be difficult — sometimes impossible. For those situations, try this hand-held featherboard. It's an ordinary featherboard with a handle so that you can hold it comfortably while you work.

To make the featherboard, select *clear* ¾"-thick stock. Rip the stock to the proper width and cut it a little long. The extra length will help you to control the workpiece while you cut the "feathers." Using a table saw, cut ⅛"-wide kerfs, ⅛" apart and 4" long on one end of the stock. Then cut the shape of the handle in the other end. Round the edges of the handle.

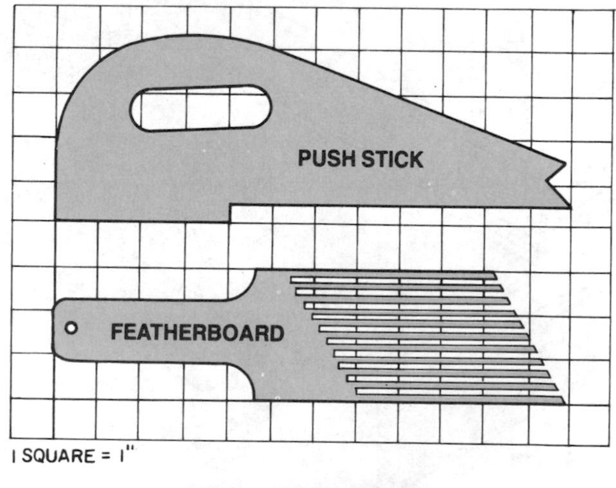

TOOL PATTERNS

BILL OF MATERIALS — Two New Safety Tools

Finished Dimensions in Inches

A.	Two-way push stick	¾ x 4½ x 12
B.	Hand-held featherboard	¾ x 3 x 12

Designed and built by Nick Engler.

Adirondack Settee

For relaxing out-of-doors, there's nothing quite so comfortable.

If you've never relaxed in an Adirondack chair, you don't know what you're missing. You don't just sit down; the chair almost captures you. You realize immediately that you'll never want to get up again. You just lean way back, face to the sky, and soak up the summer sunshine.

This particular version of the classic Adirondack chair has a few twists to enhance your comfort and sense of well-being. The back is braced to keep the structure sturdy for many years. The seat and the back are curved to fit the contours of your body. The arms are wide and flat so that you can set drinks, plates, and books on them. And finally, the design is double-wide so that two people can enjoy the experience. In fact, it's really not a chair any longer — it's a settee.

Despite the intricate curves and angles, this settee is quite simple to build. There are no joints to make. Just cut the parts to shape and put them together. Because the construction is so simple, we were able to put this settee together in just two evenings.

Paradoxically, the absence of joinery also *lengthens* the useful life of the project. There are no grooves, dadoes, or mortises to collect and hold water. Consequently the rain runs off the settee and it dries quickly. The wood does not rot, and the project stays sound longer. (Water promotes the growth of wood-eating bacteria.)

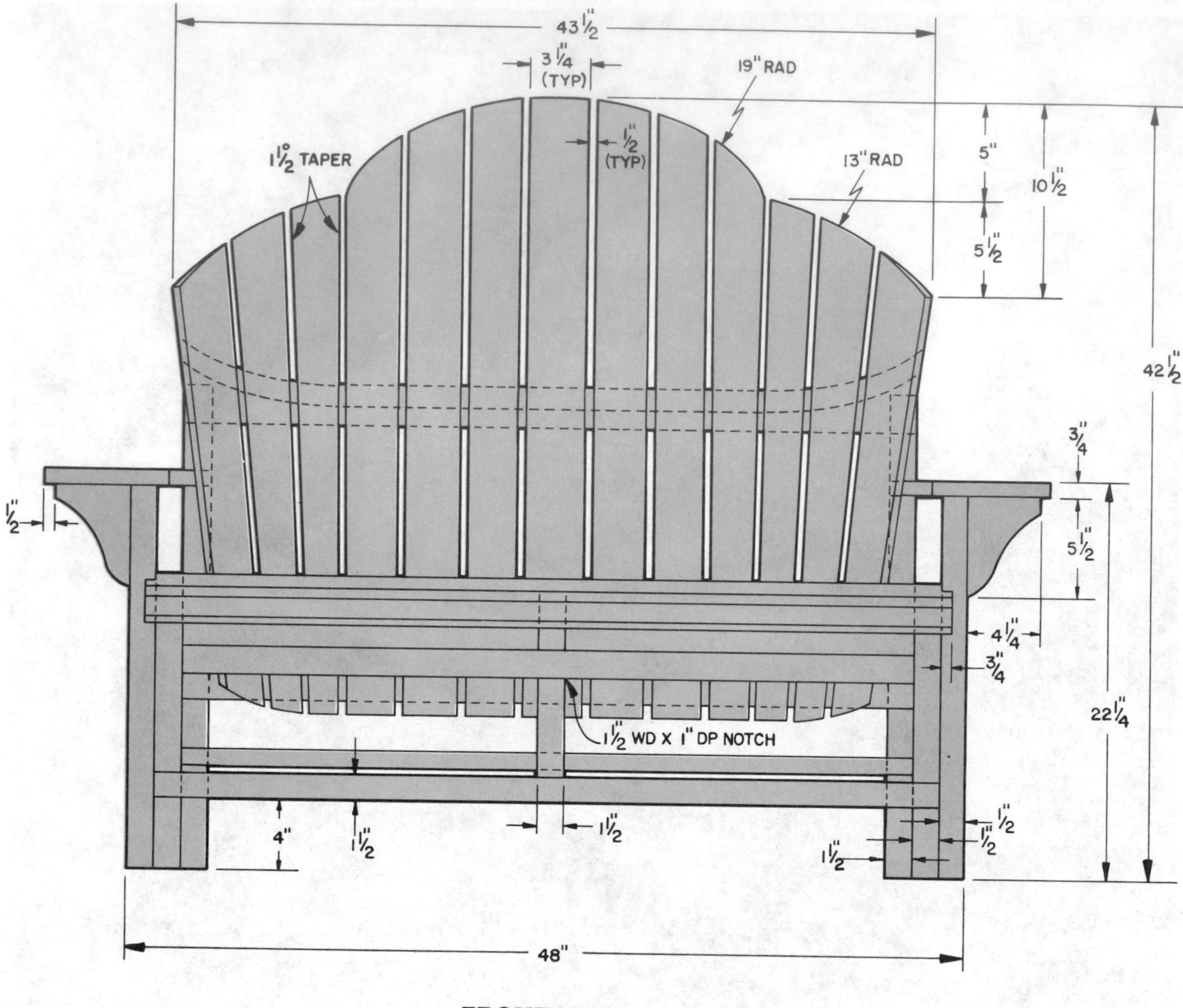

FRONT VIEW

Choosing Your Materials

The settee will last even longer — and look better — if it is made from the proper materials for the out-of-doors. The best outdoor woods, bar none, are mahogany and teak. Although very expensive, these imported woods are impregnated with natural oils that resist rainwater and rot for decades.

Several domestic woods will last almost as long, and cost far less — western red cedar, Atlantic white cedar (juniper), redwood, and cyprus. These, too, are weather-resistant because of the natural oils in the woods. As long as you get relatively clear lumber, these will serve you well. You can also use ordinary yellow pine, as long as you coat the parts with wood sealer before you put them together.

Avoid pressure-treated lumber. This chemically-treated wood is intended for outdoor construction, not for furniture. Even if you get some fairly good-looking boards, chances are they will warp or check, distorting and possibly ruining the project. Pressure-treated lumber is often very high in moisture content, and the wood is swollen. After it sits for a while in the sunshine, it shrinks drastically, sometimes splitting and distorting as it does so.

You also need to take some care in selecting hardware. Purchase brass, stainless steel, or galvanized screws. Other fasteners, even those that advertise themselves as "weather-resistant," may rust. Brass, stainless steel, and galvanized metal are weather*proof.*

Making the Frame

With a single exception (the lower back support), the frame of this settee is made from "two-by" stock, just like a house. Since these support most of the load, select straight, clear lumber for these parts — as clear as you can get, anyway.

Rip and cut the frame parts to the sizes indicated in the Bill of Materials. Cut the upper ends of the back braces at a 55° angle, as shown in the *Side View.* Enlarge the

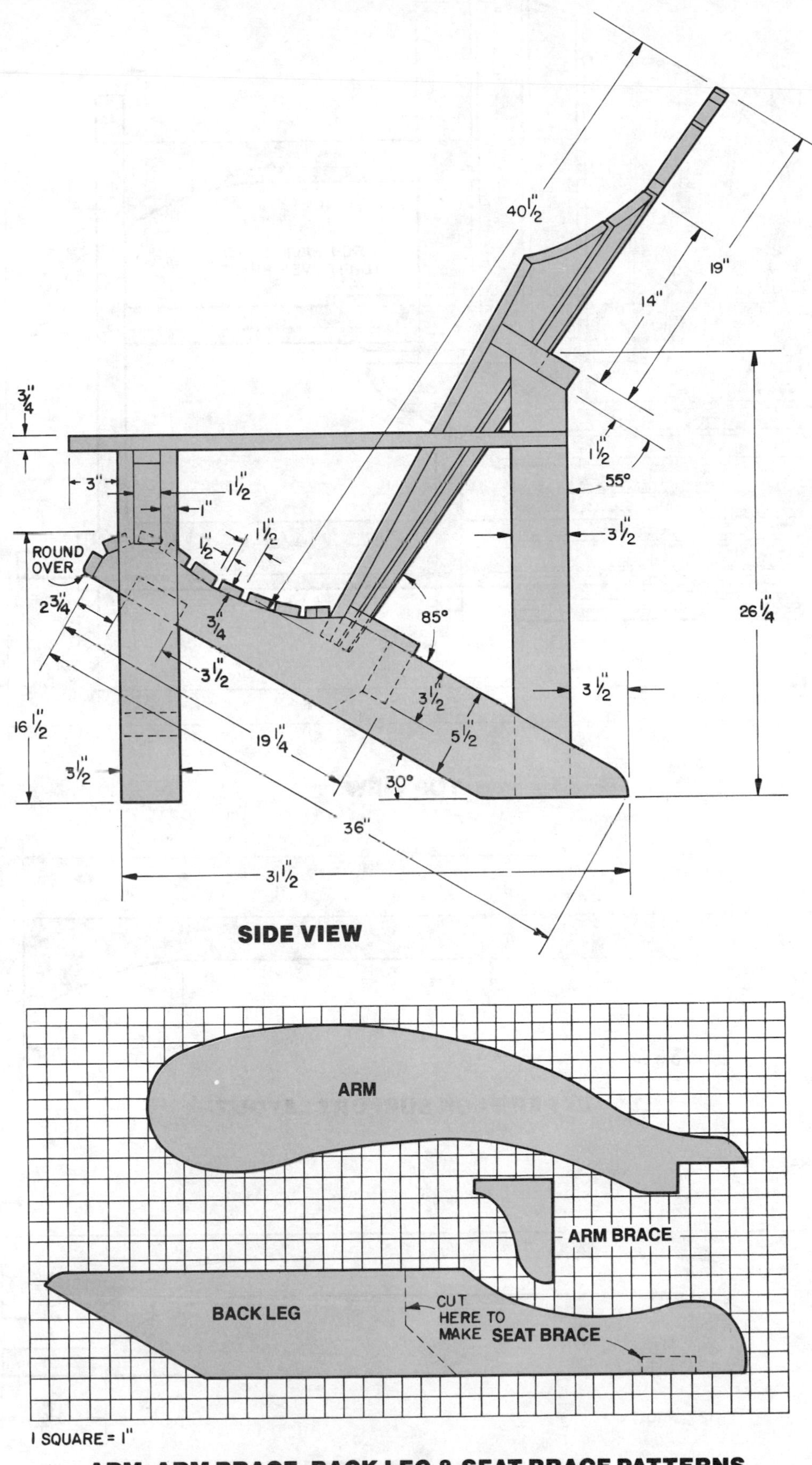

SIDE VIEW

ARM, ARM BRACE, BACK LEG & SEAT BRACE PATTERNS

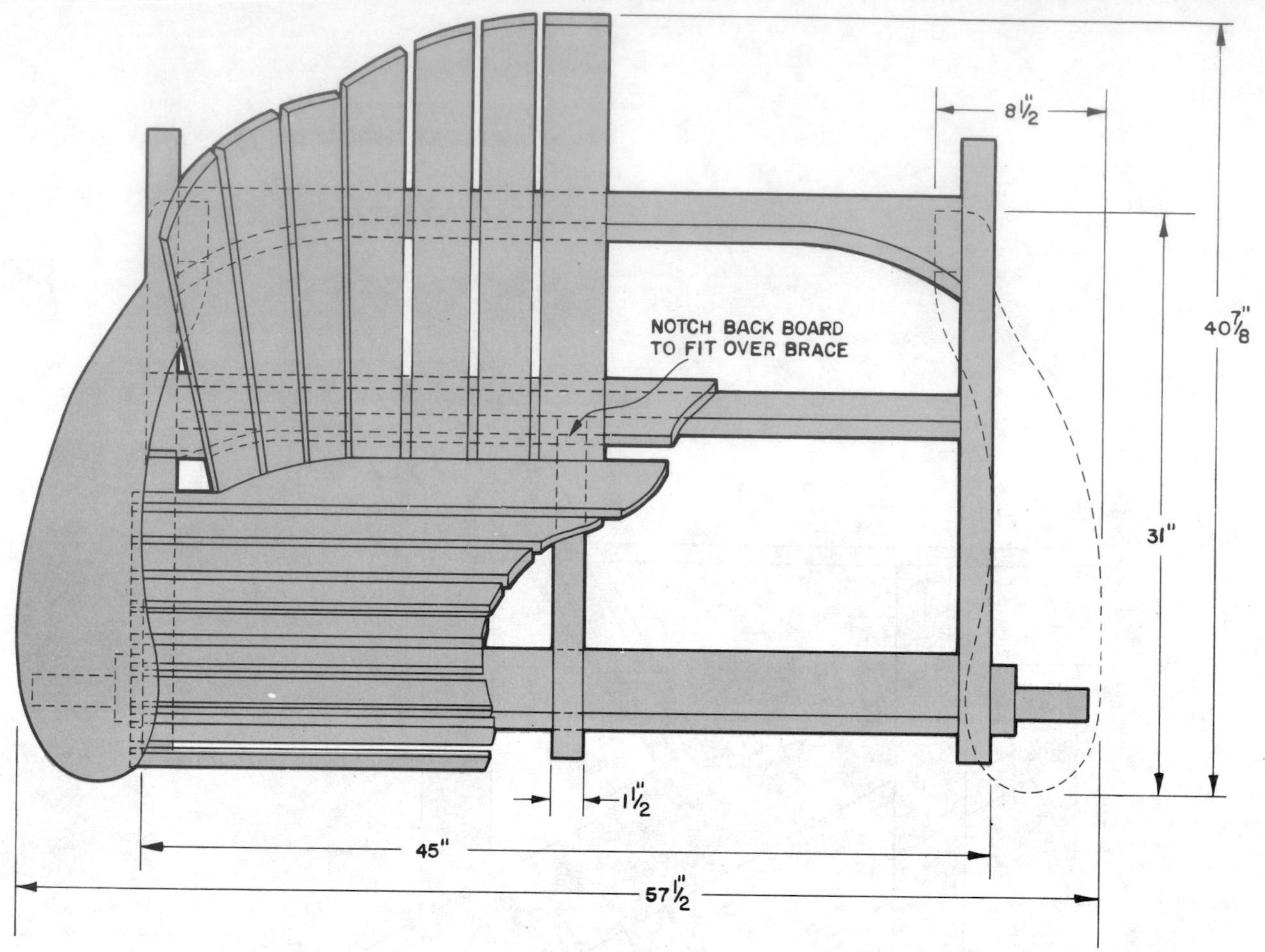

TOP VIEW

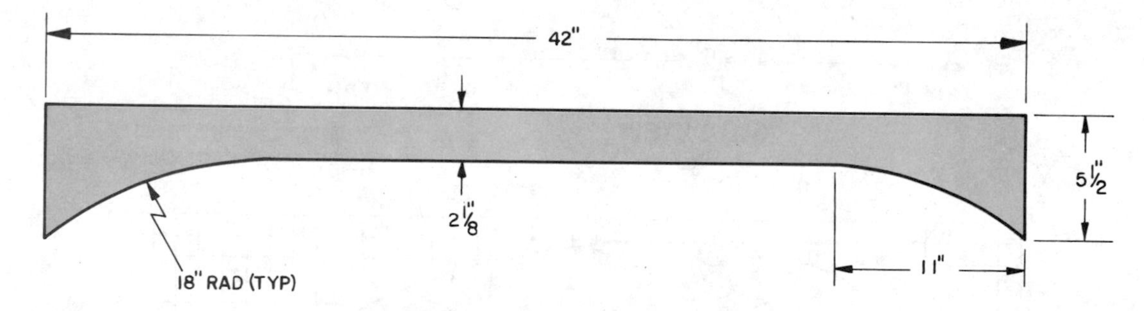

UPPER BACK SUPPORT LAYOUT

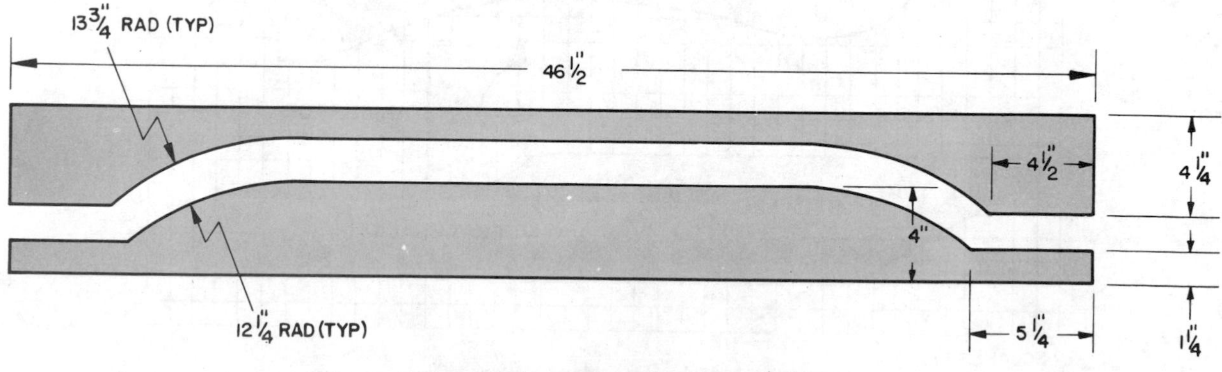

LOWER BACK SUPPORT LAYOUT

patterns for the back leg and seat brace and trace them on the stock. Also, lay out the shapes of the upper back support and lower back support. Cut the shapes on a bandsaw, and sand the edges to remove the saw marks.

Tip ◆ As you assemble the frame, you'll find it easier to work with a helper. There are a good many parts, and they all have to be held at odd angles while you fit other parts to them.

Put together the frame parts in this order: Attach the back legs to the back braces. Then secure the upper back support and the two seat stretchers, joining the leg/brace assemblies. Attach the front legs to the back legs, and join the front legs with the leg stretcher. Secure the seat brace to the seat stretchers, and attach the lower back support to the seat brace, seat stretcher, and back legs.

Use #12 x 2½" flathead wood screws to join all the 1½"-thick parts, and #10 x 1¾" flathead wood screws to attach the one ¾"-thick part. *Do not* use glue, even waterproof glue. It won't do any harm, but there's no sense in it, either. It won't contribute appreciably to the overall strength of the finished project.

Making the Arms

The arms are actually part of the frame — they help support the back, as well as add to the looks and comfort of the settee. For this reason, they should be attached to the project *before* you add the back or the seat.

Enlarge the patterns for the arms and arm braces, and trace them on the stock. Cut out the shapes with a bandsaw, and sand the saw marks from the cut edges.

Attach the arm brace to the front legs, using #12 screws. Then dry assemble the arms to the frame. Depending on how accurately you've put the project together up to this point — and how straight the wood is — you may have to do a little handwork to properly fit the arms to the frame. In particular, the angle of the notch at the back end of the arms may have to be changed slightly.

When you're satisfied that the arms fit as they should, secure them to the frame with wood screws. Use #12 x 2½" wood screws to attach the arms to the back brace, and #10 x 1¾" wood screws to attach them to the front leg and arm brace.

Making the Back

Cut the slats for the back — six pieces ¾" x 3¼" x 35½" and seven pieces ¾" x 3¼" x 40½". The six shorter pieces must be tapered at 1½°, from top to bottom. To do this, you'll either need a commercial tapering jig, or you can make your own as shown in the *Tapering Jig Layout.* Both these jigs hold the boards at an angle on the table saw, off parallel to the saw blade.

Figure 1. Using a tapering jig, cut a 1½° taper in one side of the short back boards. Save the waste.

Figure 2. Use the waste from the first taper cut as spacers to properly position the boards in the jig for the second taper cut.

To cut the tapers, place the L-shaped tapering jig so that the upright of the "L" rests against the rip fence on your table saw. Put a board in the jig and adjust the rip fence so that the saw blade just touches the upper corner of that board. Turn the saw on and push the board forward. (See Figure 1.) Save the waste!

Turn the saw off. Flip the board over in the jig and put the waste between the sawn edge of the board and the jig. The waste will serve as a spacer while you cut the other side of the taper. (See Figure 2.) Once again, turn the saw on and push the jig forward.

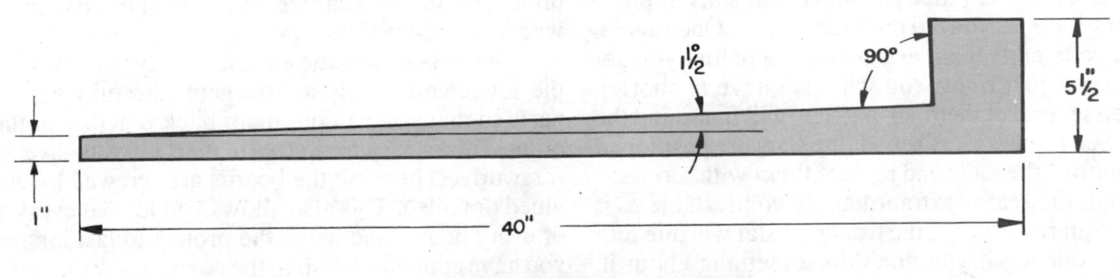

TAPERING JIG LAYOUT

Figure 3. Cut the shape of the back with a sabre saw.

Figure 4. Some of the seat slats must be cut short or notched so that they will fit around the front legs.

Figure 5. Round over the front-most corner of the front seat slat so that the hard, square corner will not bite into the back of your legs.

Cut a 1½″-wide, 1″-deep notch in the bottom end of the middle back board, so that it will fit over the seat brace. Tack this back board to the upper and lower back supports with 4d finishing nails. Then tack the rest of the boards in place, starting at the middle and working out toward the ends of the settee. Do not drive the nails home. Let the heads protrude so that you can easily remove them and shift the boards around if you have to. It will take some experimentation to get all the boards properly spaced and positioned on the frame.

When the back boards are properly placed and spaced, remove the nails one at a time and replace them with #10 x 1¾″ flathead wood screws. Be sure to countersink the screws — you don't want the heads to rub against your back.

Use a string compass to mark the shape of the back. Then cut the shape with a sabre saw. (See Figure 3.) Clean up the sawn ends and remove any saw marks with a hand-held belt sander or block sander.

Making the Seat

Lay out the shape of the back seat slat and cut it out on your bandsaw. Also, rip and cut to length the eight ¾″ x 1½″ x 46½″ seat slats that you need.

Secure the back seat slat to the back legs with #10 x 1¾″ wood screws. Then tack the other seat slats in place with finishing nails, as you did the back boards. Once again, you may have to shift them around a little before you get them positioned just right. You will also have to shorten and/or notch several of them, so that they will fit around the front legs. (See Figure 4.) When all the slats are positioned correctly, remove the nails and replace them with screws.

Although the seat is extraordinarily comfortable as it is, the hard, square corner of the front seat slat will bite into the back of your leg if you don't do something about it. Using a hand plane, round over this corner. (See Figure 5.)

Finishing Up

Using a block sander, round over all the remaining hard corners on the settee, particularly those on the arms and the upper edge of the back. Carefully inspect the surface of all the back boards, seat slats, and arm for any defects that might throw splinters, and sand these out.

If you've built this project from a weather-resistant wood such as mahogany or redwood, then the settee is completed. There's no need to apply a finish — the wood will wear just fine without one. But if you've made the settee from pine or some other wood that needs extra protection in the weather, you'll need to coat the project with a protective finish.

The best — and the easiest — way to do this is to take the settee completely apart again, carefully marking the parts so that you can put them back together in the same order. This is easy to do (particularly if you have a power screwdriver) because the boards are screwed together, not glued or nailed. This also allows you to coat every surface of every board, and helps the project to last longer. Once you have applied a finish to the parts, screw the settee back together again.

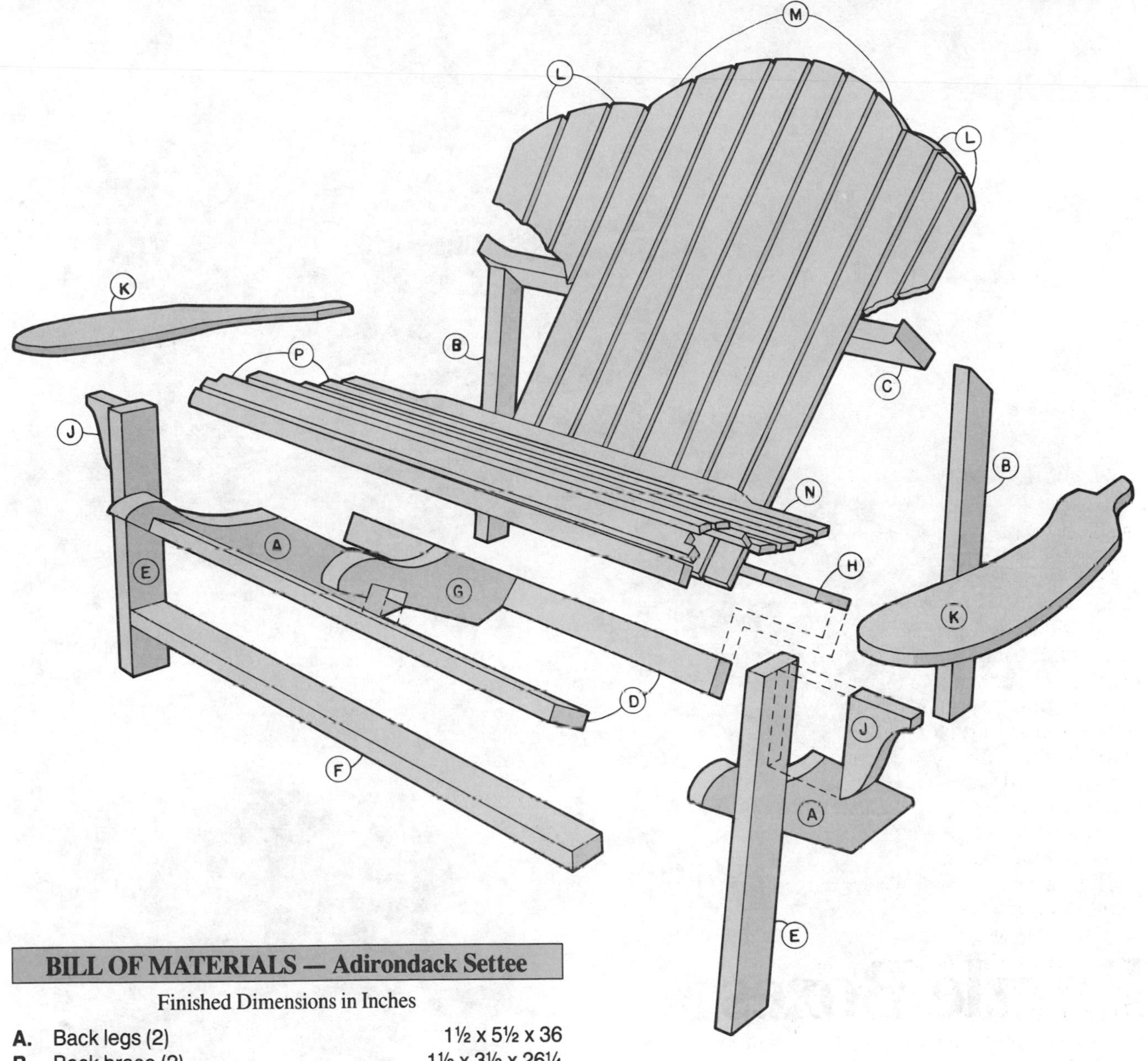

BILL OF MATERIALS — Adirondack Settee

Finished Dimensions in Inches

A.	Back legs (2)	1½ x 5½ x 36
B.	Back brace (2)	1½ x 3½ x 26¼
C.	Upper back support	1½ x 5½ x 42
D.	Seat stretchers (2)	1½ x 3½ x 42
E.	Front legs (2)	1½ x 3½ x 21½
F.	Leg stretcher	1½ x 3½ x 45
G.	Seat brace	1½ x 5½ x 17¾
H.	Lower back support	¾ x 4¼ x 46½
J.	Arm braces (2)	1½ x 4¼ x 5½
K.	Arms (2)	¾ x 8½ x 31
L.	Short back boards (6)	¾ x 3¼ x 35½
M.	Long back boards (7)	¾ x 3¼ x 40½
N.	Back seat slat	¾ x 4 x 46½
P.	Seat slats (8)	¾ x 1½ x 46½

HARDWARE

4d Finishing nails (¼ lb.)
#10 x 1¾″ Flathead wood screws (60-72)
#12 x 2½″ Flathead wood screws (36-42)

Puzzle Boxes

You have to solve the puzzle to open the box — or close it again.

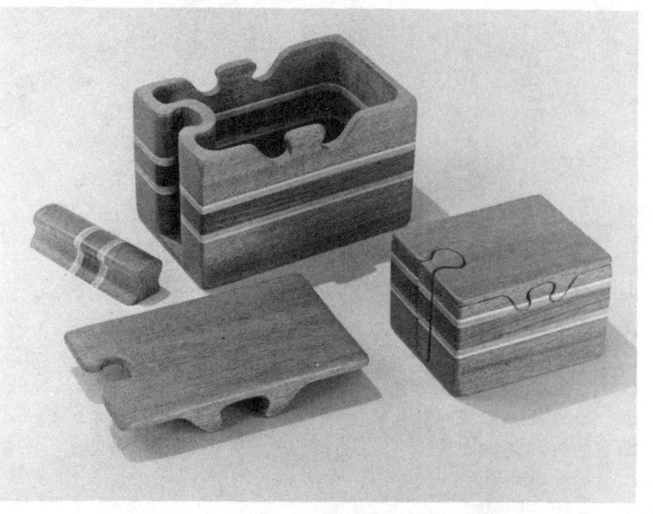

Designed by Chris Walendzak. Made by Nick Engler and Chris Walendzak.

Each box appears to be just a single block of wood. Actually, it *was* a single block of wood at one time. But it has been cut into four interlocking parts — bottom, lid, sides, and a "key." The parts fit together like a three-dimensional wooden puzzle. The lid slides onto the two ears cut in the sides, then the key drops in place, locking the parts together.

And not only are these boxes made from a single block of wood; they're made using just one tool — a bandsaw. They require no hardware — no hinges, clasps, or locks. The only additional materials and tools you need besides a block of wood and a bandsaw is a little bit of glue, some sandpaper, some clamps, and a finish.

Preparing the Wood

When choosing stock for this project, keep in mind that the block of wood from which you cut the box must be shorter and more narrow than the depth of cut of your bandsaw. The length can be greater, but the other two dimensions cannot. This is why the two boxes shown here are both less than 6″ tall and wide. The depth of cut of an average home workshop bandsaw is 6″. If your bandsaw has a larger capacity, you can make larger boxes, of course.

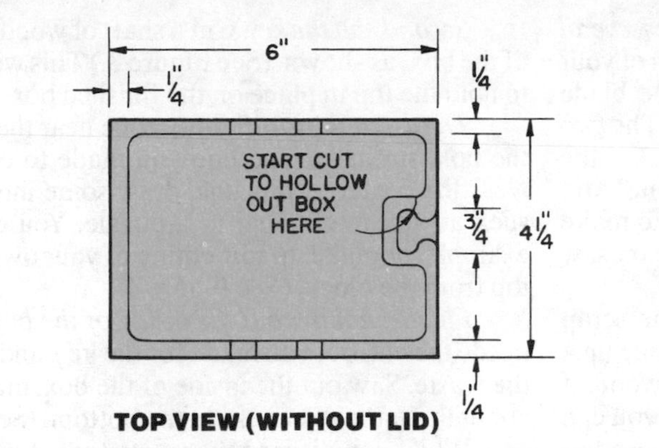

SMALL BOX

1/4"
3/4"
3 1/4
3/4"
1/4"
6"

FRONT VIEW

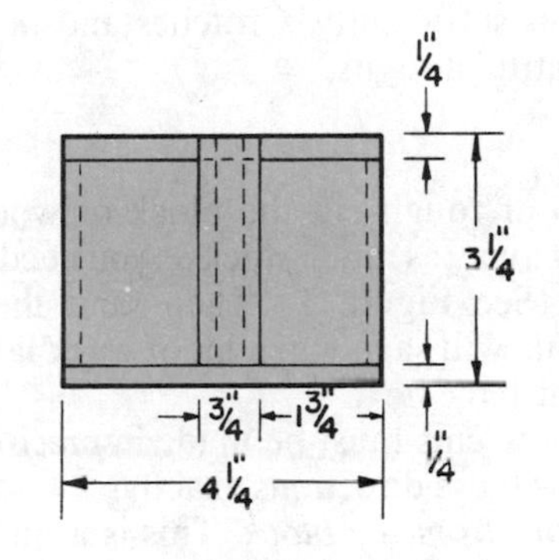

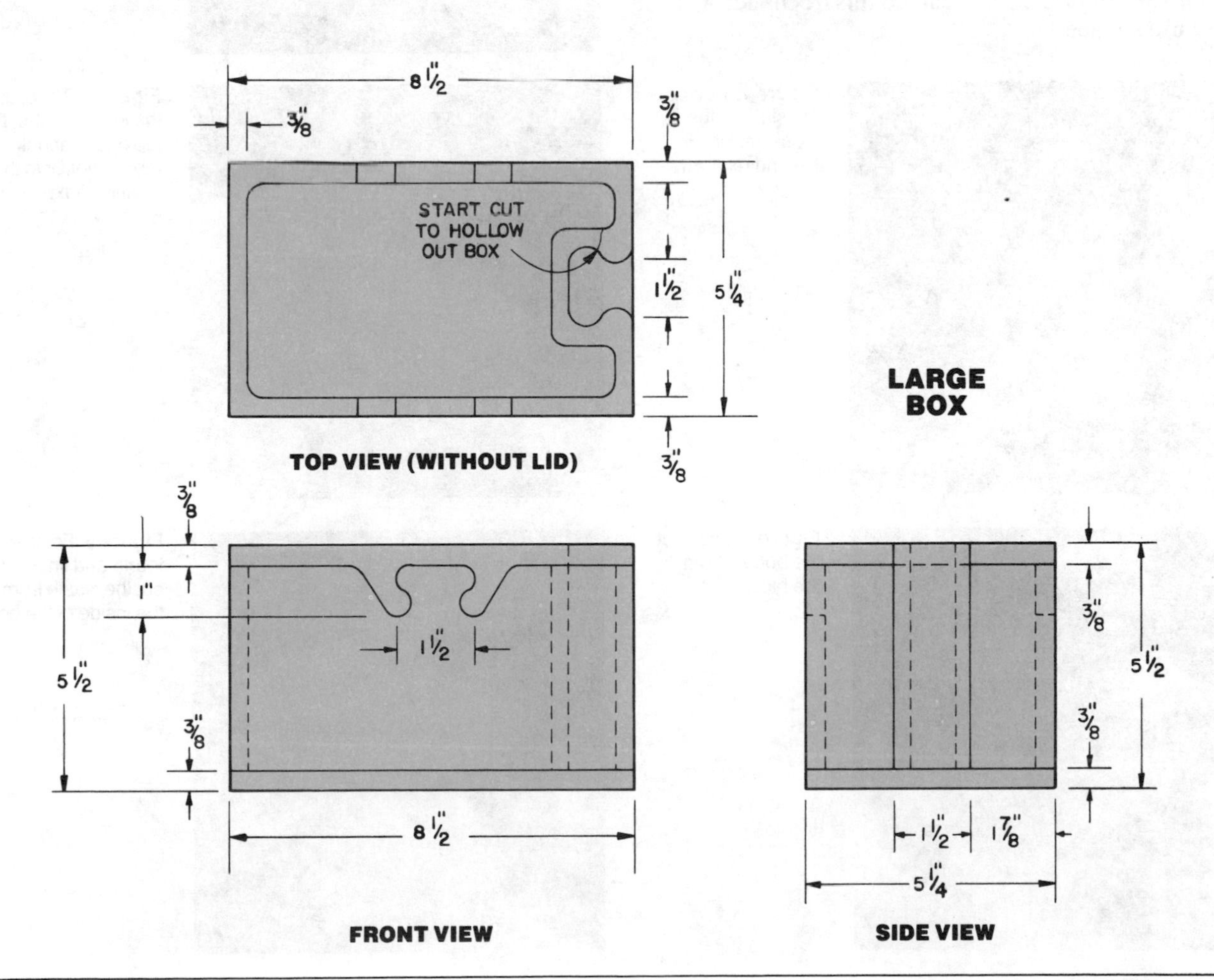

Also remember that one block will make *several* boxes, depending on the size of block and the width of your bandsaw blades. (When making small boxes, the blade must be narrow enough to turn the sharp corners.) The two boxes shown here were both cut from the same block —the small one was made from the scrap of the large one. And there was a big enough scrap from the small box to make yet another, even smaller box — if our ⅛″ wide bandsaw blade hadn't been as dull as a butter knife.

When selecting the stock, consider using the scrap that you have sitting around, as we did. You can glue up a large block easily enough from smaller pieces of wood. If you use different species — contrasting colors — you can create an attractive design in the block. You can also use blocks of wood cut from firewood and old logs, as long as the wood has dried out sufficiently. Crotches and burls make particularly beautiful designs.

Cutting the Parts

After you've glued up or rough-cut the block of wood, square up the sides. Cut away as much stock as you need to true up the surfaces. (See Figure 1.) Then sand them smooth on a sander. This will save you a lot of work later on, when it's time to finish the box.

Each of the bandsaw cuts must be made in *precisely* the right order, so follow these directions exactly:

First, cut the bottom from the block. This is a bit of resawing. Scribe a line to follow, and cut a slab off the bottom. (See Figure 2.) You can do this freehand, or, if you prefer, use a fence.

Second, cut the key. Cut a shaft of wood from one edge of the box, as shown. (See Figure 3.) This will later be used to hold the top in place on the finished box.

Third, cut the top. Scribe a line near the top surface of the box, similar to the line you made to cut the bottom. Near the center of this line, draw some interlocking tabs, such as you might find in a puzzle. You can follow our example, or make up something of your own. Then cut the top from the block. (See Figure 4.)

Finally, hollow out the inside of the box. Start the cut inside the cut-out you made for the key, and cut through to the waste. Saw out the inside of the box, making the sides about the same thickness as the bottom. (See Figure 5.)

When you discard the waste (or set it aside to make another box), you should be left with four pieces — bottom, key, top, and sides.

Figure 1. True up the sides of the block, making it flat and relatively square.

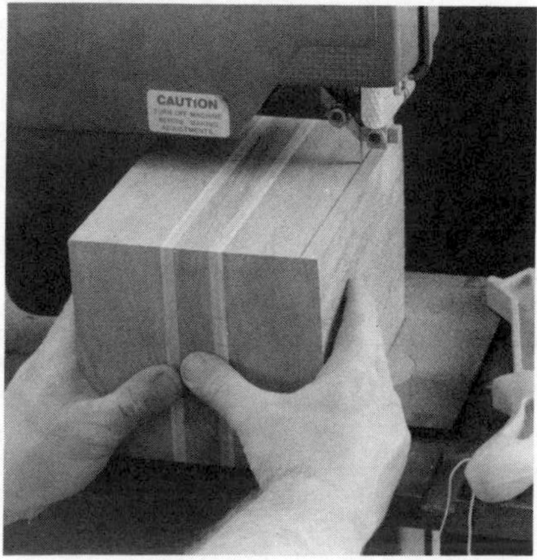

Figure 2. First, cut the bottom from the block.

Figure 3. Second, cut the key.

Figure 4. Third, cut the top. Note that the top has interlocking tabs to hold it to the finished box.

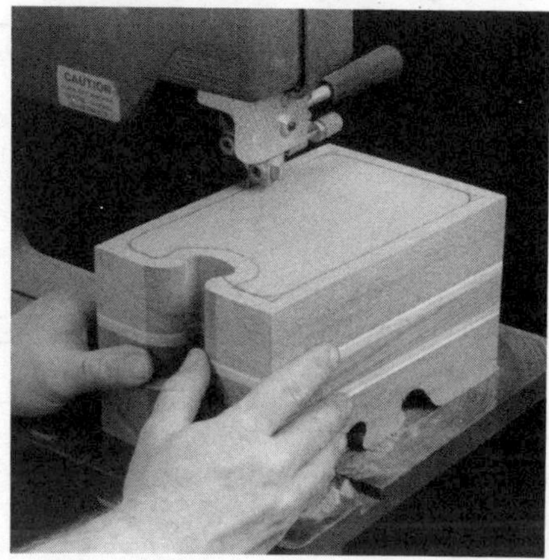

Figure 5. For the fourth and final cut, cut the waste from the inside of the box.

Figure 6. Glue the gap in the sides closed.

Figure 7. Finally, glue the bottom back onto the box.

Assembling and Finishing the Box

The cut you made to hollow out the box will have left a small gap in the sides. Fill this gap with glue and clamp it together. (See Figure 6.) This will distort the box a little, but not enough to do any damage.

After the glue in the gap cures, sand the bottom edge of the sides and the top surface of the bottom perfectly flat with a belt sander or disc sander. You could also joint them flat on a jointer, if you prefer. But be very careful when jointing the bottom because it's such a small part — use a push shoe to protect your fingers.

Also, sand the inside surface of the sides to get rid of the saw marks. Then glue the bottom to the sides. (See Figure 7.) When the glue dries, sand the outside surfaces of the box assembly, the top, and the key. Round over the corners, to give the project a "soft," contemporary look.

Apply a penetrating oil finish, such as tung oil or Danish oil. Avoid finishes that build up on the surface of the wood (such as varnish). This will interfere with the sliding action of the top and the key when you open the box or close it up again.

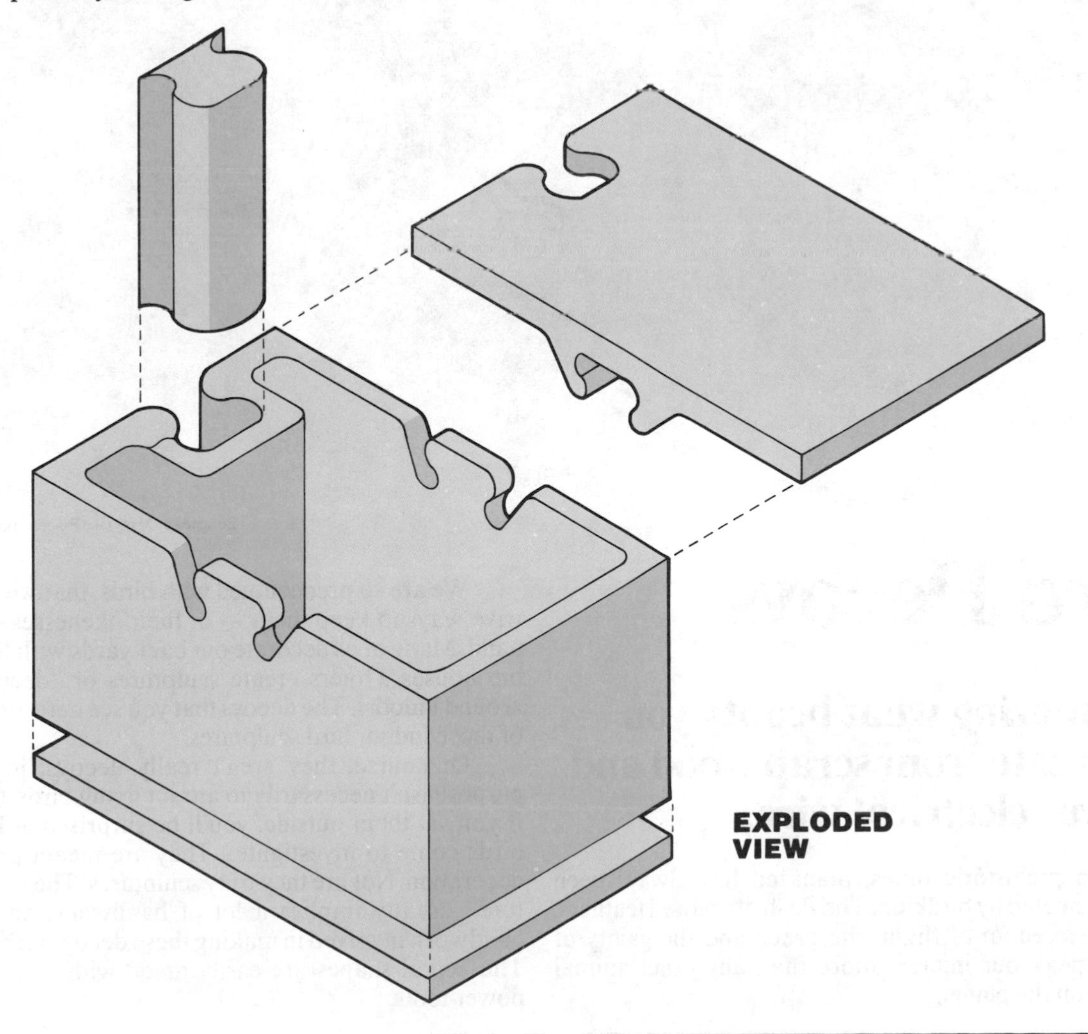

Designed by Mary Jane Favorite. Built by Nick Engler.

Bird Decoys

It's amazing what beauty you can create from scrap wood and leftover electrical wire.

From prehistoric times, mankind has always been fascinated by birdkind. The flash of colored feathers, the freedom of flight, the grace and the gaiety of birds all peak our interest more than any other animal kingdom on the planet.

We are so preoccupied with birds, that we often contrive ways to keep them — or their likenesses — close at hand. Many of us decorate our backyards with feeders and birdhouses. Others create sculptures or "decoys" to set around indoors. The decoys that you see here are examples of those indoor bird sculptures.

Of course, they aren't really decoys, in that their purpose isn't necessarily to attract living birds. (Although, if you set them outside, you'll be surprised at how many birds come to investigate.) They are meant primarily as decoration. Nor are they truly sculptures. The word "sculpture" usually implies a lot of handwork, and the only handwork involved in making these decoys is the painting. The actual shapes are easily made with a few ordinary power tools.

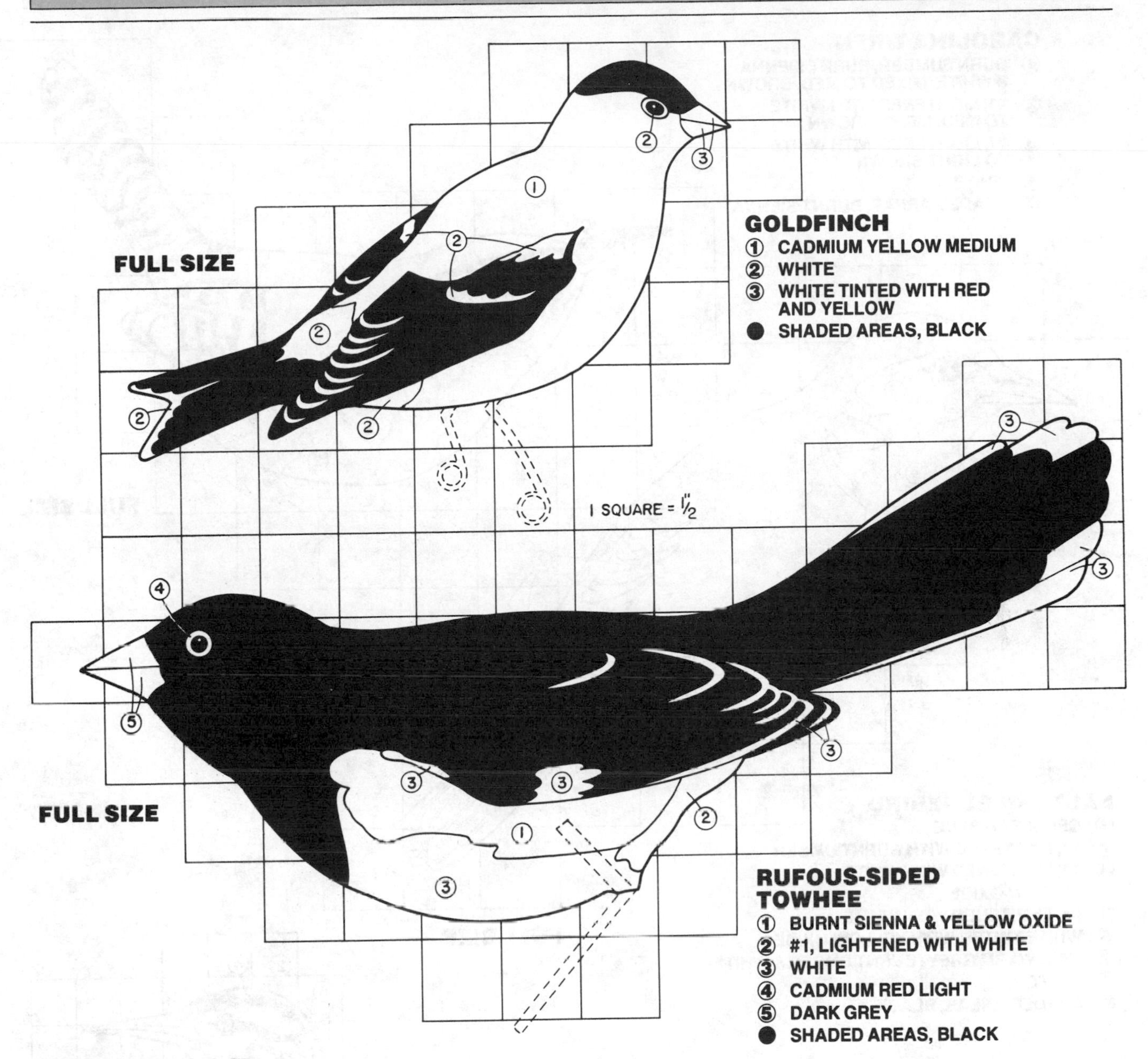

Making the Bird Shapes

Select the wood for the bird shapes. Remember, you are going to sand these wooden parts to a rough bird shape after you saw the silhouette. For this reason, choose fairly soft woods — avoid denser stock, or stock with knots and burls. Three readily-available woods are well-suited for this project — mahogany, basswood, and white pine. All of these can be sanded to shape easily. The birds you see here are made from mahogany.

Once you have chosen the wood, make *two* photocopies of each of the bird patterns that you want to make. Since these patterns are fairly complex, we have reproduced them full-size in this book so that you won't have to worry about enlarging them. Just take the book to a library, quick-print shop, or some other place with a photocopy machine, and make the copies you need.

Once you have chosen the wood, enlarge and/or make copies of the bird patterns. Many of the patterns printed here are full size — 100%. These don't have to be enlarged — just make copies of them. The other patterns are shown at 57%. To enlarge these, just take them to a quick-print shop that has a copier that can enlarge and reduce documents. Have the operator select the "letter-to-legal-size" enlargement setting. (On most copiers, this is about 121%.) Then enlarge each pattern *three* times. This will give you a full-size pattern. Here's the math:

.57 x 1.21 x 1.21 x 1.21 1.01 (approximately)

Make *two* photocopies of each full-size pattern.

Affix one of the copies to the wood with rubber cement or spray adhesive. Using the photocopy as a guide, cut out the outside shape of the bird with a bandsaw or a scroll saw. Also, cut the bird base at this time. Mark the locations of the feet on the underside of the bird shape and drill two ⅛"-diameter, ¾"-deep stopped holes. Drill two similar holes in the base. Later on, you will insert wire in these holes to make the legs and feet.

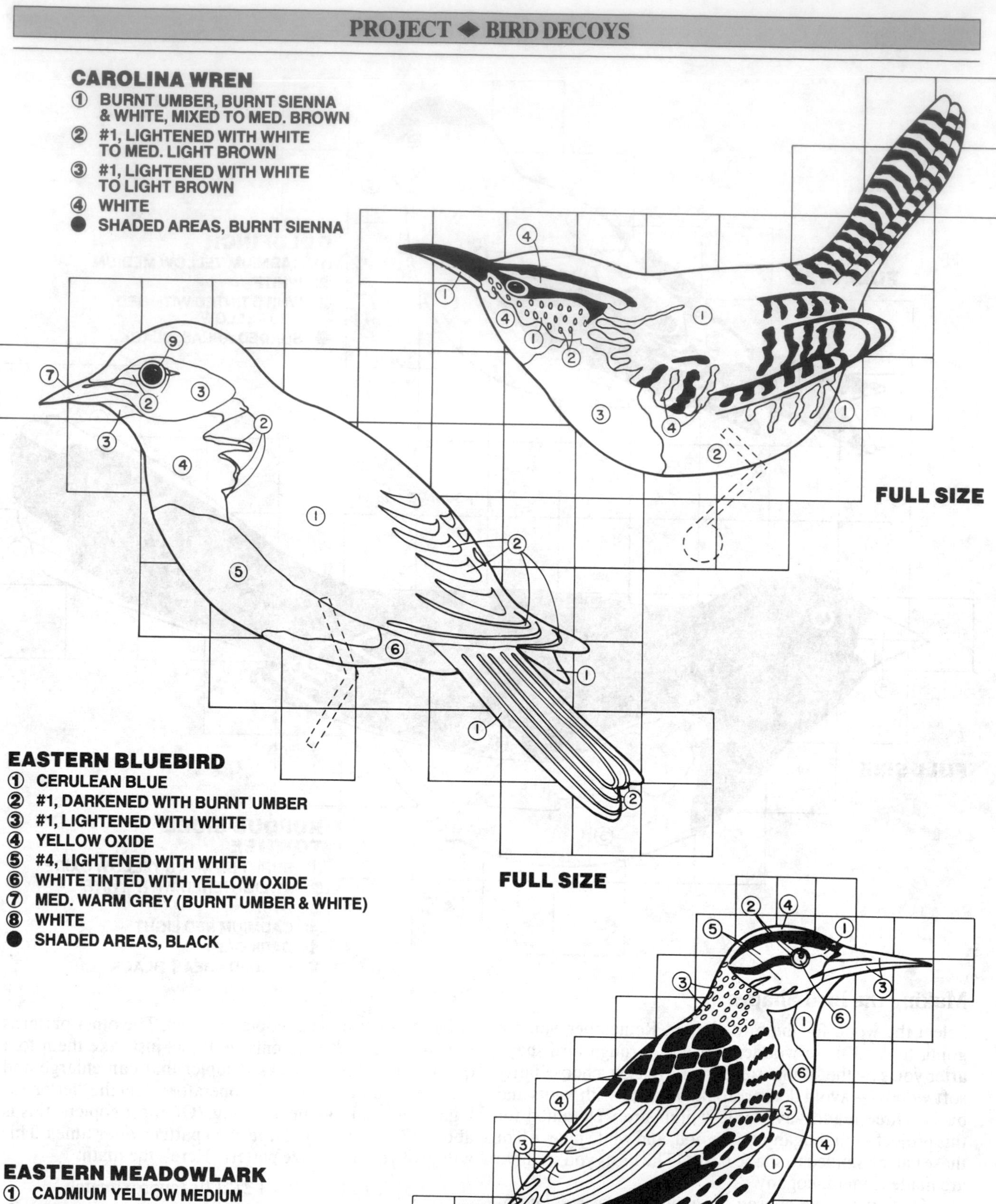

CAROLINA WREN

① BURNT UMBER, BURNT SIENNA & WHITE, MIXED TO MED. BROWN
② #1, LIGHTENED WITH WHITE TO MED. LIGHT BROWN
③ #1, LIGHTENED WITH WHITE TO LIGHT BROWN
④ WHITE
● SHADED AREAS, BURNT SIENNA

EASTERN BLUEBIRD

① CERULEAN BLUE
② #1, DARKENED WITH BURNT UMBER
③ #1, LIGHTENED WITH WHITE
④ YELLOW OXIDE
⑤ #4, LIGHTENED WITH WHITE
⑥ WHITE TINTED WITH YELLOW OXIDE
⑦ MED. WARM GREY (BURNT UMBER & WHITE)
⑧ WHITE
● SHADED AREAS, BLACK

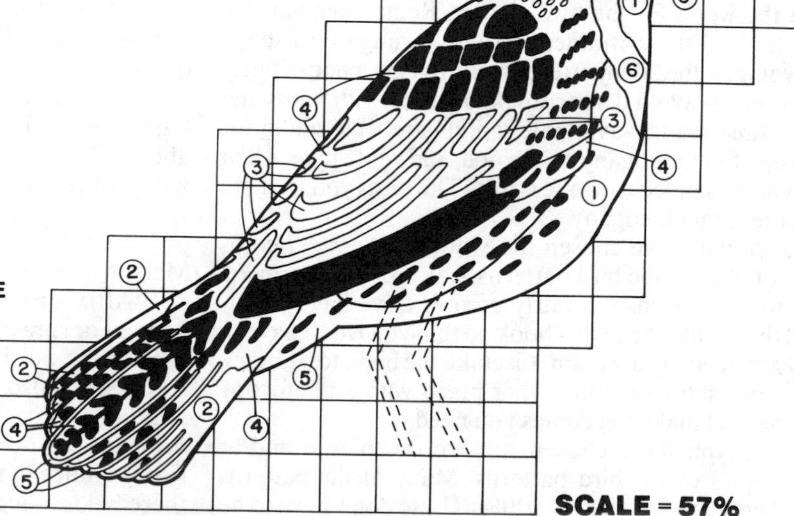

EASTERN MEADOWLARK

① CADMIUM YELLOW MEDIUM
② WHITE
③ BURNT UMBER, YELLOW OXIDE & WHITE MIXED TO MED. DARK BROWN
④ #3, LIGHTENED TO MED. BROWN
⑤ #3, LIGHTENED TO LIGHT BROWN
⑥ BLACK
⑦ BURNT UMBER & WHITE
● SHADED AREAS, BURNT UMBER

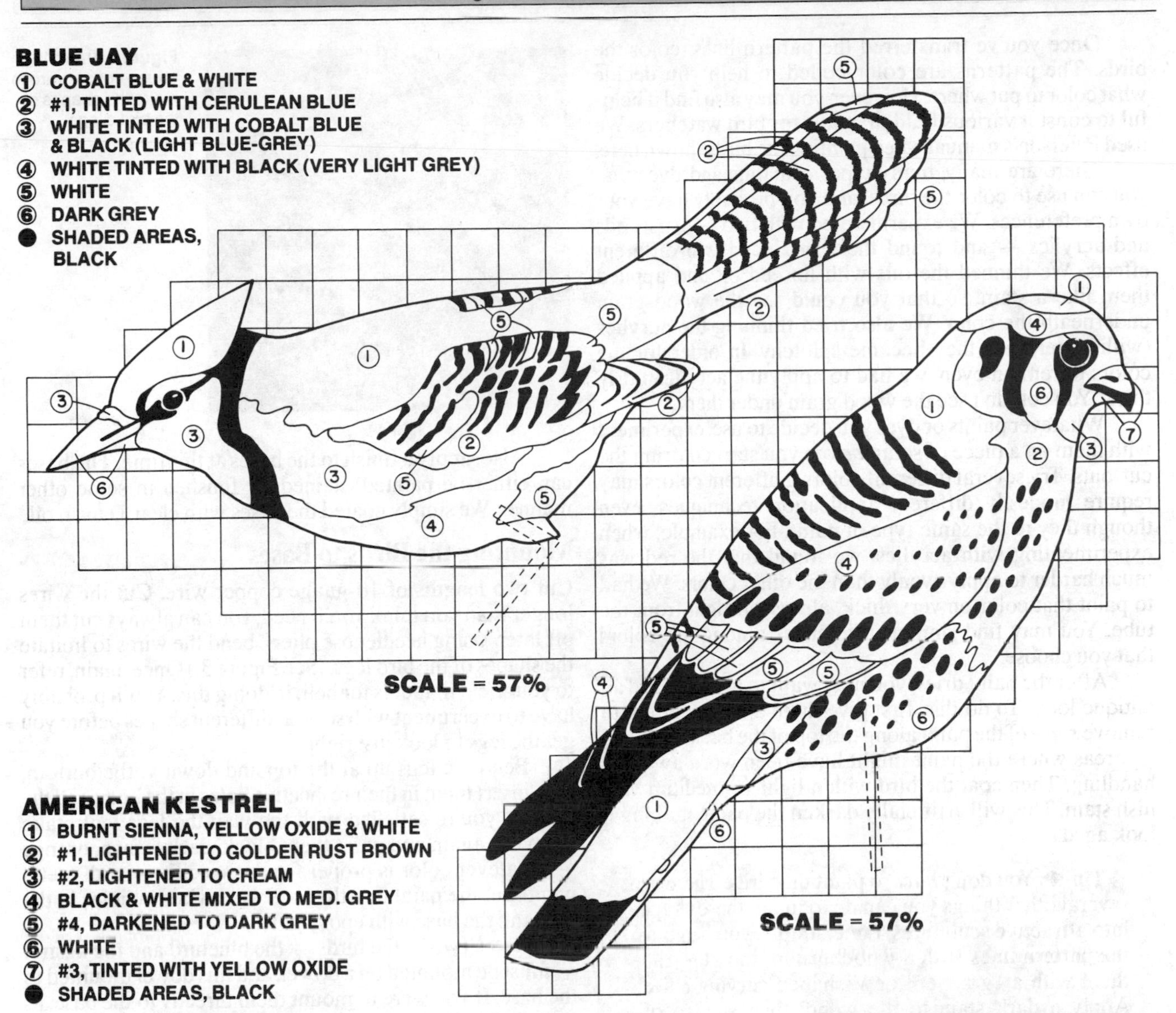

Peel the photocopy off the stock, and sand away the saw marks from the cut edges. Then begin to round over the edges of the bird shape, using rasps, files, sandpaper, and power sanders. You'll find that two power tools are particularly handy — a 1″ strip sander, and small drum sanders. (See Figures 1 and 2.)

Add a little detail, if you wish, to make the shapes more realistic. Taper the beaks with the sander. File grooves under the wings or tail feathers to emphasize these shapes. Round over the neck area more than the head and the body to give the shape the illusion of a thicker body and a bulbous head. But as you shape the bird, remember this is a decoy, a piece of folk art. It doesn't have to be realistic, it just needs to *suggest* the real bird.

Painting the Birds

Using the second photocopy of the bird, transfer the pattern lines onto the wooden shape. You can make *most* of this transfer by putting a piece of carbon paper under the photocopy, and tracing the pattern with a ballpoint pen. However, some of the lines on the rounded portions of the bird shape may have to be drawn on freehand.

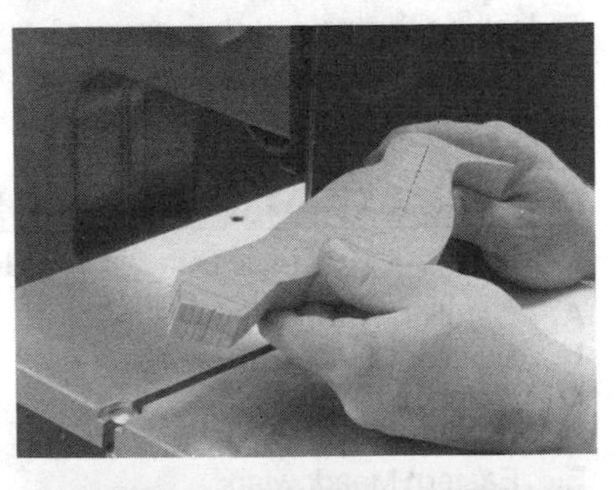
Figure 1. A strip sander makes short work of removing the saw marks from the sawn bird silhouettes.

Figure 2. If you have them, you can use small drum sanders to shape the birds.

Once you've transferred the pattern lines, color the birds. The patterns are color-coded to help you decide what color to put where. However, you may also find it helpful to consult various field manuals for bird watchers. We used Peterson's manual when painting the birds shown here.

There are many, many types of paints and dyes that you can use to color the birds, and you probably have your own preferences. We experimented with two — artists oils and acrylics — and found these produced two different effects. We thinned the oils with linseed oil and applied them like a stain, so that you could see the wood grain underneath the color. We also tried thinning the acrylics (with water), but they became splotchy. In order for the colors to remain even, we had to apply the acrylics fairly thick. You couldn't see the wood grain under them.

Whatever paints or dyes you decide to use, experiment with them on a piece of scrap *before* you start coloring the cut-outs. Try several different colors. Different colors may require modestly different application techniques, even though they're the same type of paint. For example, when experimenting with acrylics, we found that the red was much harder to apply evenly than the other colors. We had to paint that color on very thick, almost straight from the tube. You may find similar differences among the colors that you choose.

After the paint dries, you may want to give the bird an antique look. To do this, first give them a light sanding to remove *some* of the paint along the top of the back and head — areas where the paint might have been worn away by handling. Then coat the bird with a light-to-medium varnish stain. This will artificially darken the paint, making it look aged.

Tip ◆ You don't *have* to paint the birds. There are several other things you can do to make these shapes into attractive sculptures. For example, you can burn the pattern lines with a woodburning tool. Or trace them with a "groover" or V-shaped carving chisel. Apply a dark stain to the wood; then sand it off, leaving the stain in the grooves.

Figure 3. Bend 10-gauge copper wire to make the shapes of the bird's legs.

Also, apply a finish to the bases at this time. The bases can either be painted, stained, or finished in some other manner. We simply coated the bases with clear Danish oil.

Mounting the Birds to Bases

Cut two lengths of 10-gauge copper wire. Cut the wires longer than you think you'll need; you can always cut them off later. Using needlenose pliers, bend the wires to imitate the shapes of the bird legs. (See Figure 3.) Once again, refer to your field manuals for help in doing this. You'll probably have to experiment with several different shapes before you get the legs to look just right.

Bend the legs up at the top and down at the bottom, then insert them in their respective holes in the body and the base. If you're satisfied with the way the legs look, take them out again and paint them black, dark brown, orange — whatever color is proper for the species — with metal paint. Let the paint dry, then affix the wires in holes in the bird and the base with epoxy glue.

Note: Two of the birds — the bluebird and the kestrel — must be mounted on a dowel, and this dowel mounted to the base. If you were to mount them directly to the base, as the other birds are mounted, their tails would prevent you from mounting them at the correct angle.

BILL OF MATERIALS — Bird Decoys

Finished Dimensions in Inches

A.	Carolina Wren	¾ x 2¼ x 4¼
B.	Eastern Bluebird	¾ x 1¾ x 5
C.	Goldfinch	¾ x 1¾ x 4
D.	Rufous-Sided Towhee	¾ x 2½ x 6¾
E.	Eastern Meadowlark	¾ x 2¾ x 8⅝
F.	American Kestrel	¾ x 3⅛ x 9½
G.	Blue Jay	¾ x 3⅝ x 10½
H.	Small bases* (3)	2½ dia. x ¾
J.	Medium bases* (2)	3 dia. x ¾
K.	Large bases* (2)	4 dia. x ¾
L.	Small dowel**	¾ dia. x 2
M.	Large dowel**	1¼ dia. x 3

* *Use the small bases for A, B, and C; the medium bases for D and E; and the large bases for E and F.*

** *Use the small dowel to mount B, and the large dowel to mount F.*

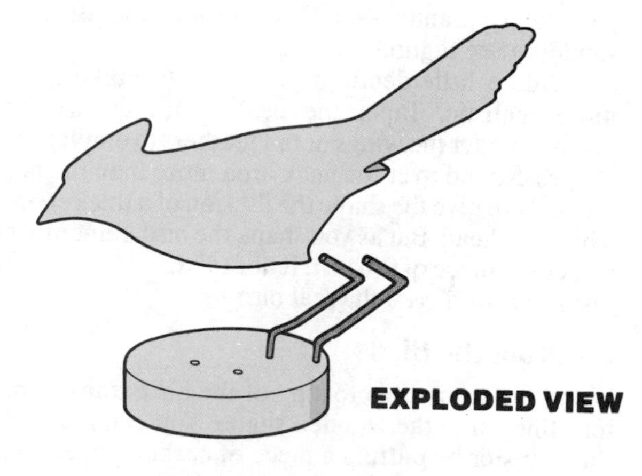

HARDWARE

10-gauge Electrical wire (approximately 5′)

Designed by Nick Engler. Built by Jim McCann.

Hook-and-Ladder

This toy fire engine will delight any kid — young or old!

Even with all the plastic figures, fortresses, and spaceships that crowd the shelves of toy stores today, a fire engine remains one of the most exciting toys that you can give to your children or grandchildren. And the hook-and-ladder is the most exciting fire engine of all.

This particular toy hook-and-ladder is designed for plenty of action. The hook section detaches from the ladder section. The extension ladder reaches upward almost two feet, locks into position, and swivels 360°. There are two accessory ladders, one on each side, that can also be detached. Finally, the hose can be let out or reeled in — just like the real thing. As you can see, there's plenty to keep the kids occupied.

Cutting the Body Parts

Select a clear, hard, close-grained wood to make this wooden toy. Some of the parts — the ladders, in particular — are fairly slender. In order to stand up to the type of

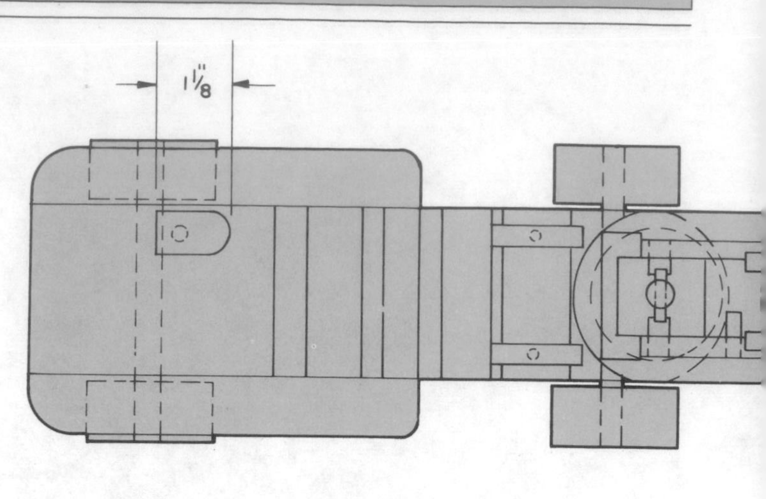

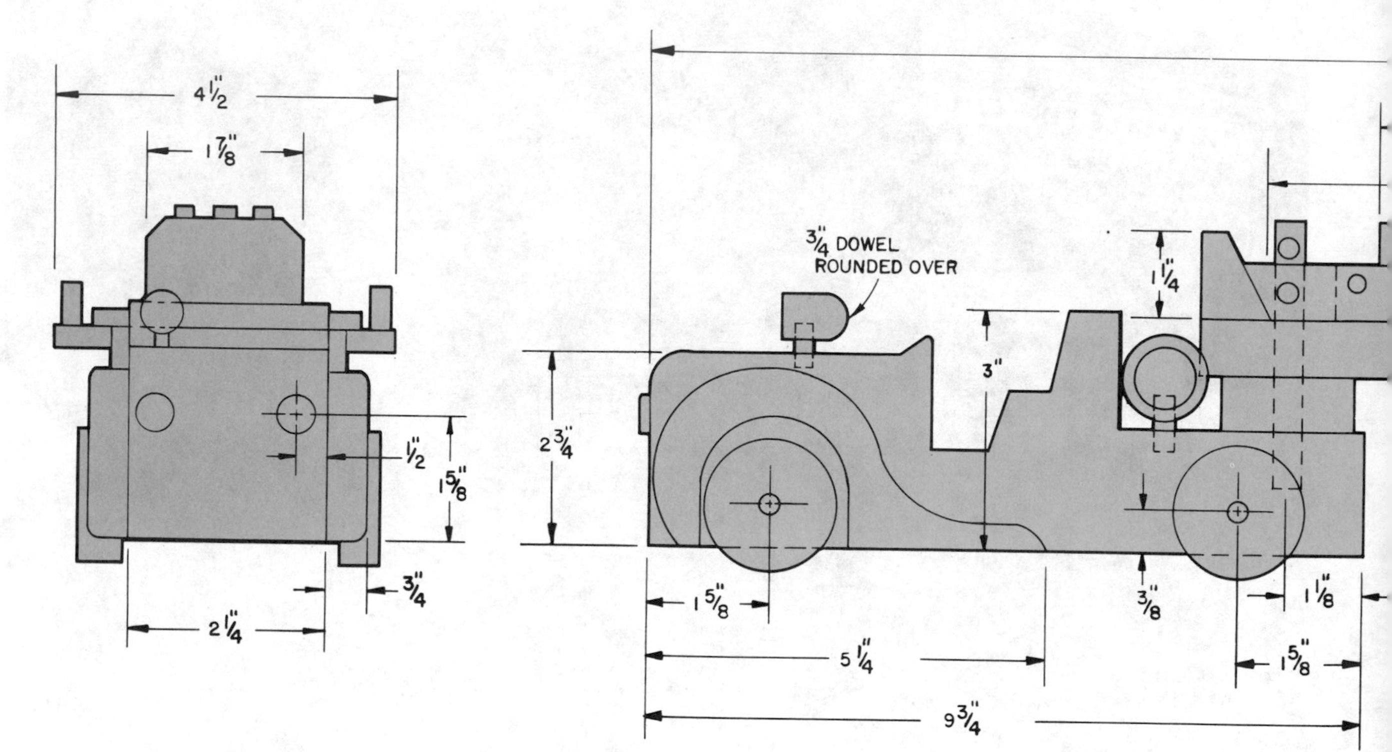

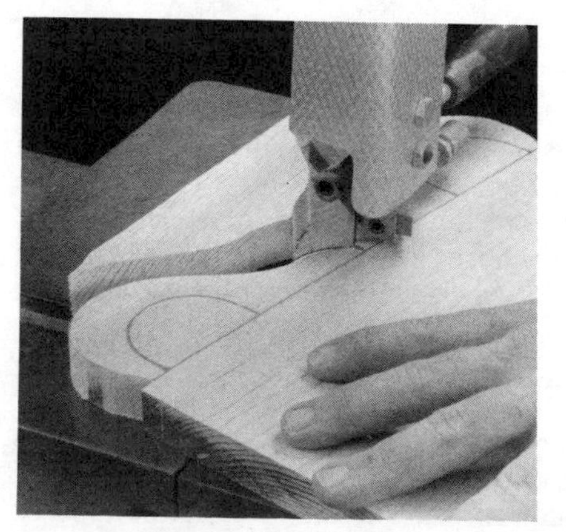

Figure 1. Cut the top edge of the fender shape in a long piece of stock. Don't cut the fender free until after you've shaped the edge.

punishment kids can deal out, they must be made from a strong material. We used poplar to make the fire engine you see here, but maple, birch, and cherry would also be good choices.

Cut the hook body, platforms, and reel supports to the sizes shown in the Bill of Materials. Cut a board 3/4" x 5 1/2" x 12" to make the fenders — you'll see why later. If you don't have a large, thick block of wood to make the hook body, glue up one 2 1/4" x 3" x 9 3/4" from three pieces of 3/4"-thick stock. Let the glue dry thoroughly before cutting.

Enlarge the patterns for the hook body and the fenders, then trace them on the stock. Position the fenders patterns so that they are drawn at either end of the board you have cut, with the top edges close to the ends. Using a

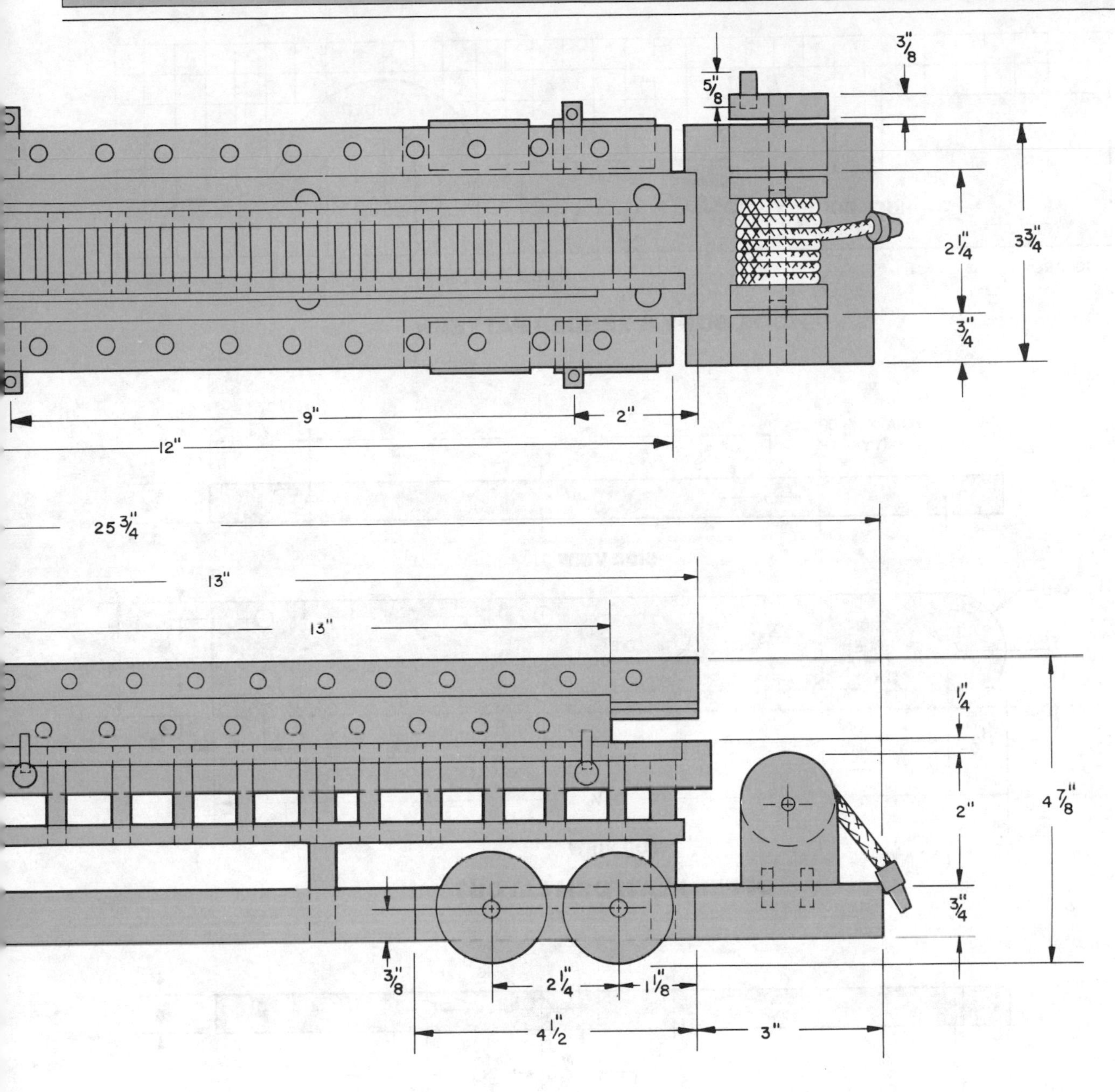

bandsaw, cut out the shape of the hook body and just the *top edge* of the fender shapes. (See Figure 1.) Leave the fenders attached to the board; don't cut them free yet.

Round the top edges of the fenders with a sander or router. (See Figure 2.) Leaving the fenders attached to a large board allows you to do this safely. You can shape the edge of the fender without getting your hands too close to the power tool. (If you cut the fenders free of the stock, they would be too small and too hard to hold onto while you shaped them.) Once the top edge of the fenders are rounded, cut them free of the stock.

Use this same technique to make the siren and the hose nozzle. Using a sander or a file, round the end of a long ¾"-diameter dowel to make the siren, and taper the end of a

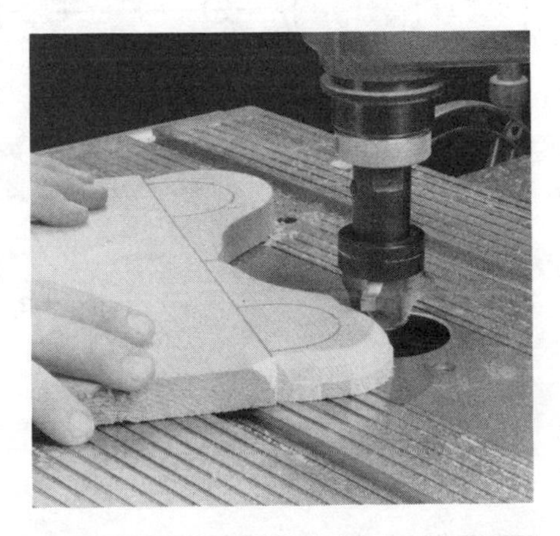

Figure 2. Round over the upper edge of the fender, *then* cut it free from the stock.

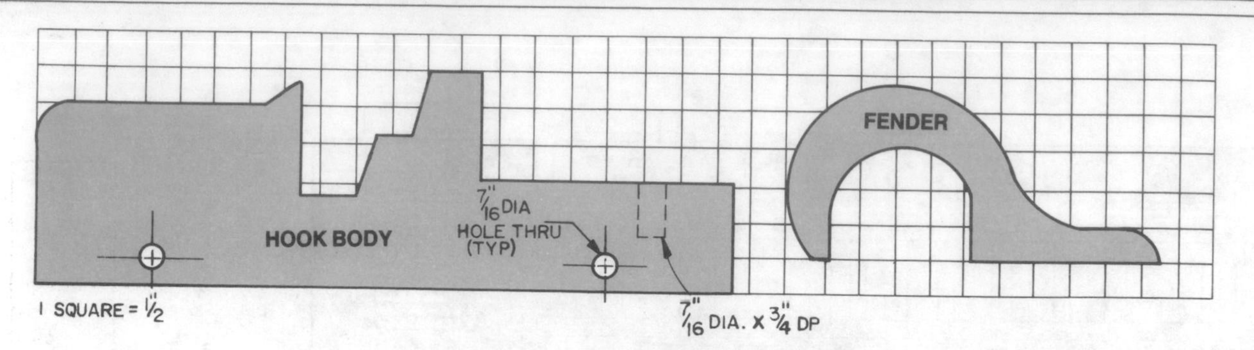

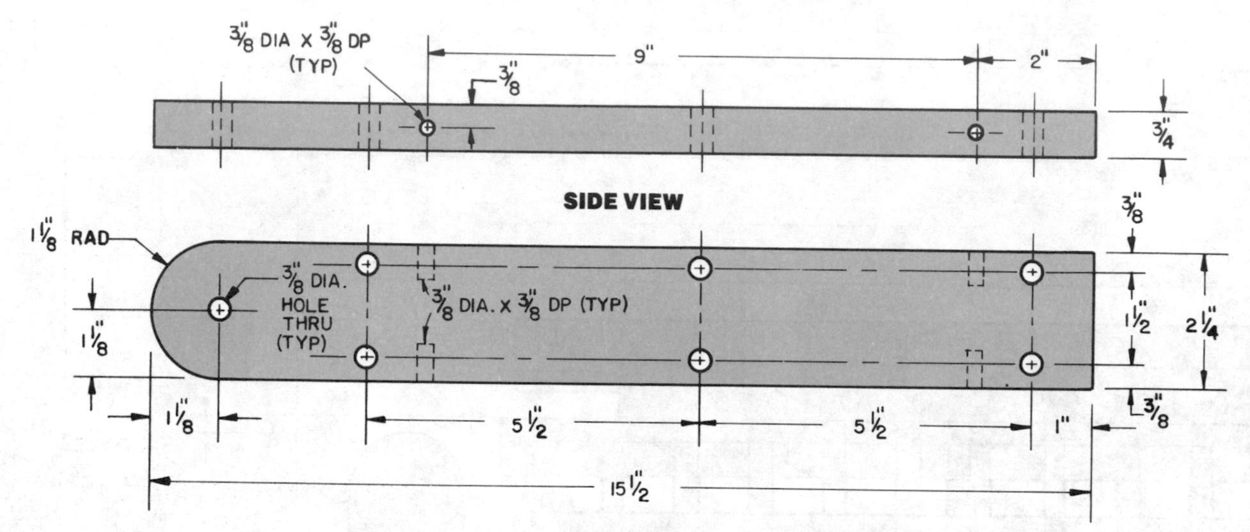

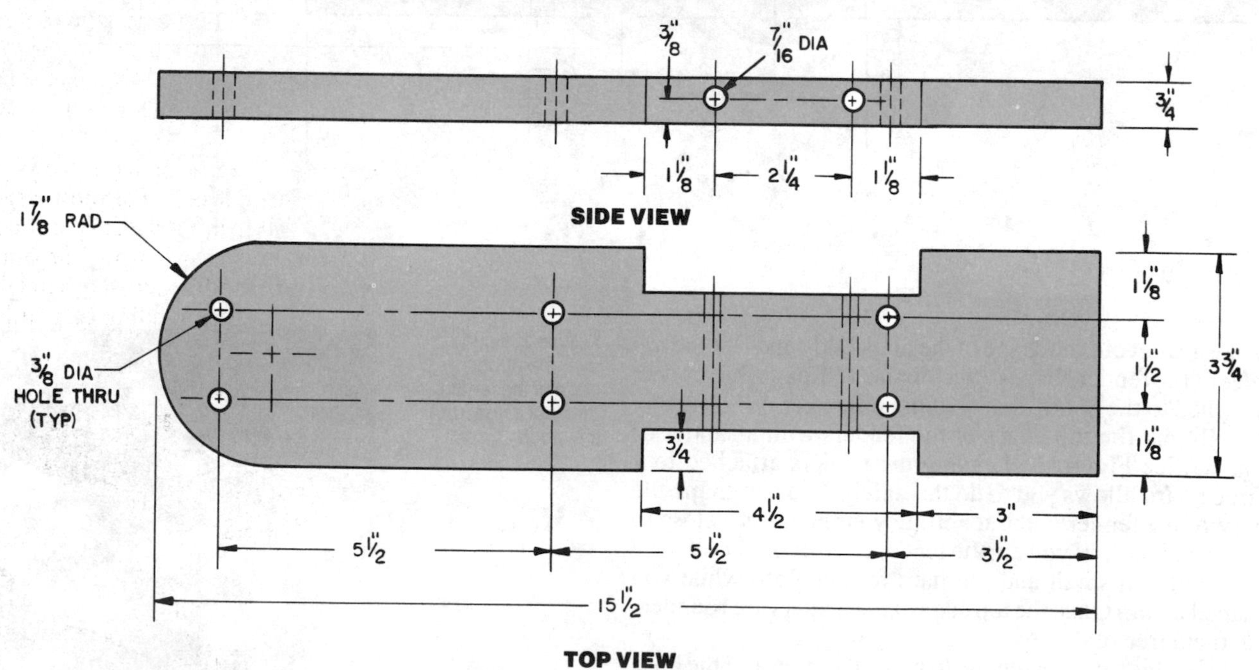

LOWER PLATFORM LAYOUT

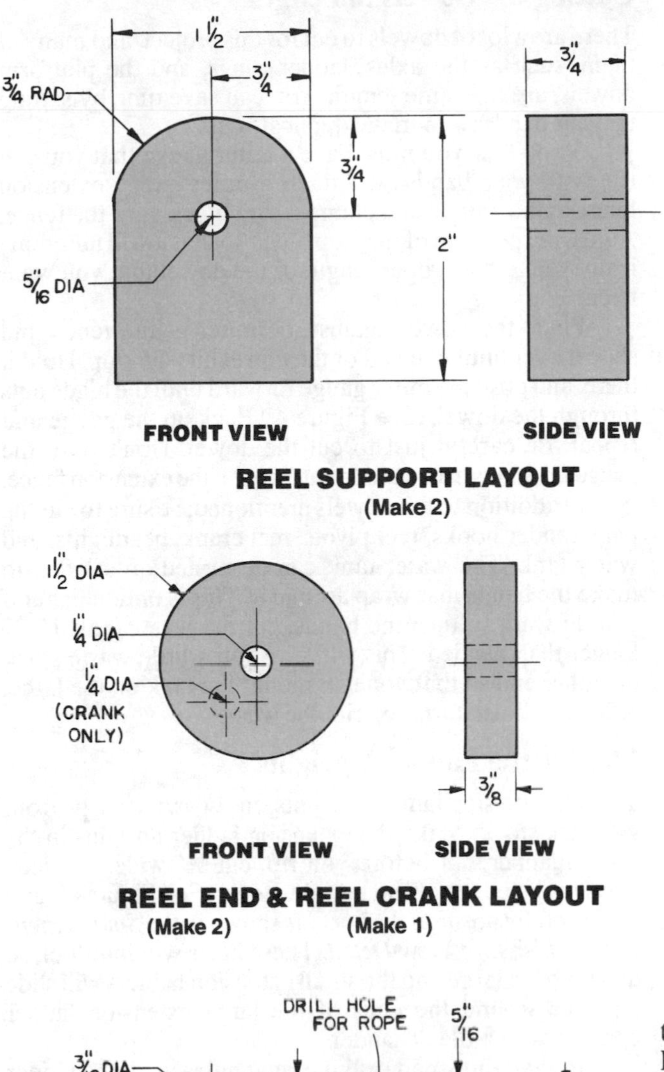

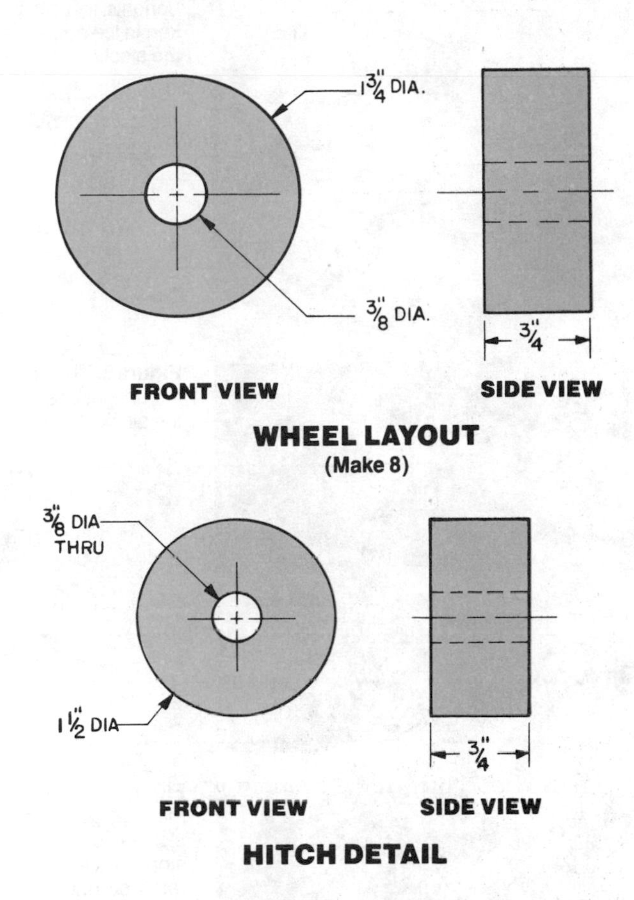

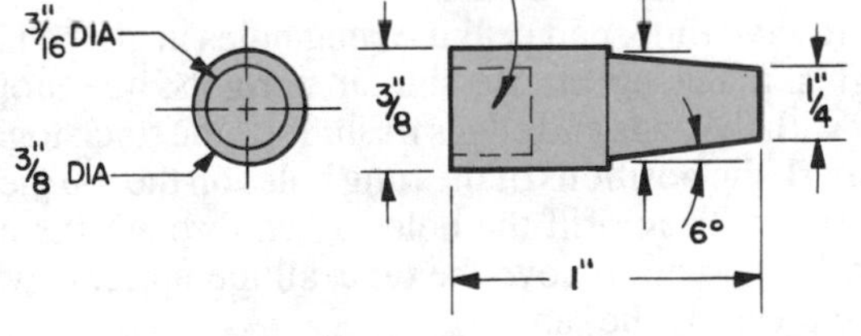

⅜"-diameter dowel to make the nozzle. *Then* cut the siren and the nozzle from the shaped dowel ends. If you tried to shape one end of these parts after you cut them to length, you'd find them difficult (if not impossible) to hold onto.

Lay out the shapes of the upper platform, lower platform, and reel support on the stock, and cut the shapes with a bandsaw. Sand away any saw marks.

Making the Round Parts

You can cut all the round parts, including the wheels, hitch, hose reels, and hose crank, with holesaws. Select saws that are approximately ¼" larger in diameter than the final diameter that you want to cut. Mount the holesaw in your drill press, and set the stop on the press to stop the saw within ⅛" of cutting completely through the stock.

Saw each round part in two steps. First, cut *almost* all the way through the stock, until the drill stop halts the saw. Retract the saw, flip the stop over, and complete the cut from the other side. Use the pilot hole to help line up the saw for the second cut. This two-step procedure will reduce the amount of chipping and tear-out at the edges of the sawn wheel or other round part.

Select a short length (3"–4") of dowel that is the same diameter as the pilot drill in the holesaw. (For most larger saws, this will be 3/16" or ¼".) Clamp this dowel in the chuck of your drill press. Friction-fit the sawn wheel or other round part on this dowel and turn the drill press on. Sand the sawn edges of the part as if you were sanding on a lathe. (See Figure 3.)

Figure 3. Sand the edges of the wheels and the other round parts on your drill press, as if you were sanding on a lathe. Clamp a dowel in the drill chuck and friction-fit the wheels to this dowel.

Figure 4. To make the extension ladder uprights, first cut a kerf in the edge of the stock.

Figure 5. Then rip the upright free of the stock.

Figure 6. Use a miter gauge extension fence and a stop block to accurately cut duplicate lengths of dowel stock.

Cutting the Dowels to Length

There are a lot of dowels to cut for this project, and many of them, such as the axles, ladder rungs, and the platform dowels, are the same length. You can save time by setting up your bandsaw to make duplicate cuts.

To do this, you must have a miter gauge that you can use with your bandsaw. Attach a miter gauge extension fence to the gauge, and clamp a stop block onto the fence. Adjust the position of the stop block so that it will automatically gauge the proper length of the dowel that you want to cut.

Place the dowel against the miter gauge fence and slide it over until one end of the dowel hits the stop. Hold it there, and push the miter gauge forward until the blade cuts through the dowel. (See Figure 4.) Back up the gauge and repeat. Be careful just to cut the dowel. Don't push the gauge far enough forward to cut through the extension fence.

In addition to the dowels mentioned, be sure to cut the pegs, ladder hooks, reel pivots, reel crank, headlights, and water tank. The water tank can be turned on a lathe, to make the bands that wrap around it. This is optional; but if you do want to turn the bands, cut the water tank 1″–2″ longer than needed. This will give you a little waste stock on either end so that you can mount the tank on the lathe. After you finish turning, trim the waste.

Making the Ladder Uprights

To make the side ladder uprights, rip ¼″-wide strips from ¾″-thick stock. Make the extension ladder uprights in the same manner, but before you rip, cut ⅛″-wide, ⅛″-deep kerfs in the edges of the upright stock. (See Figures 5 and 6.) Carefully position the kerfs as shown in the *Small Extension Ladder, End View Detail.* These kerfs will interlock so that both the large and the small extension ladders will slide together. Round the ends of the large extension ladder uprights with a file or sander.

To save time, pad drill the rung holes in all the ladder uprights. Stack up all the similar uprights, one atop the other with the ends and edges flush. Tape the stack together and mark the positions of the rung holes on the top piece in each stack. Then drill the holes down through the entire stack. When you remove the tape, all the uprights will be drilled precisely the same.

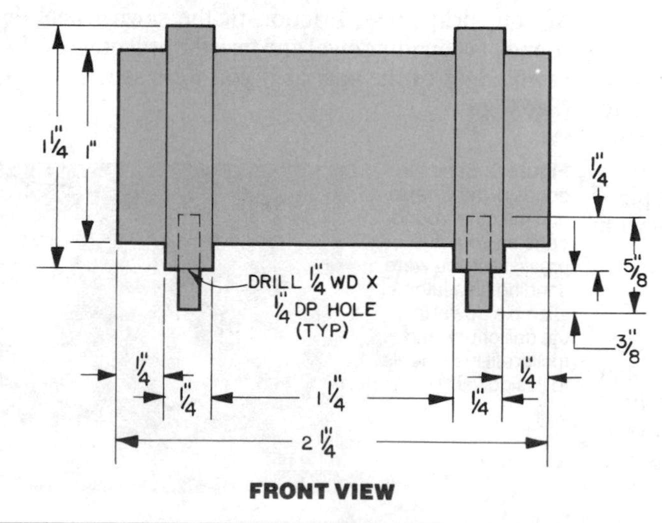

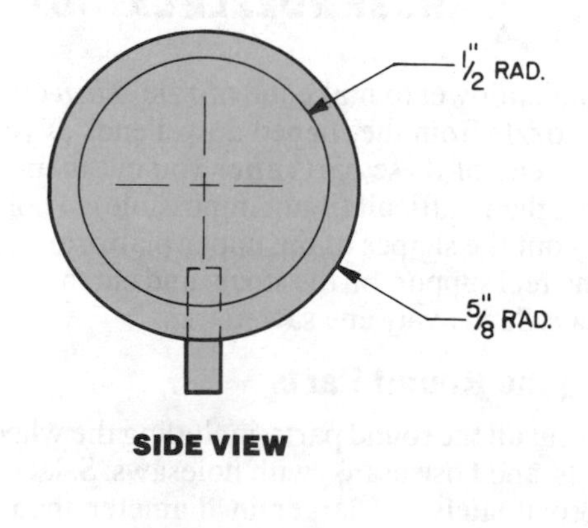

WATER TANK

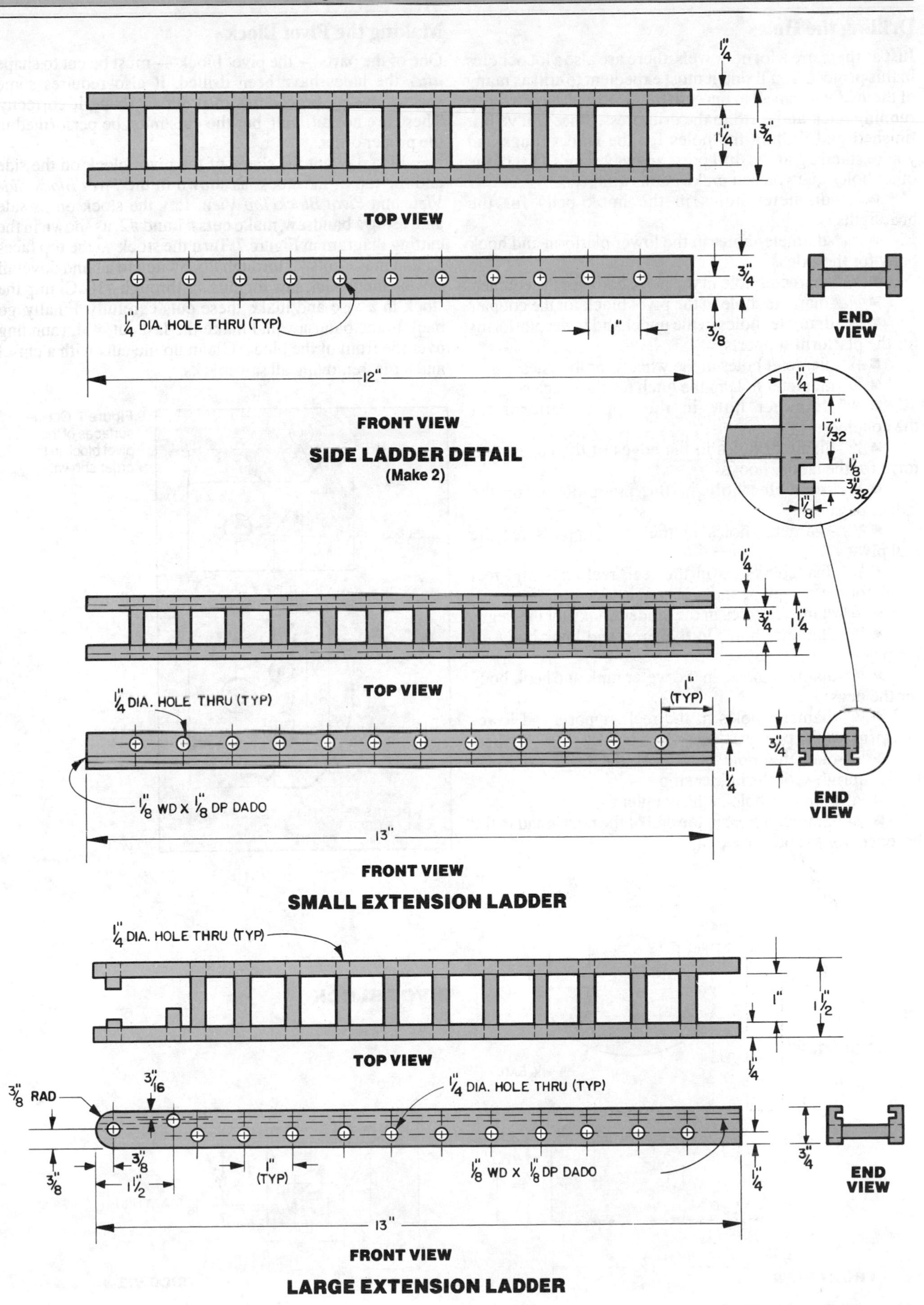

1/4"
1 3/4"
1 1/4"
TOP VIEW
3/4"
END VIEW
1/4 DIA. HOLE THRU (TYP)
3/8
1"
12"
FRONT VIEW
SIDE LADDER DETAIL
(Make 2)
1/4"
17/32"
1/8"
3/32"
1/8"
1/4"
3/4"
1 1/4"
TOP VIEW
1/4 DIA. HOLE THRU (TYP)
1" (TYP)
3/4
1/4
END VIEW
1/8 WD X 1/8 DP DADO
13"
FRONT VIEW
SMALL EXTENSION LADDER
1/4 DIA. HOLE THRU (TYP)
1"
1 1/2
TOP VIEW
1/4
3/8 RAD
3/16
1/4 DIA. HOLE THRU (TYP)
3/8
3/8
1 1/2
1" (TYP)
1/8 WD X 1/8 DP DADO
3/4
1/4
END VIEW
13"
FRONT VIEW
LARGE EXTENSION LADDER

Drilling the Holes

Just as there are a lot of dowels, there are also a lot of holes in this project. You'll find it most expedient to drill as many of them as you can all at once, so that you don't have to keep running back and forth to the drill press. Since you've just finished pad drilling the holes for the ladder rungs and you're standing at the drill press anyway, here's a list of the other holes that you can make at this time:

- ½″-diameter holes in the hook body for the headlights
- 7/16″-diameter holes in the lower platform and hook body for the axles
- 7/16″-diameter hole in the hook body for the coupler
- 7/16″-diameter hole in the pivot block for the coupler
- ⅜″-diameter holes in the upper and lower platforms for the platform supports
- ⅜″-diameter holes in the wheels for the axles
- ⅜″-diameter hole in the hitch for the coupler
- ⅜″-diameter hole in the upper platform for the coupler
- ⅜″-diameter holes in the edges of the upper platform for the ladder hooks
- 5/16″-diameter hole in the pivot block for the ladder pegs
- 5/16″-diameter holes in the reel supports for the reel pivot
- ¼″-diameter holes in the reel, reel ends, and reel crank for the reel pivot and reel handle
- ¼″-diameter holes in the ladder hooks for the pegs
- ¼″-diameter holes in the siren and hook body for the peg
- ¼″-diameter holes in the water tank and hook body for the pegs
- ¼″-diameter holes in the reel supports and lower platform for the pegs
- ¼″-diameter hole in one of the large extension ladder uprights for the ladder stop
- ¼″-diameter hole in the coupler for a peg
- 3/16″-diameter hole in the end of the nozzle and in the hose reel for the hose/rope

Making the Pivot Block

One of the parts — the pivot block — must be cut to shape *after* the holes have been drilled. It also requires some special sawing procedures in order to shape it correctly. These are not difficult, but the cuts must be performed in the proper order.

First, lay out the shape of the pivot block on the side and the top of the stock, as shown in the *Pivot Block/Side View* and *Pivot Block/Top View.* Lay the stock on its side and, using a bandsaw, make cuts #1 and #2, as shown in the cutting diagram in Figure 7. Turn the stock so the top faces up and make cuts #3 through #6. Switch to a hand dovetail saw or small back saw for cuts #7 through #10. Clamp the stock in a vise and make these cuts carefully. Finally, go back to the bandsaw and make the last cut, #11, rounding over the front of the block. Clean up the cuts with a chisel and a file, removing all saw marks.

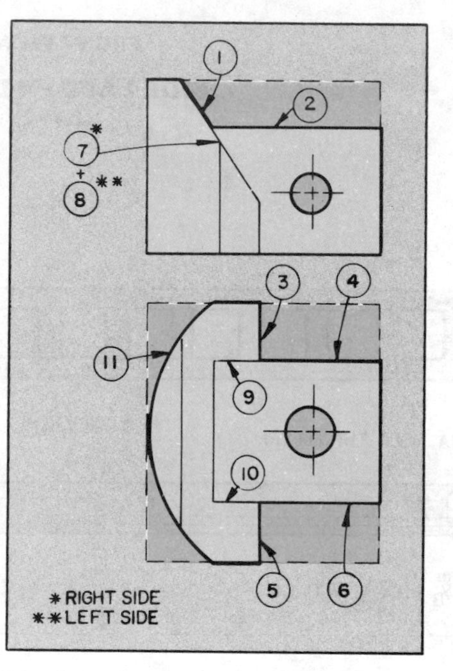

Figure 7. Cut the surfaces of the pivot block in the order shown.

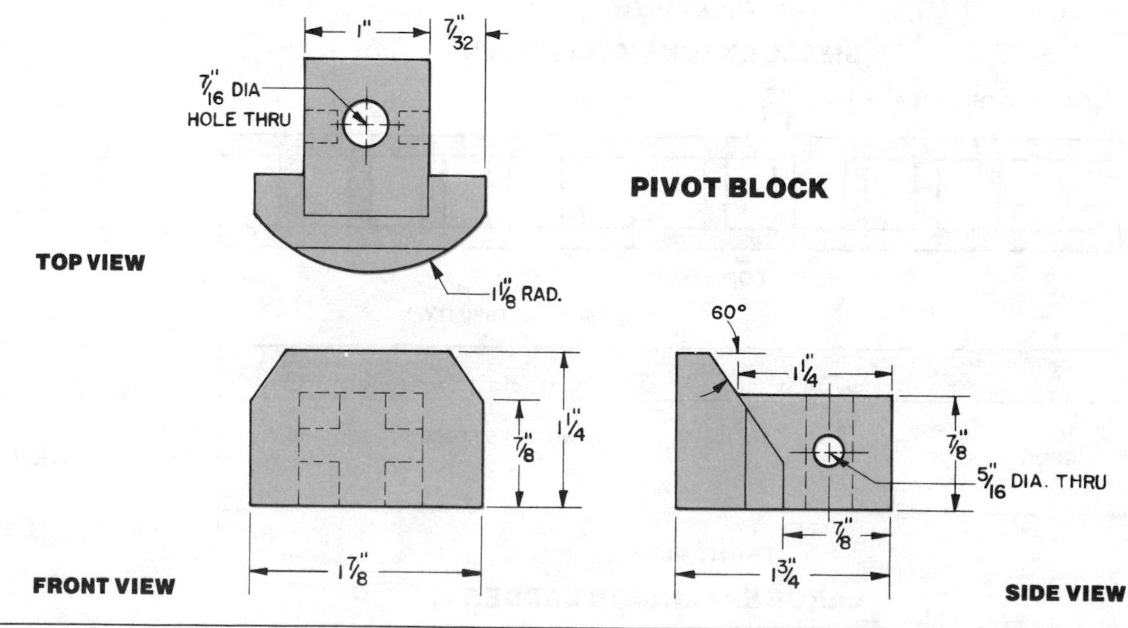

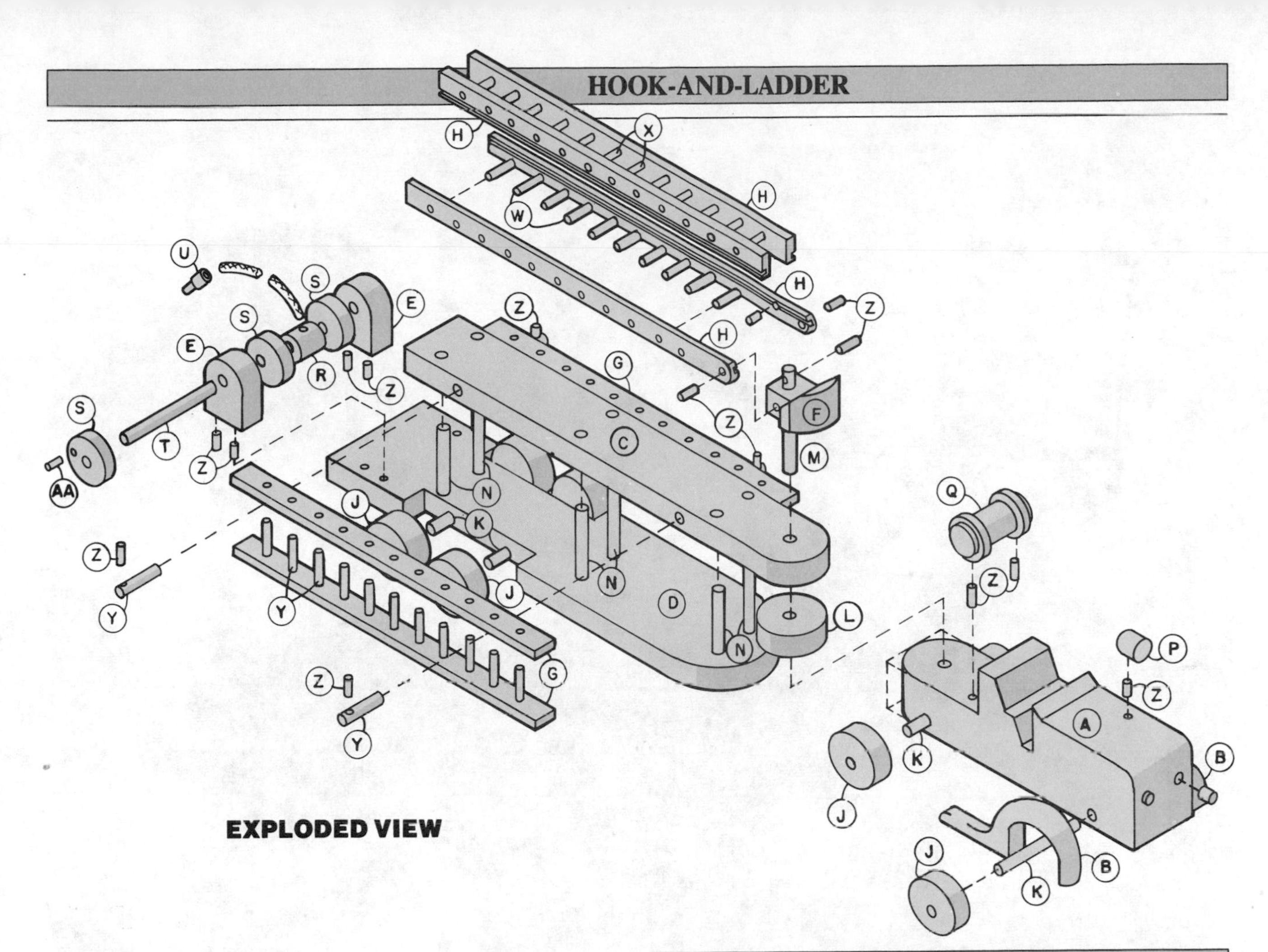

Assembly and Finishing

Surface sand all the parts you have made, and then begin to glue them together. Assembly is mostly a matter of gluing various dowels in their respective holes. Be careful to evenly coat the ends of the dowels *and* the sides of the holes with glue so that you get a good bond.

Also be careful not to glue any moving parts together. The reel pivot must turn freely in the reel supports. So should the axles in the axle holes, and the pivot block on the coupler. To help these parts turn or pivot smoothly — and to prevent any excess glue from sticking to them — carefully coat the turning surfaces of the dowels with paraffin wax.

You can use ordinary carpenter's (yellow) glue for most of this project, but glue the ends of the hose to the reel and the nozzle with epoxy glue. Use a lot of epoxy — fill the holes — so that the connections will withstand a good tug if they have to.

When the fire engine is completely assembled, finish sand the surfaces and round over any sharp edges. Apply a non-toxic finish, such as mineral oil or salad bowl dressing. You can also use Danish oil, if you're not going to give this hook-and-ladder away immediately. Danish oil *becomes* non-toxic, after it has been allowed to sit for several weeks.

This project first appeared in HANDS ON! Magazine, a publication of Shopsmith, Inc.

BILL OF MATERIALS — Hook-and-Ladder

Finished Dimensions in Inches

	Part	Dimensions
A.	Hook body	2¼ x 3 x 9¾
B.	Fenders (2)	¾ x 2⅜ x 5¼
C.	Upper platform	¾ x 2¼ x 15½
D.	Lower platform	¾ x 3¾ x 15½
E.	Reel supports (2)	¾ x 1½ x 2
F.	Pivot block	1¼ x 1¾ x 1⅞
G.	Side ladder uprights (4)	¼ x ¾ x 12
H.	Extension ladder uprights (4)	¼ x ¾ x 13
J.	Wheels (8)	1¾ dia. x ¾
K.	Axles (4)	⅜ dia. x 3⅞
L.	Hitch	1½ dia. x ¾
M.	Coupler	⅜ dia. x 3½
N.	Platform supports (6)	⅜ dia. x 3
P.	Siren	¾ dia. x 1⅛
Q.	Water tank	1¼ dia. x 2¼
R.	Hose reel	¾ dia x 1⅜
S.	Reel ends/crank (3)	1½ dia. x ⅜
T.	Reel pivot	¼ dia. x 4 3/16
U.	Hose nozzle	⅜ dia. x 1
V.	Side ladder rungs (22)	¼ dia. x 1¾
W.	Large extension ladder rungs (11)	¼ dia. x 1½
X.	Small extension ladder rungs (12)	¼ dia. x 1¼
Y.	Ladder hooks	⅜ dia. x 1½
Z.	Pegs (15)	¼ dia. x ⅝

HARDWARE

3/16" Nylon rope (24")

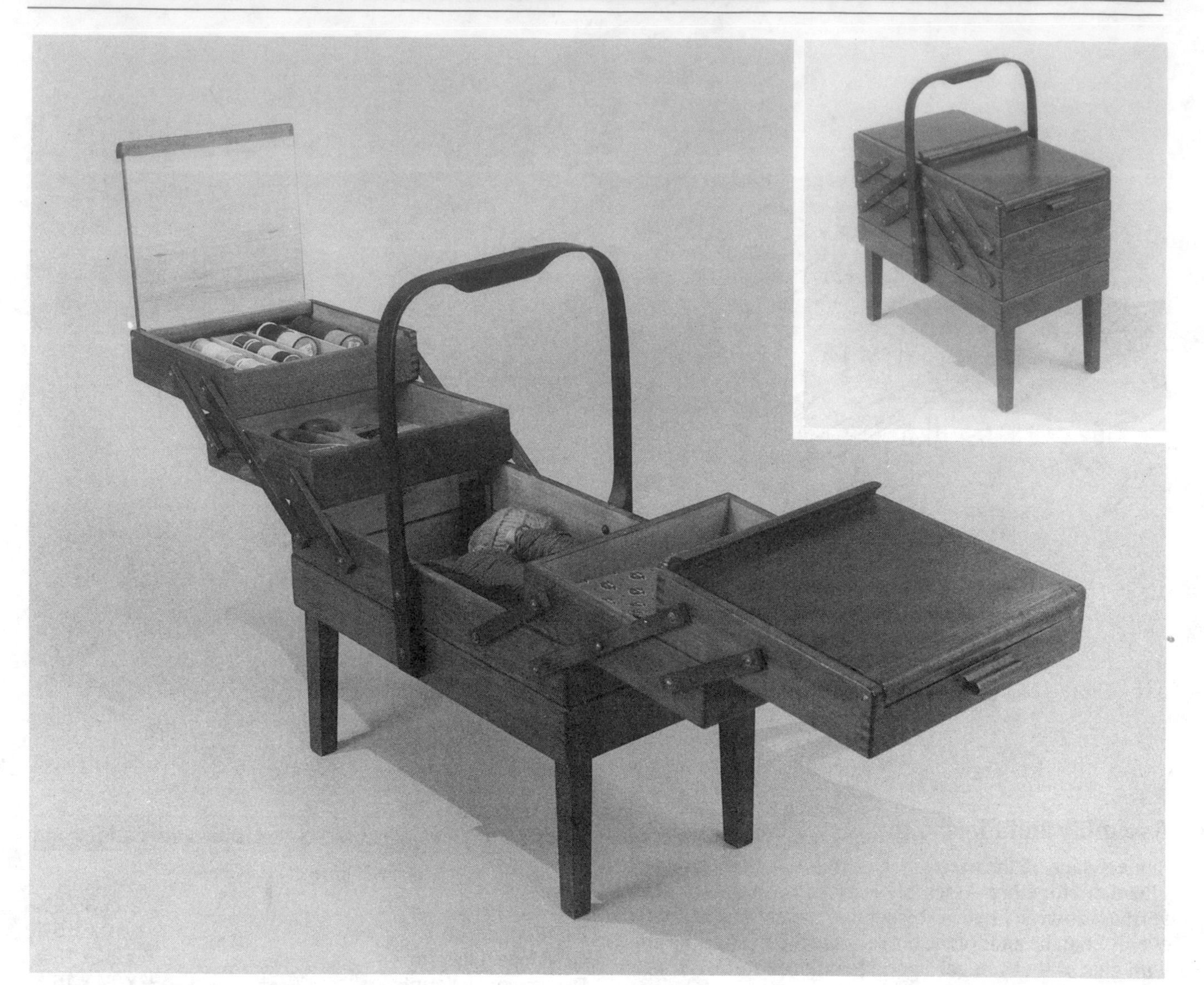

Courtesy Deborah Morgan-Lamar.

Sewing Box

This ingenious fold-out storage unit helps to organize dozens of small items.

It's called a "sewing box," but it has many other uses. It will not only store the threads, needles, and other paraphernalia associated with sewing, but also equipment and materials for model-making, leatherworking, woodcarving, stamp collecting, needlepoint, repair of electronic equipment, and dozens of other hobbies, pastimes, or chores.

The "box" consists of several trays that are hinged so that they will fold out, exposing (but not spilling) their contents. This allows you to keep many small- and medium-sized items neatly organized. You can easily reach these tools and materials at a moment's notice, then put them away again quickly. The box even has a handle, so that you can carry it from room to room.

The trays are made using classic box construction. The sides and ends are joined with finger joints (also called "box" joints), and the bottoms set in grooves. The trays stack on top of each other, but a simple system of "hinges" — actually just lengths of wood, using screws for pivots — ties them together. Pull up and out on the top tray, and the trays beneath it fan out, exposing their contents. To re-stack the trays, just push in on the same top tray.

Cutting the Parts

Select a good, cabinet grade lumber for this project, preferably something that's not too brittle. The trays are joined by multiple finger joints and the top handle is thinned out so that the stock will bend. If you choose a brittle wood, such as cherry or maple, the fingers will tear and chip when you make them, and the handle may break when you bend it. Instead, look for something supple. Poplar is a good choice. So is oak (if it hasn't been sitting too long), walnut, mahogany, and clear white pine. Other choices include butternut, birch, hickory, alder and ash.

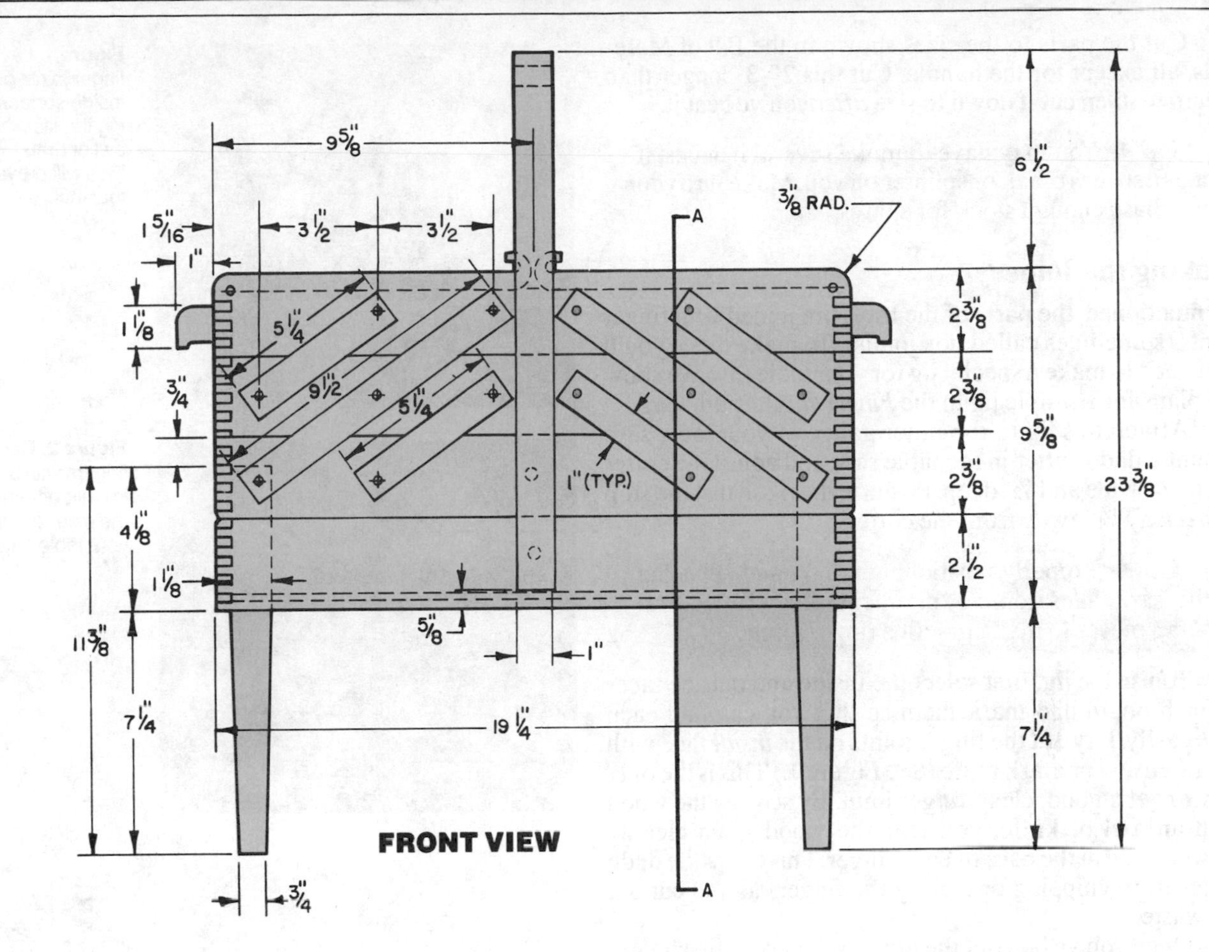
9 5/8"
1 5/16"
3 1/2"
3 1/2"
1"
1 1/8"
3/4"
5 1/4
9 1/2
5 1/4
1" (TYP.)
3/8" RAD.
A
6 1/2"
2 3/8
2 3/8
9 5/8
2 3/8
2 1/2
23 3/8"
4 1/8
1 1/8"
11 3/8"
5/8"
1"
7 1/4"
19 1/4"
7 1/4
3/4"
FRONT VIEW

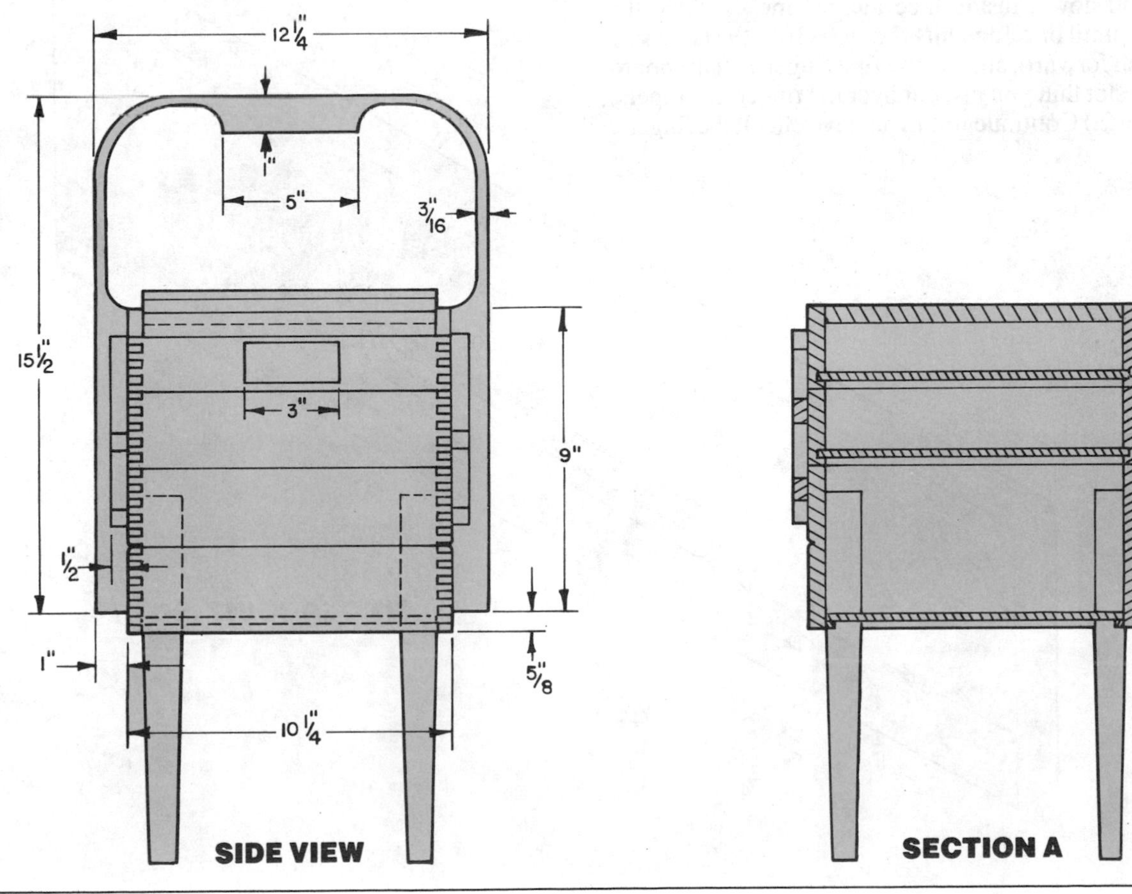
12 1/4"
1"
5"
3/16"
15 1/2"
3"
9"
1/2"
1"
5/8
10 1/4"
SIDE VIEW
SECTION A

Cut the parts to the sizes shown in the Bill of Materials, all except for the handle. Cut this 2″–3″ longer than specified, then cut it down to size *after* you've bent it.

Tip ◆ You may have to make several handles, if the first ones break or splinter on you. Make sure you purchase enough stock for spares.

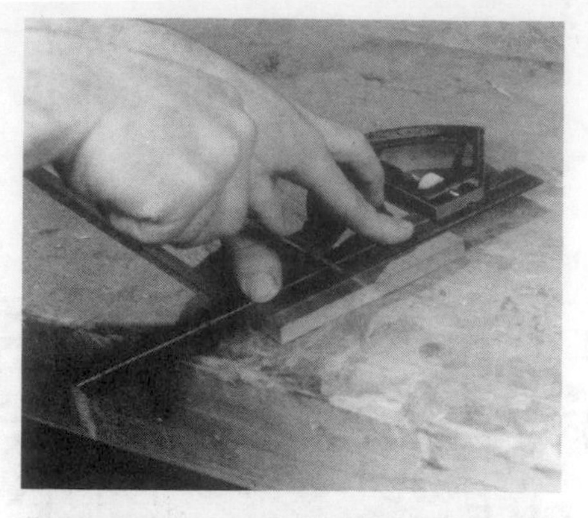

Figure 1. Lay out the finger joints on the inside surface, scoring the stock with an awl or marking knife. This will prevent tear-out.

Making the Joinery

As mentioned, the parts of the trays are joined with finger joints (sometimes called box joints). To make these, you'll first need to make a special jig for your table saw. We show the plans for a simple jig in the *Finger Joint Jig* drawing.

Attach this jig to the miter gauge of your table saw. Mount a dado cutter in the table saw, and adjust the cutter to cut 1/4″ wide and 1/2″ deep. Position the jig so that the stop is *precisely* 1/4″ away from the cutter.

Figure 2. Cut the fingers with a finger joint jig attached to the miter gauge of your table saw.

Tip ◆ Properly positioning the jig and adjusting the saw takes some experimentation. Cut several scrap pieces to make practice finger joints.

To use the jig, first select the inside and outside faces of each board and mark them so that you can find each face easily. Lay out the finger joints on the *inside* face with a scratch awl or mark knife (See Figure 1.) This is the only way to get a good, clean finger joint. By scoring the wood with an awl or knife, you tear the wood grain cleanly between and at the base of each finger. This keeps the dado cutter from chipping or tearing the fingers as you cut out the waste.

Once you've laid out the joints, select your first board. Place it end down, inside face against the jig. Slide the board over until one edge hits the stop. Turn the table saw on and push forward, cutting the first finger. Lift the board up, put the slot that you just cut over the finger, and repeat. (See Figure 2.) Continue until you have cut all the fingers.

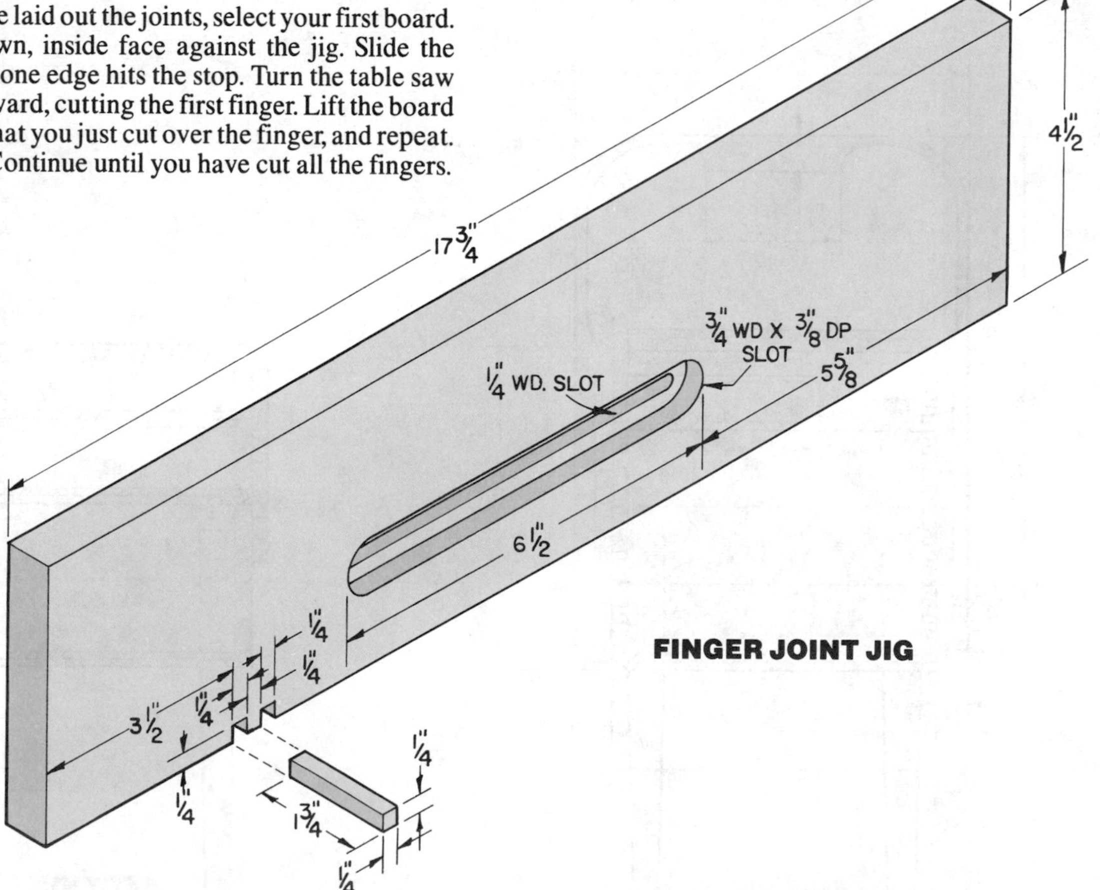

FINGER JOINT JIG

When making the fingers in the end of the board that joins the end you just cut, you'll have to adjust the position of the first finger. Make the cut with the board 1/8″ away from the stop, then continue as you did before. This will ensure that the edges of the boards line up with each other when you assemble the joints.

Note: When making the finger joints, remember that the top tray ends have no fingers in the first 1″, closest to the top edges.

In the top and middle trays, the bottoms rest in 1/4″-wide, 1/4″-deep *blind* grooves cut into the sides and ends. The easiest way to make these grooves is with a router — either an overarm router or a hand-held router mounted in a router table. Stop routing these grooves 1/4″ from each end of the boards, so that the grooves are actually closed slots. (See Figure 3.) This way, the grooves won't show on the outside of the project when you assemble the trays. Square the ends of the grooves with a chisel.

While you're making the grooves, you can also cut 1/4″-wide, 1/4″-deep dadoes in the sides of the middle and top tray parts for the horizontal dividers. (Do not cut dadoes for the vertical dividers.) Although these dadoes are the same dimensions as the grooves, you'll find it easier to use a dado cutter to make them, rather than continue to use the router.

Figure 3. Rout blind grooves in the top and middle tray parts to hold the tray bottoms.

Cut the cross lap joints in the top tray dividers, as shown in the *Top Tray/Vertical Divider Layout* and the *Top Tray/Horizontal Divider Layout.* Cut the sides of the laps with a backsaw, then remove the waste with a chisel.

Dry assemble the trays and dividers to check the fit of the joints. When you're satisfied with the fit, round over the outside corners of the top tray sides, as shown in the *Front View.* Drill 3/16″ pivot holes near those same corners to hinge the lids to the top trays. Then finish sand all the parts and assemble the trays with glue.

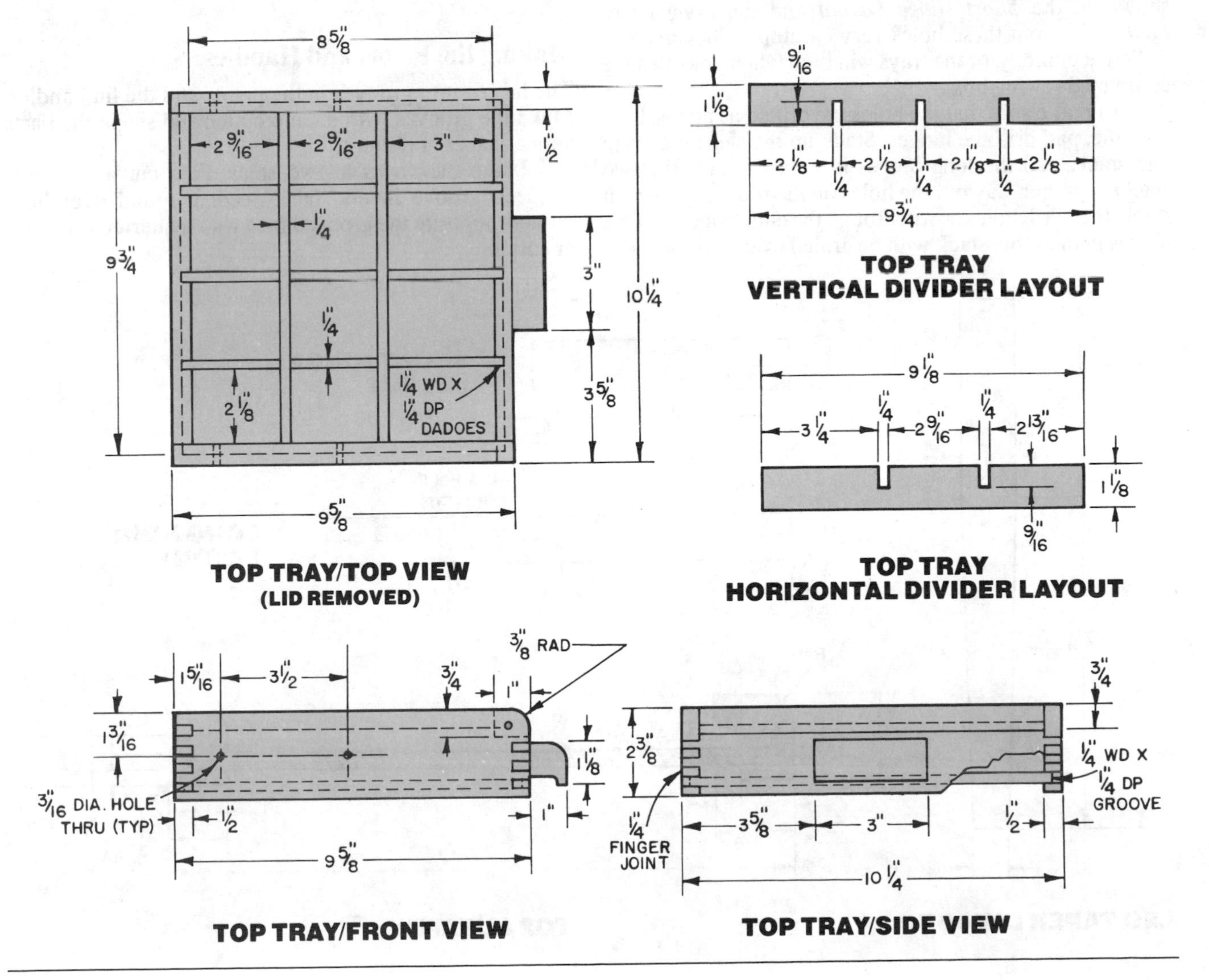

Tapering the Legs

While the glue is drying on the trays, taper the legs on your table saw. To do this, you'll either need a commercial tapering jig, or you can make your own. These jigs hold the boards at an angle on the table saw, off parallel to the saw blade.

To cut the tapers, place the L-shaped tapering jig so that the upright of the "L" rests against the rip fence on your table saw. Put a board in the jig and adjust the rip fence so that the saw blade starts to cut the leg stock 4⅛" down from the top end. Turn the saw on and push the board forward. (See Figure 4.) Save the waste!

Turn the saw off. Flip the board over 180° in the jig and put the waste between the sawn edge of the board and the jig. The waste will serve as a spacer while you cut the other side of the taper. Once again, turn the saw on and push the jig forward. And once again, save the waste.

Tape the waste back onto the stock to make it reasonably square, then repeat the process, cutting the two remaining sides. (See Figure 5.) When you remove the tape, the leg should be tapered on all four sides. Joint and sand the tapers smooth.

Figure 4. Cut the tapers in two opposite sides of the legs, Save the waste.

Figure 5. Tape the waste back to the legs, and cut the tapers in the two remaining sides.

Making the Hinges

With a 3/16"-diameter bit, drill the holes in the hinges, as shown in the *Short Hinge Layout* and the *Long Hinge Layout.* Lay out these holes very carefully. They *must* be drilled accurately, or the trays will bind when you open the completed sewing box.

To make sure that the holes are drilled as precisely as possible, pad drill the hinges. Stack up the short hinges in one stack, and the long hinges in another. Tape the two stacks together. Lay out the holes on the top hinge in each stack, then drill holes down through the entire stack. All the hinges in the same stack with be drilled exactly the same.

Making the Pivots and Handles

The lids fit into grooves in the pivots and the lid handles. Make the grooves with a dado cutter, and shape the parts with a shaper or router.

Make the *pivots* in two steps. First cut a ¼"-wide, ½"-deep groove in one face. Second, round over both corners opposite the grooved face with a quarter-round bit or cutter.

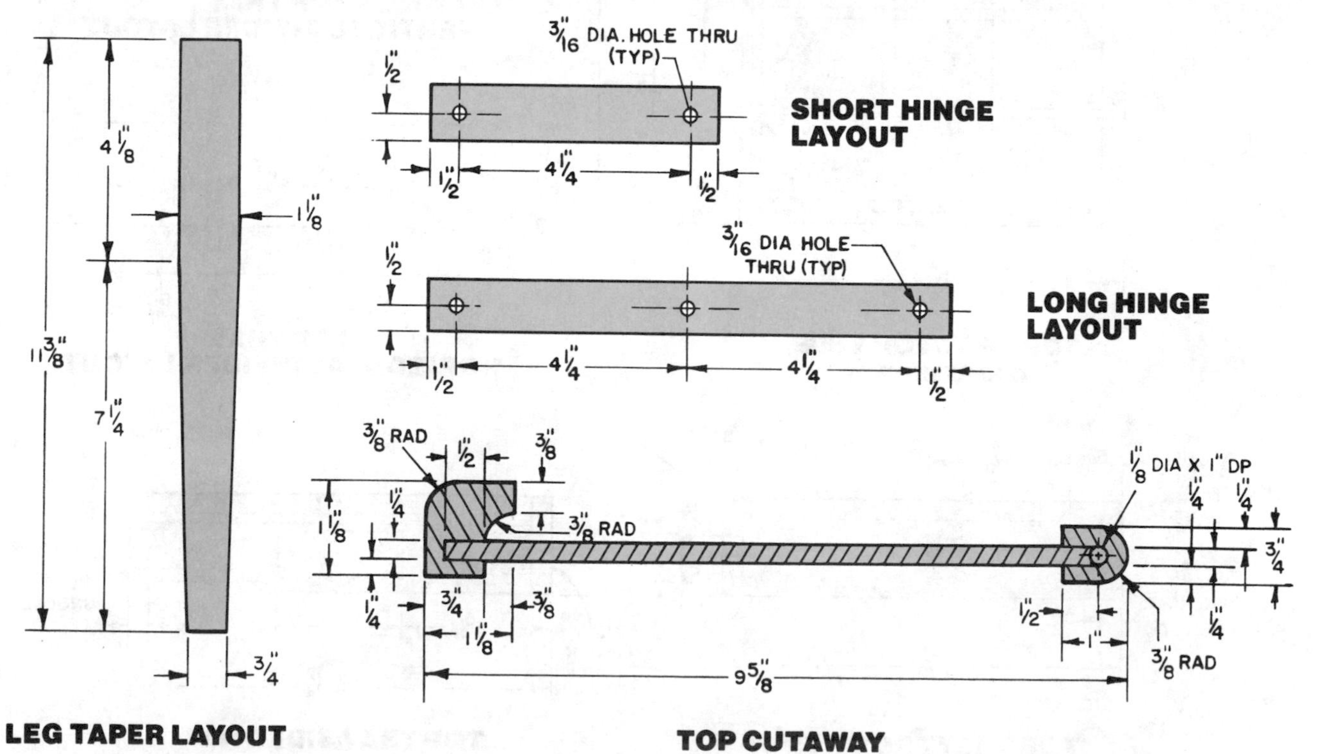

The *lid handles* require four steps. First, cut a ¼″-wide, ⅞″ deep groove in one face. Second, round over one corner opposite the grooved face. Third, make a ½″-wide, ⅜″-deep rabbet in that same face, using a table saw or jointer. (This will reduce the groove to ½″ deep.) Fourth, cut a cove on the inside of that rabbet. (See Figure 6.)

Make the *side handles* in a similar manner to the way you made the lid handles, but omit the grooves. First, round over one corner. Second, cut a ½″-wide, ⅜″-deep rabbet in the face opposite the rounded corner. Third, cut a cove on the inside of the rabbet.

The *large handle* is not made using any of these tools or techniques. It's made completely on a bandsaw. Use the saw to thin out the stock to 3/16″-thick, where shown on the *Side View.* (See Figure 7.) Remove the saw marks with a drum sander. Then carefully bend the handle to shape. Hold it in place with a band clamp until you're ready to attach it to the sewing box assembly.

Tip ◆ If the top handle stock wants to crack or split, soak it in water for a few days before bending it.

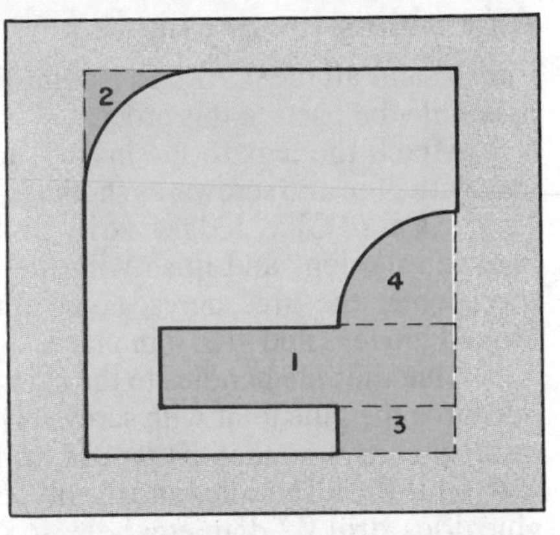

Figure 6. Make the cuts to form the lid handles in the order shown. Use the same procedure to make the side handles, but omit the grooves.

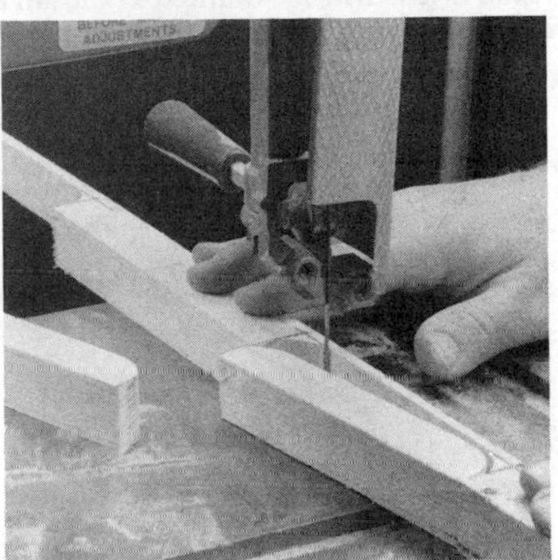

Figure 7. To make the bends in the top handle, thin out the stock with a bandsaw.

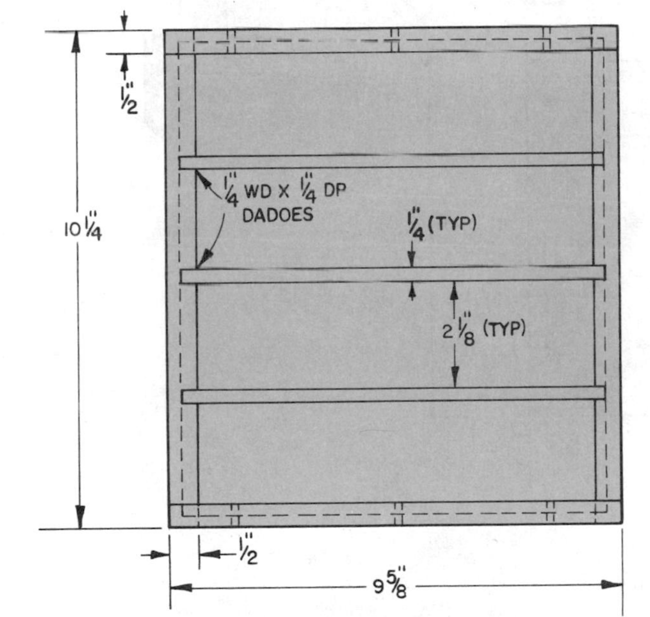

MIDDLE TRAY/TOP VIEW

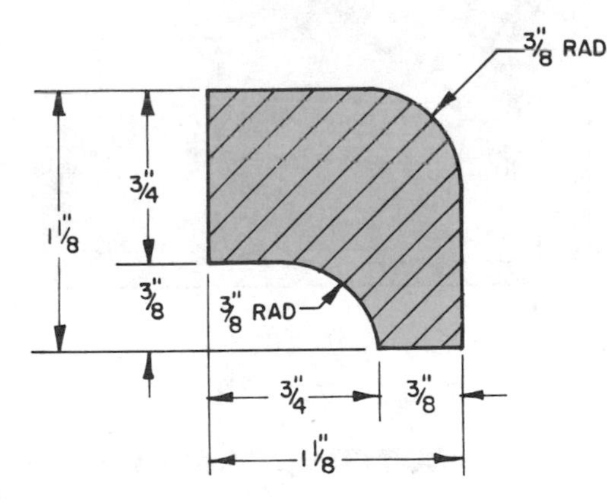

HANDHOLD PROFILE

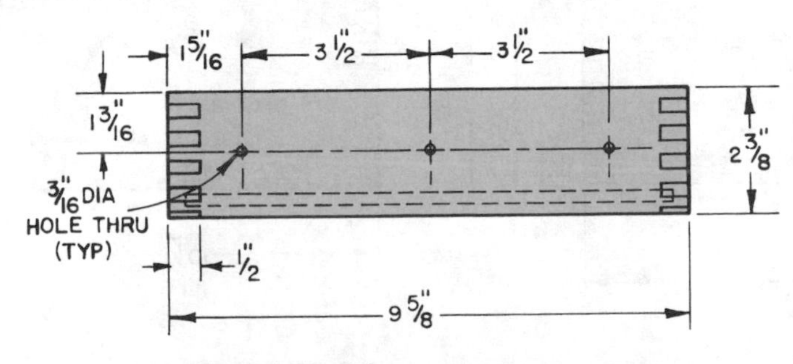

MIDDLE TRAY/FRONT VIEW

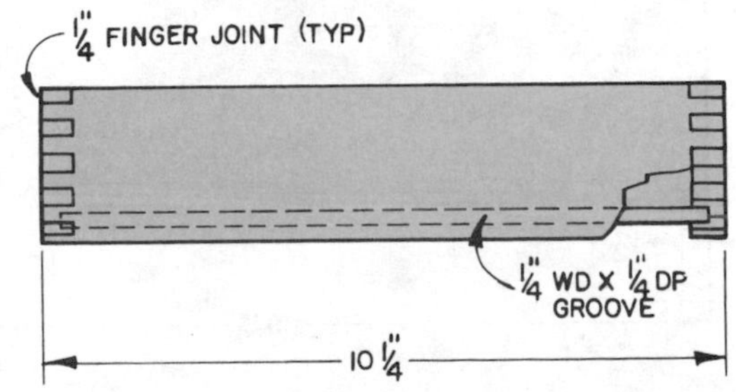

MIDDLE TRAY/SIDE VIEW

Assembling the Sewing Box

Finish sand all the parts and assemblies that need it. Then assemble the parts in this order:

Attach the legs to the inside surfaces of the bottom tray with glue and screws, as shown in the *Bottom Tray/Top View Detail.* Glue ledger strip to the inside surfaces, between the legs and flush with the bottom edges of the tray. When the glue cures, notch the tray bottom to fit around the legs and glue it in place.

Glue the side handles to the sides of the top trays, and reinforce the glue joint with screws. Drive the screws from inside the trays, so that the screws won't show.

Glue the lid handles and the pivots to the lid. When the glue dries, drill 1/8"-diameter holes in the pivots. Attach the lid assemblies to the top trays with roundhead wood screws and washers, driving the screws through the trays and into the pivots. Don't tighten the screws too tight. Leave them loose enough so that the lids open and close smoothly.

Stack the middle and top trays on top of the bottom tray and clamp the stack together with bar clamps so that the trays won't shift around. Carefully mark where the hinges will be attached to the trays, and drill 1/8'-diameter pilot holes, 3/8" deep. Secure the hinges to the trays with roundhead wood screws and washers. Once again, don't tighten the screws too tight.

Check the action of the hinges, making sure that the sewing box opens up properly. If any part of the assembly binds, you may have to loosen the screws that hold the hinges or sand away some stock from the inside surfaces of the hinges.

Finally, attach the top hinge to the bottom tray. Clamp it in position, and mark where you want to cut off the ends. Cut the handle to the proper length, and secure it with flathead wood screws and glue. Drive the screws from inside the tray so that they won't be seen.

Remove all the roundhead screws, and disassemble the trays and lids. Do any necessary touch-up sanding and apply a finish to the completed project. When the finish dries, reassemble the sewing box.

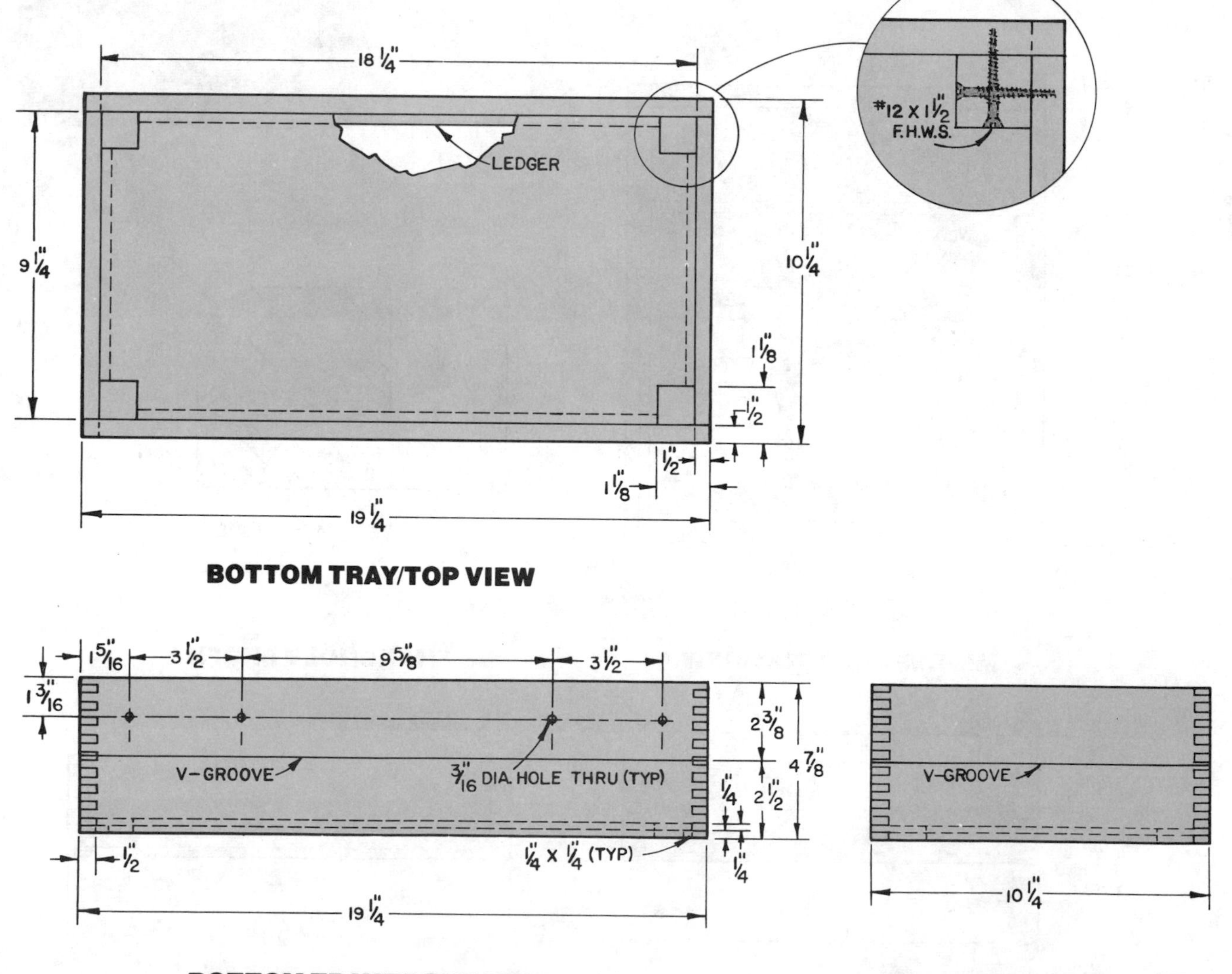

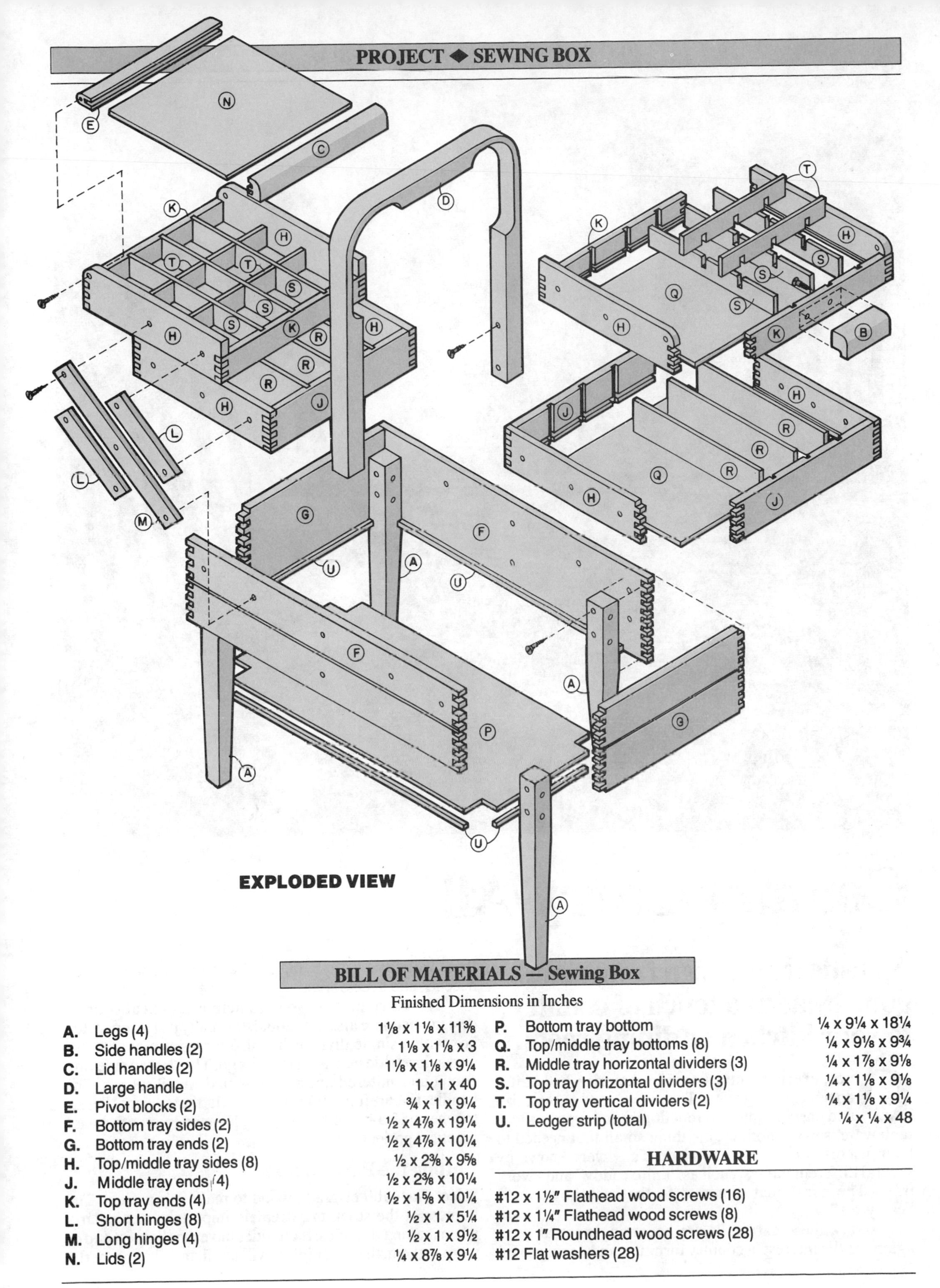

EXPLODED VIEW

BILL OF MATERIALS — Sewing Box

Finished Dimensions in Inches

Part		Dimensions
A.	Legs (4)	1⅛ x 1⅛ x 11⅜
B.	Side handles (2)	1⅛ x 1⅛ x 3
C.	Lid handles (2)	1⅛ x 1⅛ x 9¼
D.	Large handle	1 x 1 x 40
E.	Pivot blocks (2)	¾ x 1 x 9¼
F.	Bottom tray sides (2)	½ x 4⅞ x 19¼
G.	Bottom tray ends (2)	½ x 4⅞ x 10¼
H.	Top/middle tray sides (8)	½ x 2⅜ x 9⅝
J.	Middle tray ends (4)	½ x 2⅜ x 10¼
K.	Top tray ends (4)	½ x 1⅝ x 10¼
L.	Short hinges (8)	½ x 1 x 5¼
M.	Long hinges (4)	½ x 1 x 9½
N.	Lids (2)	¼ x 8⅞ x 9¼
P.	Bottom tray bottom	¼ x 9¼ x 18¼
Q.	Top/middle tray bottoms (8)	¼ x 9⅛ x 9¾
R.	Middle tray horizontal dividers (3)	¼ x 1⅞ x 9⅛
S.	Top tray horizontal dividers (3)	¼ x 1⅛ x 9⅛
T.	Top tray vertical dividers (2)	¼ x 1⅛ x 9¼
U.	Ledger strip (total)	¼ x ¼ x 48

HARDWARE

- #12 x 1½″ Flathead wood screws (16)
- #12 x 1¼″ Flathead wood screws (8)
- #12 x 1″ Roundhead wood screws (28)
- #12 Flat washers (28)

Designed and built by Nick Engler.

Country Carry-All

A rustic tray design from times gone by adds a touch of country to your kitchen or dining room.

Once, every country home in America had half a dozen carrying trays. They were used to organize and carry many different domestic items — tools, tableware, sewing notions, anything small that needed to be transported from place to place. They were known by several different names, such as "knife caddy" and "work tray." The name that seems to fit the best, however, is "carry-all."

Today, these carry-alls are becoming popular once again. As the interest in country furniture and decor grows, these wood trays are being used as country centerpieces, accents, and accessories.

The carry-all that you see here is a typical country design — simple and functional. It's really just an open-top box with a single divider that also serves as a handle. It's also a *formal* design, as carry-alls go. The slanted sides are compound-mitered and joined with dovetail splines. The handle is carefully scalloped to fit the fingers. These touches add a bit of homespun elegance to an otherwise practical project.

Cutting the Parts to Size

Select *flat,* cabinet-grade wood to make this project. The flatness of the stock is extremely important, particularly when making the sides. If the sides have the slightest cup or warp in them, the miter joints will not fit together properly.

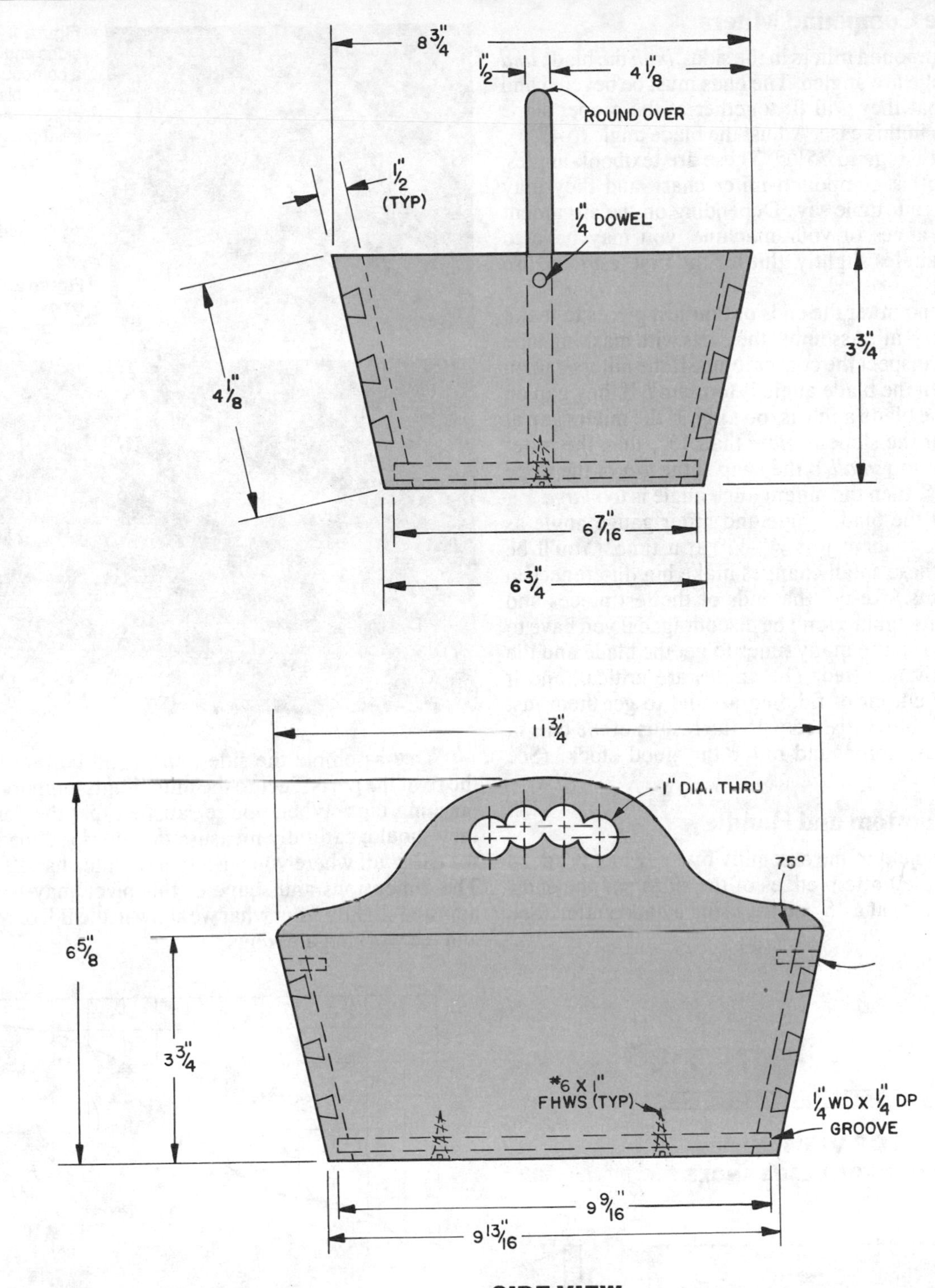

SIDE VIEW

Most country furniture was made from domestic woods. The most popular furniture wood was white pine, but country craftsmen also used walnut, maple, butternut, hickory, and birch for special projects. In some cases, the craftsmen would use two or more contrasting species of woods to emphasize the design. The carry-all you see here is made from cherry with walnut splines.

Cut the handle/divider and bottom to the sizes shown in the Bill of Materials. Make the sides and the ends 1″–2″ longer than specified, so that you have room to make the miters. Bevel-rip the upper and lower edges of the sides at 15°.

Tip ◆ Make extra sides and ends from scrap wood — enough to make a second carry-all. You can use these as test-pieces when you adjust the table saw to make the compound miters.

Cutting the Compound Miters

To cut the compound miters in the sides, *both* the blade *and* the miter gauge are angled. The ends must be beveled and mitered so that they will fit together at the proper slope angle — 15°, in this case. Adjust the blade angle to 43¼°, and the miter gauge to 75½°. These are textbook angles, taken right off a compound-miter chart, and they may not work on your table saw. Depending on the alignment and the tolerances of your machine, you may have to readjust the angles slightly. But for the first test cuts, use these angles.

Compound miter the ends of four test pieces to make a practice carry-all. Assemble the parts with masking tape and carefully inspect the corner joints. If the miters gap on the *inside,* then the blade angle is too *small.* If they gap on the *outside,* the blade angle is too *large.* If the miters gap at the *bottom,* or the slope is *more* than 15°, then the miter gauge angle is too *small.* If they gap at the *top,* or the slope is *less* than 15°, then the miter gauge angle is too *large.*

Readjust the blade angle and miter gauge angle as necessary. Move them just ¼°-½° at a time. (You'll be surprised — these small changes make big differences in the miter joints.) Re-cut the ends of the test pieces and check the joints again. Don't be discouraged if you have to repeat this procedure many times to get the blade and the gauge properly adjusted. The angles are critical, and it may take quite a bit of fiddling around to get them just right. When you're satisfied with the results of the cuts in the test pieces, compound-miter the good stock. (See Figure 1.)

Figure 1. Join the sides and ends with a compound miter. Set the blade angle to 43¼°, and the miter gauge angle to 75½°.

Figure 2. Cut the groove for the bottom at a 15° angle.

Fitting the Bottom and Handle

The bottom is held in the assembly by ¼"-wide, ¼"-deep grooves near the bottom edges of the sides and the ends. Cut these grooves at a 15° angle, using a dado cutter. (See Figure 2.)

Dry-assemble the sides, ends, and bottom to check the fit of the parts. Secure the miter joints temporarily with masking tape. When you're satisfied that the parts fit as they should, carefully measure the interior dimensions of the carry-all where you wish to mount the handle/divider. The dimensions and shape of this piece may have to be adjusted slightly from what we show in the Bill of Materials and the working drawings.

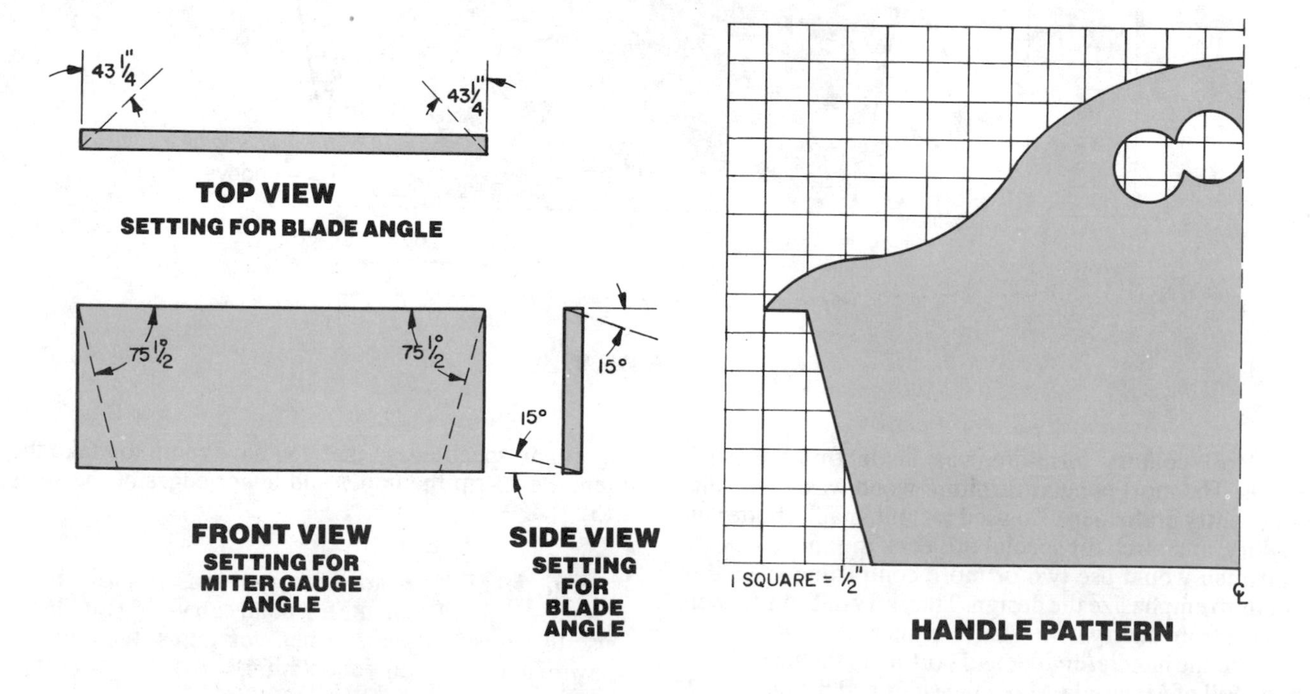

Figure 3. To make the opening in the handle, drill four overlapping 1″-diameter holes.

Figure 4. To hold the assembly together while the glue cures in the miter joints, wrap band clamps around the carry-all like ribbons around a package.

Enlarge the *Handle Pattern,* and make any necessary changes. Then transfer this pattern to the stock, and cut out the shape on a bandsaw. Sand the sawn edges of the handle smooth.

To make the opening in the handle, drill four overlapping 1″ holes. (See Figure 3.) To help prevent tear-out around the edges of the holes, use a brad-point bit and drill from *both* sides. Drill the first side until the point of the bit — but not the flutes — penetrates the other side of the stock. Turn the wood over, and complete the hole from the other side. Use the tiny pin-hole created by the brad-point to center the bit properly.

Assembling the Carry-All

Apply glue to the mitered ends of the sides and ends, and assemble these parts with the bottom in place. *Do not* apply any glue to the bottom. Let it float in the grooves, free to expand and contract with changes in the weather.

Tape the joints together with masking tape. This will hold them while you slip band clamps over the assembly. Use two band clamps perpendicular to each other — wrapped around the assembly like ribbons around a package — to hold the miter joints securely until the glue dries. (See Figure 4.)

Surface sand the assembly and clean up the miter joints. Don't do any finish sanding or round any corners just yet — that will come after you install the dovetail splines and the handle/divider.

Installing the Splines

To install the splines, you need a router, a router table, and a dovetail router bit. You also need to make a special jig to hold the carry-all while you rout the slots for the splines. The *Dovetail Spline Jig* drawing shows how to make this fixture. Note that the faces of the cradle in the jig are 100°

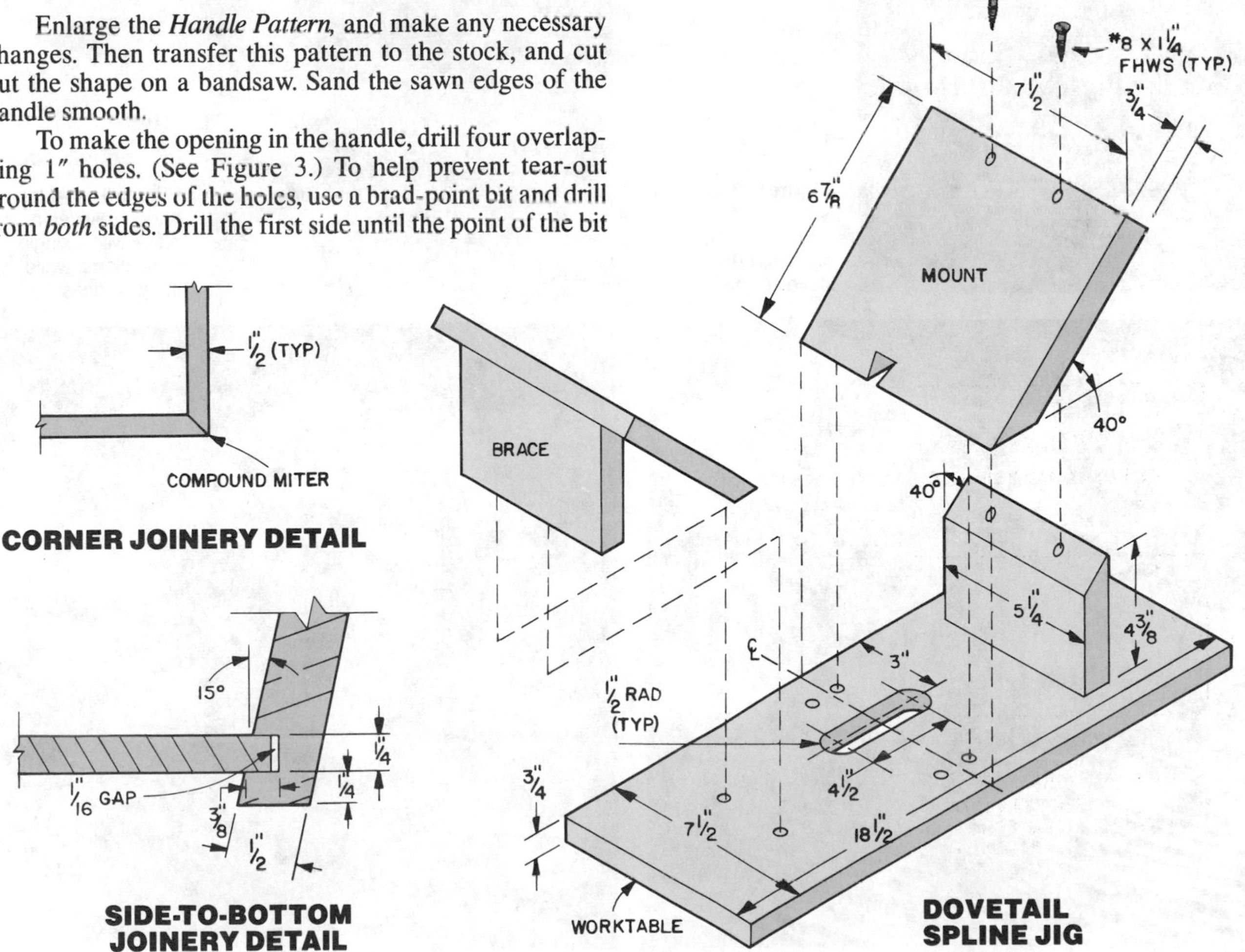

apart, not 90°, as you might expect. This is because the sides of the carry-all are sloped. If you cut the slots with the carry-all cradle in a 90° jig, the completed dovetails will seem slightly out of kilter. The 100° angle compensates for the sloped sides of the carry-all, and the dovetails line up properly.

To use the jig, first mount your router to a router table. Secure a dovetail bit in the router chuck, and adjust the height of the bit so that the top is approximately ½" above the base of the jig — 1¼" above the router table surface. Attach a fence or a straightedge to the router table to guide the jig across the bit.

Clamp the carry-all in the jig and cut a slot in one corner. Readjust the position of the carry-all in the cradle, and repeat. Continue until you have cut three slots in each corner. (See Figure 5.)

To make the splines that fit in the slots, remove the jig from the router table. Readjust the position of the fence and the height of the dovetail bit. Rout one side of a piece of ¾"-thick stock, turn it over, and rout the other side. (See Figure 6.) This will make a dovetail-shaped tongue in the edge of the wood. Using a bandsaw, cut the tongue free of the stock and cut it up into 1" lengths to make the keys.

Glue these keys in the slots. After the glue cures, cut away *most* of the stock that protrudes from the sides and ends, using a backsaw or dovetail saw. Sand or file the keys down until they are perfectly flush with the surfaces of the carry-all. (See Figure 7.)

Attaching the Handle and Finishing Up

After installing the splines, glue the handle/divider to the ends and the bottom. Hold the handle in place with a single band clamp until the glue dries. (See Figure 8.)

Figure 5. Cut the dovetail slots in the corners of the assembly with a special jig. You can build this jig from scraps of plywood.

Figure 7. Glue the keys in the slots, cut off the excess wood, and sand them flush with the surface of the carry-all.

Figure 6. Use the same dovetail bit that you used to make the slots to cut the dovetail keys.

Figure 8. Hold the handle/divider in place with a single band clamp while the glue dries.

Reinforce the joint with screws and dowels. Drive two #6 x 1″ screws up through the bottom into the handle/divider, as shown in the *Side View* and *End View.* Also drill two ¼″-diameter stopped holes through the ends and into the handle/divider. Glue hardwood dowels in these holes.

Finish sand the completed carry-all, rounding over the hard corners to give it a used look. Apply a clear finish to bring out the grain of the wood. We used an old country finish — beeswax and turpentine. Soak ¼″ of beeswax chips in an equal amount of turpentine overnight. This will make a soft paste. Apply the paste with a soft rag — it will begin to build up on the surface of the wood like a french polish. Let it build up for a few minutes, let it dry a few minutes more, then buff it out with a clean rag. Repeat until the finish is as deep as you want it. Apply a new coat of beeswax each year to renew the shine.

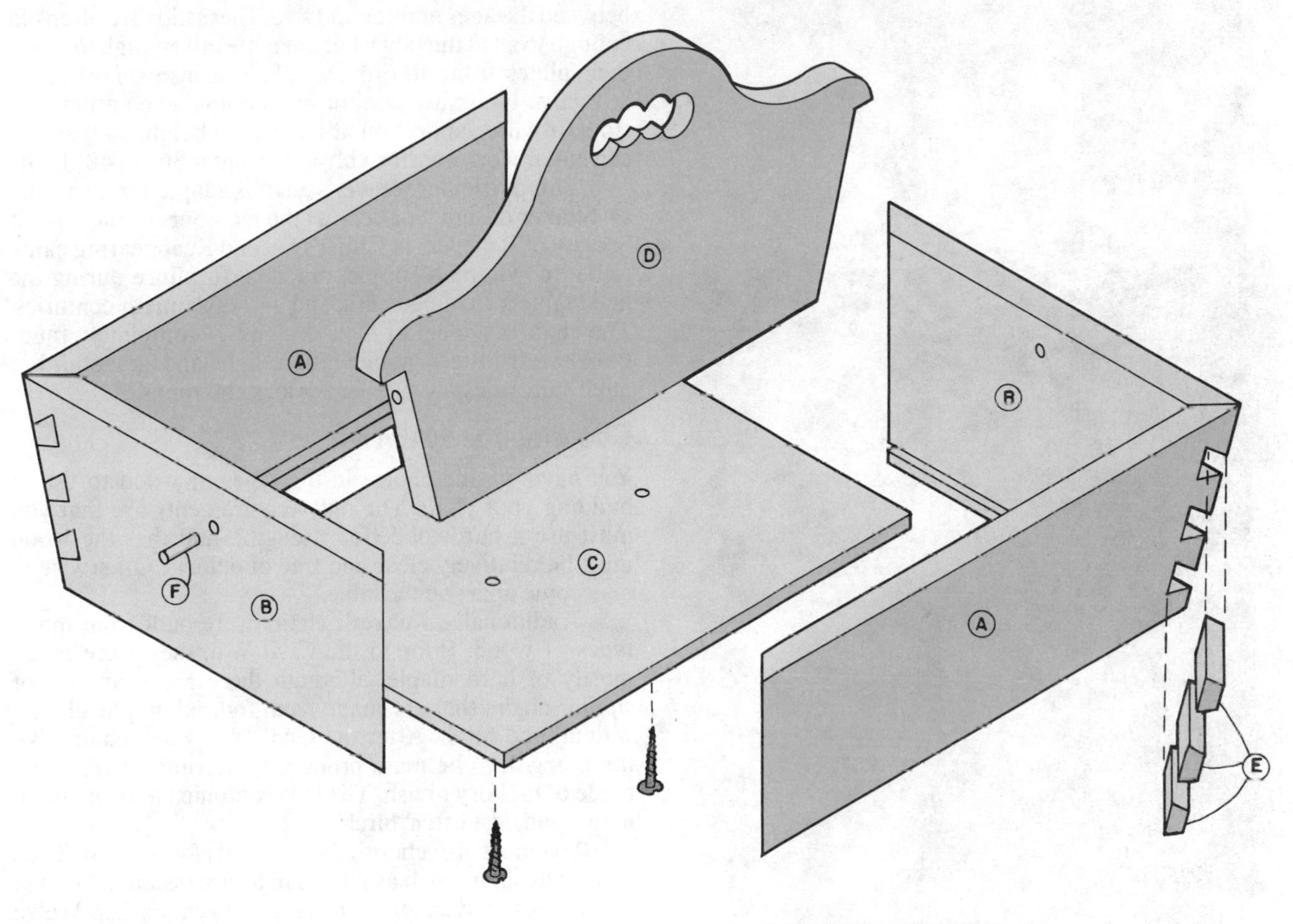

EXPLODED VIEW

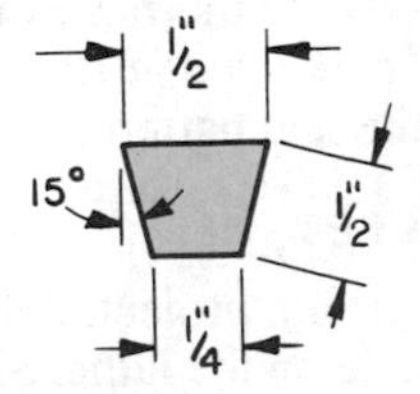

KEY
END VIEW

BILL OF MATERIALS — Country Carry-All

Finished Dimensions in Inches

A.	Sides (2)	½ x 4⅛ x 11¾
B.	Ends (2)	½ x 4⅛ x 8¾
C.	Bottom	¼ x 6⁷⁄₁₆ x 9⁹⁄₁₆
D.	Handle/divider	½ x 6⅛ x 11¾
E.	Dovetail keys (12)	½ x ½ x 1
F.	Dowels (2)	¼ dia. x 1

HARDWARE

#6 x 1″ Flathead wood screws (2)

Built by Nick Engler from a traditional Shaker design.

Weaver's Chair

An old country design makes a great youth chair or breakfast stool.

Long ago, when cloth was woven by hand, weavers sat at their looms on special chairs. The chairs were higher than normal so that the weavers could easily reach their work. But as high as they were, these weren't simply stools; the chairs had backs to help support the backs of the men and women who had to sit all day, weaving cloth and other goods.

Today, the weaver's chair has found other uses. It makes a good "youth chair" — a chair for children between the ages of three and five. These kids are often old enough to sit at the table, but not quite tall enough to reach their plates from an ordinary chair. It also serves as an attractive breakfast stool or bar stool — even a drafting stool. It will support you at the proper height so that you can eat or work comfortably at a counter 36″ to 40″ high.

This particular weaver's chair is adapted from a classic Shaker design. Shakers, as the members of the United Society of Believers in Christ's Second Reappearing came to be known, built simple, practical furniture during the late eighteenth, nineteenth, and early twentieth centuries. The chair is typical of their designs — completely functional with little ornamentation, light and graceful, but quite sturdy despite the slender legs and rungs.

Choosing the Materials

You have a wide choice in the types of wood to use in building your chair. The only requirements are that you must use a hardwood (for strength), and that the wood must be relatively clear and free of defects. Otherwise, it may come apart on the lathe.

Traditionally, weaver's chairs were built from many types of wood. Prior to the Civil War, they were made mostly of hard maple, although there are examples of similar chairs that are made from figured maple, cherry, walnut, and birch. After the Civil War, when chairs like these began to be mass produced, the rungs were often made of hickory or ash. The legs continued to be made of maple and, less often, birch.

You must also choose the materials for the seat. Seats on turned chairs such as these can be upholstered with the splint, rush, woven straw, cane, and even leather. We've upholstered ours with a cloth tape. This was first developed in the late 1830's by the Shakers. The worsted tape or "listing" can be woven onto the chair frames in several simple patterns. Often, a seat-maker will use two different colors of tapes to emphasize the seat pattern.

Turning the Rungs and Legs

A chair like this is mostly a turning project. All the parts except the backrest can be made on the lathe. Since these parts have little or no decoration, the turning procedures are straightforward. The only beads and coves to worry about are the acorn finials at the ends of the back legs.

For simplicity, all of the rungs are straight. The Shakers most likely would have made the front and the side rungs *slightly* tapered. If you want to add this bit of decoration, go ahead. All the rungs have ½″-diameter tenons with ⅛″ shoulders. This adds strength to the chair frame.

It is extremely important that these tenons be turned to *precisely* the diameter shown in the *Rung and Tenon Detail.* If they are too small, the joint will have too much

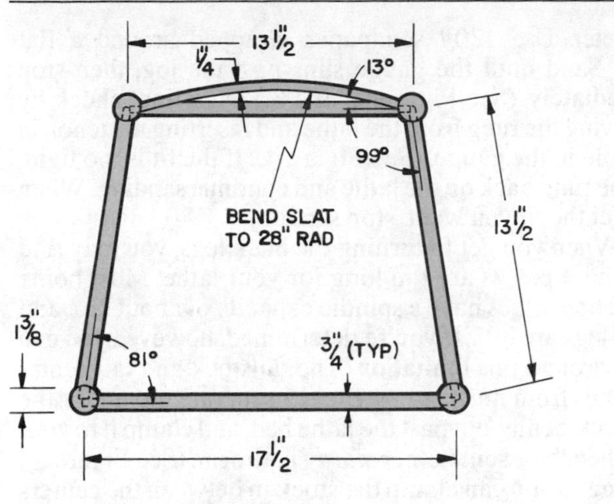

TOP VIEW

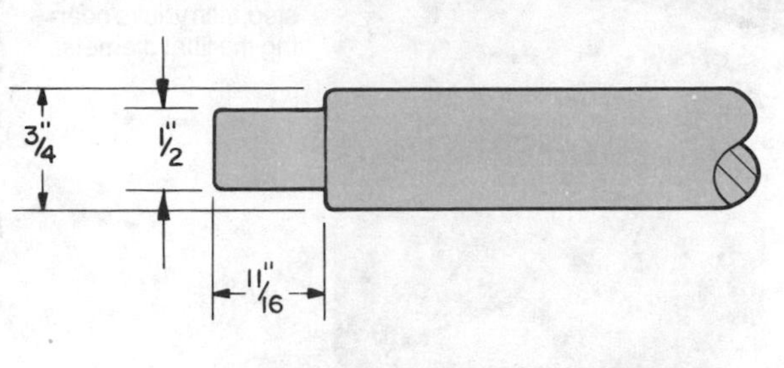

RUNG & TENON DETAIL

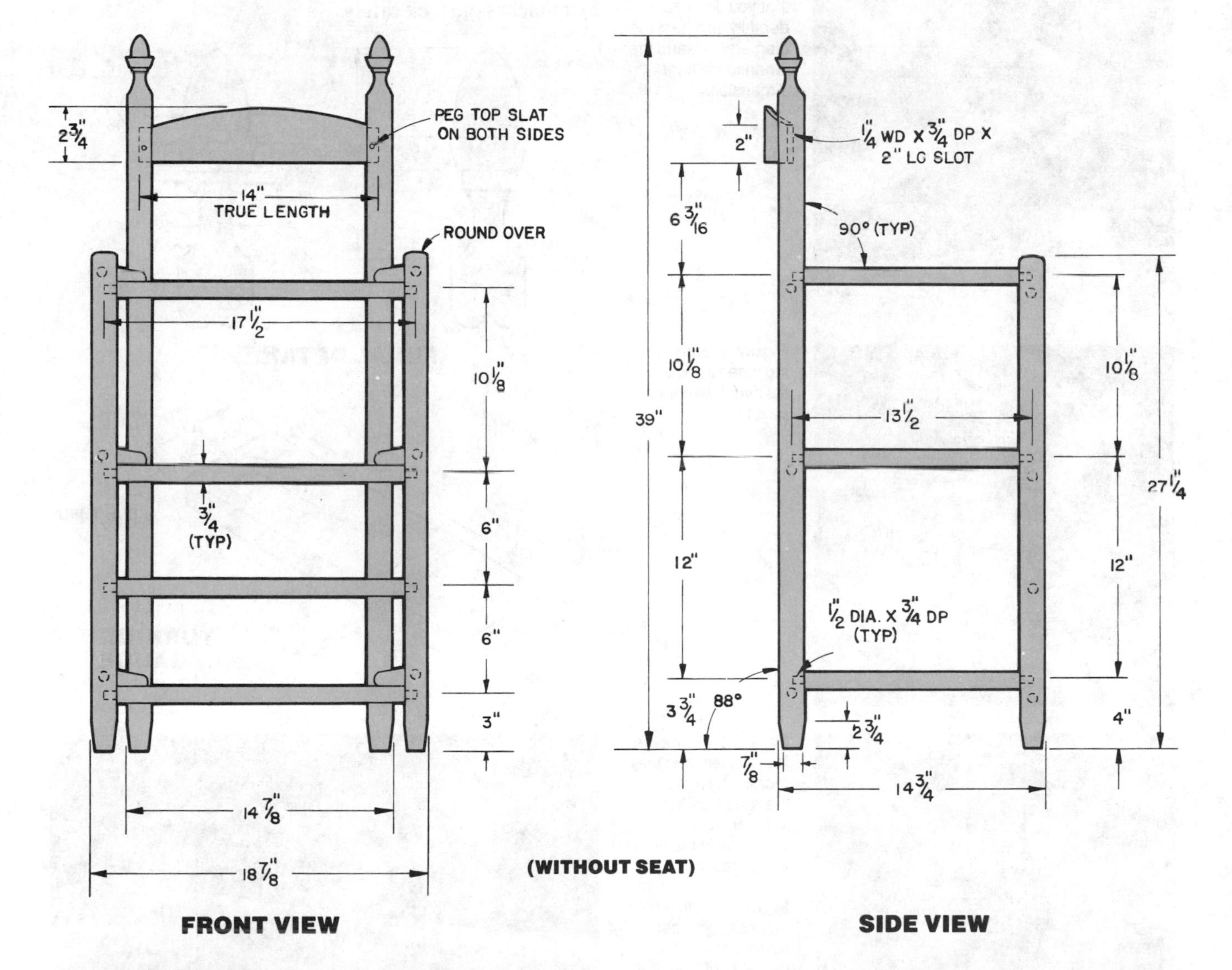

FRONT VIEW

SIDE VIEW

slop and this will weaken the chair. Eventually, it will cause the chair to come apart.

To aid in turning the tenons to a precise diameter, make a turning gauge from a scrap of wood. This gauge is really just a fixed caliper for a ½" diameter. Use it constantly to check the diameter of the tenon as you work. The gauge will tell you when you're getting close — it also has a built-in warning device, a tiny jog in one side of the gauge. When the gauge slips over the tenon up to the jog, the tenon is nearing its final diameter. (See Figure 1.)

At this point, proceed very carefully. Some turners prefer to set their tools aside and *sand* the tenon to its final

Figure 1. When the gauge slips over the tenon up to the jog or step, then you're nearing the final diameter.

Figure 2. To remove stock slowly — so that you don't accidentally turn past the diameter — sand the tenon to the final dimension.

Figure 3. Stop sanding when the gauge fits over the tenon past the jog.

Figure 4. Check the fit of the tenon in the mortise by removing the rung from the lathe and inserting the tenon in the hole in the gauge.

Figure 5. With a little ingenuity, you can safely extend the capacity of a lathe a few inches by making an auxiliary mount for the tailstock and/or center. This shows how we extended the capacity of our Shopsmith.

diameter. Use 120# sandpaper, wrapped around a flat edge. Sand until the gauge slips past the jog, then stop immediately. (See Figures 2 and 3.) Do a final check by removing the rung from the lathe and inserting the tenon in the hole in the gauge. (See Figure 4.) If the fit is too tight, put the rung back on the lathe and continue sanding. When you get the fit you want, stop sanding.

When you get to turning the back legs, you may find that these pieces are too long for your lathe. Most home workshop lathes have a spindle capacity of about 26", and these legs are 39". If you're determined, however, you can work around this limitation. The tailstock and tail center detaches from most lathes. Build a separate mount for the tailstock/center out past the lathe bed, and clamp it to your workbench or some other *sturdy* platform. (See Figure 5.) As long as you can clamp the stock in between the centers securely and you work at low speeds, you can turn several extra inches of stock safely.

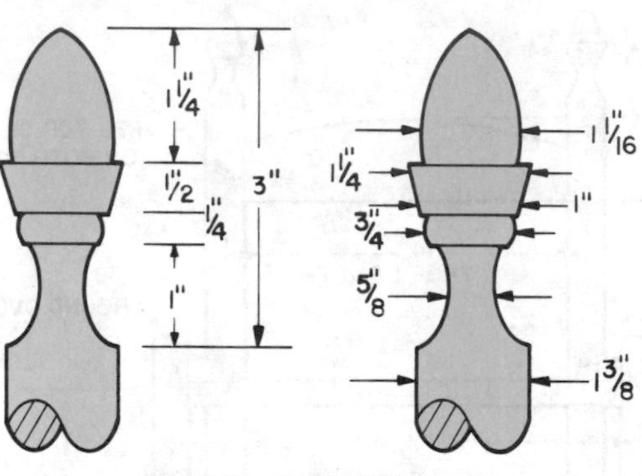

FINIAL DETAIL

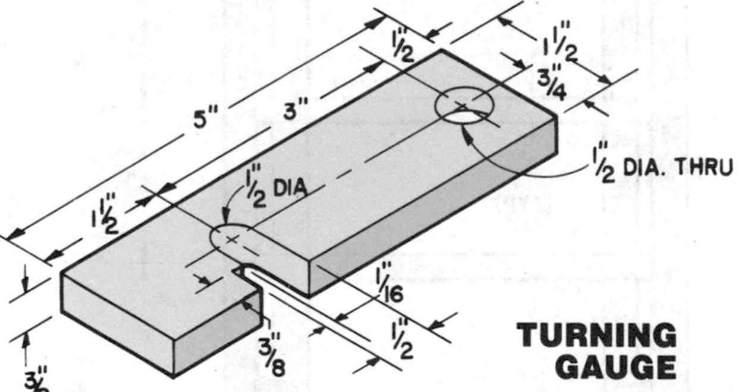

TURNING GAUGE

One more turning tip: Remember, all the parts are fairly slender — the largest finished diameter is just 1⅜". Because of this, you must be careful that the spindles don't whip or bow on the lathe. Use just enough tailstock pressure to keep the stock firmly mounted between the centers. When turning the long back legs, use a steadyrest to keep them from whipping. (See Figure 6.)

Bending the Backrest

The backrest is bent slightly to fit your back. This piece is thin enough (¼") that you can bend it easily in a home workshop without making a steamer. There are two methods that you can use:

The first requires a woodstove. Cut the backrest 4"- 6" longer than needed, and cut the shape on a bandsaw. Soak it in water overnight. The next day, light a fire in the stove and press the wet workpiece against the hot stove pipe. (**Caution:** Before attempting this, make sure your stovepipe is sturdy enough to withstand the pressure.) Hold the slat by both ends, press forward gently, and rock the wood back and forth to heat it evenly. Be careful not to char the wood! As the stock heats up, you'll feel the stock "give." Keep pressing forward until you have a little more curve than you want. Let the wood cool and cut off the backrest to the proper length.

If you don't have a woodstove, boil the backrest in a roasting pan for 45 to 60 minutes, then clamp it in a simple bending jig. (See Figure 7.) Let the wood dry a few weeks in the form. You can expect the backrest to spring back roughly 20% when it comes out of the jig. Compensate for this by making the curve of the form slightly more pronounced than the desired final curve of the backrest.

Figure 6. When turning the back legs, use a steadyrest to keep the long, slender turning from whipping on the lathe.

Figure 7. Use a simple bending jig — just a block of wood with a curve cut into it — to bend the backrest to the proper curve after you've heated it up in boiling water.

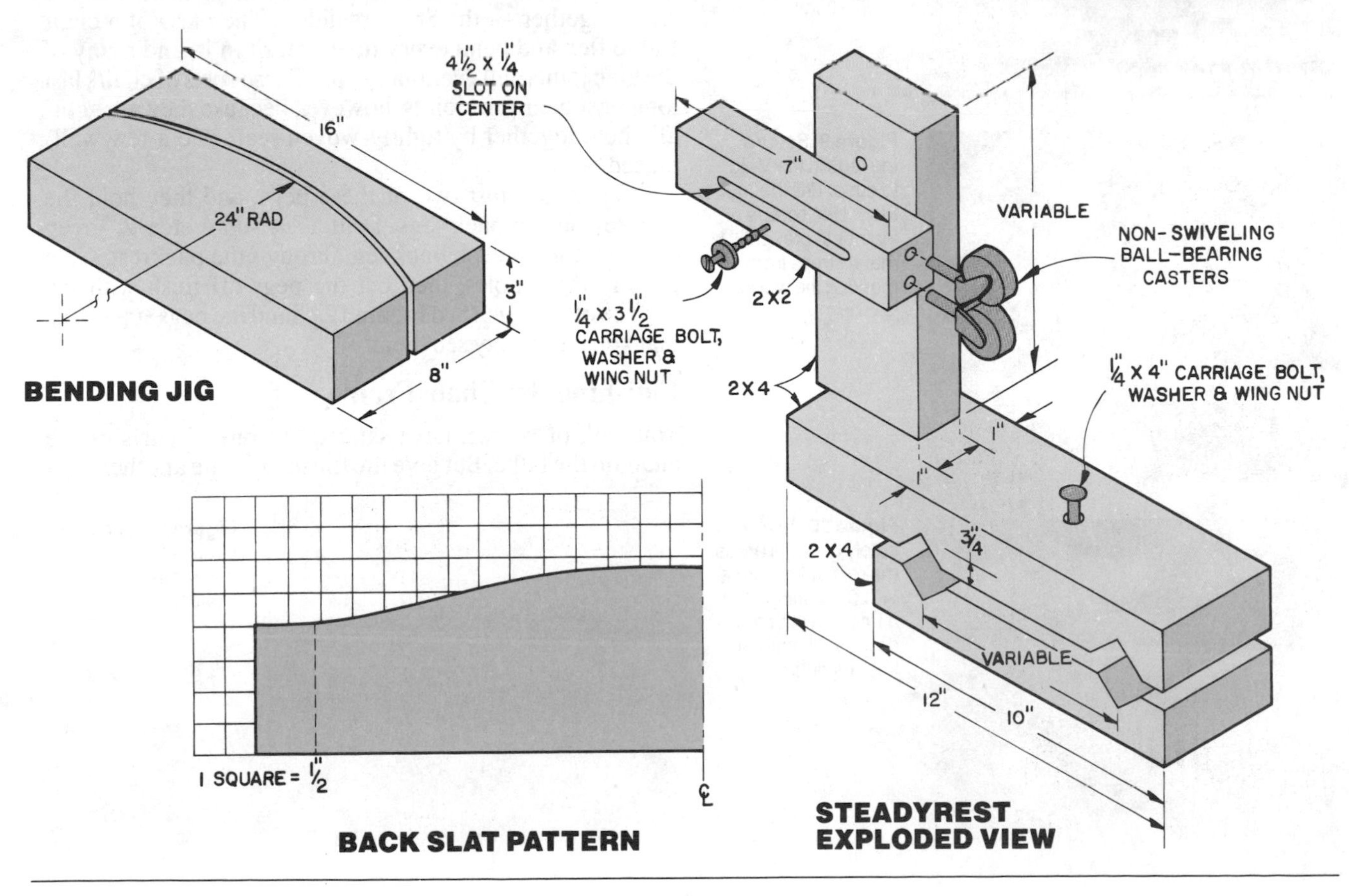

Mortising the Legs

The mortises in the legs must line up with each other. There are two "lines" of mortises in the front leg (front rungs and side rungs), and three lines in the back legs (side rungs, back rungs, and backrest). Each line of holes must be drilled at the proper angle to the other lines. It's fairly easy to mark these angles on the ends of the legs, but how do you transfer these marks down the length of stock so that you can keep the holes in the same line? The simplest way is with a long V-shaped jig. Rest the stock in the jig and use one side of the "V" as a straightedge. (See Figure 8.)

The V-jig also comes in handy when it's time to drill holes for the rungs or cut slot mortises for the backrest. Secure the leg in the jig with metal straps and wood screws. This will keep the stock properly aligned with the bit or cutter. (See Figure 9.) When cutting the slots, clamp a fence to the worktable to guide the jig.

Make the holes on a drill press with a ½" bit, and cut the slot mortises for the backrest on an overarm router with a ¼"-diameter straight bit. If you don't have an overarm router, you can use a drill press for both operations, provided you take certain precautions. An ordinary drill press

Figure 8. Use a V-jig as a straightedge to mark the "lines" of mortise holes on the legs.

Figure 9. Secure the legs in the V-jig to cut or drill the mortises. Use scraps of leather to prevent the metal straps from marking the wood.

Figure 10. To rout safely on a drill press, make a collet from a ¼" I.D. bushing. With a hacksaw, cut a slot down the length of the bushing.

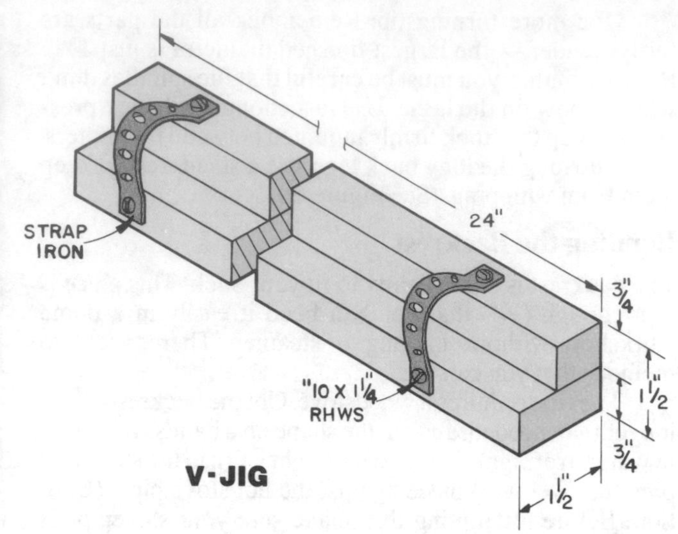

chuck won't support the shank of a router bit against lateral (sideways) thrust, and the bit may bend or break. To prevent this, make a collet from a ¼" I.D. bushing. (See Figure 10.) Cut a slot down one side of the bushing. Mount the router bit in the collet, and clamp the collet in the drill chuck. After routing the mortise, square the ends of the slot with a chisel.

Assembling the Chair Frame

Once you've made all the parts and cut the joints, assemble the chair without glue to check the fit. If you're satisfied, apply glue and assemble the parts permanently. Use band clamps to hold the frame together while the glue dries. (See Figure 11.) But don't depend on glue alone to hold the chair together — the Shakers didn't. The parts of a chair frame flex and bend every time you sit in it, and many of the glue joints will eventually pop. These sorts of chairs last long past their glue joints, however, because they are actually held together by tightly-woven seats and a few well-placed pegs.

There are just two of these pegs, and they hold the backrest in the back legs. Drill a 3/16"-diameter, ¾"-deep stopped hole in each back leg, through the backrest. Glue pegs in these holes, then cut the pegs off flush with the surface of the legs. (See Figure 12.) Sand the pegs smooth so that you can barely see them.

Finishing the Chair Frame

You will, of course, have sanded the turned parts of the chair on the lathe. But give the finished frame another light

Figure 11. Use band clamps to hold the chair frame together while the glue dries.

sanding to remove any nicks or scratches that may have developed during assembly. Then apply a finish.

Traditionally, the Shakers and other country craftsmen covered their wooden chair frames with a variety of finishes. The earliest weaver's chairs were painted with milk paint, usually a deep red. Later, the country craftsmen thinned the paint and used it as a stain so that the grain of the wood showed through the color. Some chairs were left their natural color and finished with a clear varnish, shellac, or linseed oil. Some post-Civil War manufacturers also stained the chair frames, or coated them with colored varnishes. We finished our frame with a simple tung oil.

Let the finish dry completely, then rub it down with a rag to make sure there are no tacky spots. It must be completely cured before you can attach the seat.

Weaving the Seat

Weaving a chair seat is another entire chapter in itself. Furthermore, the information applies not just to weaver's chairs, but to all sorts of frame chairs. So we've elected to develop a chapter in the *Techniques* section on just that subject — "Weaving a Chair Seat."

When you're ready to make your chair seat, turn to that chapter and follow the step-by-step instructions. We show how to weave two popular sorts of country-style seats — rush and tape. If you would like to attempt to do other types of seats, such as splint, consult your local library.

Figure 12. Peg the backrest in the mortises in the back legs. This will help hold the chair together even after the glue joints give way.

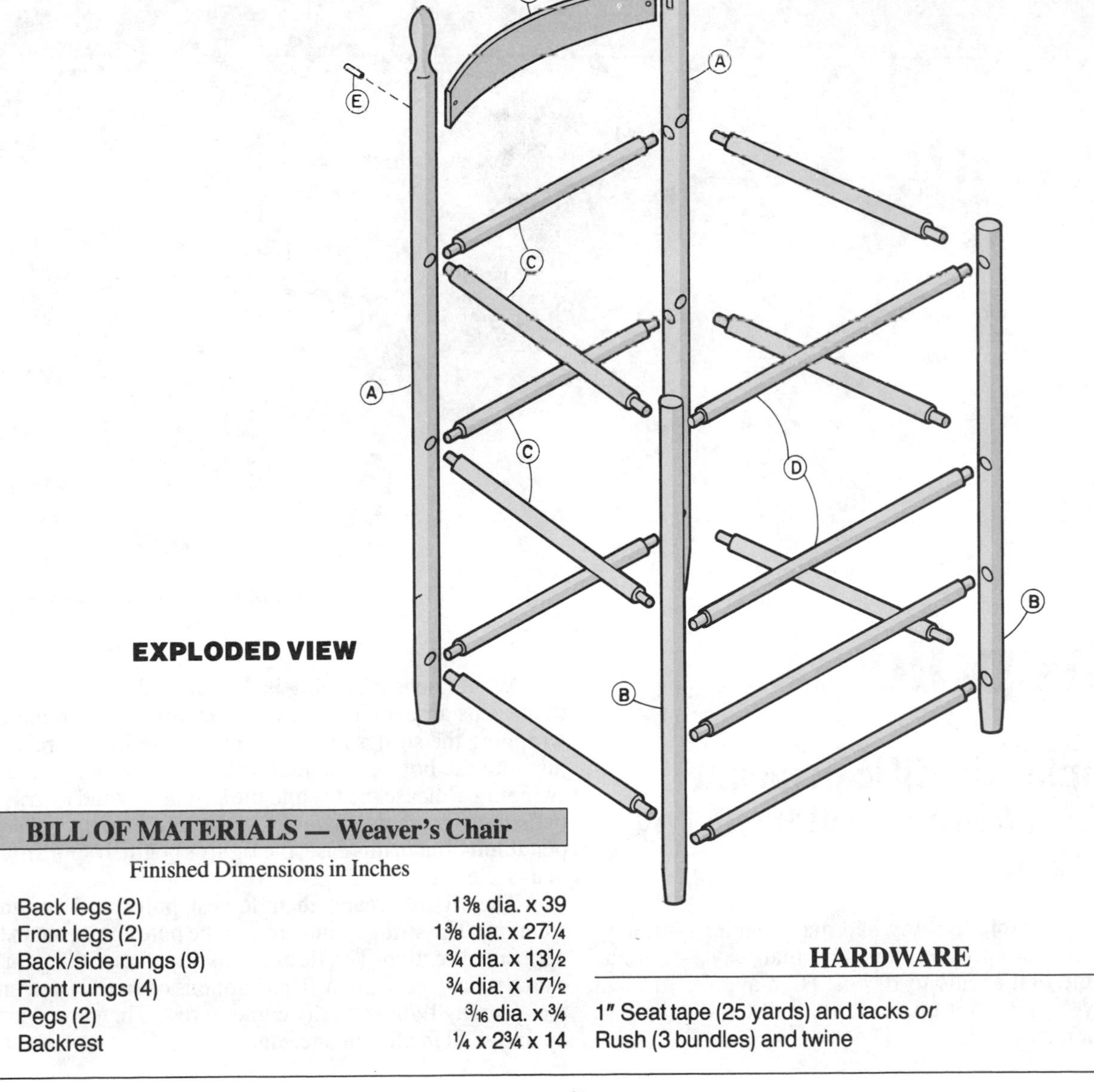

BILL OF MATERIALS — Weaver's Chair

Finished Dimensions in Inches

	Part	Dimensions
A.	Back legs (2)	1⅜ dia. x 39
B.	Front legs (2)	1⅜ dia. x 27¼
C.	Back/side rungs (9)	¾ dia. x 13½
D.	Front rungs (4)	¾ dia. x 17½
E.	Pegs (2)	3/16 dia. x ¾
F.	Backrest	¼ x 2¾ x 14

HARDWARE

1" Seat tape (25 yards) and tacks *or*
Rush (3 bundles) and twine

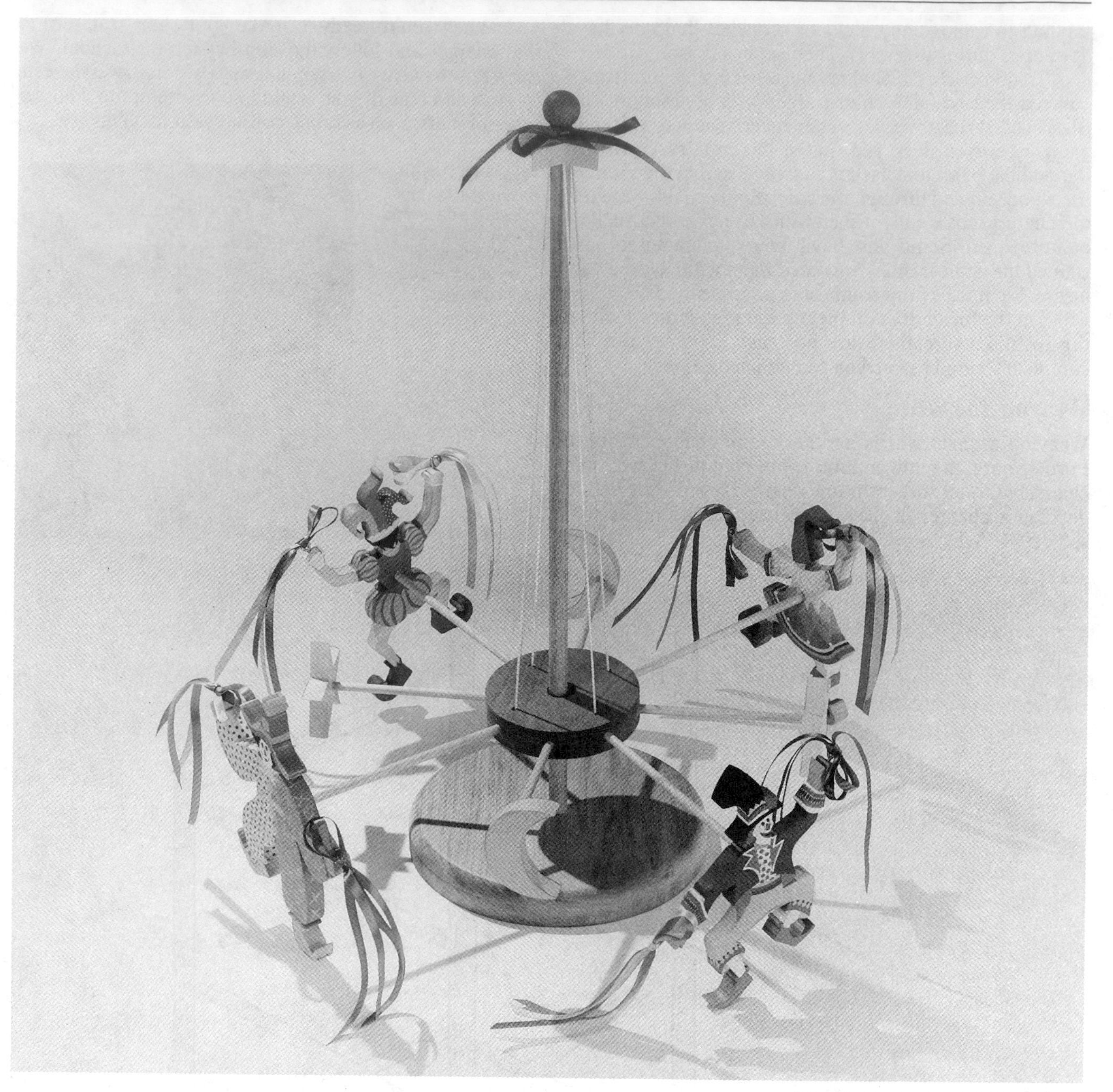

Designed by Mary Jane Favorite. Built by Nick Engler.

Maypole

A simple scientific principle sets this old-time children's toy in motion.

This venerable folk toy had many names — merry-go-round, carousel, this-way-that-way — but the name that seems to fit best is "maypole." It is an action toy. You wind it up, let it go, and it will remain in motion for a long time.

What keeps it moving is the same physical principle that keeps a pendulum moving. As you wind up the toy, wrapping the strings around the pole, the figures raise up just like the bob of a pendulum is raised when you set it swinging. Release the toy and the strings unwind as gravity pulls the figures downward — just like gravity pulls the pendulum. But in this case, the figures begin to spin around in a circle.

The figures reach their lowest point and continue spinning. The strings wind around the pole again, but in the opposite direction. The figures raise up, then fall again — exactly like a pendulum. This happens over and over, until the spinning figures finally come to rest. Then you wind it up and set it in motion once again!

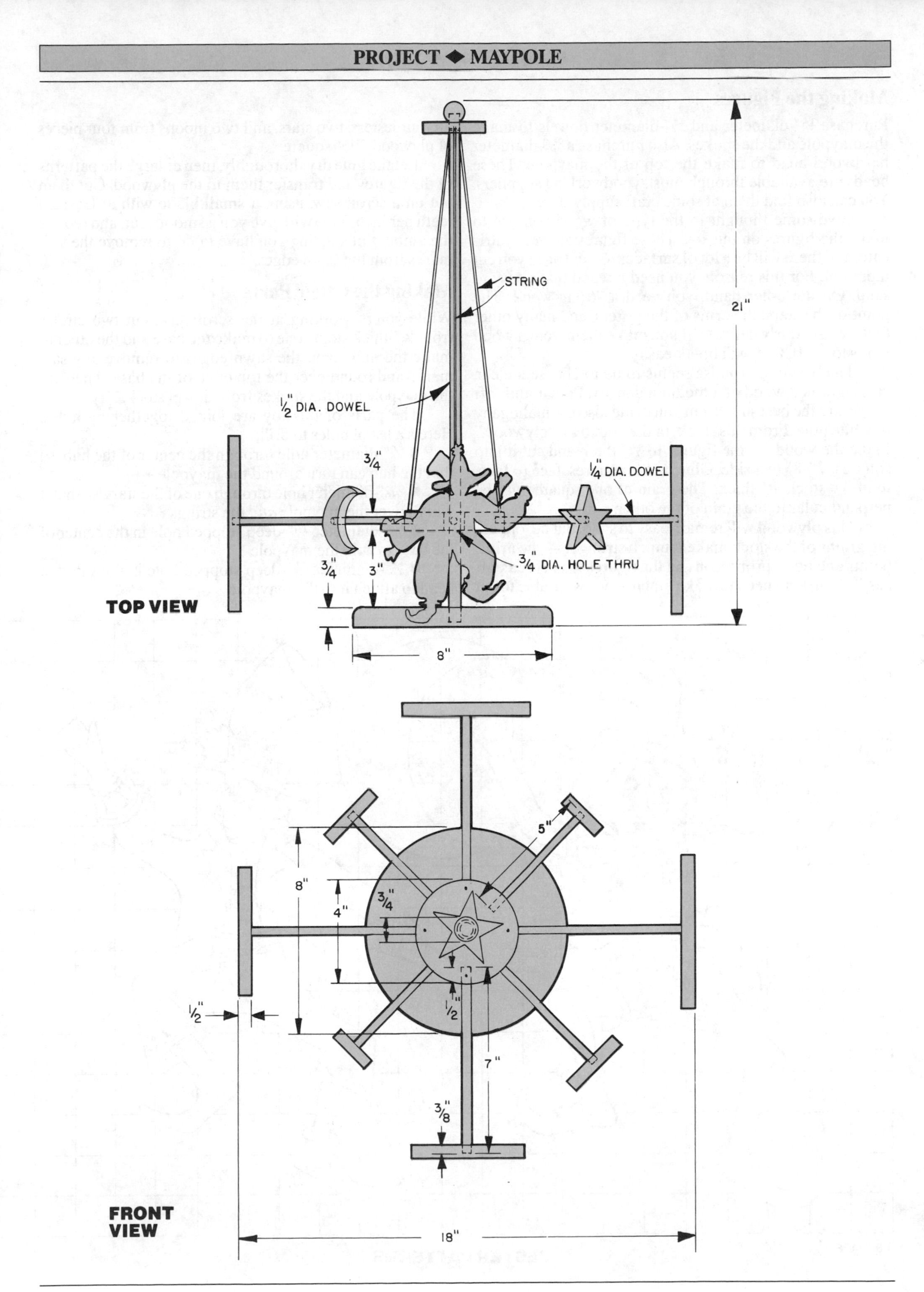
STRING
21"
1/2" DIA. DOWEL
3/4
1/4" DIA. DOWEL
3/4
3"
3/4" DIA. HOLE THRU
TOP VIEW
8"
5"
8"
3/4
4"
1/2"
1/2"
7"
3/8"
FRONT VIEW
18"

Making the Figures

Purchase ¼″-diameter and ½″-diameter dowels to make the maypole and the spokes. Also purchase a ¾″-diameter hardwood bead to make the top of the maypole. These beads are available through most woodworking suppliers. You can also find them at some craft supply stores.

Give some thought to the type of wood you use to make the figures on this toy. These figures are very intricate, and there will be a lot of surfaces to sand once you cut them out. For this reason, you need a wood that's easy to sand. On the other hand, you need a strong wood. The point of the stars, the arms of the jesters, and many other features are fairly delicate. If you make them from a wood that's too soft, they will break easily.

The best compromise seems to be to choose a clear, close-grained wood of a medium density. Poplar and soft maple are the best suited, but you could also use mahogany or white pine. From this stock, make your own "plywood." Plane the wood for the figures to ¼″ thick and cut it into squares, 7″–8″ to a side. Glue up the squares, face to face, to make stock ½″ thick. The grain of one square *must* be perpendicular to the grain of the other.

This plywood will remain easy to sand, but the opposing grains of the stock make it much stronger — the arms, points and other protrusions on the figures won't break off easily. You don't need to make much — we were able to cut all four jesters, two stars, and two moons from four pieces of plywood, 7½″ square.

Let the glue dry thoroughly, then enlarge the patterns of the figures and transfer them to the plywood. Cut them out on a scroll saw, using a small blade with at least 20 teeth per inch. This will give you a smooth cut, and reduce the amount of sanding you have to do to remove the saw marks from the sawn edges.

Making the Other Parts

While you're working at the scroll saw, cut two circles from ¾″-thick stock, one to make the base and the other to make the hub. Sand the sawn edges to remove any saw marks and round over the top edge of the base. Then cut the maypole and the spokes from dowel stock.

The parts of this toy are joined together by holes. Here's a list of holes to drill:

- ⅝″-diameter hole through the center of the hub, so that the hub can turn around the maypole
- 9/16″-diameter hole through one of the stars, so that it will fit over the maypole *and* the strings
- ½″-diameter, ½″-deep stopped hole in the center of the base to hold the maypole
- ½″-diameter, ⅜″-deep stopped hole in the wooden bead to attach it to the maypole

JESTER PATTERNS

■ 1/4″-diameter, 1/2″-deep stopped holes around the edge of the hub to hold the spokes. The positions of these holes are shown in the *Top View.*

■ 1/4″-diameter, 3/8″-deep stopped holes in the back of the figures, to attach them to the spokes. The positions of these holes are shown in the patterns.

■ 1/8″-diameter holes through the maypole to hold the string

■ 1/8″-diameter holes through the hub to attach the end of the string. The positions of these holes are shown in the *Top View.*

Tip ◆ Use V-jigs to aid in drilling the maypole, hub, and wooden bead. (See Figures 1 and 2.)

Figure 1. Use a long V-block to drill the holes in the wooden bead and the maypole.

Figure 2. A "V" cut into a 3/4″-thick scrap of wood to make a flat V-jig helps to hold the hub while you drill holes in the edge.

Assembling and Painting

Finish sand all the parts of the maypole, then dry assemble the toy to check its operation. Cut the lengths of string that you need to hang the hub, and tie them in place with *slip knots* so that you can untie them easily. When you're satisfied that the toy works properly, take it apart again.

You'll find it easier if you assemble the toy *partially,* paint all the parts, then finish the assembly. Glue the maypole in the base, but do *not* glue the star or the wooden bead to the top of the pole. Glue the spokes in the hub, and glue

JESTER PATTERNS

the moons and the other stars to the short spokes, but do *not* glue the jesters to the long spokes.

Paint all the parts according to your own tastes. We used acrylic paints to color the wood, but here, too, you have a choice. Use whatever paints or stains that you're comfortable using.

Let the paint dry completely, then glue the jesters to the long spokes. Put the hub over the maypole and hang the hub assembly from the strings so that the feet of the jesters just clear the ground. Tie knots in the ends of the strings to keep them from slipping through the holes. It will take you some experimentation to get these knots positioned just right. Not only must the jesters hang at the right height, but the hub and spokes must be level. When you do get the knots right, put a drop of glue on each knot to keep it from coming undone.

Glue the star with the hole in the center over the strings, where they go through the maypole. This will keep them from shifting. Then glue the wooden bead to the top of the maypole.

Do any necessary touch-up painting, then attach the ribbons to the figures with glue and small tacks. And that's it! There's nothing left to do but wind the jesters 'round the pole and let 'em go.

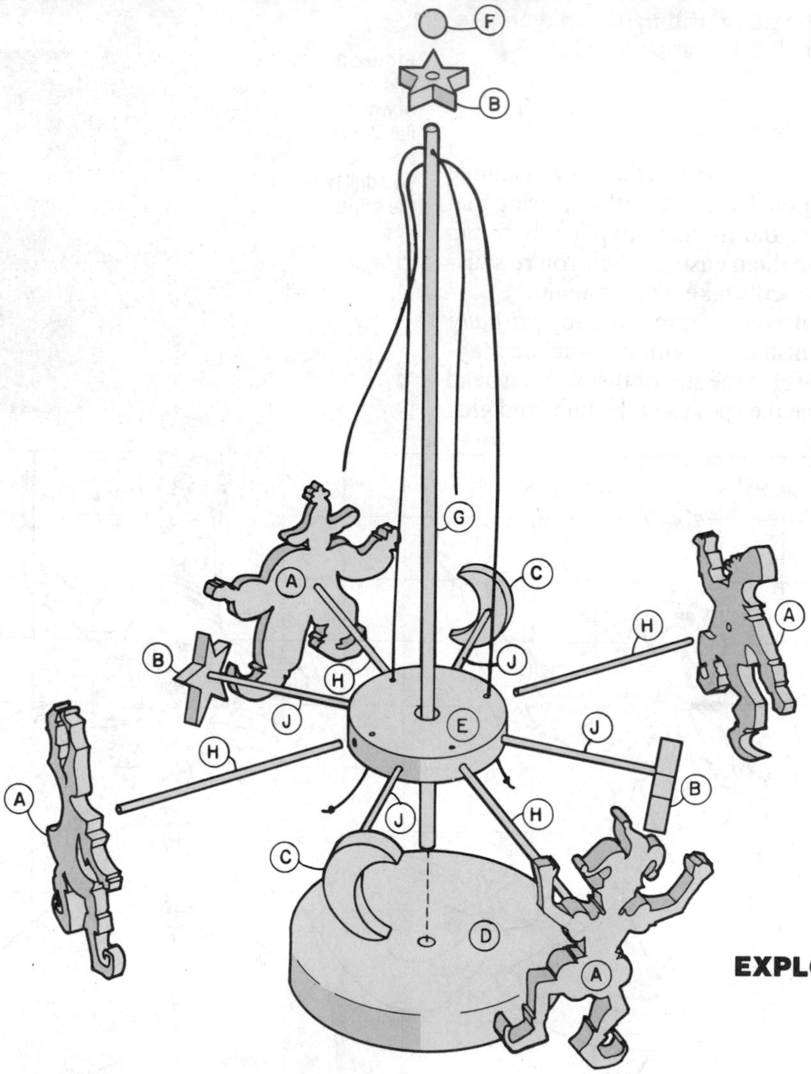

EXPLODED VIEW

BILL OF MATERIALS — Maypole

Finished Dimensions in Inches

Part	Name	Dimensions
A.	Jesters* (4)	½ x 5⅝ x 6¾
B.	Stars (3)	½ x 2½ x 2⅞
C.	Moons (2)	½ x 1¾ x 2½
D.	Base	8 dia. x ¾
E.	Hub	4 dia. x ¾
F.	Bead	¾. dia.
G.	Maypole	½ dia. x 20
H.	Long spokes (4)	¼ dia. x 7
J.	Short spokes (4)	¼ dia. x 5

HARDWARE

$^{3}/_{32}$" dia. Nylon twine (two 40" lengths)
Ribbons (as needed)
Brass tacks (8)

** These are the dimensions of the largest jester. Others will be slightly smaller.*

Chimney Hutch

This traditional country design takes up half the floor space of most hutches.

There are two possible explanations as to how this country storage unit got its curious name. The first is obvious — it looks like a chimney, complete with mantle and fireplace. The second is that this piece of furniture often occupied the narrow space between the fireplace and the nearest wall.

Whatever the reason for the name, the chimney hutch remains a useful piece of furniture, even today. Because it occupies so little floor space, it can be used in areas where you ordinarily couldn't put a full-size hutch. Yet it still provides a good deal of storage space for china, books, collectibles — whatever you have to store.

This particular chimney hutch was built by W. R. Goehring, a professional cabinetmaker in Gambier, Ohio. Rick specializes in "country-derived" pieces such as this. He studies the country forms, particularly those ethnic groups such as the Shakers, Moravians, and Amish, then builds his own interpretation of those forms. The hutch is Rick's interpretation of a traditional Shaker design.

Cutting the Parts

Select cabinet-grade stock to make this project. Traditionally, these hutches were built from white pine, poplar, maple, cherry, or walnut. Rick decided on a non-traditional species — the chimny hutch you see here is made from ash.

Cut all the parts to the sizes shown in the Bill of Materials, except for the bead and the cove moldings. Later on, you'll make these moldings from larger stock. Note that each side is made from two pieces of wood. This is done for convenience, to make it easier to cut and fit the dovetails that join the short sides and the counter.

Joining the Sides and Counter

Rick made these through dovetails by hand, using a dovetail saw and bench chisels. This is not a difficult procedure, it just takes some patience and careful layout. It also requires some very sharp tools. Both your saw and your chisels must be properly sharpened.

Start by making the tails. Use a sliding T-bevel to lay them out. You can use the measurements shown in the — *Counter Dovetail Layout* — or use some variation of your own. Saw the sides of the tails with a dovetail saw, following the marks. (See Figure 1.) If you wish, use a small square to help get the saw started just right.

Remove the waste between the tails with a bench chisel. This is the only real trick to making through dovetails — removing a large amount of waste with a chisel. Most woodworkers think of chisels as tools for removing small amounts of wood. But the sides and the counter parts are ¾″ wide!

Designed and built by W.R. Goehring.

The trick is simple: First make sure your chisel is properly sharpened, as we said before. To test your chisel to see if it's really sharp, shave a piece of end grain with it. It should cut the end grain cleanly with no tearing. The second part of the trick is in how you use the chisel. You must use it as both a cutting *and* a prying tool. Tap the chisel into the stock along the line where you want to cut the waste. Cut down about 1/16″ (not very far), then pry out with a chisel. (See Figure 2.) A small flake of wood will separate from the waste and fall out. If it doesn't — if the

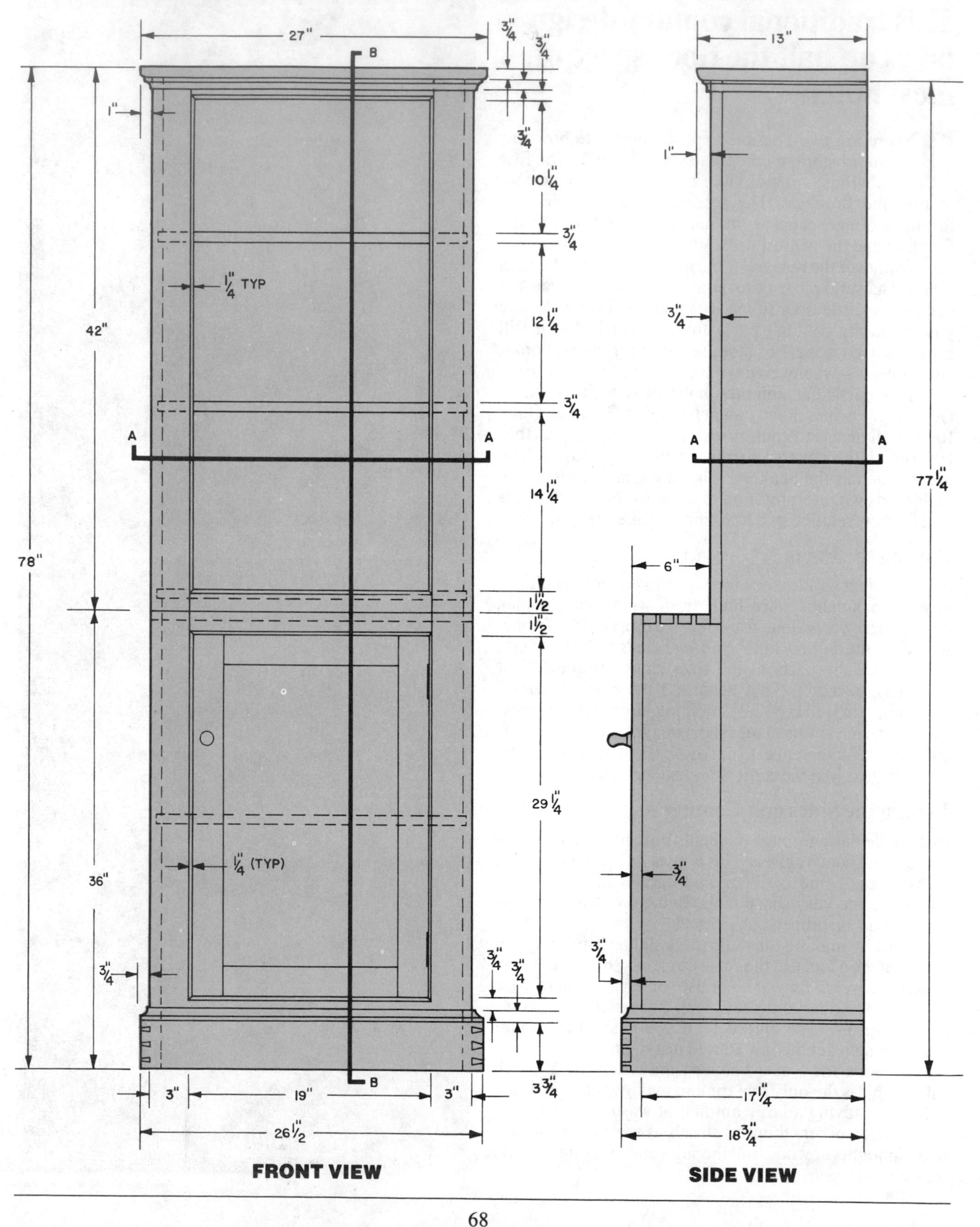

wood is tough to split — then try another tack: After cutting down 1/16", use the chisel to split the waste along the edge of the stock. (See Figure 3.)

Work your way halfway through the stock, removing half the waste between each tail. Then flip the stock over and repeat this procedure, removing the remainder of the waste. If the chisel is properly sharpened, the bottom of the gullet between the tails will be cleanly cut.

Use the tails as templates to lay out the pins on the side stock. That way, you'll get a precise match. Cut the sides of the pins with your saw, staying to the outside of the line. (Some woodworkers prefer to stay 1/64" to the outside of the line. Later on you can remove this extra stock with a chisel and get a perfect fit.) Remove the waste between the pins in the same manner that you removed the waste between the tails. Just be careful to follow the slope of the pins with your chisel.

Check the fit between the tails and the pins. If necessary, remove a little stock from the pins with a chisel or a file. Remember that the fit should be snug — but not too snug. If it is, there won't be any room for glue.

After cutting and fitting the dovetail, glue the short sides to the long sides, edge to edge, as shown in the *Side View.*

Cutting the Joinery in the Sides and Panels

Carefully lay out the dadoes and the rabbets on the inside faces of the sides, as shown in the *Side Layout.* Remember, the sides must be mirror images of each other. To help ensure that they are, line them up back edge to back edge and mark the joinery across *both* pieces at the same time.

Cut the joints with a router and a 3/4" straight bit. Cut the dadoes first. Clamp a straightedge to the workpieces to help guide the router while you cut. (See Figure 4.) Then make the rabbets, using a guide attached to the router base to control the cuts. Make each joint in several passes, cutting just 1/8"-1/4" deeper with each pass.

Tip ◆ You can save time and make the dadoes more accurately if you cut them the same way you marked them — with the sides lined up back edge to back edge.

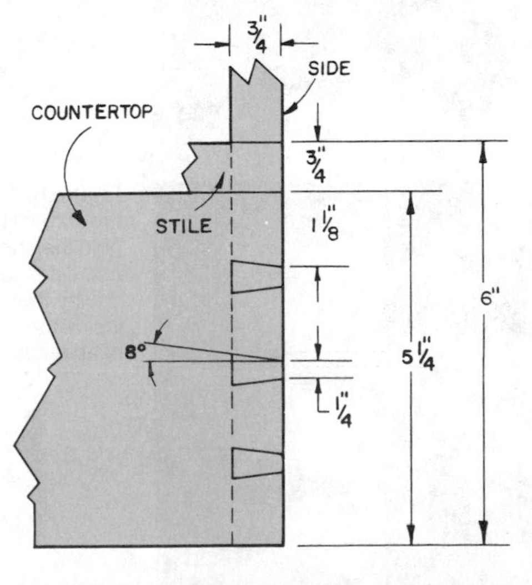

COUNTER DOVETAIL LAYOUT

Figure 1. Cut the tails with a dovetail saw. If you want, use a square to help start the saw.

Figure 2. Remove the waste with a sharp bench chisel. Cut down about 1/16", then pry off a slivver of waste. Cut half the waste from between the tails, then turn the board over and do the other half.

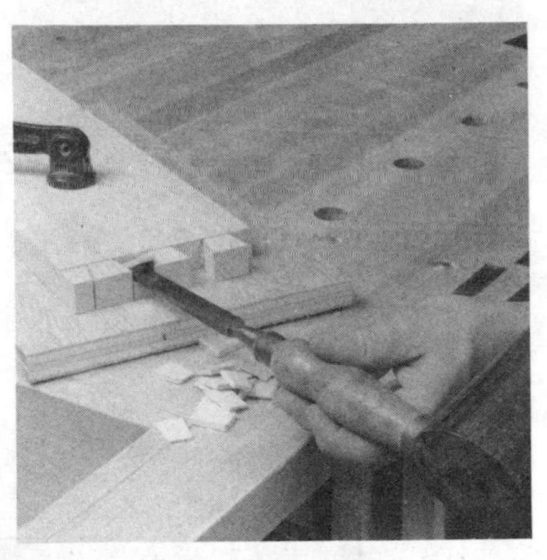
Figure 3. If the waste won't split off when you pry out, you may have to split it off from the edge of the board.

Figure 4. When you cut the dadoes, use a straightedge to guide the router.

While you're set up to make rabbets, cut the rabbets in the back panels, as shown in *Section A*. With a molder, cut a bead in the left and right back panels, next to the shoulder of the rabbet, as shown on the drawings. (See Figure 5.)

Dry assemble the sides, shelves, counter, and back panels to check the fit of the case parts. Make any adjustments that are necessary, then leave the case assembled — held together with band clamps or bar clamps — for the time being.

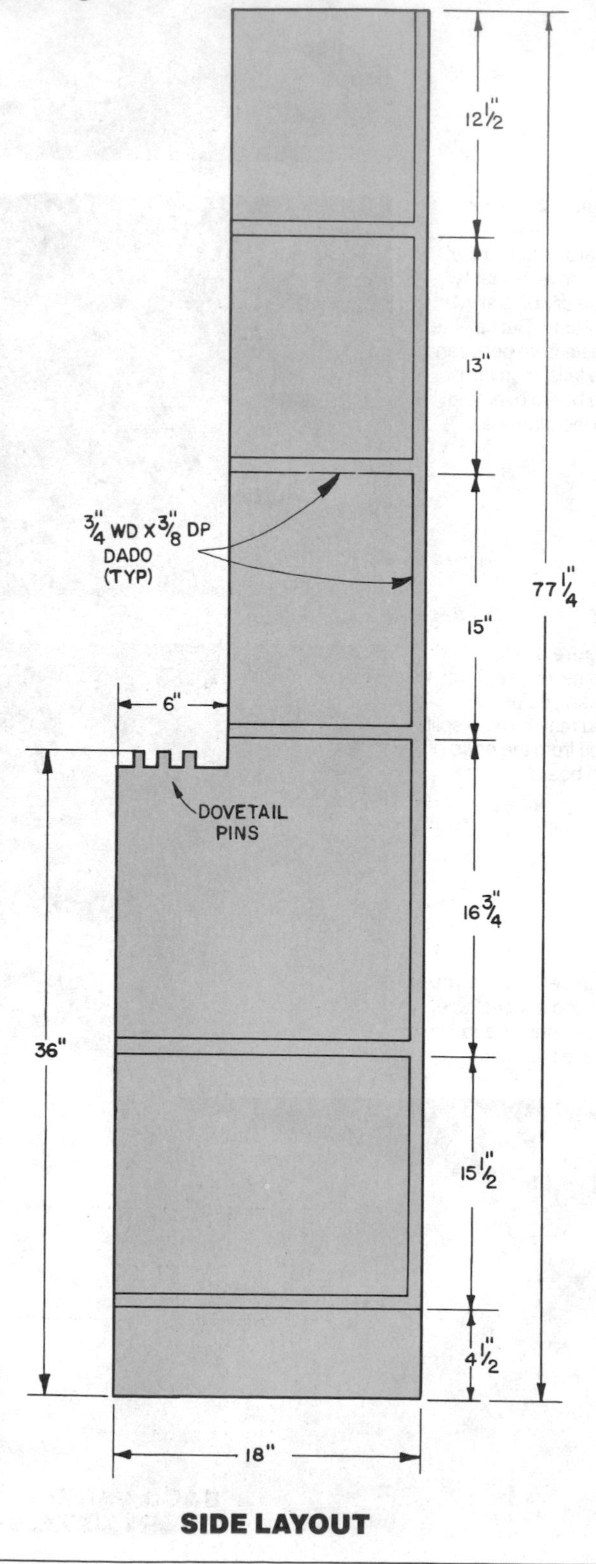

SIDE LAYOUT

Making the Face Frames

Join the rails and stiles of the face frames with dowels. Use a doweling jig to position the holes in the edges and the ends of the frame members. Dry assemble the parts to check the fit. Hold the frames up against the case to make sure that these frames fit, too. If the fit is satisfactory, glue the frames together.

Note: While Rick specifies dowels to hold the face frame parts together, you can use a variety of other methods. Traditionally, craftsmen used mortise-and-tenon joints or lap joints. You may also want to consider using a newly-developed device, the plate or "biscuit."

Assembling the Case

While the glue dries on the face frame, disassemble the case. Finish sand all the parts, then reassemble them with glue and screws. Make sure the case is square as you clamp the parts together. Do *not* glue the back panels to each other, and don't glue them to the backs of the shelves. Instead, drive a single screw through the middle of each panel at each shelf. This will let the panels expand and contract with changes in temperature and humidity.

Tip ◆ Stain the inside shoulders and cheeks of the rabbets in the panels a dark color before you attach the panels to the case. When the wood shrinks, the joints will be less noticeable.

"Toenail" the screws that hold the shelves to the sides. Drive them in at an angle, up through the shelf from the bottom and into the side. (See Figure 6.) This way, they won't show on the outside of the case.

Figure 5. Use a molder to cut the bead in the left and right back panels.

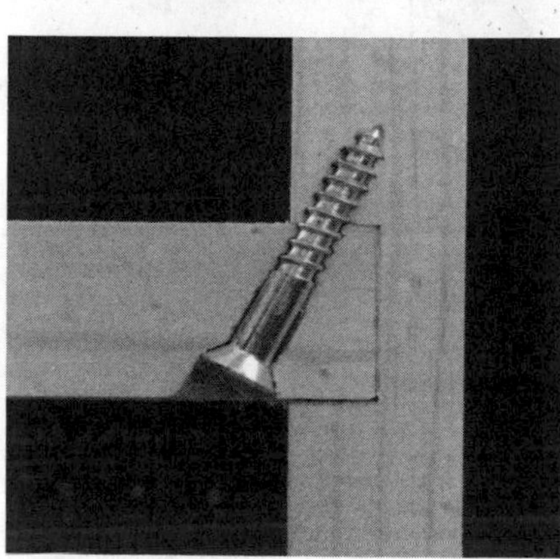
Figure 6. "Toenail" the screws that hold the shelves and sides together, driving them from inside the cabinet at an angle.

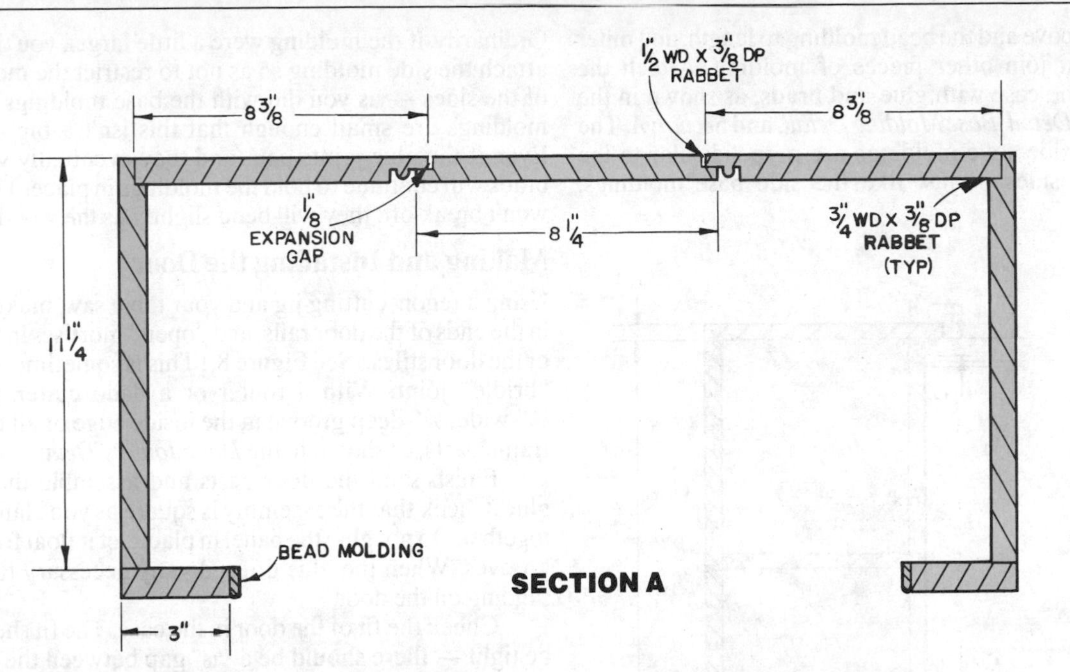

Finish sand the face frames and glue these to the case. You don't need screws to hold them in place. Since the grain direction of the sides and the stiles are parallel, a glue joint should be sufficient.

After the glue dries on the case, do any necessary touch-up sanding. Then attach the top with screws, driving the screws down through the top and into the sides, back panels, and face frame rail. Counterbore and countersink these screws, then cover the heads with wood plugs. Sand the plugs flush with the surface of the wood.

Making and Attaching the Molding

The bead and the cove moldings can both be made with a similar procedure. Cut the shape of the molding with a router, shaper, or molder in wide stock. Then rip the narrow molding from the wider stock on a table saw. (See Figure 7.) Take care that you don't set up your table saw so that the narrow molding is caught between the fence and the blade. If this happens, the molding is liable to kick back as you finish the cut.

Warning: Never try to shape narrow, thin, or small pieces of wood. When you need delicate moldings, always cut the shape in the edge of a large board *first,* then cut the shape from the board.

Cut the dovetails that join the base moldings in the same manner that you cut those that join the sides and the counter. Finish sand all the moldings, then attach the base moldings to the case with roundhead screws. Drive the screws from inside the case into the base molding, so the screws won't be noticeable from the outside. Make the screw holes in the sides of the case slightly larger than the shaft of the screws (but make the pilot holes in the moldings the normal size — slightly smaller). This will allow the sides to expand and contract.

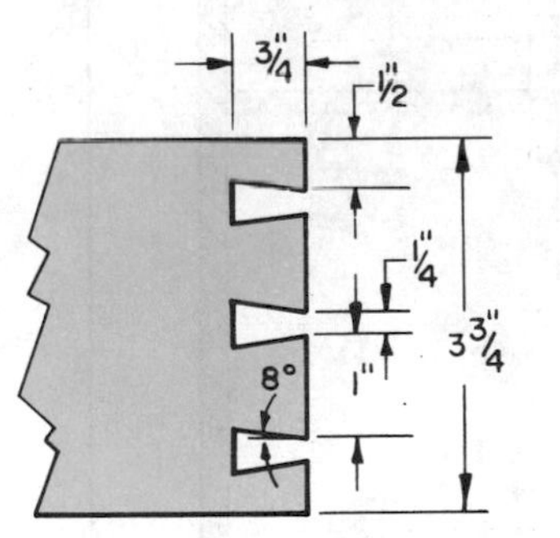

Figure 7. Cut the shape of the cove and the bead moldings in a large board, then rip the moldings free of the stock.

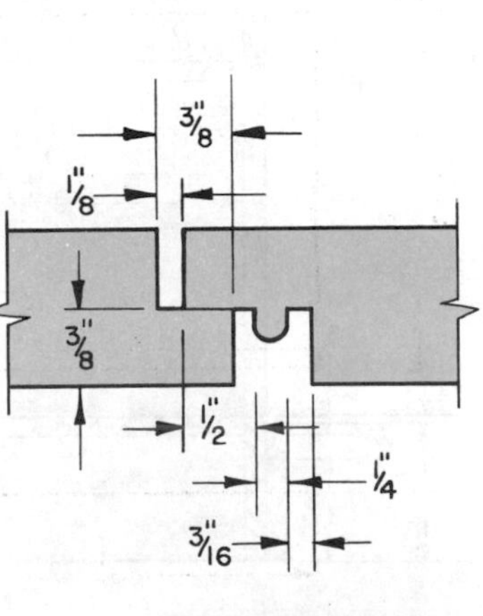

Cut the cove and the bead molding to length, and miter the ends that join other pieces of molding. Attach the molding to the case with glue and brads, as shown in the *Top Molding Detail, Base Molding Detail,* and *Section A.* The grain of the side cove moldings are perpendicular to the grain of the sides — just like the side base moldings. Ordinarily, if the molding were a little larger, you'd have to attach the side molding so as not to restrict the movement of the sides — as you did with the base moldings. But the moldings are small enough that this isn't a big concern. Even if the glue joints pop (and they eventually will), the brads will continue to hold the moldings in place. The brads won't break off; they will bend slightly as the wood moves.

Making and Installing the Door

Using a tenon-cutting jig and your table saw, make tenons in the ends of the door rails, and "open" mortises in the ends of the door stiles. (See Figure 8.) This is sometimes called a "bridle" joint. With a router or a dado cutter, make a 1/4″-wide, 1/4″-deep groove in the inside edge of all the door frame parts, as shown in the *Door Joinery Detail.*

Finish sand the door parts and assemble them with glue. Check that the assembly is square as you clamp them together. Do not glue the panel in place; let it float free in the grooves. When the glue dries, do any necessary touch-up sanding on the door.

Check the fit of the door in the case. The fit should not be tight — there should be a 1/16″ gap between the edge of the door and the opening in the face frame. If the door is too tight, use a plane or a *very* sharp chisel to pare away the edge of the door where needed.

When the door fits to your satisfaction, mortise one edge for the hinges. Then mount the door in the case. Install a bullet catch to keep the door closed. These spring-loaded catches are much less obtrusive than ordinary magnetic or friction catches. You can barely see them when the door is open.

Turn the pull on the lathe, or carve one from a scrap of wood. (The shape shown here is what Rick used. You may prefer a different shape.) Attach it to the door with a roundhead wood screw. Drive the screw through the door and into the pull from the inside surface — the back of the door — so that the screw won't be visible on the outside.

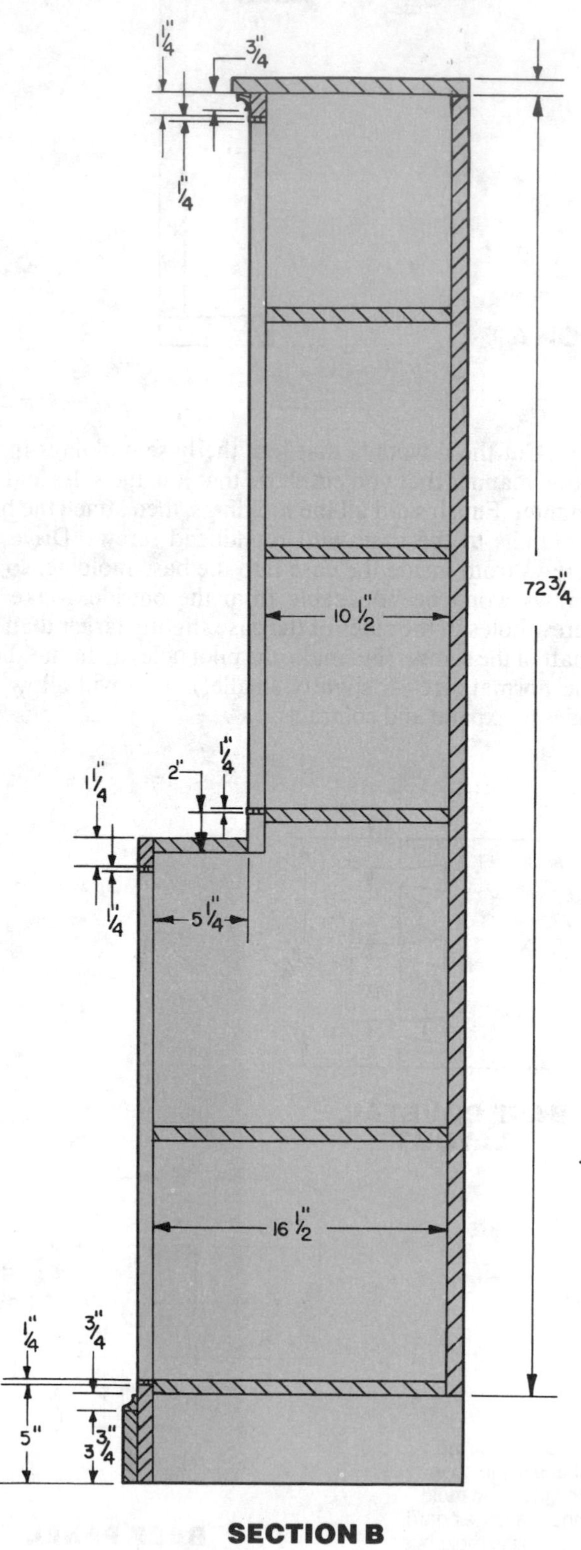

SECTION B

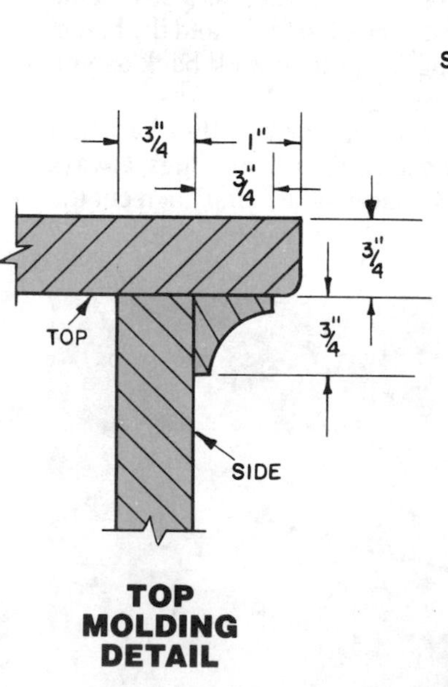

TOP MOLDING DETAIL

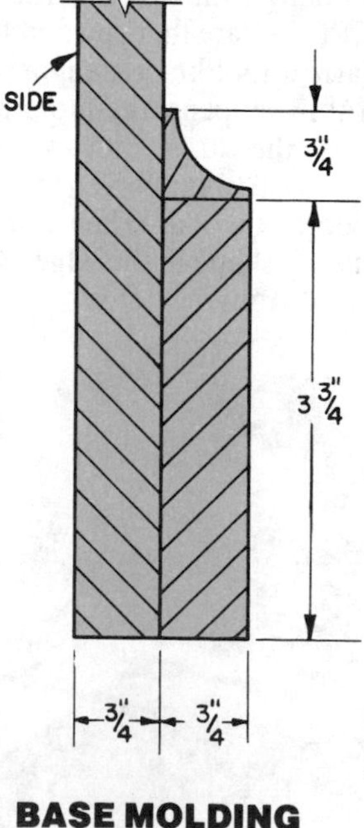

BASE MOLDING DETAIL

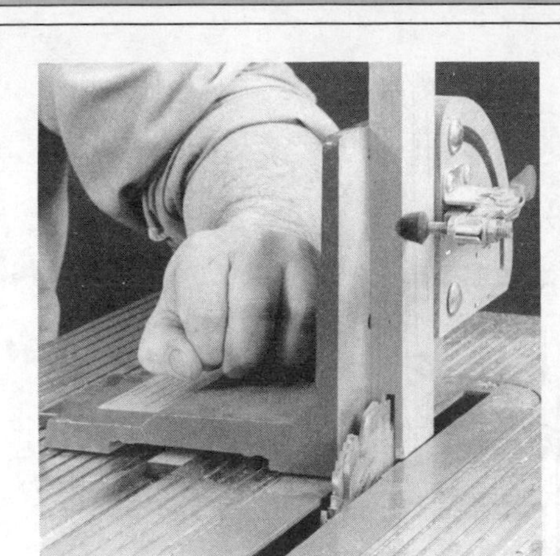

Figure 8. Cut the mortises and the tenons that hold the door frame together with a tenon cutting jig. The jig shown here is commercially-made, but you can easily make one from scrap wood.

Finishing the Hutch

Remove the door and any hardware from the completed chimney hutch. Do any necessary touch-up sanding. (For a really smooth sanding job, wet the wood down with a damp rag to raise the grain slightly. Let the hutch dry overnight, then sand it down with very fine sandpaper.) Apply a finish. Be careful to apply as many coats to the inside of the hutch as you do to the outside. This will help prevent warping, and will ensure that all the parts shrink and swell evenly.

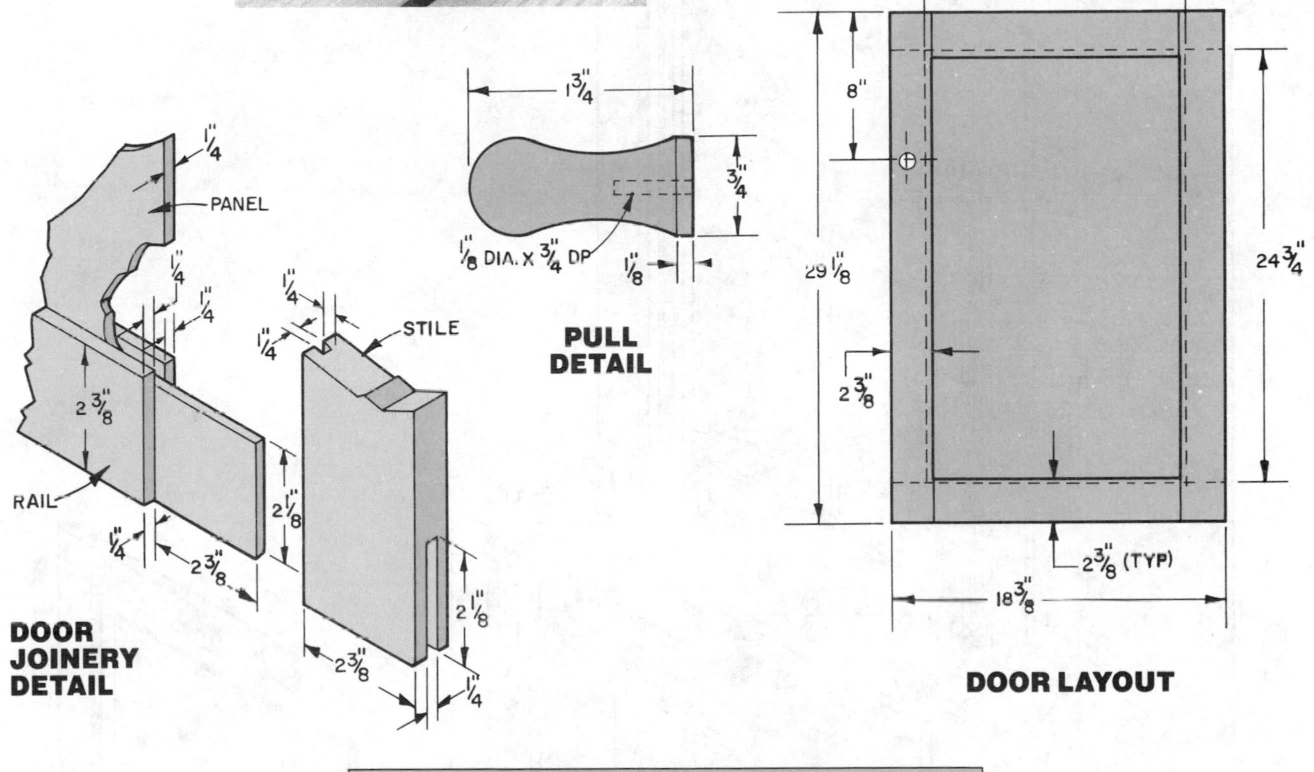

BILL OF MATERIALS — Chimney Hutch

Finished Dimensions in Inches

Part	Description	Dimensions
A.	Long sides (2)	¾ x 11¼ x 77¼
B.	Short sides (2)	¾ x 6 x 36
C.	Top shelves (3)	¾ x 10½ x 24¼
D.	Bottom shelves (2)	¾ x 16½ x 24¼
E.	Top	¾ x 13 x 27
F.	Counter	¾ x 5¼ x 25
G.	Left/right back panels (2)	¾ x 8⅜ x 72¾
H.	Middle back panel	¾ x 8¼ x 72¾
J.	Top face frame stiles (2)	¾ x 3 x 42
K.	Upper top face frame rail	¾ x 1¼ x 19
L.	Lower top face frame rail	¾ x 2 x 19
M.	Bottom face frame stiles (2)	¾ x 3 x 36
N.	Upper bottom face frame rail	¾ x 1¼ x 19
P.	Lower bottom face frame rail	¾ x 5 x 19
Q.	Top vertical bead molding (2)	¼ x ¾ x 38¾
R.	Bottom vertical bead molding (2)	¼ x ¾ x 29¾
S.	Horizontal bead molding (4)	¼ x ¾ x 19
T.	Door stiles (2)	¾ x 2⅜ x 29⅛
U.	Door rails (2)	¾ x 2⅜ x 18⅜
V.	Door panel	¼ x 14 x 24¾
W.	Pull	¾ dia. x 1¾
X.	Front cove moldings (2)	¾ x ¾ x 26½
Y.	Top side cove moldings (2)	¾ x ¾ x 12¾
Z.	Bottom side cove moldings (2)	¾ x ¾ x 18¾
AA.	Front base molding	¾ x 3¾ x 26½
BB.	Side base moldings (2)	¾ x 3¾ x 18¾
CC.	Dowels (16)	⅜ dia. x 2

HARDWARE

#8 x 1¼" Flathead wood screws (42-48)
#8 x 1¼" Roundhead wood screws (6-8)
#10 x 1½" Roundhead wood screw and washer (1)
1½" x 2½" Brass butt hinges and mounting screws (1 pair)
Bullet catch

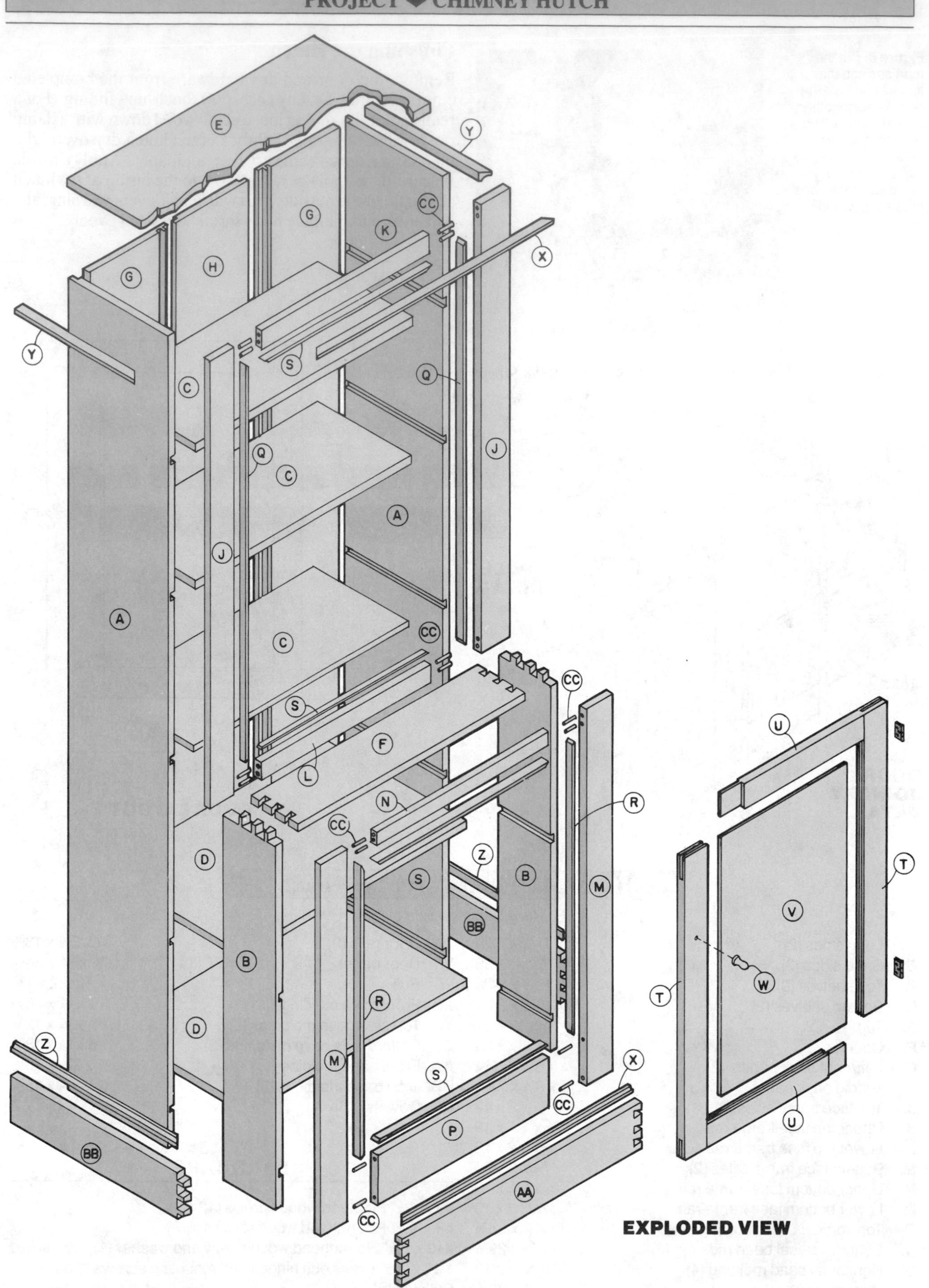

EXPLODED VIEW

Designed and built by Nick Engler.

Purple Martin House

An apartment house for birds helps to keep the local bug population under control.

Did you know that a single purple martin eats up to *two thousand* mosquitoes a day? It's no wonder that some people build birdhouses especially designed for martins. Several pairs of martins in residence can keep your backyard almost pest-free.

Purple martins are one of the few species of small meadow birds that prefer to nest in colonies. For this reason, the best martin house is actually an "apartment" house. The birdhouse that you see here will accommodate a dozen nesting pairs — 24 birds in all.

Martins also like to have fresh, clean spots to build their nests each year. They rarely come back to an old nest. So we have designed this birdhouse so that it can be easily cleaned. Just loosen four bolts and it comes apart, allowing you to remove the old nests. To put it back together, tighten the bolts again.

Selecting the Site

Before you go to the trouble of building and erecting a martin house, be sure you have a good site for the project. To attract purple martins you not only need the right house, you need the right backyard. There should be no trees or other obstructions for 40 yards around the spot where you plan to put the birdhouse. Martins swoop and glide to their nesting place, and they need plenty of open space. A nearby pond or stream, an open meadow, and telephone wires (for perches) will also help to attract the birds.

Selecting Materials

Once you have selected a site, choose your building materials. The wood and hardware must withstand the elements. For this reason, use redwood, cedar, or cypress lumber. These woods are naturally resistant to damage caused by moisture and insects. Purchase hardwood dowels to serve as perches, and soak them in tung oil to help them weather the outdoors. Also purchase brass, stainless steel, or galvanized hardware. These metals do not rust.

Avoid pressure-treated lumber. This lumber is usually treated with chromated copper arsenate, an arsenic compound. Although many lumber companies claim their treated lumber will not harm wildlife, arsenic in any form is *potentially* hazardous. Many carpenters who work with CCA-treated lumber for long periods of time report rashes and other skin irritations. Birds — because they are smaller — are more susceptible to environmental poisoning than carpenters, so draw your own conclusions. It may be fine to build decks and gazebos from treated lumber, but birdhouses should be built of untreated lumber. After all, birds live in trees; trees are made of *untreated* wood.

Making the Parts

Many of the parts in this project are wider than common 1 x 12 stock. For these parts, you'll have to glue up wider stock, edge to edge, using waterproof resorcinol or epoxy glue. When you've glued up all the stock you need, cut all the pieces to size.

Drill ¼" holes in the floors and the top for drainage, ventilation, mounting perches, and connecting the separate assemblies of the birdhouse, as shown in the *Front View, Side View,* and *Floor Plan* drawings. (The top won't get holes for perches, of course, but it does need ventilation and connecting holes.) Also, drill ¼" ventilation and 2½" entrance holes in the sides and ends, where shown. Use a hole saw to make the entrance holes.

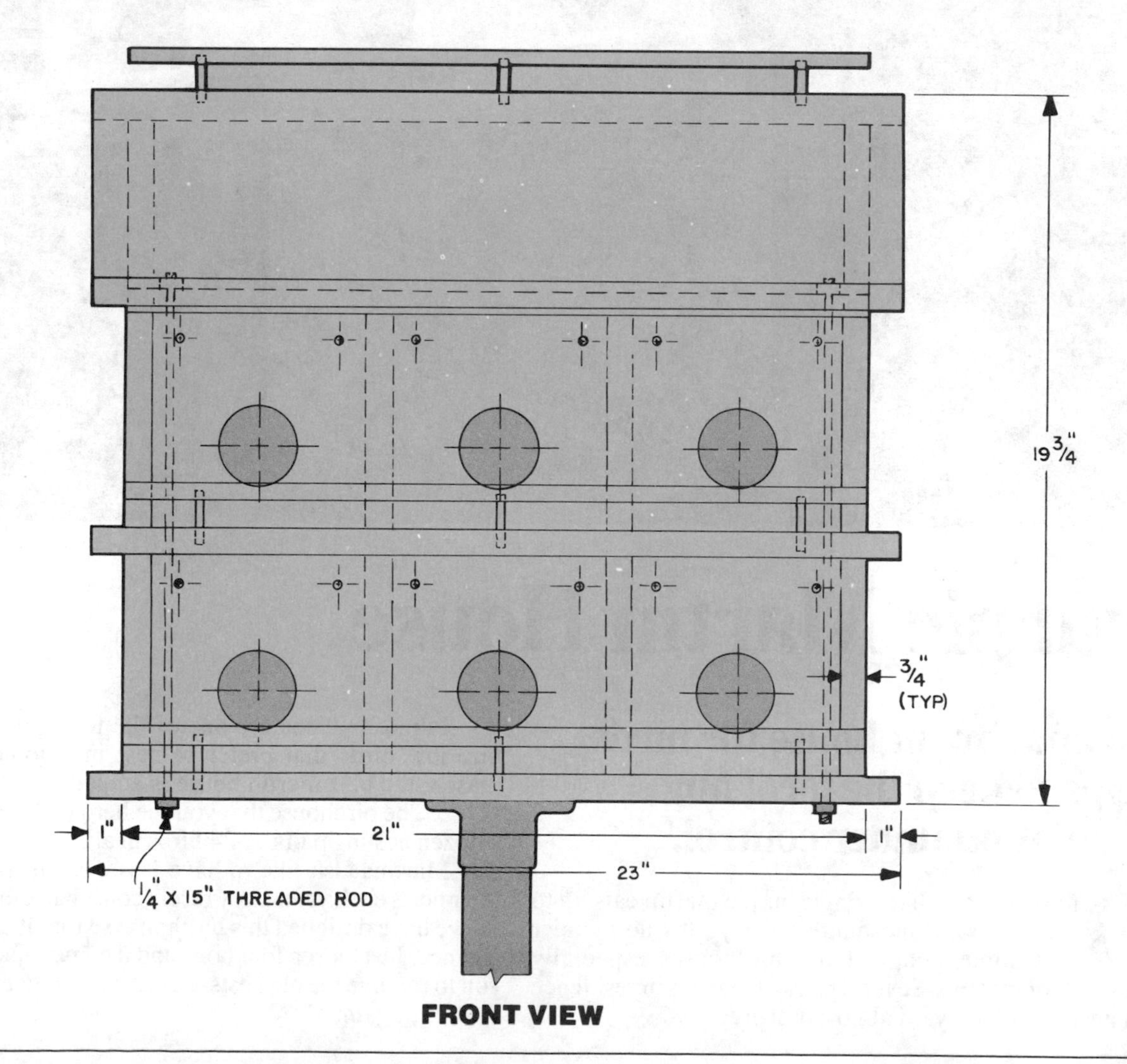

FRONT VIEW

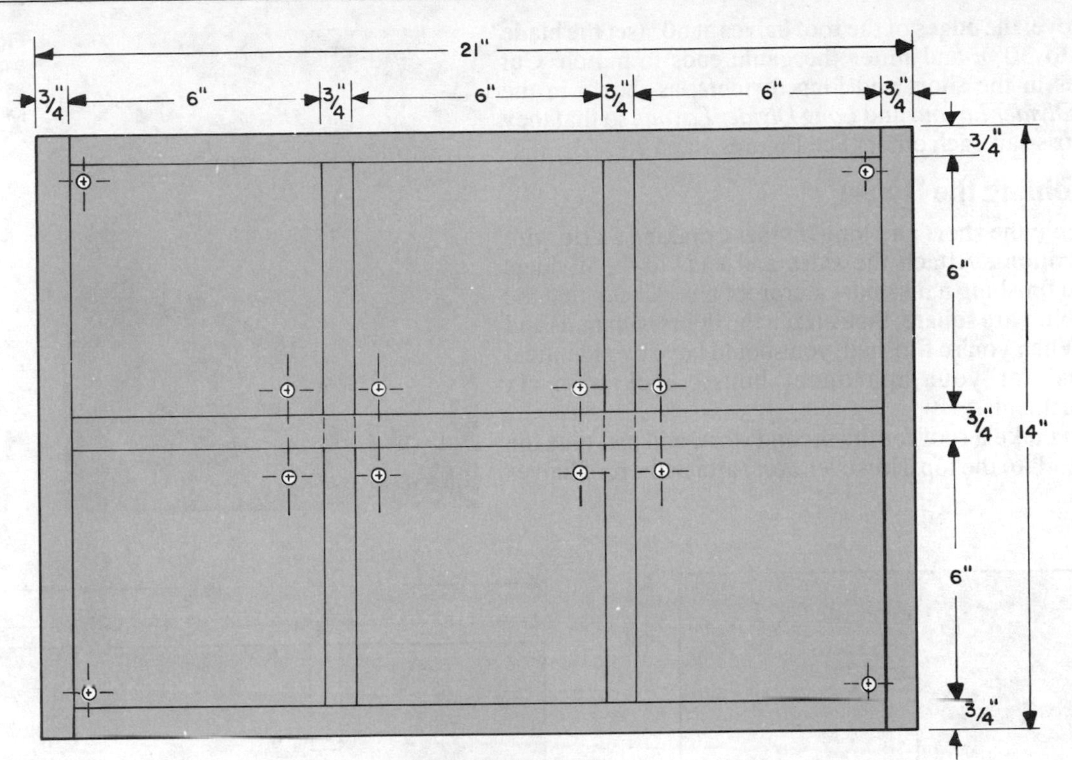

FLOOR PLAN

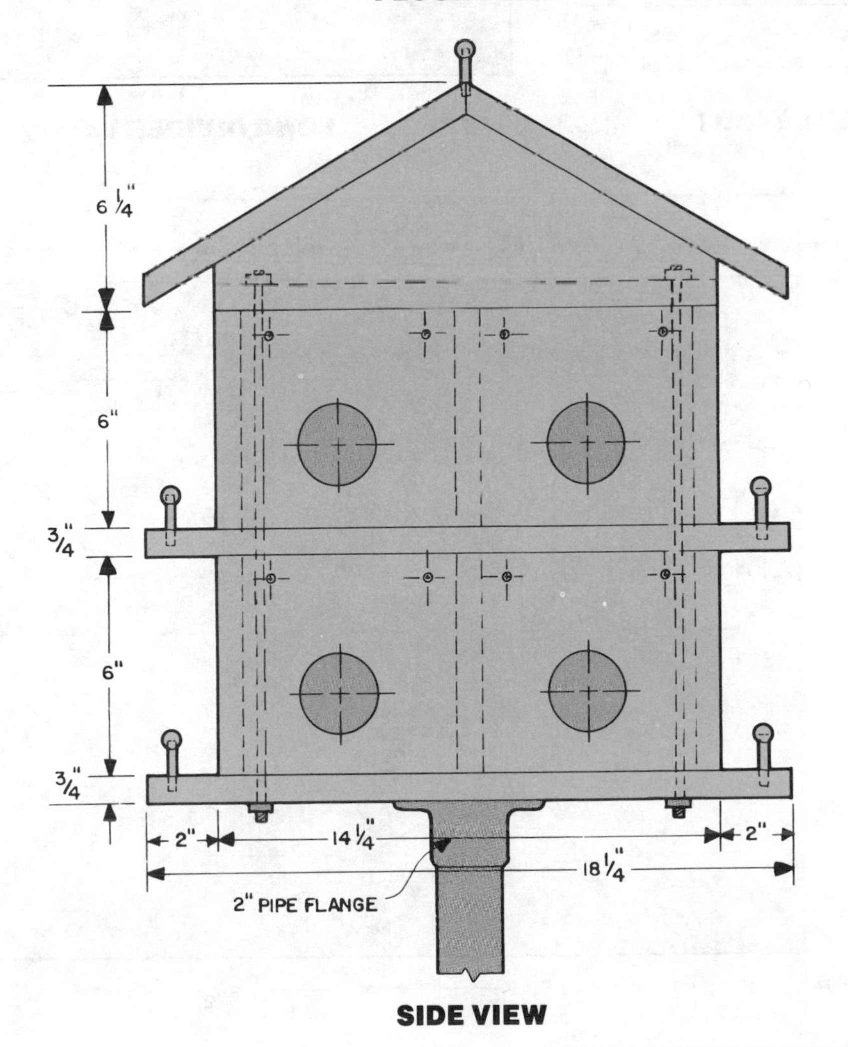

SIDE VIEW

Bevel the edges of the roof halves at 60° (set the blade angle to 30°), and miter the gable ends to match. Cut notches in the short and long dividers, as shown in the *Short Divider Layout* and *Long Divider Layout*, so that they will cross-lap each other. (See Figures 1 and 2.)

Figure 1. To make a cross lap joint, first saw the side of the joint.

Assembling the House

Assemble the short and long dividers, making a grid with six partitions. Attach the sides and ends to the dividers with 6d finishing nails and waterproof glue. Check that the assemblies are square; then attach the floors with nails and glue. When you're finished, you should have two identical 'stories' for your apartment house, each with six compartments.

To make a roof for the second story, nail and glue the gable ends to the top. However, *don't* attach the roof halves just yet.

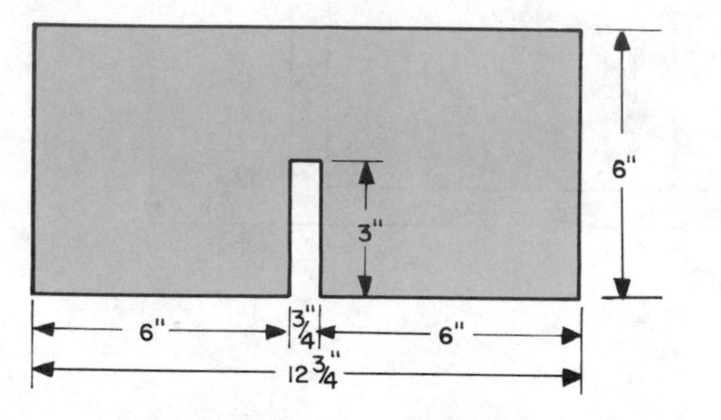

SHORT DIVIDER LAYOUT

LONG DIVIDER LAYOUT

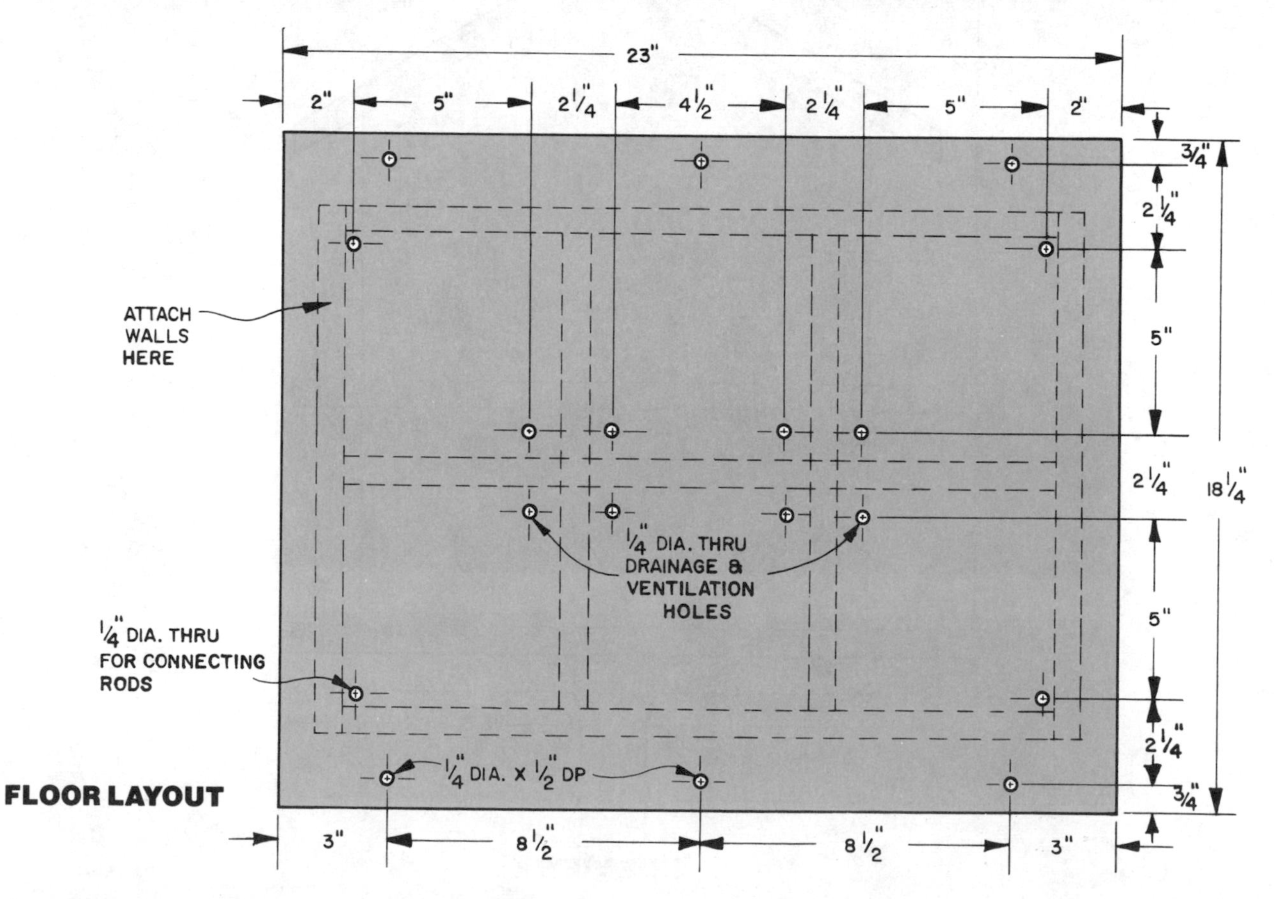

FLOOR LAYOUT

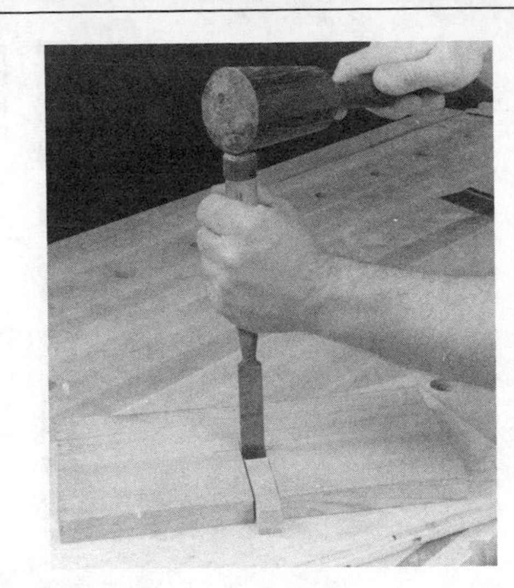

Figure 2. Then remove the waste with a sharp chisel.

Cut four pieces of ¼″ threaded rod, 15″ long. Put a nut and a flat washer on one end of the rods; then insert the rods through the connecting holes in the top, then those in the second story, then those in the first story. With the top and both stories stacked atop one another, put flat washers and nuts on the other ends of the threaded rods and tighten the nuts. Finally, *screw* the roof halves in place on the gable ends.

Note: To take the apartment house apart to clean it, all you have to do is remove the roof (just loosen the screws). Using two wrenches, hold the nuts on the top from turning and remove the nuts at the *bottom* of the assembly, under the first floor. Remove the stories one at a time. When you've cleaned all the apartments, stack the stories back on the threaded rods and tighten the nuts.

Adding the Perches

Cut lengths of hardwood dowel rod to make the perches. Drill three ¼″ holes in each length of ½″ rod to match the holes you've already drilled in the floors of the apartment house. If you wish, also drill holes in the roof to mount a perch at the roof peak. Glue the ¼″ dowels in the mounting holes; then glue the ½″ dowels to the smaller dowels, as shown in the *Perch Detail* drawing.

Tip ◆ Don't glue the perch at the roof peak in place. If you do, you won't be able to easily remove the roof. Instead, just friction-fit the dowels to their holes. After the first rain, the ¼″ dowels will swell up in their holes, and the perch will be secure without glue.

¼" DIA. VENTILATION HOLES
2½" DIA. ENTRANCE HOLE
¾"
3"
6"
2¼"
3"
3"
6"

SIDE LAYOUT

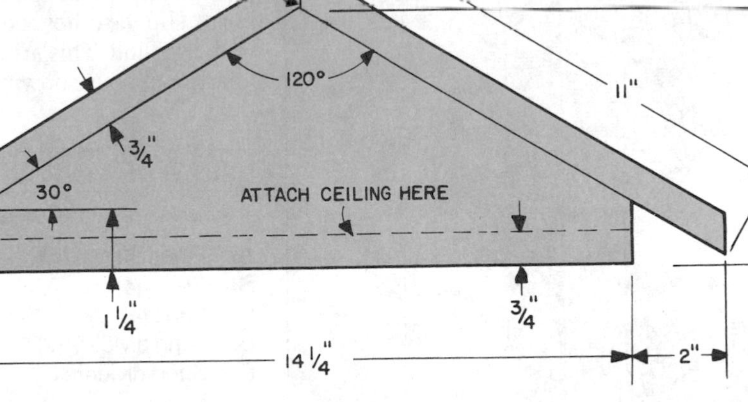

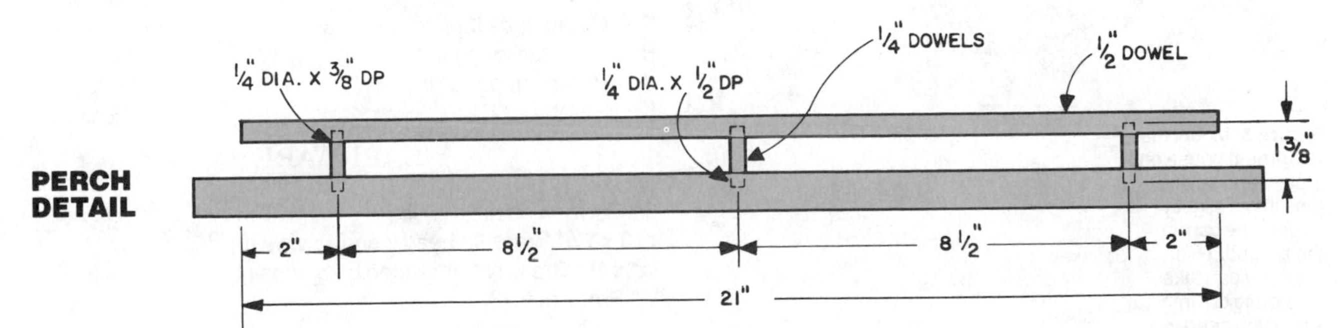

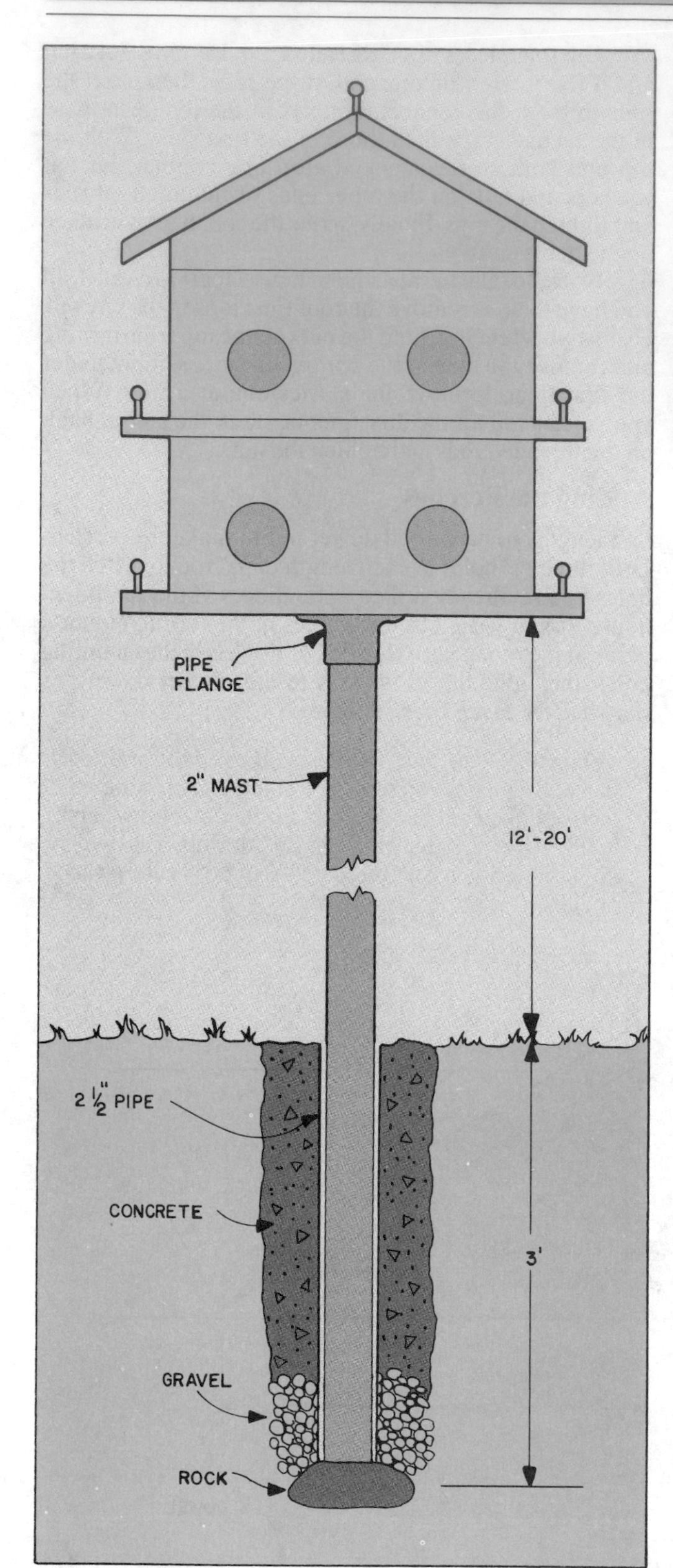

Figure 3. Mount the apartment house on a pipe, and set the pipe into a slightly larger pipe cast in the ground. This way, you can take the house down when you need to.

Figure 4. Attach the apartment house to the mast with a pipe flange.

Finishing and Mounting the House

Because the cedar, redwood, and cyprus are all naturally weather resistant, the birdhouse doesn't need to be painted or otherwise finished. However, you may want to paint it anyway to match the architecture on your property or for other aesthetic reasons. If this is so, be careful to only paint the *outside*. Allow the house to sit for at least three weeks after you paint it so that the smell from the paint will dissipate. This smell will keep birds away.

When you're ready to mount the apartment house, purchase a 2″ pipe flange, a 3′ length of 2½″ pipe, and two 10′ lengths of 2″ 'mast', with couplers. Dig a 3′ deep hole and place a large rock in the bottom. Set the 2½″ pipe on the rock, and throw some gravel in the hole for drainage. Fill the rest of the hole with concrete. (See Figure 3.) Attach the pipe flange to the bottom of the apartment house with flathead wood screws, and screw the threaded end of the 2″ pipe into the pipe flange. (See Figure 4.) When the concrete cures, slip the other end of the 2″ pipe into the 2½″ pipe, set in the ground. This arrangement will allow you to take the apartment house down from time to time for cleaning.

BILL OF MATERIALS — Purple Martin House

Finished Dimensions in Inches

	Part	Dimensions
A.	Floors (2)	¾ x 18¼ x 23
B.	Sides (4)	¾ x 6 x 19½
C.	Ends (4)	¾ x 6 x 14¼
D.	Long dividers (2)	¾ x 6 x 19½
E.	Short dividers (4)	¾ x 6 x 12¾
F.	Top	¾ x 14¼ x 19½
G.	Gable ends (2)	¾ x 5⅜ x 14¼
H.	Roof halves (2)	¾ x 11 x 23
J.	Perch supports (15)	¼ dia. x 1⅜
K.	Perches (5)	½ dia. x 21

HARDWARE

6d Galvanized nails (¼ lb.)
#10 x 1½″ Brass flathead wood screws (6)
¼″ x 15″ Brass rod, threaded both ends (4)
¼″ Brass nuts (8)
¼″ Brass flat washers

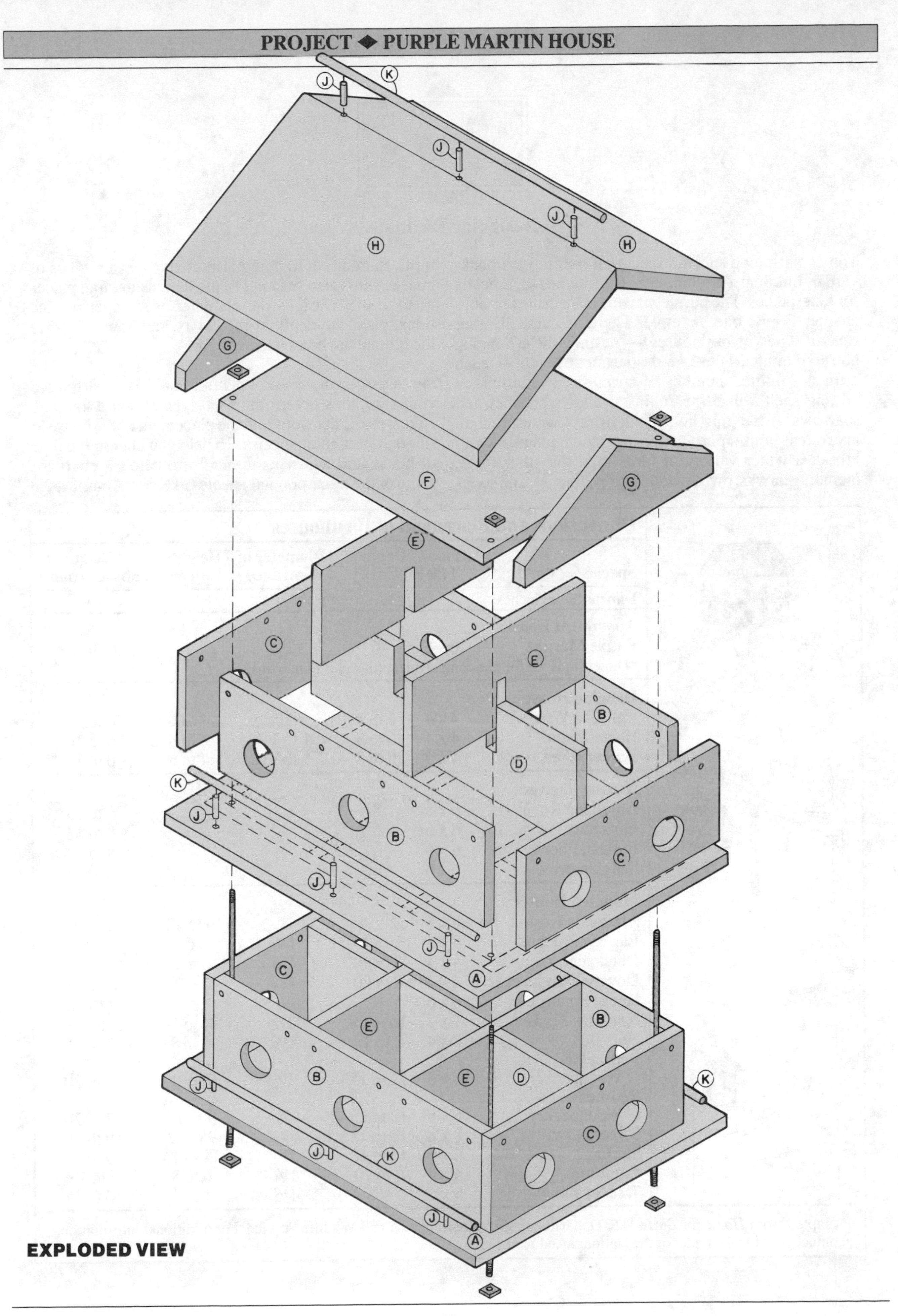

EXPLODED VIEW

Designing Birdhouses

You can attract a specific species of bird to your backyard by building a birdhouse that is designed specifically for that species. The purple martin house in the previous chapter is just one example. There are actually four *general* types of birdhouses — nesting shelf, hanging house, mounted house, and apartment house — each attract a limited number of species. For example, a nesting 'shelf' will attract robins, swallows, phoebes, and sparrows. A hanging house will attract wrens, and an apartment house, purple martins. Mounted houses will attract a wider variety of birds than the other three, including hawks, owls, woodpeckers, finches, and songbirds. In addition to being attracted to certain types of houses, birds also respond to the dimensions and placement of the house — the diameter of the opening, the floor space, the depth of the cavity, and how far above the ground the house is mounted.

◆ Decide what species of birds you'd like to attract to your yard; then determine what type of house to build. Adjust the dimensions and the placement of the house to suit that particular species. To help you choose the type of house and adjust its dimensions, here's a chart for some of the more popular species in North America.

Dimensions and Placement of Birdhouses

Species	Floor Size	Depth of Cavity	Diameter of Entrance	Height of Entrance	Height above ground
Dimensions in Inches					Feet
Apartment House:					
Purple Martin*	6 x 6	6	2½	1	12 to 20
*Dimensions are for one compartment (one pair of martins).					
Hanging Houses:					
Carolina Wren	4 x 4	6 to 8	1½	4 to 6	6 to 10
House Wren	4 x 4	6 to 8	1 to 1¼	4 to 6	6 to 10
Winter Wren	4 x 4	6 to 8	1 to 1¼	4 to 6	6 to 10
Nesting Shelves:					
American Robin	6 x 8	8			6 to 15
Barn Swallow	6 x 6	6			8 to 12
Eastern Phoebe	6 x 6	6			8 to 12
Song Sparrow	6 x 6	6			1 to 3
Mounted Houses:					
American Kestrel	8 x 8	12 to 15	3	9 to 12	10 to 30
Eastern Bluebird	5 x 5	8	1½	6	5 to 10
Chickadee	4 x 4	8 to 10	1⅛	6 to 8	6 to 15
Downy Woodpecker	4 x 4	8 to 10	1¼	6 to 8	6 to 20
House Finch	6 x 6	6	2	4	8 to 12
Northern Flicker	7 x 7	16 to 18	2½	14 to 16	6 to 20
Nuthatch	4 x 4	8 to 10	1¼	6 to 8	12 to 20
Red-bellied Woodpecker	6 x 6	12 to 15	2½	9 to 12	12 to 20
Red-headed Woodpecker	6 x 6	12 to 15	2	9 to 12	12 to 20
Screech Owl	8 x 8	12 to 15	3	9 to 12	10 to 30
Starling	6 x 6	16 to 18	2	14 to 16	10 to 25
Titmouse	4 x 4	8 to 10	1¼	6 to 8	6 to 15
Tree Swallow	5 x 5	6	1½	1 to 5	10 to 15

Adapted from *Home for Birds,* U.S. Department of the Interior, Fish and Wildlife Service. For additional information, contact your local chapter of the National Audubon Society.

Designed and built by Nick Engler and Mary Jane Favorite

Knock-Down Tables

Knock-down fasteners make these contemporary pieces simple, portable, and sturdy.

Looking for a place to set your home computer? Or a stand to place the sewing machine? A desk for the kids to do their homework? These two worktables will accommodate all of those things. The utter simplicity makes them incredibly versatile.

And versatility isn't their only virtue. Although they look quite solid, these tables come apart so that you can easily store or move them. Each of these pieces of contemporary furniture are assembled with knock-down fasteners. To take them apart, just loosen a few screws.

These same fasteners also make the tables easy to build. Using knock-down hardware eliminates the need for complex joinery. Instead, the table tops, legs, and braces are all assembled with ordinary butt joints. The only rabbets, grooves, or dadoes that you'll find in this project are those that join the drawer of the storage table.

Selecting the Materials

These tables — and the CRT stand — are all made from 1″-thick stock. This extra-thick stock adds stability that you can't get if you use ordinary ¾″-thick materials. The thinner stock would bow under moderate-to-heavy loads, and the butt joints would have a tendency to wobble. The thickness of the stock is important.

The thick stock is also more expensive than the thin stock. You'll have to find a lumberyard that carries five-quarter (1¼″-thick) rough-cut lumber, and plane it down to 1″. You could also purchase eight-quarter (2″) stock, but it would be even more expensive, and — unless you resaw every piece — almost half the lumber would be wasted.

There is one inexpensive alternative, but it requires some patience. Look around for some decent two-by (1½″) construction-grade lumber. You can probably find some pretty good-looking stock. However, you won't be

Figure 1. Round over the edges with a router and a quarter-round bit.

Figure 2. Install the threaded inserts in their holes with a screwdriver.

able to use it right away. Construction lumber is usually only cured to 30% moisture content, while cabinet lumber is cured to 7%–8%. If you use this lumber right away, it will warp and twist, ruining the project.

Instead, you'll have to set the lumber aside for eight months to a year, so that it has time to dry out properly. Don't bring it indoors into a heated environment — it will dry out too fast. Let it sit in your garage or storage barn. Stack the lumber flat with small sticks in between each layer of wood so that the air circulates around every board.

After the lumber has time to dry out, plane it down to 1/16" thick. Let it sit in the shop for a few weeks to get used to the climate, then plane off that last 1/16". Glue up the width of stock you need, and cut all the parts to the sizes shown in the Bill of Materials.

Making the Tables

All of the pieces, including the CRT stand, are made in precisely the same manner. After cutting the parts to size, round the edges and the corners that *don't* butt up against other parts. Use a sabre saw to round the corners, and a router with a ½" quarter-round bit for the edges. (See Figure 1.)

Carefully mark where you want to install the knock-down fasteners. (We used threaded inserts and roundhead bolts to make this project, but there are many other types of knock-down fasteners available.) Use three fasteners along each edge of the wide parts, such as the tops, and two fasteners per edge in the smaller parts. Then *nail* the parts together with 8d nails, placing one nail every place you want to put a fastener. Don't drive the nails all the way home; let the heads protrude slightly so that you can easily remove them.

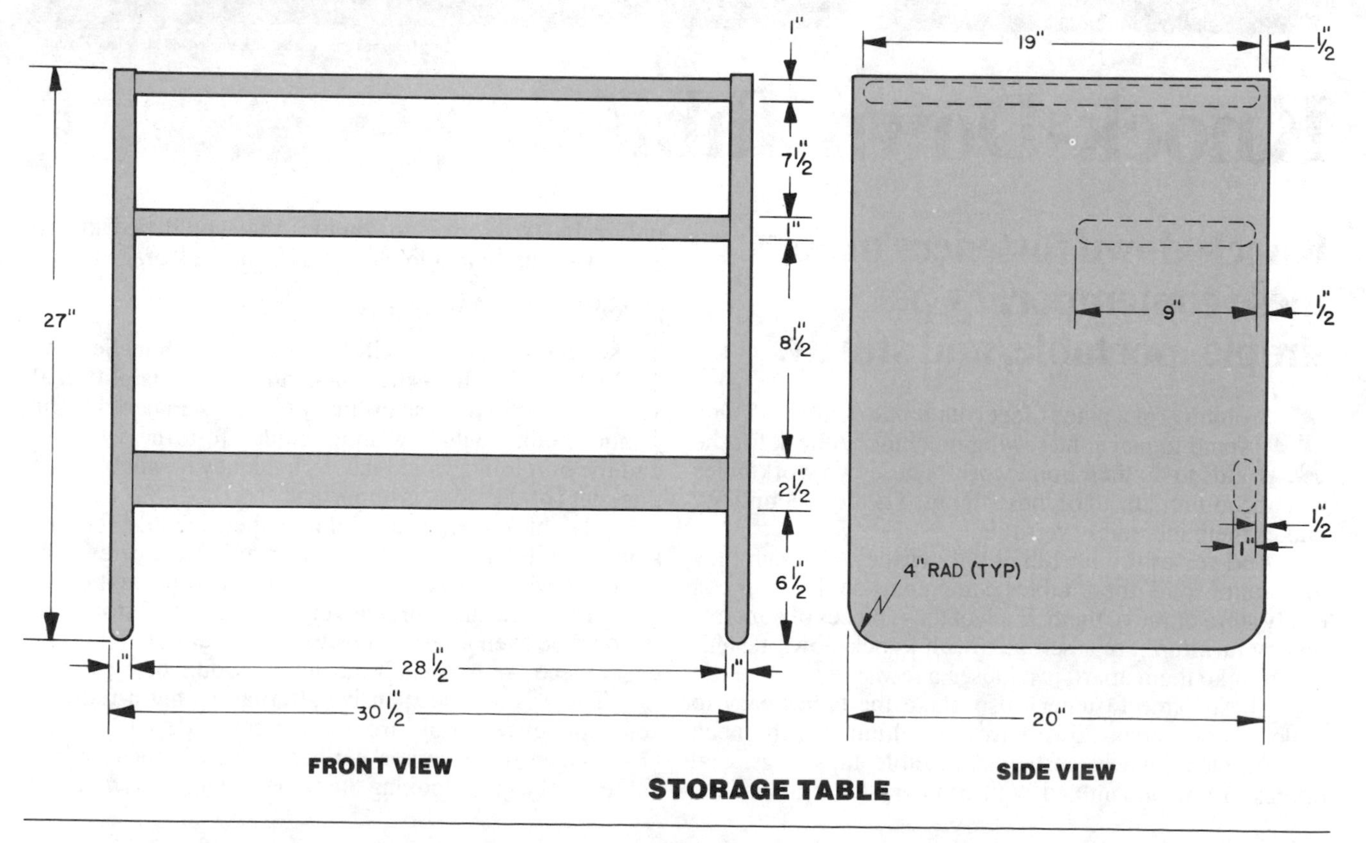

Pull the nails out and disassemble the table. The nail holes will mark where you want to make the counterbores and install the fasteners. Drill ¾″-diameter, ½″-deep counterbores and 5/16″-diameter shaft holes in the faces of the parts, and 7/16″-diameter, ¾″-deep stopped holes in the edges.

Install threaded inserts in the 7/16″-diameter holes, using a screwdriver. (See Figure 2.) Then reassemble the parts, using 5/16″ bolts and flat washers. Put a washer on each bolt, then insert the bolt through a counterbore and into a threaded insert. Tighten the bolt so that the head is snug in the counterbore. Then cover the head with a ¾″ screw button. (These large buttons are available through most mail-order woodworking suppliers.)

When you're satisfied that all the parts fit together properly, disassemble the table. Finish sand all parts and apply a finish. Then reassemble the table with the bolts. Glue the screw buttons in place with rubber cement or spray adhesive. This will let you easily remove the button, should you ever want to take the table apart.

Making and Installing the Drawer

There is one feature on one of the tables that is not assembled in this manner — the drawer on the storage table. This drawer requires a few simple joints. All of these can be cut with a router and straight bit:

- ¾″-wide x ½″-deep dadoes in the sides for the drawer glides — cut a matching notch in the ends of the drawer back
- ¾″-wide x ⅜″-deep rabbets in the drawer front and back to attach the sides
- ¼″-wide, ¼″-deep grooves in the drawer front, back, and sides to hold the bottom

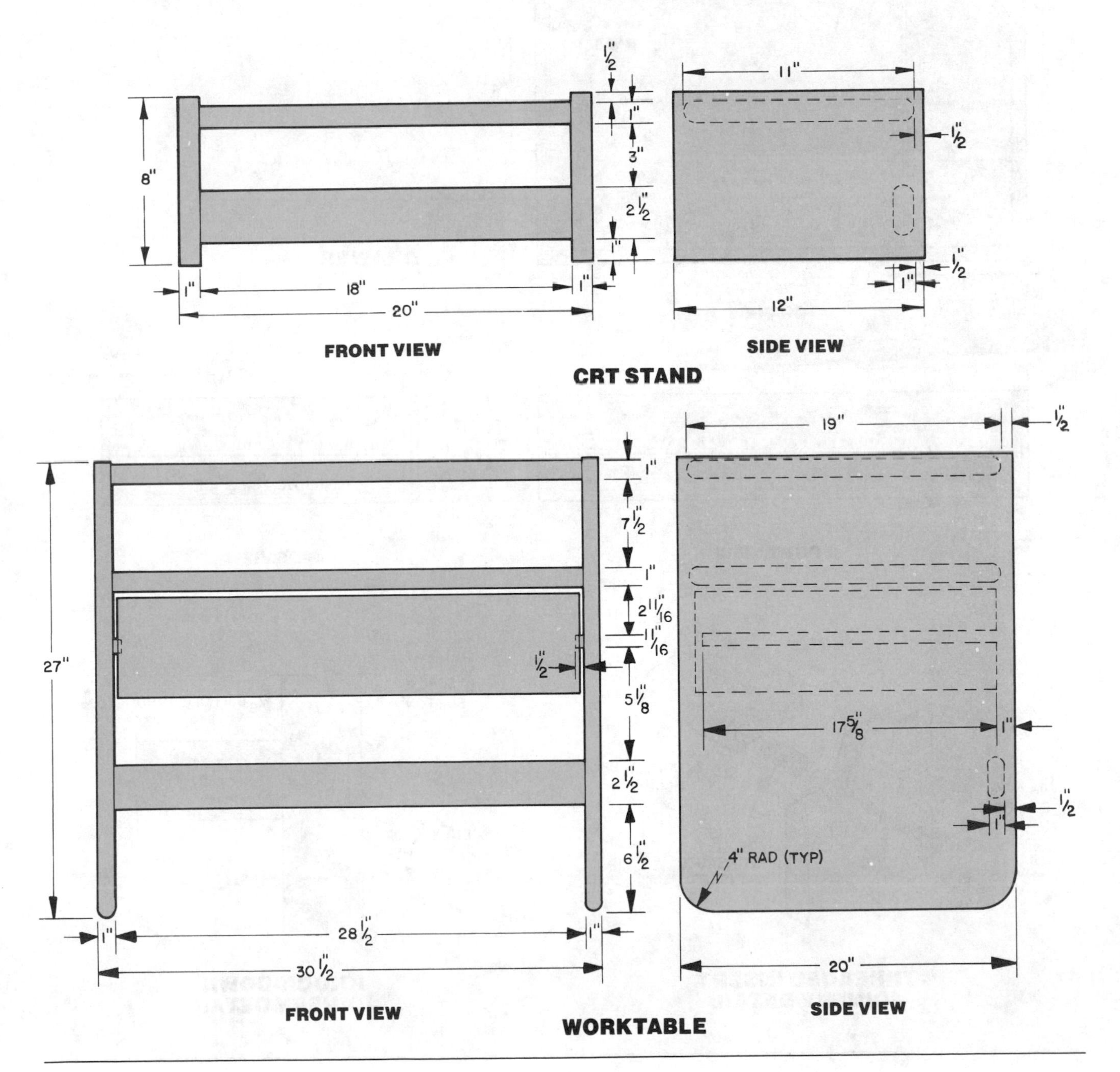

■ ¼″-wide, ¼″-deep dadoes in the front and back to hold the divider

Refer to the *Drawer/Top View, Side View,* and *Front View* for the positions of these joints.

Dry assemble the drawer to check the fit of the parts. When you're satisfied, disassemble the drawer and finish sand all the parts. Reassemble them with glue and 4d finishing nails. Use the nails to reinforce the rabbet joints that hold the sides to the front and back. *Do not* glue the drawer bottom or the divider in place. Let them float in their respective grooves or dadoes.

Attach drawer glides to the legs of the table, as shown in the *Storage Table/Front View* and *Side View.* Use flathead screws — no glue — to hold the glides in place. Drill the screw holes in the glides slightly larger than the shaft. This will allow the legs to expand and contract without buckling or breaking the slender glides.

Sand and finish the drawer when you finish the table. Then slide the drawer into position on the glides. The drawer front will serve as a stop. So that the drawer slides as easily as possible, coat the glides with paraffin wax. (Just rub the block of wax over the faces of the glides.)

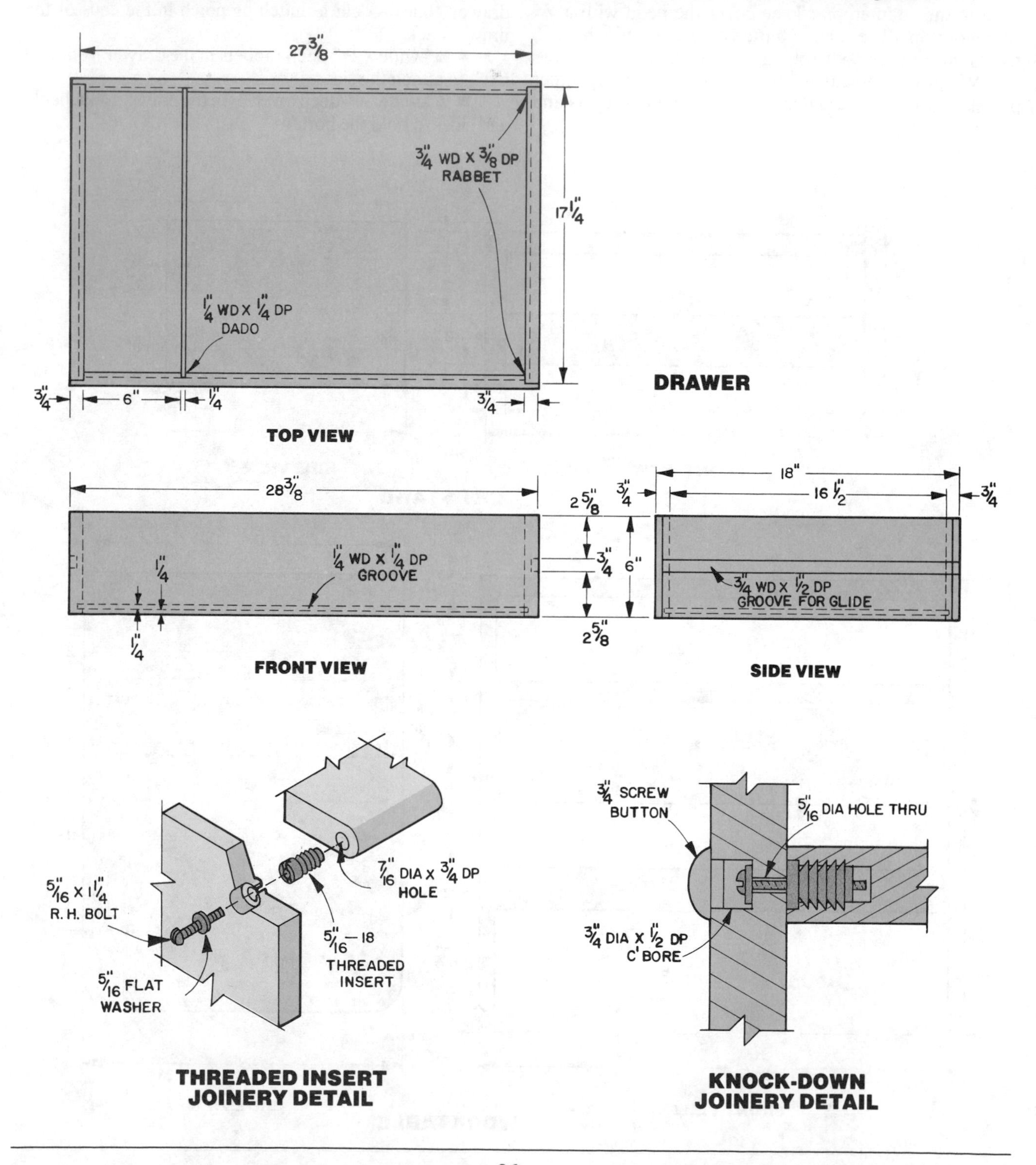

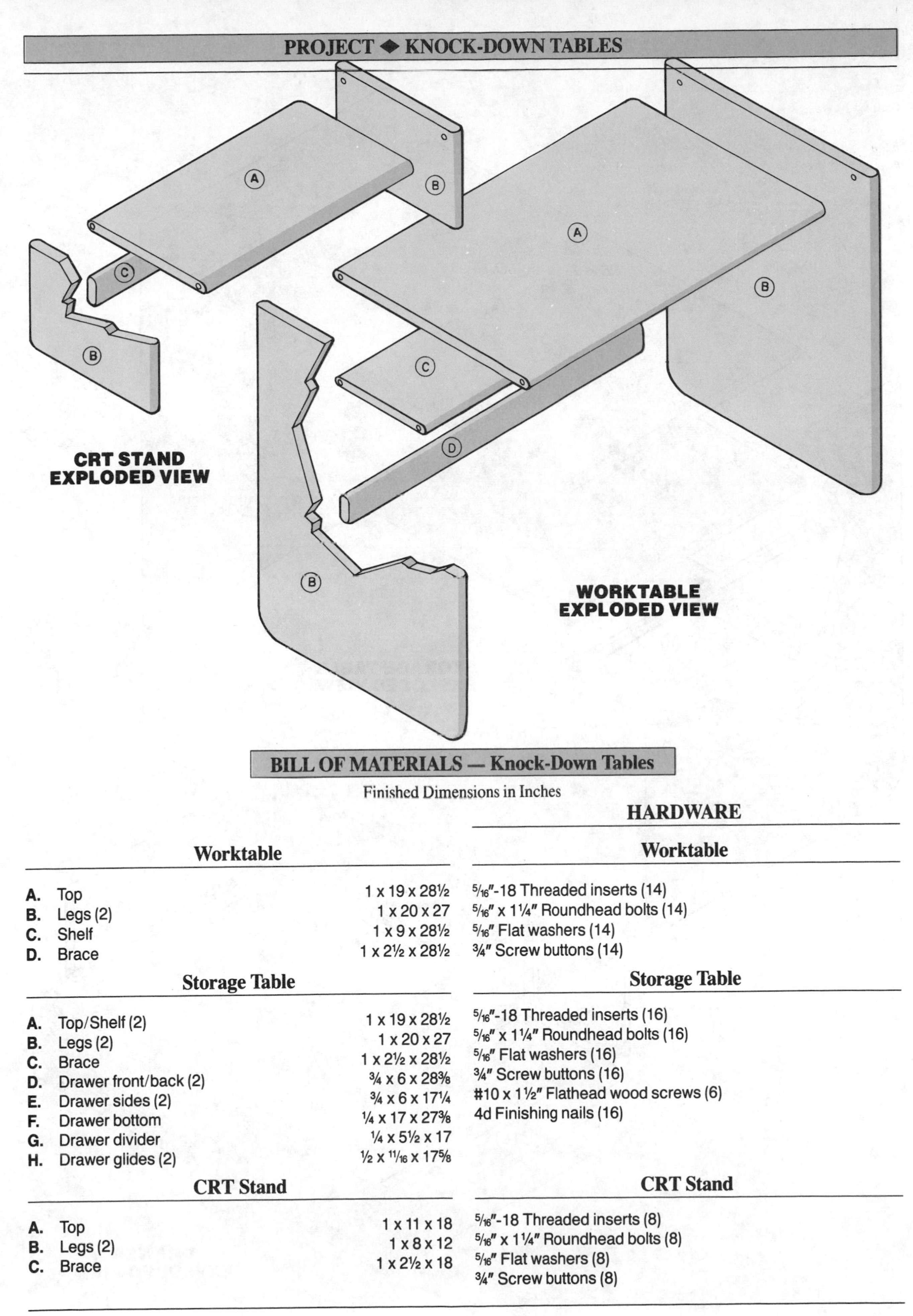

BILL OF MATERIALS — Knock-Down Tables

Finished Dimensions in Inches

Worktable

	Part	Dimensions
A.	Top	1 x 19 x 28½
B.	Legs (2)	1 x 20 x 27
C.	Shelf	1 x 9 x 28½
D.	Brace	1 x 2½ x 28½

Storage Table

	Part	Dimensions
A.	Top/Shelf (2)	1 x 19 x 28½
B.	Legs (2)	1 x 20 x 27
C.	Brace	1 x 2½ x 28½
D.	Drawer front/back (2)	¾ x 6 x 28⅜
E.	Drawer sides (2)	¾ x 6 x 17¼
F.	Drawer bottom	¼ x 17 x 27⅜
G.	Drawer divider	¼ x 5½ x 17
H.	Drawer glides (2)	½ x 11/16 x 17⅝

CRT Stand

	Part	Dimensions
A.	Top	1 x 11 x 18
B.	Legs (2)	1 x 8 x 12
C.	Brace	1 x 2½ x 18

HARDWARE

Worktable

5/16″-18 Threaded inserts (14)
5/16″ x 1¼″ Roundhead bolts (14)
5/16″ Flat washers (14)
¾″ Screw buttons (14)

Storage Table

5/16″-18 Threaded inserts (16)
5/16″ x 1¼″ Roundhead bolts (16)
5/16″ Flat washers (16)
¾″ Screw buttons (16)
#10 x 1½″ Flathead wood screws (6)
4d Finishing nails (16)

CRT Stand

5/16″-18 Threaded inserts (8)
5/16″ x 1¼″ Roundhead bolts (8)
5/16″ Flat washers (8)
¾″ Screw buttons (8)

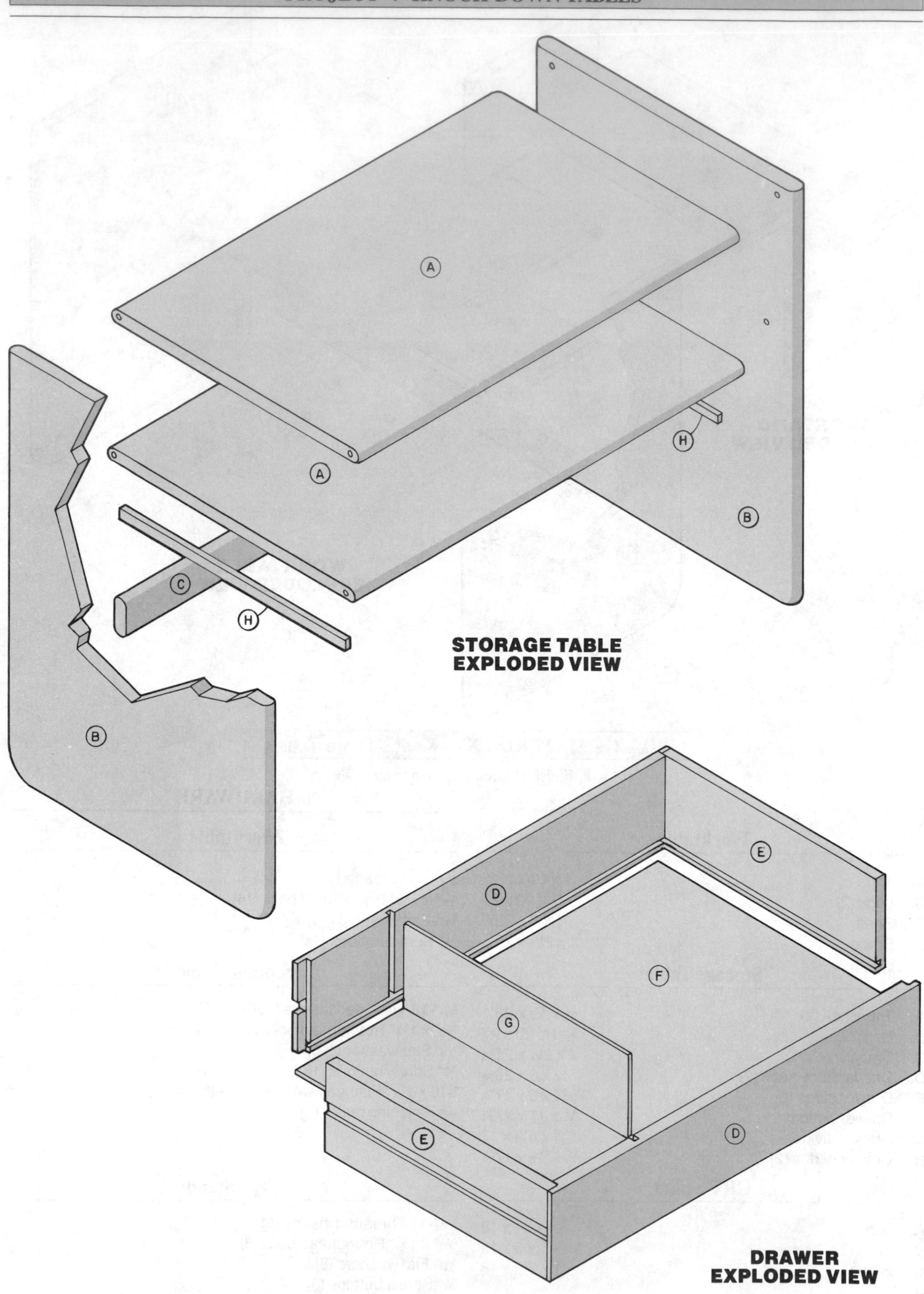
A
A
H
B
C
H
B
STORAGE TABLE
EXPLODED VIEW
E
D
F
G
E
D
DRAWER
EXPLODED VIEW

Designed and built by Nick Engler.

Computer Diskette File

An old, old design finds new uses.

Although it has a long, fancy name, this computer diskette file is really just a wooden box. It's built like a small version of a classic six-board chest: The sides and ends are dovetailed together, while the top and bottom rest in grooves. There is one distinctive, non-traditional feature, however. The way in which the lid is cut from the box makes it easy to reach frequently-used diskettes, and reduces the amount of desk space that the box occupies when open.

The choice of materials makes this box decorative as well as functional. To emphasize the dovetails, the sides and the ends are made from contrasting woods. We've built this project from cherry and curly maple, but you could also use cherry and walnut, maple and walnut, cherry and birch, mahogany and poplar, oak and ash, and many other similar combinations. The parts of the box are small enough that you can use up scraps of many different woods leftover from previous projects.

Selecting the Wood

You'll need three different thicknesses of wood to make this box — ½″ for the sides, ends, and top, ¼″ for the bottom, and ⅛″ for the dividers. Since all of these pieces are fairly small, you can use up some of those odd scraps that have been sitting around your shop since the last Ice Age. We managed to use a beautiful cherry burl that we had been saving.

You can also use several different species of wood. The different colors and textures emphasize the joinery. We used three different woods in the box shown here — curly maple for the ends, cherry for the sides, and walnut for the top, bottom, and dividers. When you decide on the stock you want to use, plane it to the proper thickness and cut it to the sizes shown in the Bill of Materials.

Cutting the Blind Grooves

The bottom and the top are held in place by "blind" grooves in the sides and ends. These grooves are double-blind — stopped just short of the ends of the boards — so

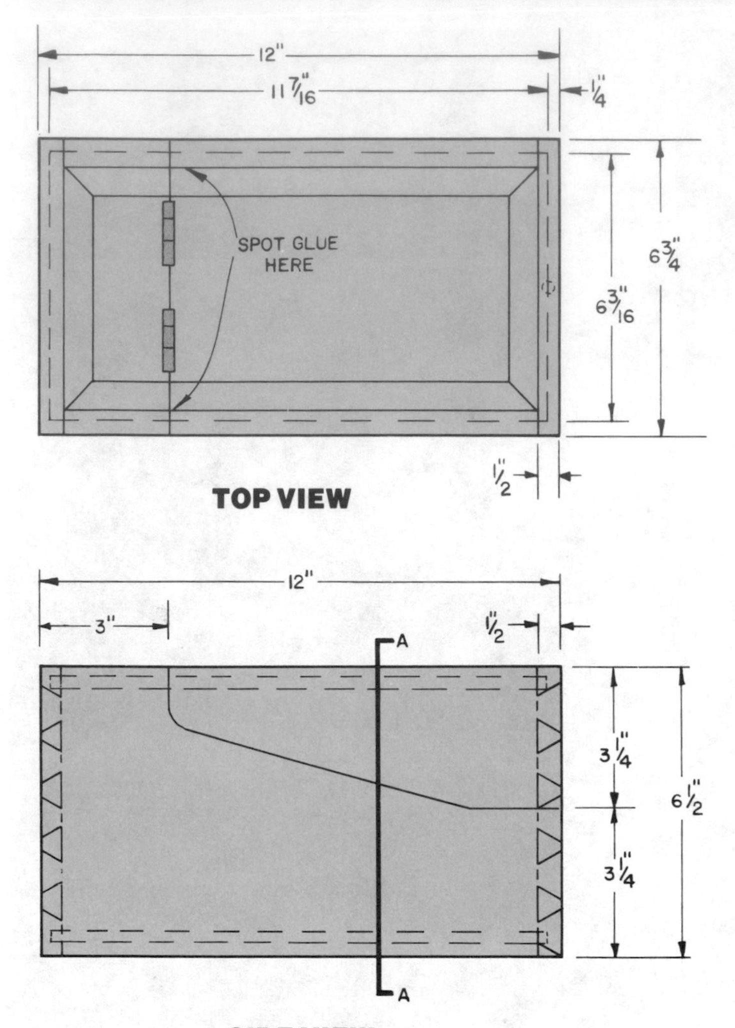

TOP VIEW

SIDE VIEW

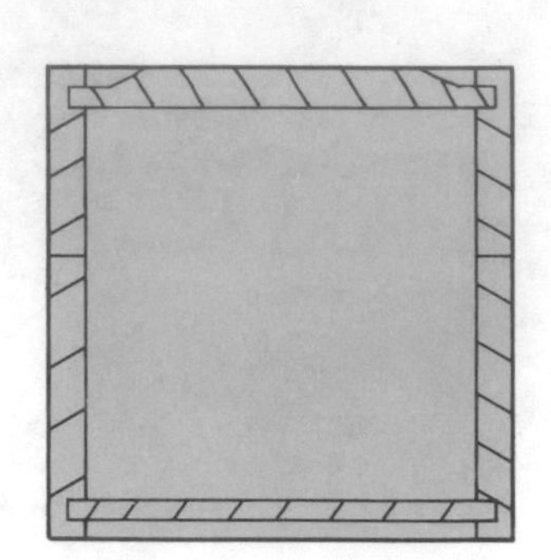

SECTION A

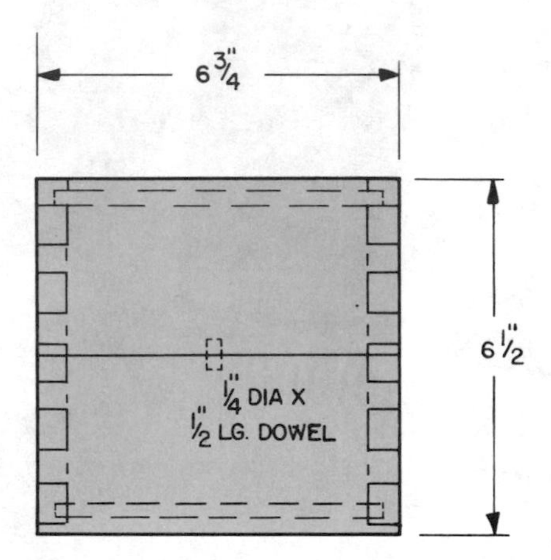

FRONT VIEW

that you won't see them when the box is assembled. Make these grooves *before* you cut the dovetails that hold the sides and ends together.

The best tool for making a blind groove is an overarm router. Mount a straight bit in the router and clamp a straightedge to the worktable to guide the stock. Clamp two stops to the straightedge to stop the bit from cutting 1/4" before it exits the stock. (See Figure 1.)

If you don't have an overarm router, you can also use a drill press, provided you take certain precautions. An ordinary drill press chuck won't support the shank of a router bit against lateral (sideways) thrust, and the bit may bend or break. To prevent this, make a collet from a 1/4" I.D. bushing. (See Figure 2.) Cut a slot down one side of the bushing. Mount the router bit in the collet, and clamp the collet in the drill chuck.

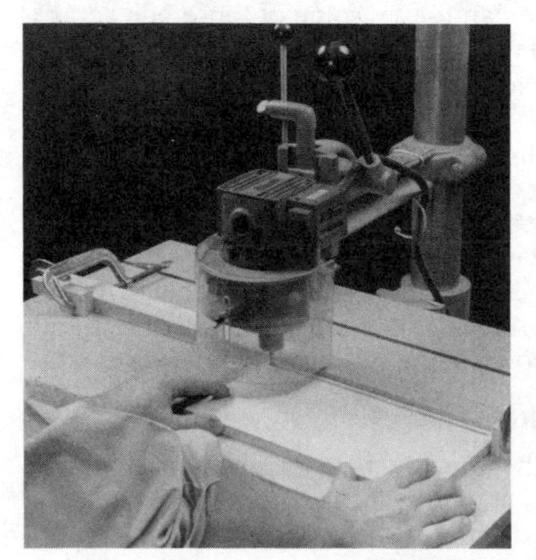

Figure 1. If you have one, use an overarm router to make the double-blind grooves. Two stops keep you from cutting through to the ends of the boards.

Figure 2. You can rout on your drill press if you make a special collet to hold the bits. To make this collet, cut a slot down the length of a 1/4" I.D. bushing.

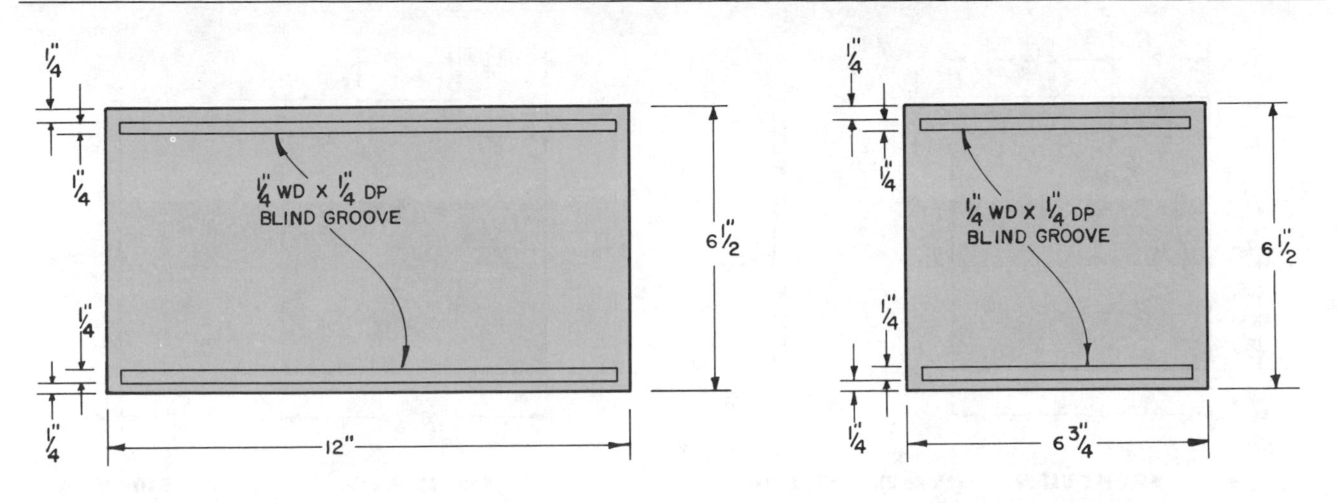

SIDE LAYOUT
(BEFORE CUTTING DOVETAILS)

FRONT LAYOUT
(BEFORE CUTTING DOVETAILS)

Adjust your drill press to run at its highest speed. Use a straightedge and stops to guide and control the cuts, just as you would if you had an overarm router. (See Figure 3.) Make each groove in several passes. Take small bites, routing just 1/16" deeper with each pass. Upon finishing the grooves, square the blind ends with a bench chisel.

Making the Dovetails

Through dovetails — dovetails that show on both the sides and the ends of a box — are typically made by hand. If you wish to make these by hand, there are many, many different methods published in woodworking books and magazines. The dovetails shown here, however, were made by machine. Two separate companies have recently developed router jigs that will make through dovetails. These are available from most mail-order woodworking catalogs, or you can write:

Leigh Industries P.O. Box 357 Port Coquitlam, B.C. Canada V3C 4K6	Keller & Co. 1327 I St. Petaluma, CA 94952

Both jigs work in a similar manner. A guide bushing, which screws into the base plate of the router, rides against the jig, controlling the cut. The tails are cut using a dovetail router bit, and the pins using a straight bit. (See Figure 4.)

Rout the tails first. Use a scrap block to back up the workpiece and to help keep the wood from chipping or tearing. (See Figure 5.) Make the pins last so that you can fit them to the tails. To make the pins larger or smaller,

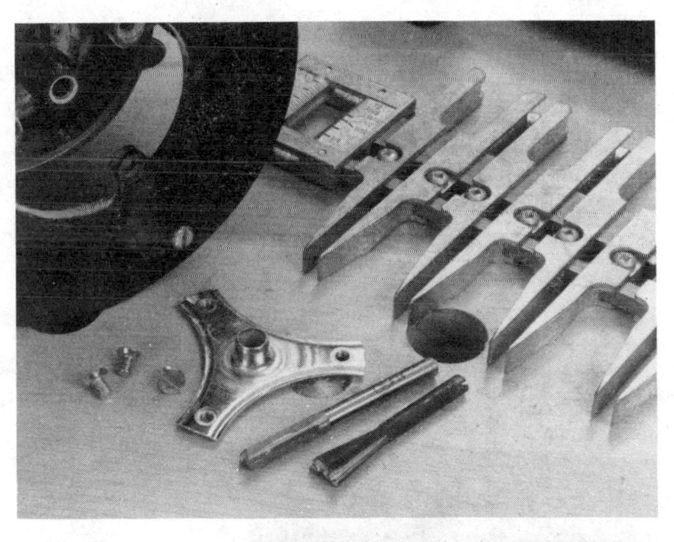

Figure 4. There are several special routing jigs that will help you cut through dovetails. In addition to the jig and a router, you also need a guide bushing, a dovetail bit, and a straight bit.

Figure 3. Rout with the speed of your drill press adjusted as high as it will go. Use stops to keep from making the grooves too long.

Figure 5. Cut the tails with the dovetail bit. The guide bushing guides the router over the jig.

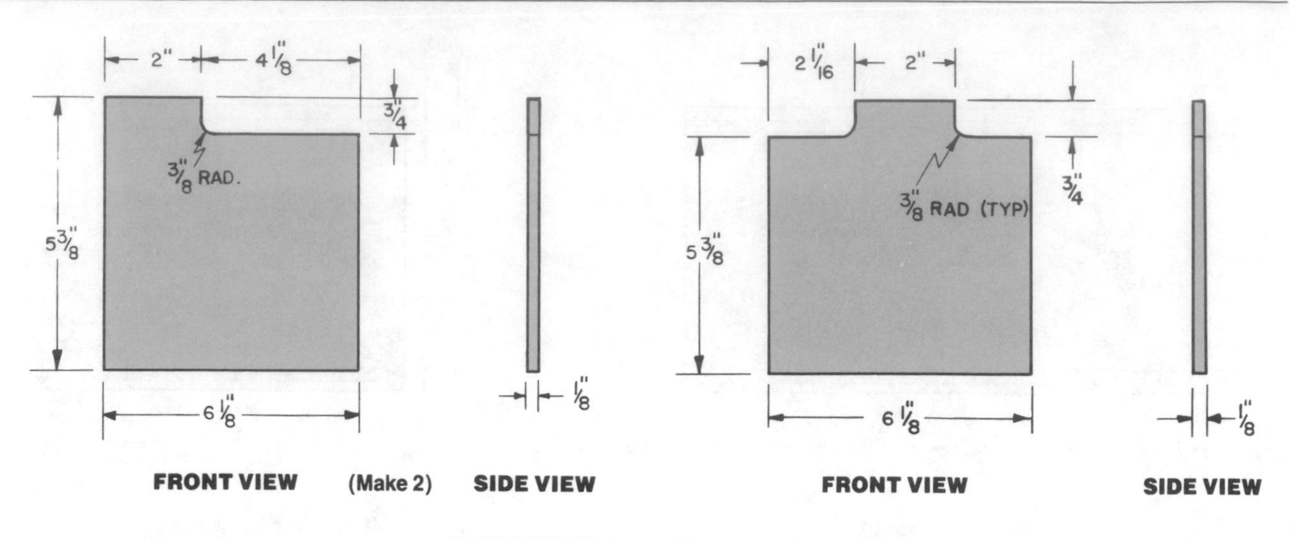

DISKETTE DIVIDER LAYOUTS

move the fingers of the jig in or out, perpendicular to the face of the board. (See Figure 6.) Dry assemble the completed pins and tails to check the fit of the joint. If the router and the jig are both properly aligned, you shouldn't have to do any handwork to adjust the fit. (See Figure 7.)

Making the Raised Panel

The top of the box is a raised panel. You can make this panel using an overarm router or the router setup that you made for your drill press.

First, use a straight bit to cut a ½"-wide, ¼"-deep rabbet in the top stock, all around the edge. Switch to a core box bit and cut a cove in the shoulder of the rabbet. Sand away any millmarks, but be careful not to sand the thinned edge much thinner than ¼". If it gets too thin, the top won't fit properly in the grooves.

Cut the raised panel in two sections, where shown in the *Top View*. Use your bandsaw to make this cut, so that the kerf is no more than 1/16" wide. Mortise each section for hinges, using a router or a dado cutter. Finish sand the two sections, but don't install the hinges. Instead, tape the sections together, spacing the sections approximately 1/32"-1/16" apart — the same distance that the hinges would space the sections apart if they *were* installed.

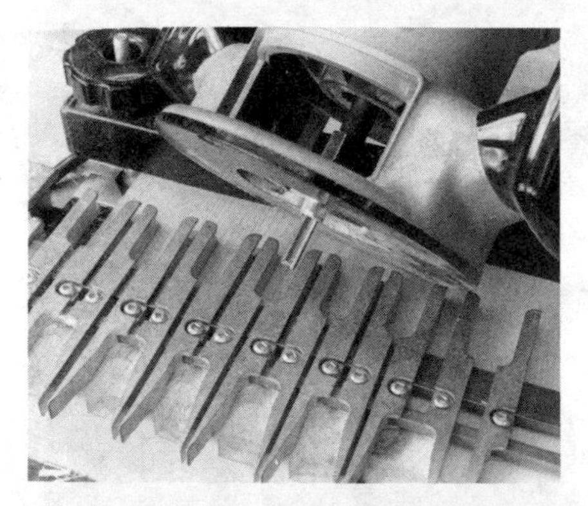

Figure 6. Cut the pins with the straight bit and the other portion of the jig.

Figure 7. Fit the pins to the tails. If the pins do not fit properly, move the jig in or out across the stock.

Assembling the Box and Cutting the Lid

Finish sand the other parts of the box — sides, ends, and bottom. Dry assemble all the parts to check the fit. If you're satisfied that everything fits properly, reassemble the box with glue. Glue the tails and the pins together, but let the bottom and *most* of the top float in their grooves without gluing them in place. Just "spot" glue the edges of the top in the vicinity of the hinges (½" on either side of the cut), where shown in the *Top View*. When the glue cures, sand all the pins flush with the surface of the sides, if necessary.

Mark the cutlines for the lids on the sides and the end of the box. Using a sabre saw, cut along these lines, separating the lid from the box. (See Figure 8.) Use a fine blade with as many teeth per inch as you can find. This will leave a smooth cut and a small kerf. Sand the sawn edges to remove the saw marks.

Figure 8. Cut the lid free from the box with a sabre saw. Use a fine blade for a smooth cut.

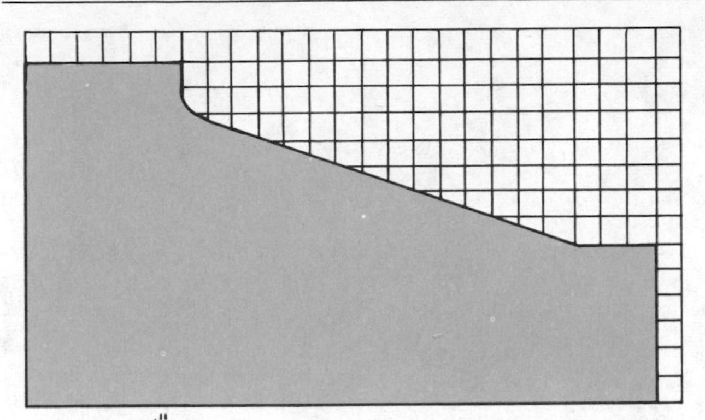

FLIP TOP PATTERN

Remove any tape and install the hinges, making sure that the lid closes properly. All the sides and ends should remain flush. To make sure that they stay flush, install an alignment pin between the two sections of the ends. Drill a 1/4"-diameter, 1/4"-deep stopped hole in the lower section, centered in the top edge. Using a dowel center, mark the position of a corresponding hole in the top section. Drill this hole 3/8" deep. Glue a 1/4"-diameter, 1/2"-long dowel in the upper hole, so that just 1/8" of the dowel protrudes. When you close the lid, this little stub of a pin will fit in the lower hole and keep the lid aligned with the rest of the box.

Do any necessary touch-up sanding to the box. If you wish, cut several wooden dividers from the 1/8"-thick stock. Finish sand these dividers, then apply a finish to the box and the dividers. After the finish dries, glue 3/8"-diameter felt pads to the lower section of the end, between the lid and the box. This will keep the lid from banging when it's shut.

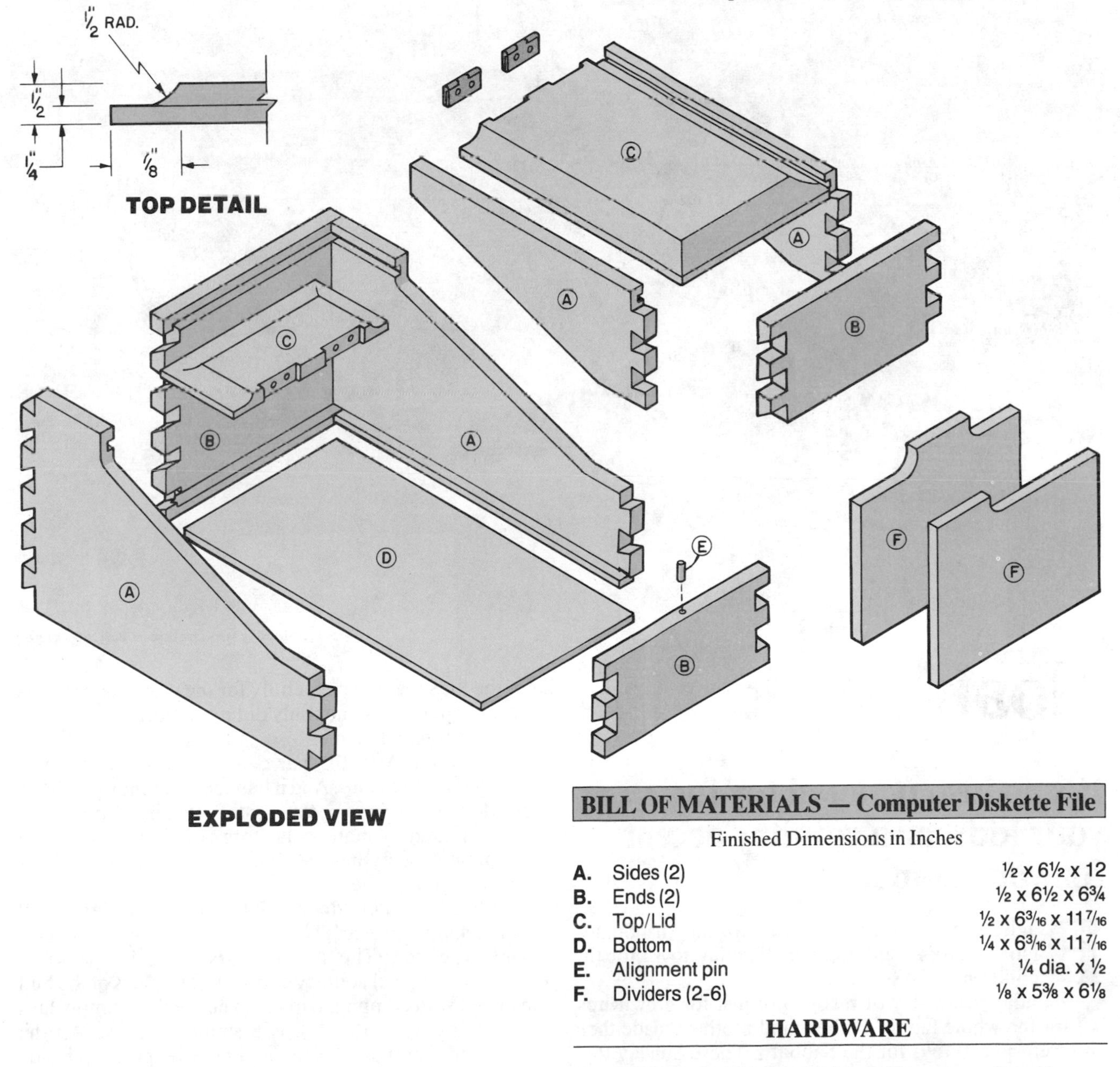

EXPLODED VIEW

BILL OF MATERIALS — Computer Diskette File

Finished Dimensions in Inches

A.	Sides (2)	1/2 x 6 1/2 x 12
B.	Ends (2)	1/2 x 6 1/2 x 6 3/4
C.	Top/Lid	1/2 x 6 3/16 x 11 7/16
D.	Bottom	1/4 x 6 3/16 x 11 7/16
E.	Alignment pin	1/4 dia. x 1/2
F.	Dividers (2-6)	1/8 x 5 5/8 x 6 1/8

HARDWARE

1" x 1 1/2" Brass butt hinges and mounting screws (1 pair)

Designed by Mary Jane Favorite. Built by Nick Engler.

Noah's Ark

It's an instructional toy for your kids, or a country accent for your home.

Back when this country was young, handmade Noah's Arks were popular "Sunday toys" for the children of the settlers.

Sunday was a day of rest — not just for grown-ups, but for the whole family. Fathers and mothers made their children special toys for the Sabbath. These Sunday toys were playthings that did not inspire boisterous activity, and kept the kids playing peacefully for the day. The Ark was especially popular — not only did it promote quiet play; it also had a Biblical theme.

Today, the Ark still makes a wonderful toy for precisely the same reasons. And it has acquired another use, as well. Homespun Sunday toys — the Ark, in particular — are now prized by many collectors of folk art. Displayed on a mantle of a shelf, a Noah's Ark adds a touch of country to your home.

Whether you build the Ark for play or display, you'll find it a simple project. The animals are simple cut-outs, slightly rounded. The Ark itself is made in the same manner as a typical country carry-all. The parts of the hull are joined with compound miters, and the deck simply lays in place. Actually, the Ark is a small toy chest. All the animals, the ramp, and Noah and his wife pack up inside the hull and the cabin of the boat.

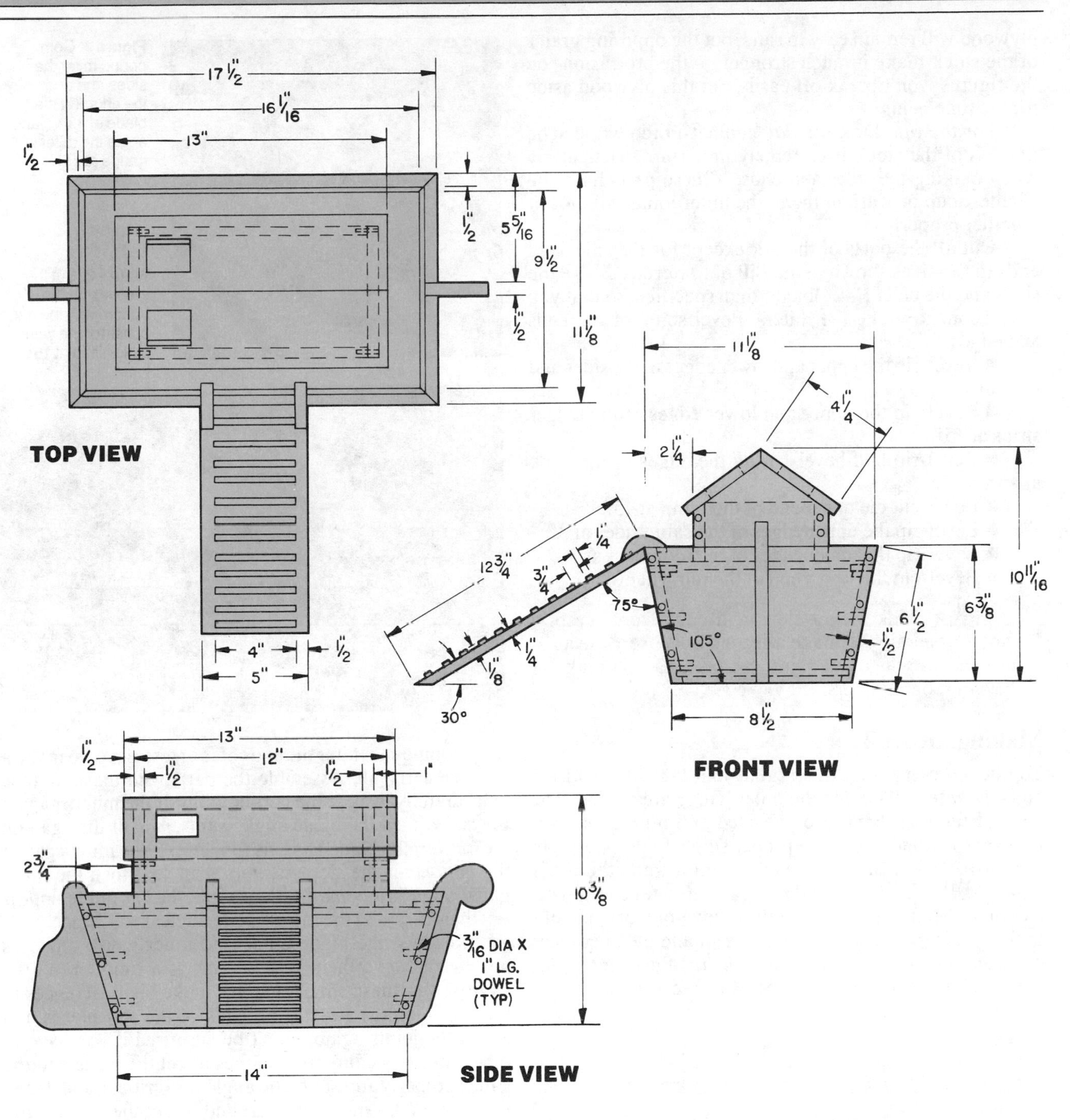

Selecting and Preparing the Stock

A Noah's Ark is actually a two-part project. The first part is to make all the animal cut-outs, and the second is to build a boat to put them in. Keep this in mind when selecting the wood you'll use to make the ark and all the animals. The design of each part puts different demands on the materials. For this reason, you may elect to make each part out of a different species of wood.

The *animal figures* are fairly intricate, and there will be a lot of surfaces to sand once you cut them out. Because of this, you'll need a wood that's easy to sand. On the other hand, you need a strong wood. The legs, trunks, tails, and other appendages are fairly delicate. If you make them from a wood that's too soft, they will break easily.

The best compromise seems to be to choose a clear, close-grained wood of a medium density. Poplar and soft maple are the best suited, but you could also use mahogany or white pine. From this stock, make your own "plywood." Plane the wood for the figures to 1/4" thick and cut it into squares. Glue up the squares, face to face, to make the 1/2"-and 3/4"-thick stock (two layers and three layers) that you need. No matter what the thickness, the grain of one square *must* be perpendicular to the grain of the other. This plywood will remain easy to sand, but the opposing grains of the stock make it much stronger — the protrusions on the figures won't break off easily. Set this plywood aside for the time being.

For the *ark,* look for *flat,* cabinet-grade wood. The flatness of the stock is extremely important, particularly when making the sides and ends. If these parts have the slightest cup or warp in them, the miter joints will not fit together properly.

Cut all the parts of the ark except for the sides and ends to the sizes shown in the Bill of Materials. Make the sides and the ends 1″–2″ longer than specified, so that you have room to make the miters. Bevel some of the ends and edges:

- Bevel-rip the upper and lower edges of the sides and ends at 15°.
- Bevel-rip the upper and lower edges of the ledger strips at 15°.
- Bevel-rip and bevel-cut *all* the edges of the deck at 15°.
- Bevel-cut the upper end of the ramp at 15°.
- Bevel-rip the upper edges of the cabin sides at 30°.
- Bevel-rip the upper edges of the roof parts at 30°.
- Bevel-cut the lower end of the ramp at 60°.

Tip ◆ Make extra sides and ends from scrap wood — enough to make a second ark. Use these as test-pieces when you adjust the table saw to make the compound miters.

Figure 1. Compound miter the sides and ends of the arks. Tilt the blade at 43¼°, and angle the miter gauge at 75½°.

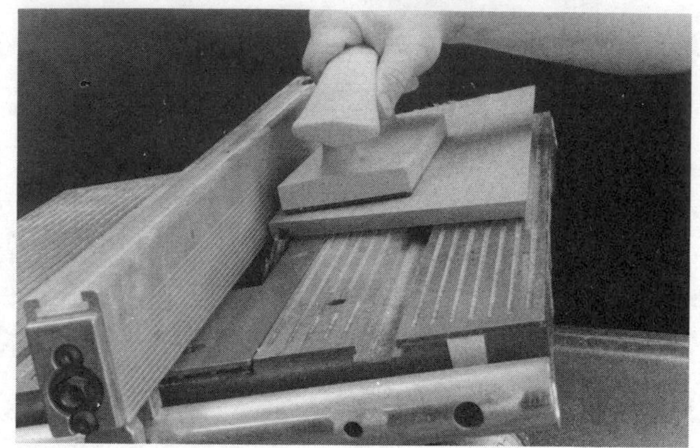

Figure 2. Cut the grooves for the bottom with the dado cutter (or the worktable) tilted at 15°.

Making the Hull

To cut the compound miters that join the sides and the ends, *both* the blade *and* the miter gauge are angled. The ends of the boards must be beveled and mitered so that they will fit together at the proper slope angle — 15°, in this case. Adjust the blade angle to 43¼°, and the miter gauge to 75½°. These are textbook angles, taken right off a compound-miter chart, and they may not work on your table saw. Depending on the alignment and the tolerances of your machine, you may have to readjust the angles slightly. But for the first test cuts, use these angles.

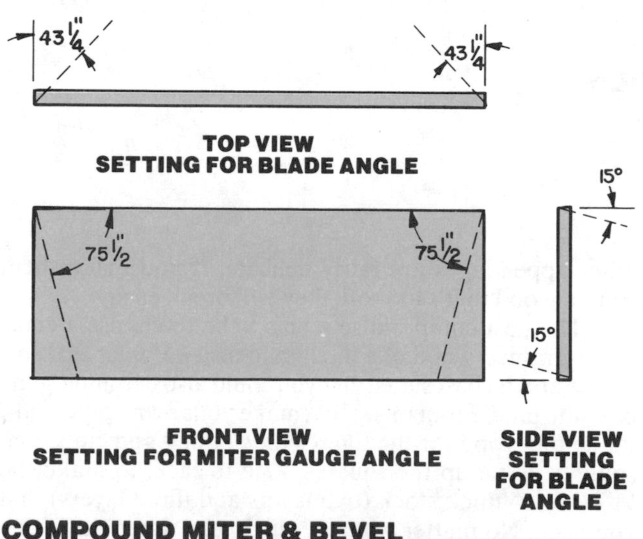

COMPOUND MITER & BEVEL CUTTING DETAILS FOR SIDES & ENDS

Compound miter the ends of four test pieces to make a practice carry-all. Assemble the parts with masking tape and carefully inspect the corner joints. If the miters gap on the *inside,* then the blade angle is too *small.* If they gap on the *outside,* the blade angle is too *large.* If the miters gap at the *bottom,* or the slope is *more* than 15°, then the miter gauge angle is too *small.* If they gap at the *top,* or the slope is *less* than 15°, then the miter gauge angle is too *large.*

Readjust the blade angle and miter gauge angle as necessary. Move them just ¼°–½° at a time. (You'll be surprised — these small changes make big differences in the miter joints.) Re-cut the ends of the test pieces and check the joints again. Don't be surprised if you have to repeat this procedure many times to get the blade and the gauge properly adjusted. The angles are critical, and it may take quite a bit of fiddling around to get them just right. When you're satisfied with the results of the cuts in the test pieces, compound-miter the good stock. (See Figure 1.)

Next, fit the bottom to the sides and ends. The bottom is held in the assembly by ¼″-wide, ¼″-deep grooves near the bottom edges of the sides and the ends. Cut these grooves at a 15° angle, using a dado cutter. (See Figure 2.)

Dry-assemble the sides, ends, and bottom to check the fit of the parts. Secure the miter joints temporarily with masking tape. When you're satisfied that the parts fit as they should, apply glue to the mitered ends and assemble these parts with the bottom in place. *Do not* apply any glue to the bottom. Let it float in the grooves, free to expand and contract with changes in the weather.

Tape the joints together with masking tape. This will hold them while you slip band clamps over the assembly.

Figure 3. Tape the compound miter joints together to hold them temporarily.

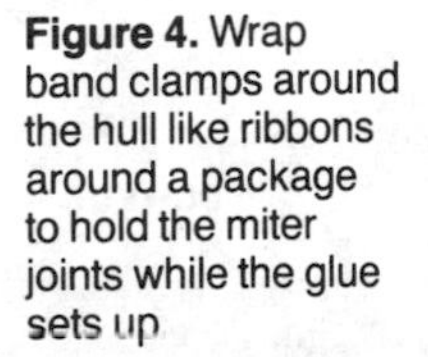

Figure 4. Wrap band clamps around the hull like ribbons around a package to hold the miter joints while the glue sets up.

Figure 5. Make a piercing cut with a scroll saw to cut out the skylights in the roof halves.

Use two or three band clamps — one perpendicular to the other two. Wrap them around the assembly like ribbons around a package. This will hold the miter joints securely until the glue dries. (See Figure 3.)

Reinforce the miter joints with 3/16"-diameter dowels. Drill three pairs of dowel holes in each corner. (See Figure 4.) Each pair of holes should be perpendicular to each other. They should not meet, however. One hole in the pair should be about 1/4"–3/8" above the other. Spread glue on the dowels, drive them into the holes, and cut them off flush with the surface of the wood.

Adding a Bow, Rudder, and Ledgers

Sand the surfaces of the hull, and remove any hardened glue. Enlarge the patterns for the bow and the rudder, and cut these from 1/2"-thick stock. Glue them to the ends of the hull, and reinforce the glue joints with flathead screws. Drive these screws through the hull and into the bow or rudder from the inside, so that the screw heads won't show on the outside.

Tip ◆ You will want to make the bow and the rudder from some of the 1/2"-thick plywood that you glued up for the animal figures. This will make these parts better able to stand up to the sort of punishment that kids can sometimes deal out.

Mark the positions of the ledger on the inside of the hull sides, then glue the ledgers in place. You don't have to attach ledgers to the ends; the side ledgers will be sufficient.

Making the Cabin

Cut the shape of the cabin ends as shown in the *Cabin and Deck Layout/Front View.* Also cut the shape of the roof braces. Using a scroll saw or a sabre saw, cut out the skylights in the roof parts. (See Figure 5.) These skylights are to accommodate the long necks of the giraffes.

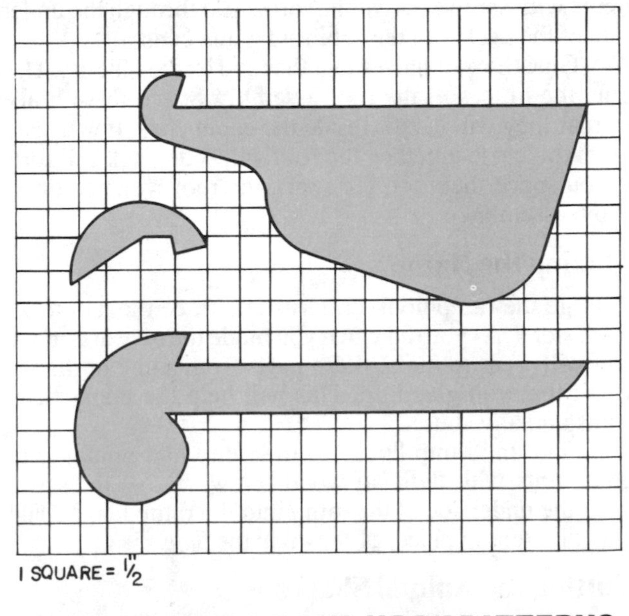

RUDDER, BOW & RAMP HOOK PATTERNS

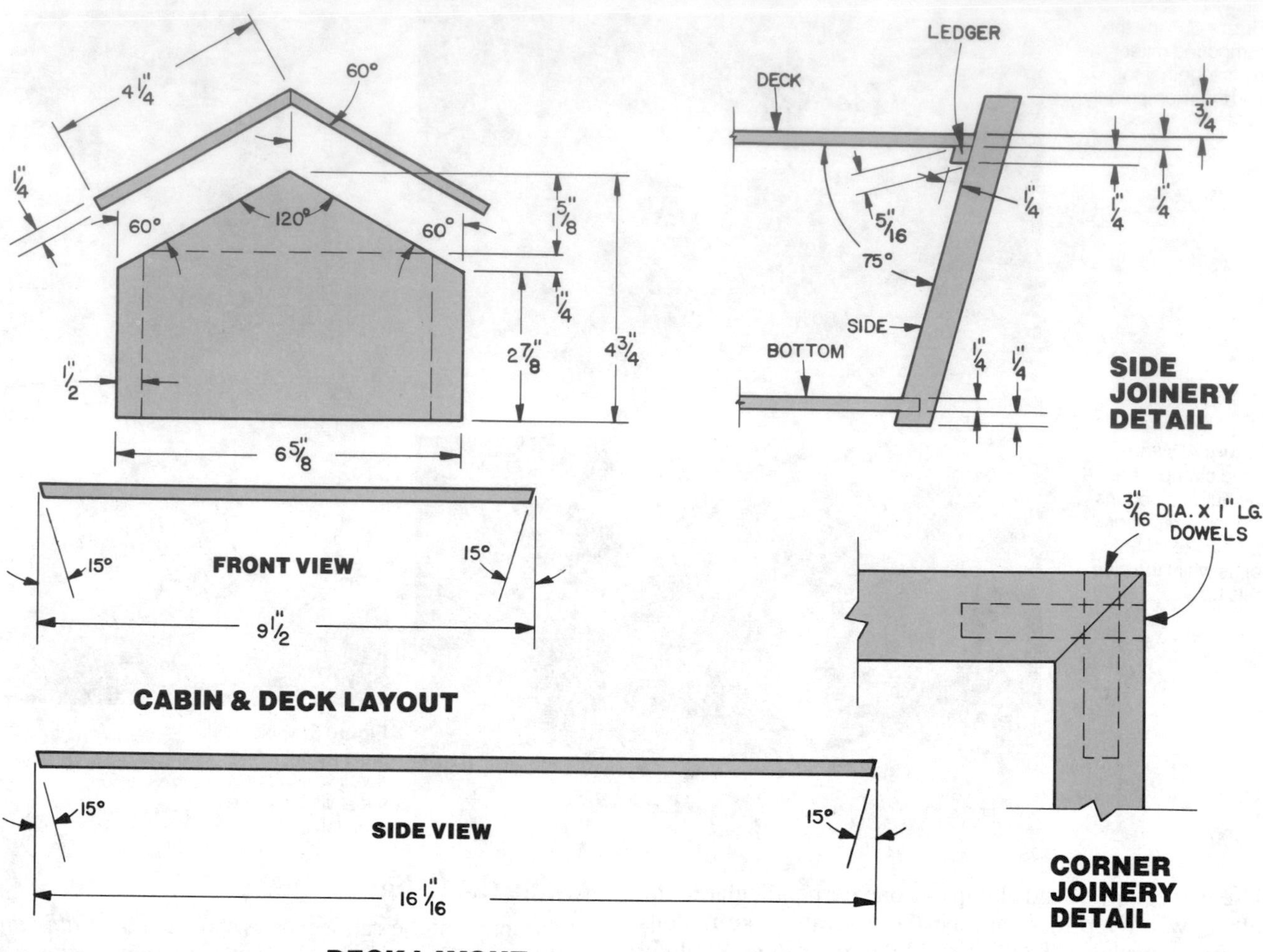

Glue the cabin ends to the cabin sides. Reinforce the glue joints with 3/16″ dowels. After the glue sets up, glue the cabin assembly to the deck. Reinforce the cabin-to-deck joints with screws. Drive the screws up through the underside of the deck into the cabin sides and ends.

Glue the roof halves together and let the glue dry. Then glue the braces to the roof assembly. Space these braces so that they will just fit inside the cabin ends. If you space them too close together, the roof will slide back and forth. If you space them too far apart, the roof won't fit on the cabin assembly.

Making the Ramp

Enlarge the ramp hook patterns and trace them onto ½″-thick stock. As you did when you made the bow and rudder, you will want to make these parts from some of the plywood that you glued up. This will help the hooks better withstand any abuse.

Glue the ramp hooks to the ramp and reinforce the glue joints with flathead wood screws. Drive the screws from the underside of the ramp into the ramp hooks. Then glue the steps in place, as shown in the *Side View.*

Cutting the Animal Shapes

Enlarge and/or make copies of the animal patterns. Most of the patterns printed here are full size — 100%. These don't have to be enlarged — just make copies of them. The other patterns are shown at 57%. To enlarge these, just take them to a quick-print shop that has a copier that can enlarge and reduce documents. Have the operator select the "letter-to-legal-size" enlargement setting. (On most copiers, this is about 121%.) Then enlarge the patterns *three* times. (See Figure 6.) This will give you a full-size pattern. Here's the math:

.57 x 1.21 x 1.21 x 1.21 1.01 (approximately).

Make *two* photocopies of each full-size pattern.

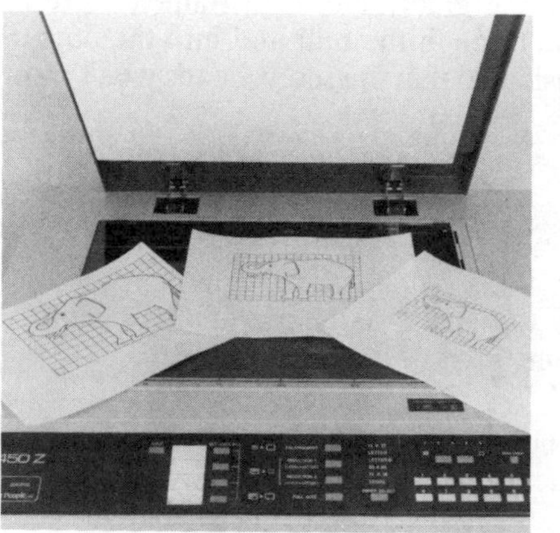

Figure 6. Using a photocopier, enlarge the 57%-size patterns three times at the "letter-to-legal" setting. This will blow up the drawings to full size.

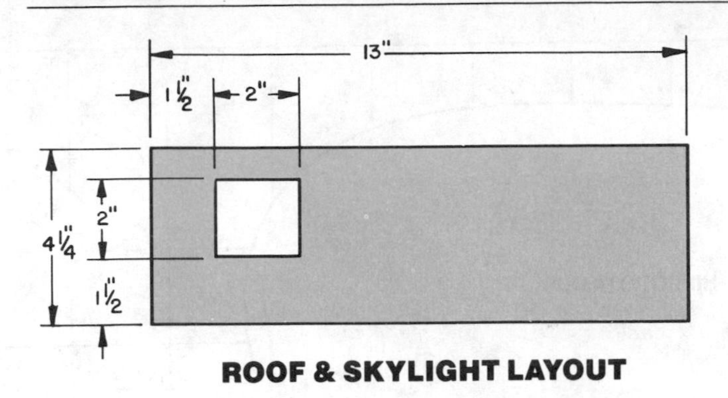

ROOF & SKYLIGHT LAYOUT

Stack up two pieces of plywood, one on top of the other. Hold the stack together with masking tape. Affix one of the copies to the top piece of plywood with rubber cement or spray adhesive. Using the photocopy as a guide, pad-saw the outside shape of the animal, cutting two identical animals at the same time. Use a scroll saw and a small blade with at least 20 teeth per inch. This will give you a smooth cut, and reduce the amount of sanding you have to do to remove the saw marks.

Peel the photocopy off the stock, and sand away the saw marks from the cut edges, using rasps, files, sandpaper, and power sanders. Round over the edges of the shapes slightly.

Painting the Ark and the Animals

Using the second photocopy of the animals, transfer the pattern lines onto the wooden shape. You can make this transfer by putting a piece of carbon paper under the photocopy, and tracing the pattern with a ballpoint pen.

Once you've transferred the pattern lines, color the animals. You may find it helpful to consult various picture books and books of wildlife photography to help you decide what color to use for what animal.

There are many, many types of paints and dyes that you can use to color the animals, and you probably have your own preferences. We experimented with two — artists oils and acrylics — and found these produced two different effects. We thinned the oils with linseed oil and applied them like a stain, so that you could see the wood grain underneath the color. We also tried thinning the acrylics (with water), but they became splotchy. In order for the colors to remain even, we had to apply the acrylics fairly thick. You couldn't see the wood grain under them. Whatever paints or dyes you decide to use, experiment with them on a piece of scrap *before* you start coloring the cut-outs.

Just as you may have chosen different materials to make the Ark and the animals, you may also choose different paints to color them. It will be tedious and time-consuming to color the broad, flat surfaces of the Ark with acrylics or oils. We suggest you use latex paints or old-fashioned milk paints.

Tip ◆ Acrylics and latex paints are much less toxic than most other commercial colors. This is important to consider if you are giving this toy to a young child who might put the pieces in his or her mouth.

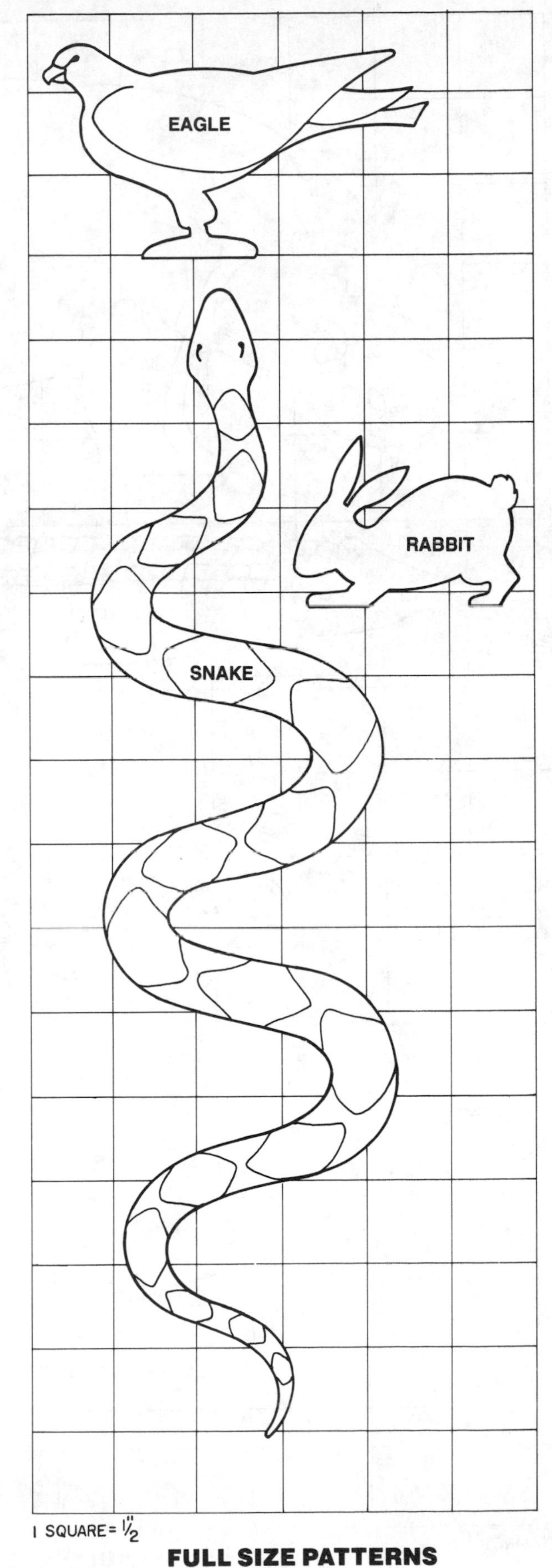

FULL SIZE PATTERNS

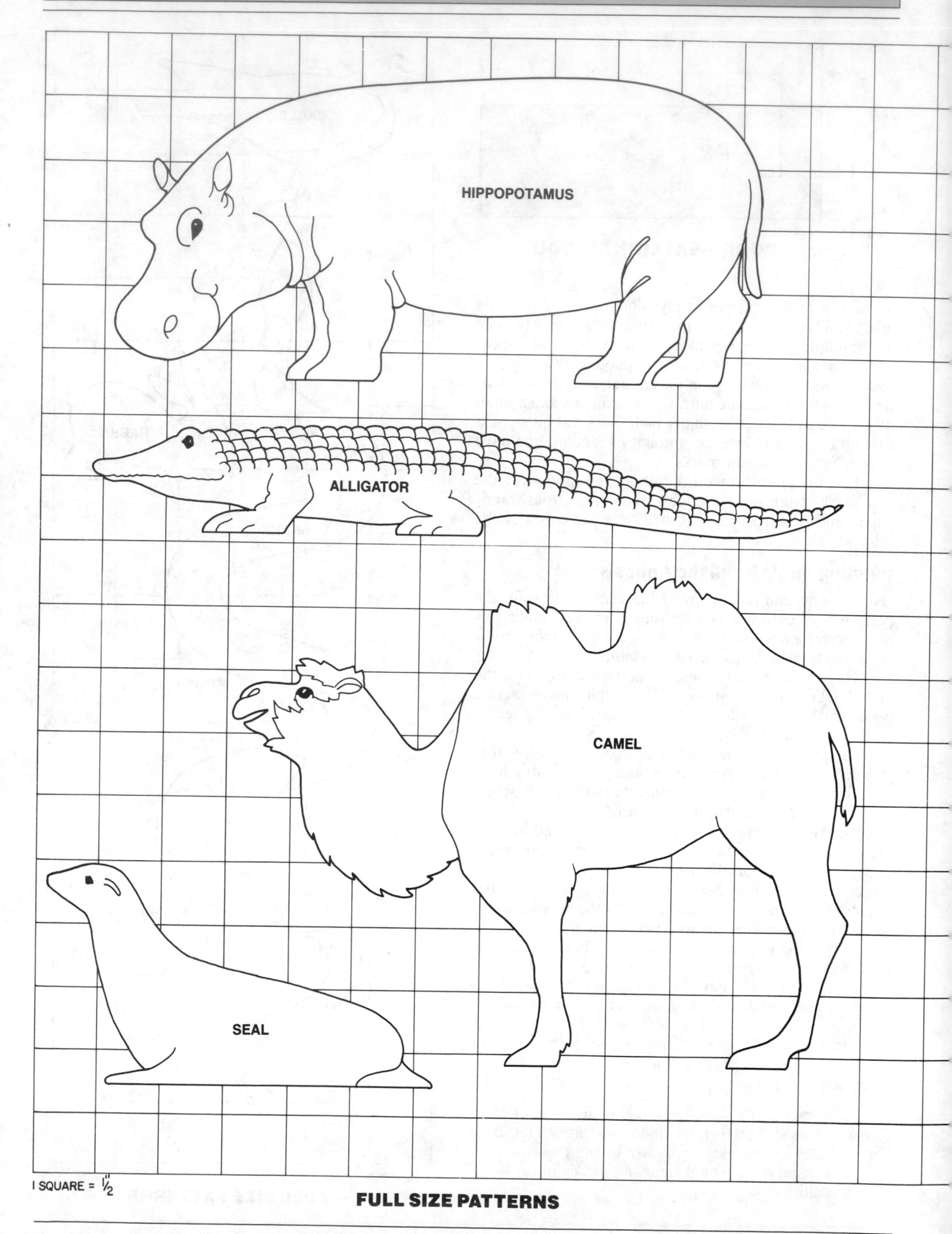

FULL SIZE PATTERNS

FULL SIZE PATTERNS

FULL SIZE PATTERNS

FULL SIZE PATTERNS

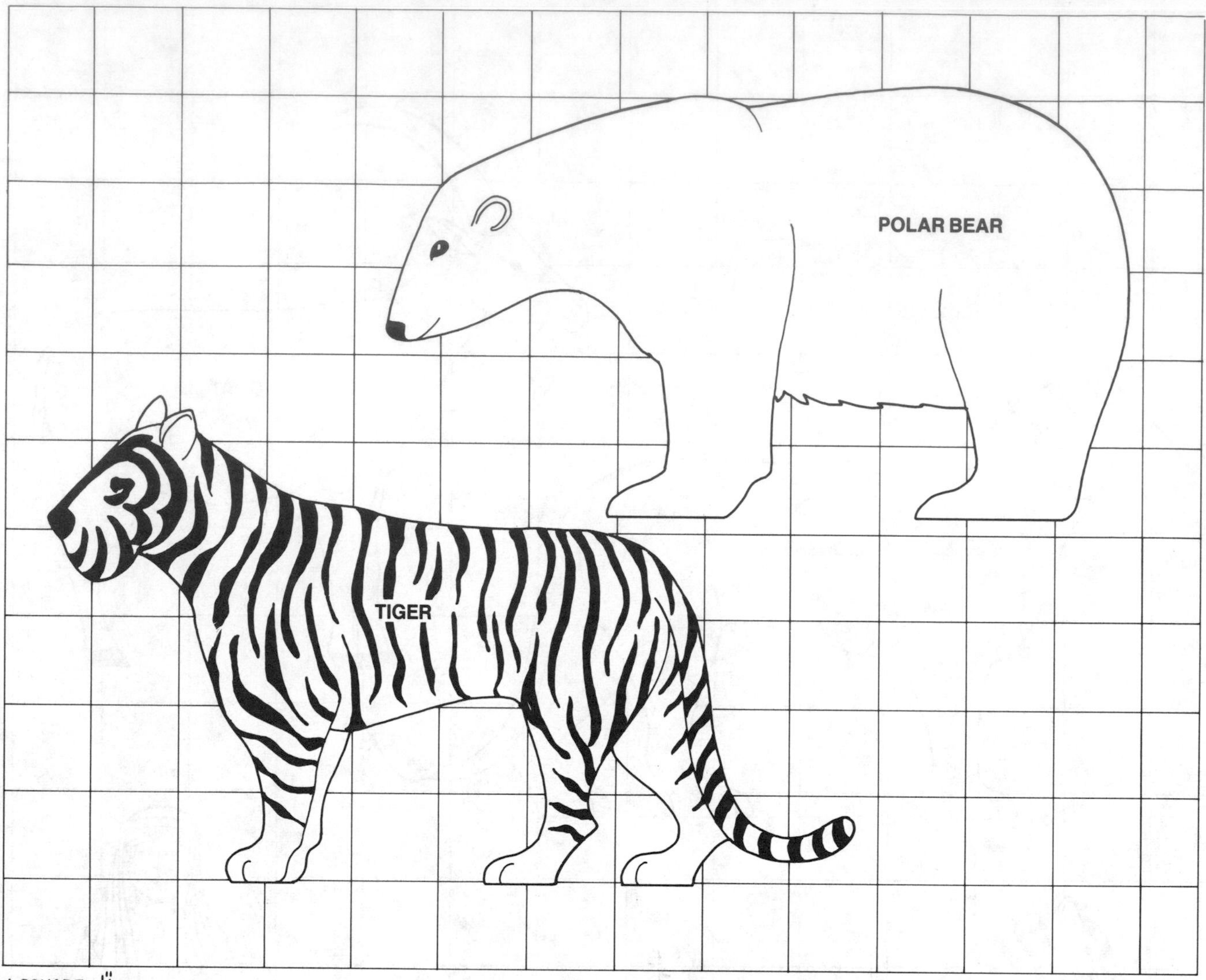

1 SQUARE = ½"

FULL SIZE PATTERNS

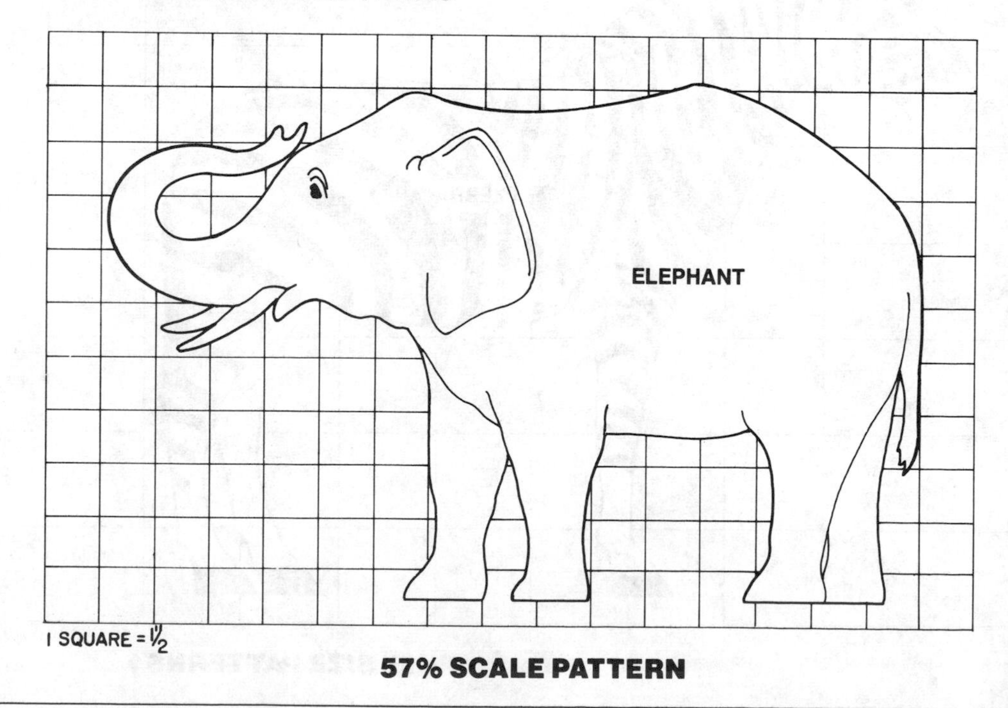

1 SQUARE = ½"

57% SCALE PATTERN

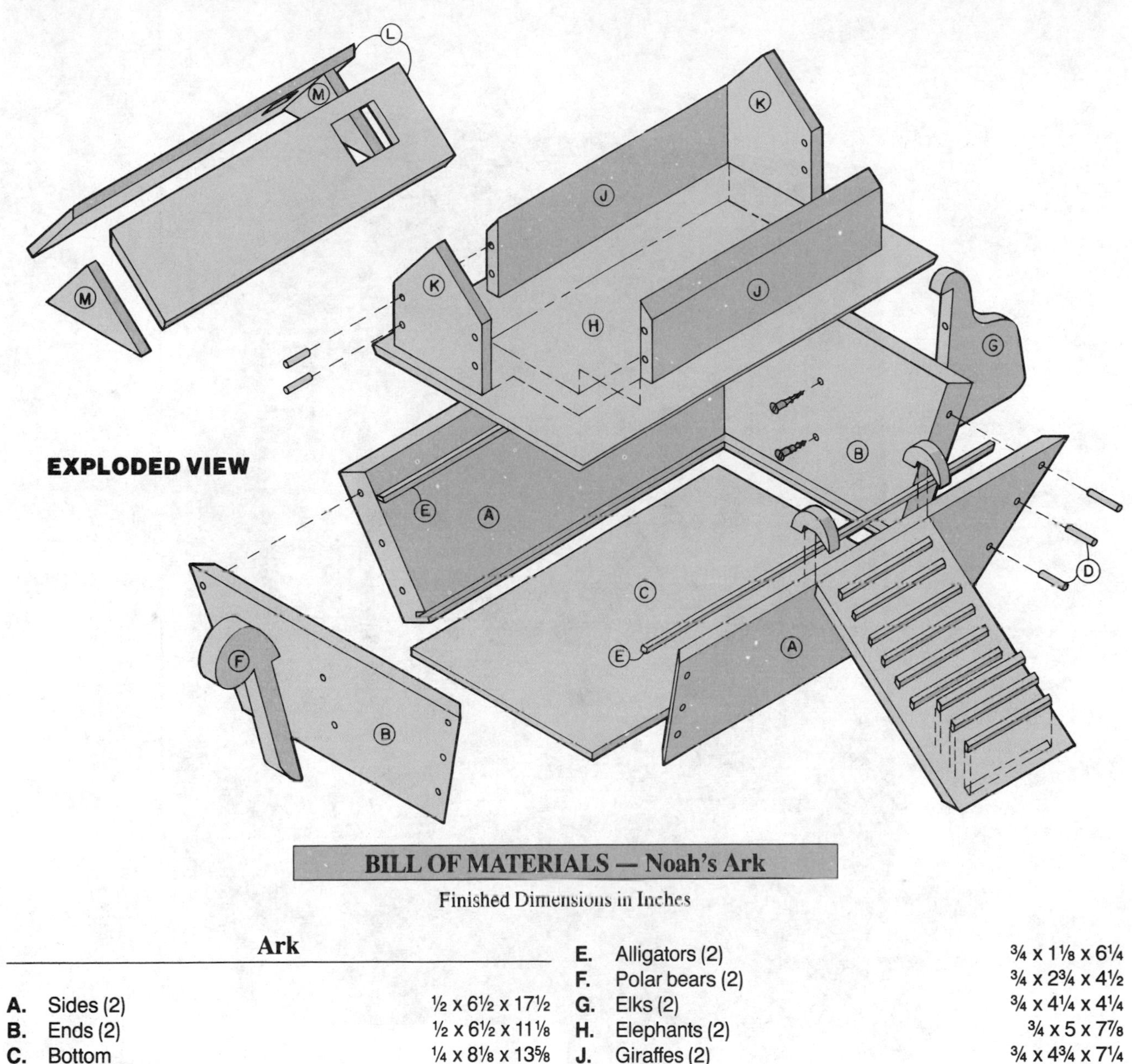

BILL OF MATERIALS — Noah's Ark

Finished Dimensions in Inches

Ark

A.	Sides (2)	½ x 6½ x 17½
B.	Ends (2)	½ x 6½ x 11⅛
C.	Bottom	¼ x 8⅛ x 13⅝
D.	Dowels (32)	3/16 dia. x 1
E.	Ledger strips (2)	¼ x 5/16 x 15 15/16
F.	Bow	½ x 2¾ x 8
G.	Rudder	½ x 3⅝ x 7⅛
H.	Deck	¼ x 9½ x 16 1/16
J.	Cabin sides (2)	½ x 3⅛ x 11
K.	Cabin ends (2)	½ x 4¾ x 6⅝
L.	Roof halves (2)	¼ x 4¼ x 13
M.	Roof braces (2)	½ x 1⅝ x 5⅝
N.	Ramp	¼ x 5 x 12¾
P.	Ramp hooks (2)	½ x 1¼ x 2⅛
R.	Steps (12)	⅛ x ¼ x 4

Animals

A.	Lion/lioness (2)	¾ x 3 x 5
B.	Zebras (2)	¾ x 4 x 4½
C.	Tigers (2)	¾ x 3 x 5
D.	Camels (2)	¾ x 4 x 5¼
E.	Alligators (2)	¾ x 1⅛ x 6¼
F.	Polar bears (2)	¾ x 2¾ x 4½
G.	Elks (2)	¾ x 4¼ x 4¼
H.	Elephants (2)	¾ x 5 x 7⅞
J.	Giraffes (2)	¾ x 4¾ x 7¼
K.	Ostriches (2)	¾ x 3¼ x 3¾
L.	Rhinoceroses (2)	¾ x 3⅜ x 6
M.	Hippopotami (2)	¾ x 2⅛ x 5⅜
N.	Goats (2)	¾ x 3½ x 3½
P.	Noah	¾ x 2¼ x 3¾
Q.	Noah's wife	¾ x 1⅜ x 3¼
R.	Seals (2)	½ x 2 x 3¼
S.	Eagles (2)	½ x 1¾ x 2⅝
T.	Rabbits (2)	½ x 1¼ x 1½
U.	Snakes (2)	½ x 2 x 7¼

HARDWARE

Ark

#6 x 1″ Flathead wood screws (12)

Animals

10-gauge Electrical wire (4″)

Portable Secretary

A traveling desk from days gone by makes an attractive cabinet.

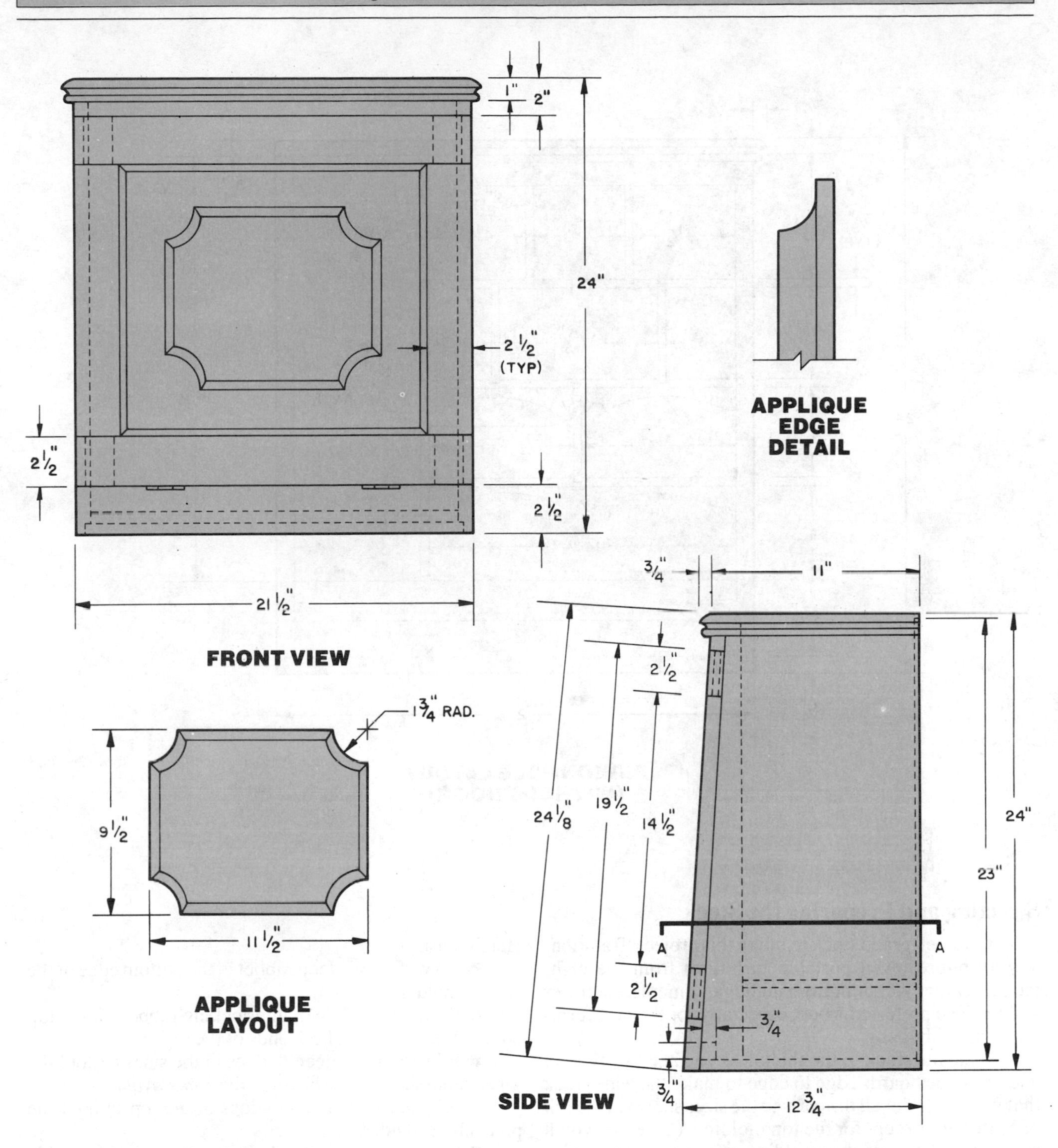

Ever since the dawn of paperwork, business travelers have devised ways to take their paperwork with them. The latest advances include electronic notebooks and laptop computers, but back in the eighteenth and early nineteenth centuries, this "portable secretary" was considered state-of-the-art technology for those people who needed to carry their business from place to place.

Although this desk is hardly what we consider portable, it can be easily moved. It's about half the size of a trunk, and fits easily in the baggage compartment behind a carriage or stagecoach. It packs up neatly, with all the papers held in various pigeonholes. Once you arrived at your destination, you simply set (or had your servants set) the desk on any handy table. The side dropped down to make a writing surface, and there was all your paperwork ready and waiting.

Today, the portable secretary still has many uses, though few of us would want to lug it around from place to place. It still makes an excellent desk for your home; the pigeonholes help to organize bills and other important papers. You can also use it as a display case for small and medium-sized collectables, a liquor cabinet, or even a work center for various hobbies.

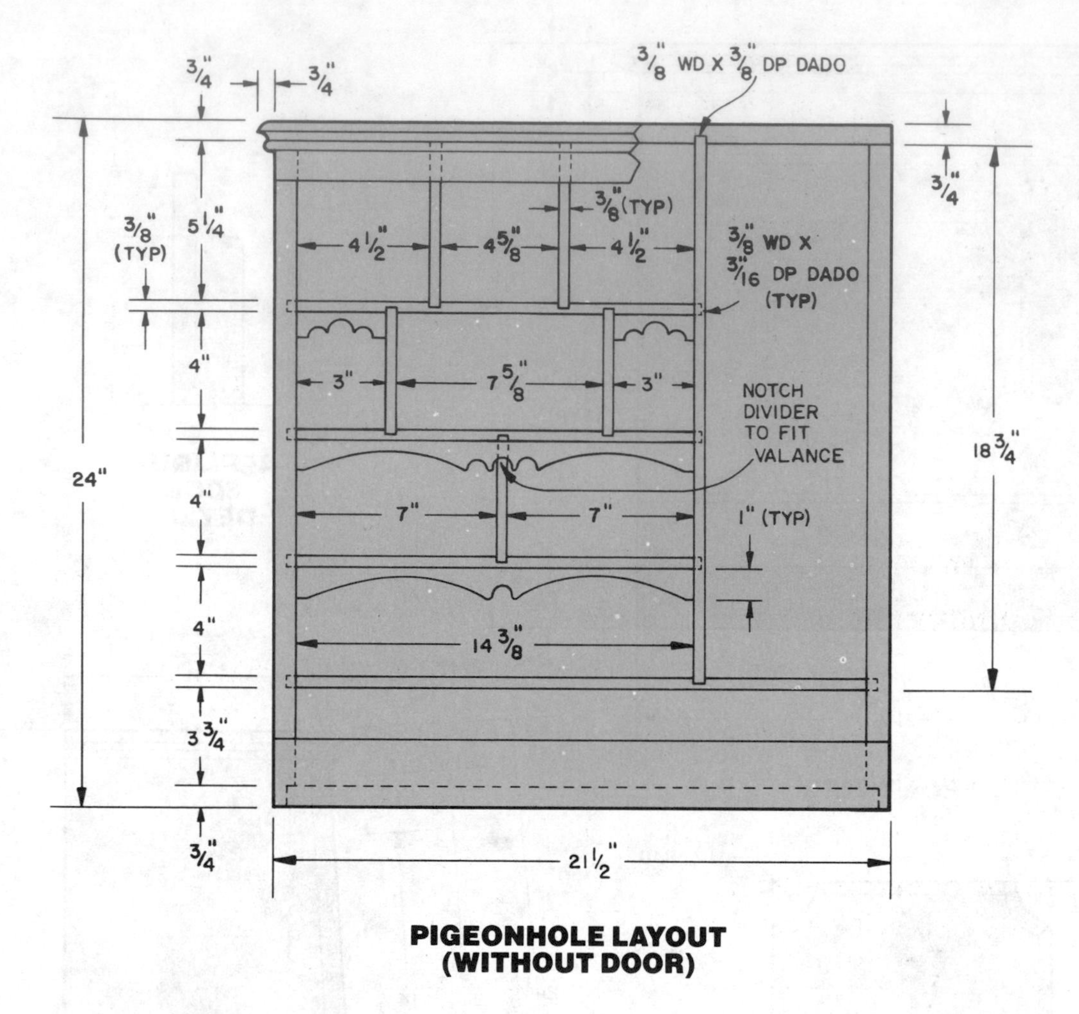

PIGEONHOLE LAYOUT (WITHOUT DOOR)

Selecting and Preparing the Stock

Select cabinet-grade stock to make this project. Traditionally, furniture (even portable furniture) from the eighteenth century was built from mahogany, maple, cherry, or walnut. The preferred wood, especially for the best furniture, was mahogany.

Plane the stock to the thickness you need — 3/4", 3/8", and 1/4". Glue boards edge to edge to make the wide stock that you need. Cut all the parts to the sizes shown in the Bill of Materials, except for the top molding. (Later on, you'll create the shape of this molding in the edge of a wide board, then rip the molding from the board.) As you cut the parts to size, bevel-rip the edges of several pieces at 85°:

- The top edge of the top rail
- The bottom edge of the bottom rail
- The front edge of the top
- The front edge of the bottom

Cutting the Case Joinery

The case and the pigeonholes are assembled with a large number of dadoes and grooves. You can make all of these using either a dado cutter or a router and a straight bit. Here's a list:

- 3/4"-wide x 3/8"-deep rabbet in the bottom edge of the sides to hold the bottom
- 3/8"-wide x 3/8"-deep interlocking rabbets in the top edges of the sides and both ends of the top
- 3/8"-wide x 3/8"-deep dadoes in the sides to hold the pigeonhole shelves, as shown in the *Side Layout*
- 3/8"-wide x 3/8"-deep dadoes in the top to hold the pigeonhole dividers
- 3/8"-wide x 3/16"-deep dadoes in the pigeonhole side to hold the pigeonhole shelves
- 3/8"-wide x 3/16"-deep dadoes in the pigeonhole shelves to hold the pigeonhole dividers
- 1/4"-wide x 3/8"-deep rabbets in the back edges of the sides, top, and bottom to hold the back
- 5/16"-wide x 1/8"-deep rabbets in the back edges of the door panel, to fit in the grooves in the door frame.

In addition, you'll need to make two more joints:

Cut a 3/4"-wide, 3/8"-deep notch in the upper front corner one of the lower pigeonhole dividers. Use a bandsaw to make this joint. The notch will hold the middle valance when the case is assembled.

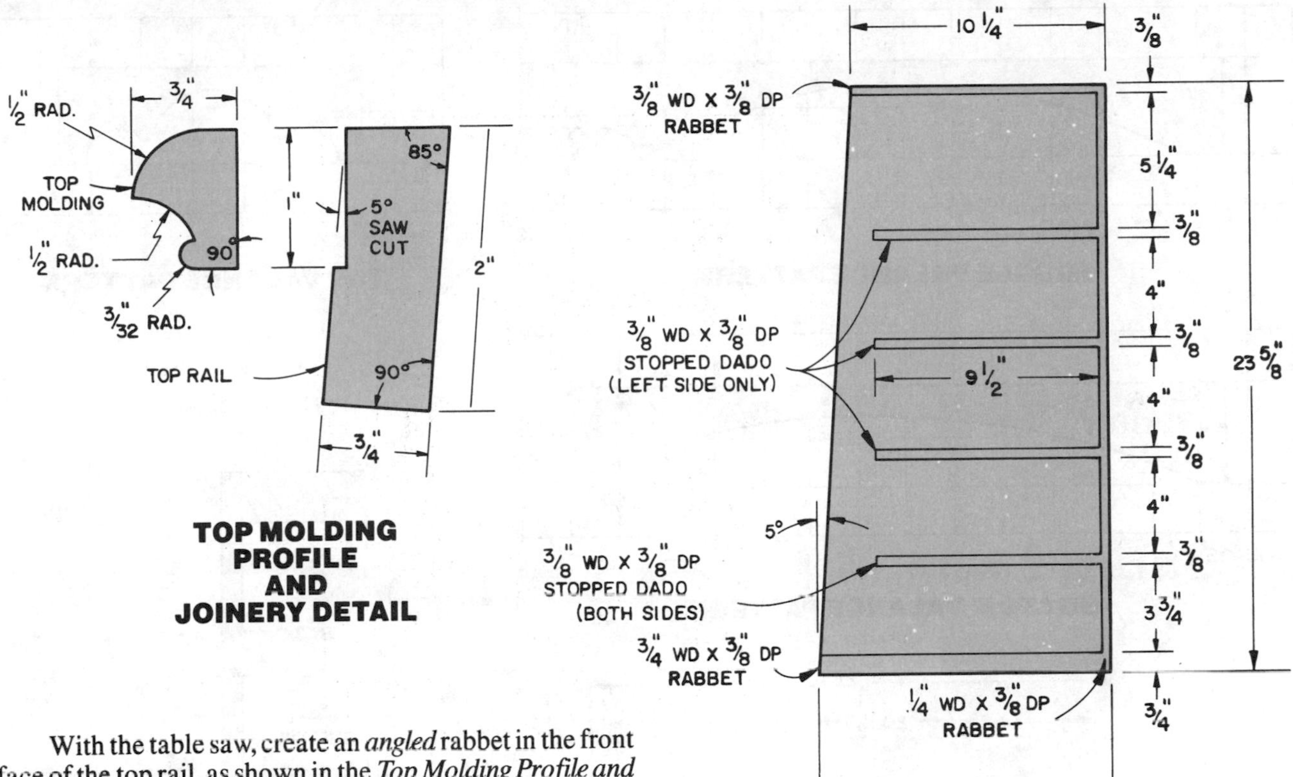

With the table saw, create an *angled* rabbet in the front face of the top rail, as shown in the *Top Molding Profile and Joinery Detail.* Tilt the blade (or table) at 5°, then cut the rabbet with an ordinary saw blade. (See Figure 1.)

Cutting the Valances and the Molding

Enlarge the patterns for the valances and trace them on 3/8"-thick stock. Cut the valance out with a bandsaw or scroll saw, and sand the sawn edges to remove the saw marks.

Make the molding from 3/4"-thick stock using a molder. Select a board 5" or more wide — something that you can get a good grip on. Mount 1/2"-radius quarter-round cutters in the molding head and round over the edge of the stock. Switch to cove cutters, and make a cove to the inside of the rounded edge. Finally, cut a bead right next to the cove, using beading cutters. (See Figures 2 and 3.) Rip the molding shape from the wide board, and use this as the top molding.

Warning: Never try to shape or mold a narrow board, especially when you have this many cuts to make. The smaller the board, the better the chance it will kick back. If it's too small, it may come apart on the machine, throwing splinters every which way.

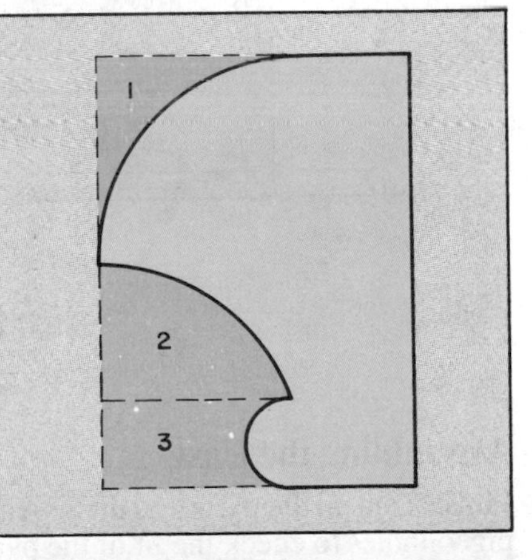

Figure 2. You'll need to use three different molding cutters to make the top molding. Cut the shapes in the order shown.

Figure 1. Cut the rabbet in the top case rail at a 5° angle with an ordinary saw blade.

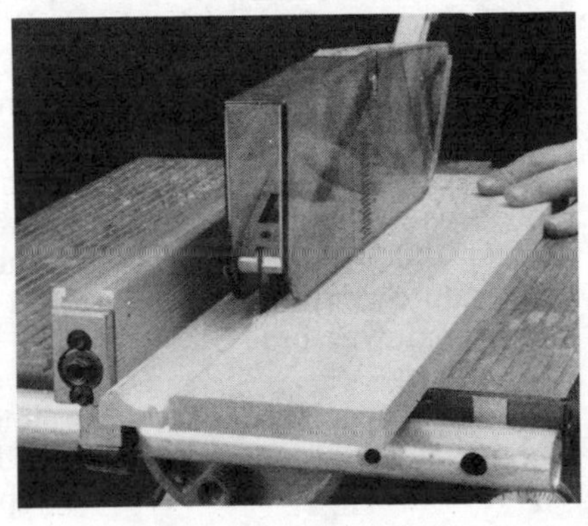

Figure 3. Cut the molding shape in a wide board, then rip the molding from the board.

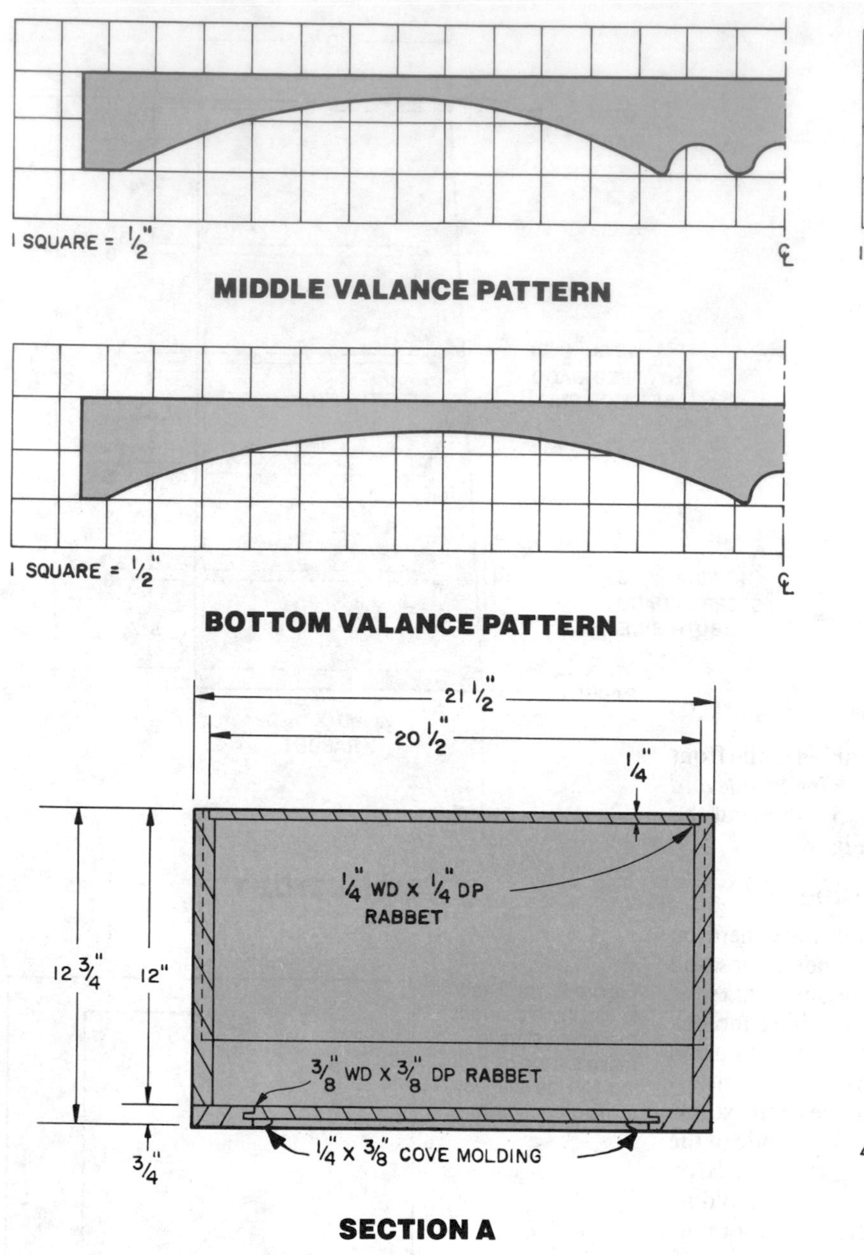

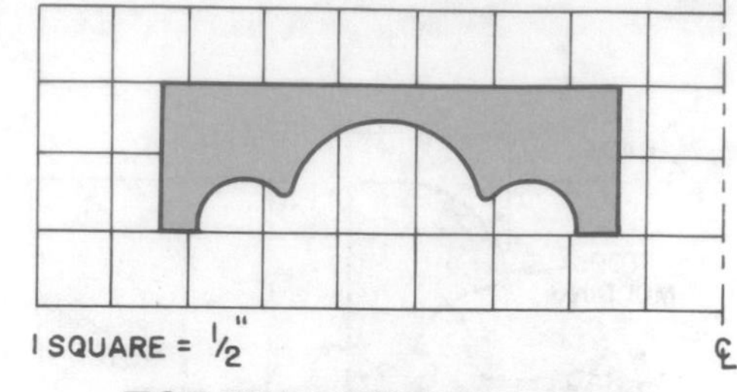

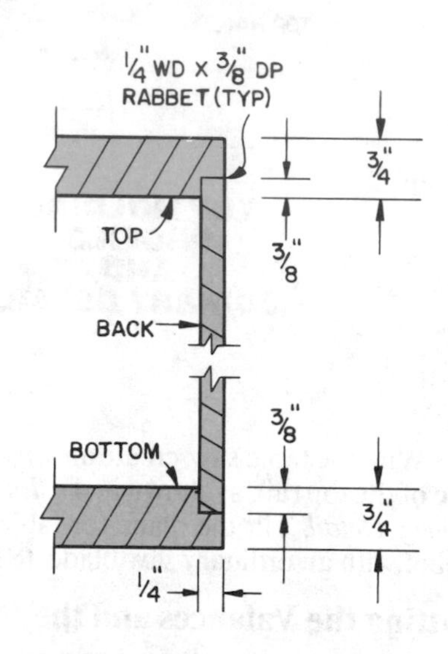

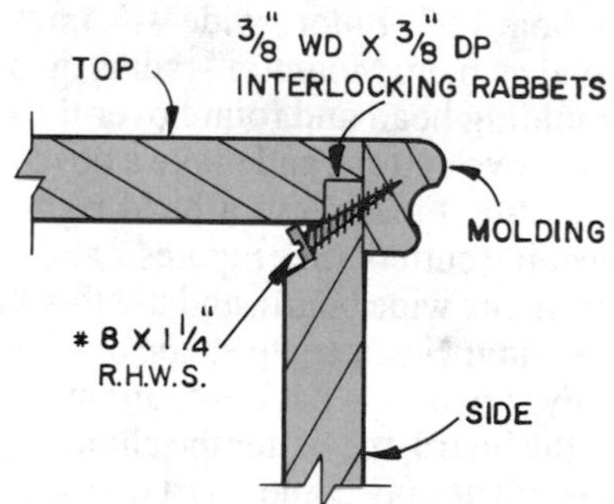

Assembling the Case

Finish sand all the parts and dry assemble the case with the pigeonholes to check the fit of the parts. Make any adjustments necessary to get a better fit. When you're satisfied that the case goes together as well as you can make it, reassemble the sides, top, bottom, and pigeonhole parts (including the valances) with glue.

Do not glue the back in place. Instead, tack it in the rabbets with 1″ brads. The back will want to "breathe" — expand and contract across the grain with changes in temperature and humidity. Glue will restrict this movement. Small wire brads, however, will bend slightly as the wood moves.

Fit the top molding to the case, mitering the ends of the molding at the front corners. Glue the front molding piece in place in the angled rabbet in the top rail. Glue the *front ends* of the side pieces in place, but not the rest of length. (If you glue the entire length of the side molding pieces to the sides, they will restrict the movement — prevent the sides from breathing — because the grain of the molding is perpendicular to the grain of the sides.) Instead, hold the side molding pieces in place with flathead wood screws. Drive these screws from inside the case into the molding, as shown in the *Top-to-Side Joinery Detail.* Drill the screw holes in the sides slightly oversize. This will allow the sides to move.

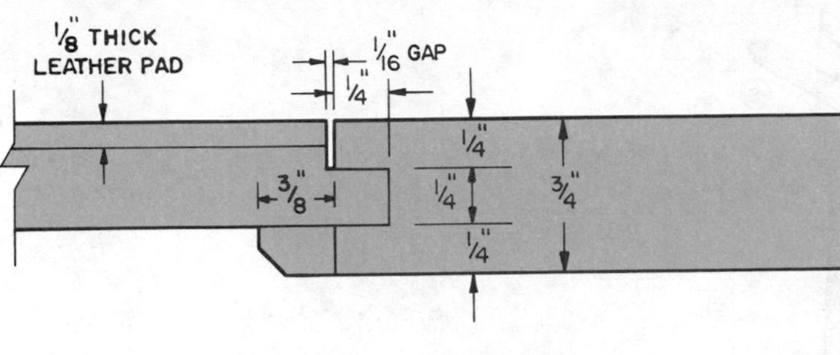

DOOR JOINERY DETAIL

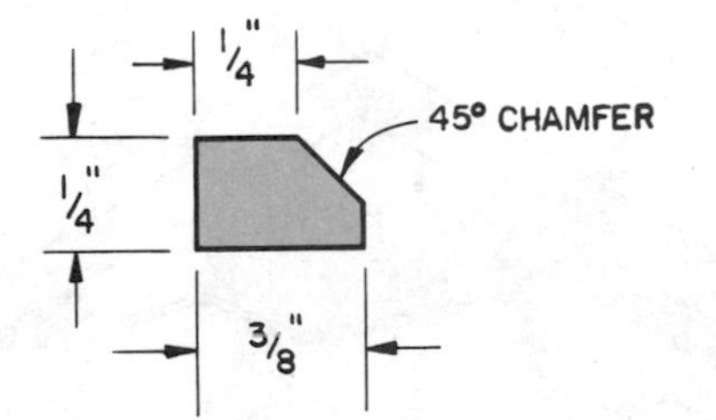

DOOR MOLDING PROFILE

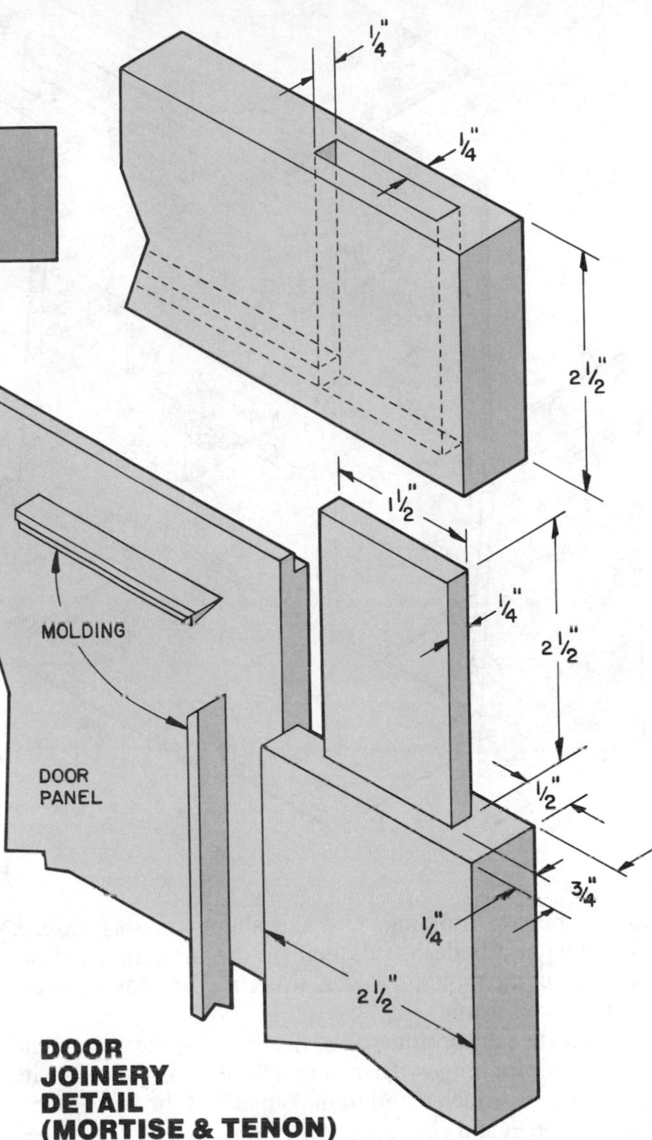

DOOR JOINERY DETAIL (MORTISE & TENON)

Making the Door

The door frame is assembled with through mortises and tenons. Make the tenons in the stiles on your table saw, with the aid of a tenoning jig. (See Figure 4.) Make the mortises by drilling a series of ¼"-diameter holes through the edge of the rails. (See Figure 5.) Clean up the edges of the mortise and square the corners with a bench chisel.

With a router and a straight bit, cut ¼"-wide, ¼"-deep grooves in the inside edges of the rails and stiles. The grooves in the rails must be *blind* — they should stop at the mortises. They must not go through to the ends of the boards.

Assemble the door frame to check the fit of the joints. When you're satisfied, reassemble the parts with glue. Some craftsmen like to pin mortise and tenon joints together with dowels. This is not necessary, but it does look nice. If this appeals to you, drill two ¼"-diameter holes in each corner of the assembled frame, through the tenons. Glue dowels in these holes.

When the glue dries, sand the frame to clean up the joints and make the dowels flush with the surface of the wood. Make the door molding in the same manner that you

Figure 4. Use a tenoning jig to cut the tenons in the door stiles.

Figure 5. Make the mortises in the rails by drilling a series of holes, then cleaning up the edges with a chisel.

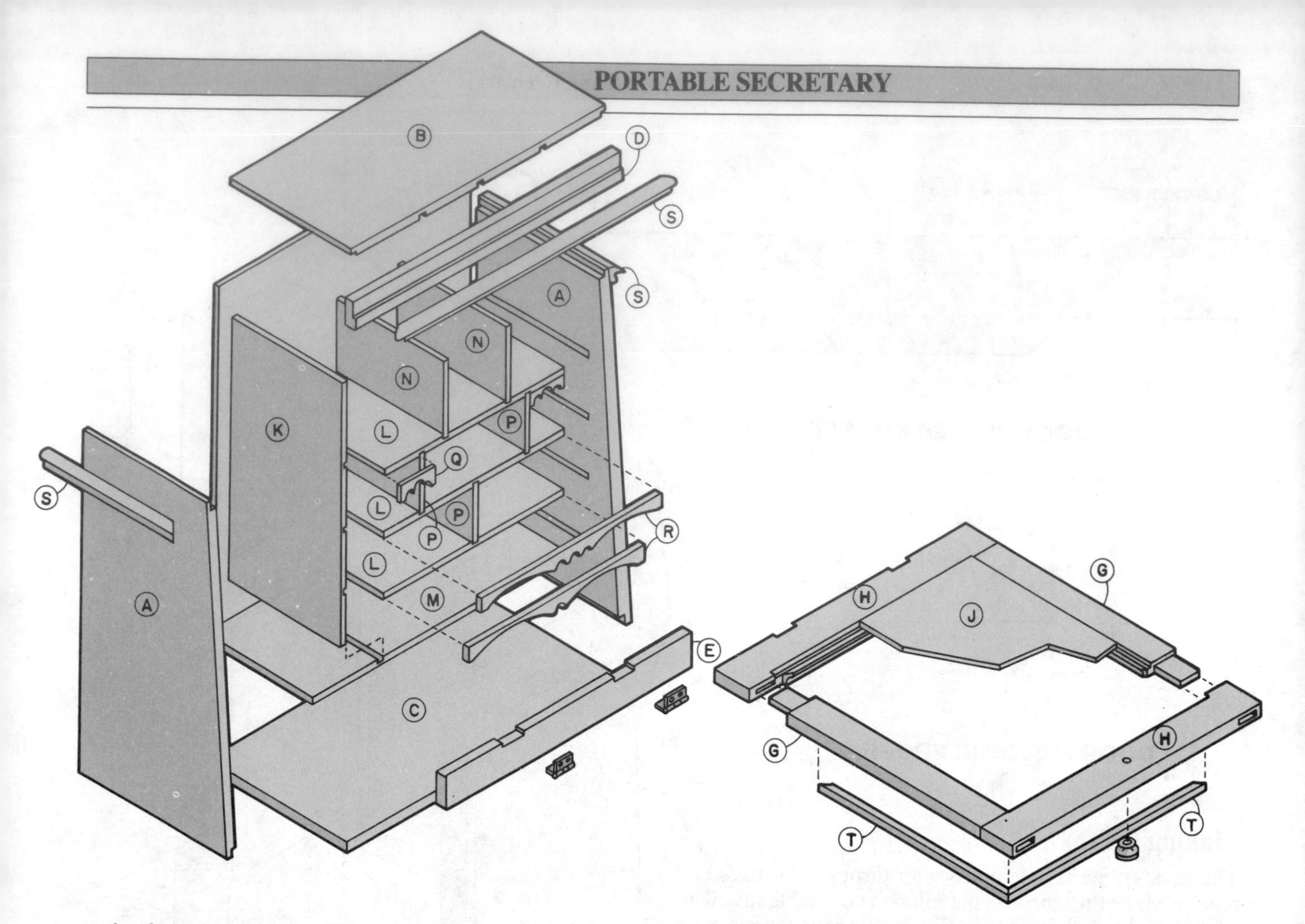

made the top molding. Cut the shape (in this case, a chamfer) in a wide board, then rip the molding from the board. Cut the molding to size, mitering the ends, and glue it to the door frame.

Mortise the bottom rail of the case and the bottom rail of the door for hinges. Then install the door in the case with butt hinges. Attach a pull to the outside of the door so that you can open and close it easily.

Gravity will hold the door closed and, if the secretary sits on a table, the table surface will hold the door at the proper angle for writing when the door is open. However, you may wish to install some additional hardware to help keep the door closed and hold it while it's open. Use a bullet catch to secure the door in the closed position, and a pair of drop lid supports to hold the door when it's open.

Finishing Up

Disassemble the completed secretary and remove all the hardware. Do any necessary touch-up sanding, and apply a finish to the wood. Be sure to apply as many coats of finish to the inside of the case as you do to the outside. This will ensure that all the parts of the project expand and contract evenly, with no tendency to warp or twist.

After the finish dries, reassemble the secretary. Using contact cement, affix a 1/8"-thick pad of leather to the back of the door panel. This will create a writing surface. (You may have to build up the back of this pad with veneer to make it a full 1/8" thick.) Be careful not to get any finish or wax on the leather.

BILL OF MATERIALS — Portable Secretary

Finished Dimensions in Inches

	Part	Dimensions
A.	Sides (2)	3/4 x 12 x 23 5/8
B.	Top	3/4 x 10 1/4 x 21 1/2
C.	Bottom	3/4 x 12 x 20 3/4
D.	Top rail	3/4 x 2 x 21 1/2
E.	Bottom rail	3/4 x 2 1/2 x 21 1/2
F.	Back	1/4 x 20 3/4 x 23
G.	Door stiles (2)	3/4 x 2 1/2 x 19 1/2
H.	Door rails (2)	3/4 x 2 1/2 x 21 1/2
J.	Door panel	3/8 x 15 x 17
K.	Pigeonhole side	3/8 x 9 1/2 x 18 15/16
L.	Pigeonhole upper shelves (3)	3/8 x 9 1/2 x 14 15/16
M.	Pigeonhole lower shelf	3/8 x 9 1/2 x 20 3/4
N.	Pigeonhole upper dividers (2)	3/8 x 5 13/16 x 9 1/2
P.	Pigeonhole lower dividers (3)	3/8 x 4 3/8 x 9 1/2
Q.	Pigeonhole top valances (2)	3/8 x 1 x 3
R.	Pigeonhole middle/bottom valances (2)	3/8 x 1 x 14 3/8
S.	Top molding (total)	3/4 x 1 x 48
T.	Door molding (total)	1/4 x 3/8 x 64
U.	Applique (optional)	1/4 x 9 1/2 x 11 1/2

HARDWARE

#8 x 1 1/4" Roundhead wood screws (4)
1" Brads (24)
1 1/2" x 2" Brass butt hinges and mounting screws (1 pair)
Bullet catch
Door pull
Drop lid supports (2)

Designed and built by Nick Engler.

Arched Bench

This sturdy stool is equally at home in both country and contemporary settings.

Need a small bench in a hurry? You can make this arched bench in just a few hours, start to finish. There are only four parts in this project, and just a few dado joints to make. It can be built from ordinary "dimension" lumber — 1 x 12 (3/4" x 11 1/4") stock — straight from the lumberyard. You don't even have to enlarge any patterns — the shapes of the legs and the brace can be laid out with a compass.

This simple bench is adapted from a traditional Shaker design. The Shakers, as the United Society of Believers in Christ's Second Reappearing were known, manufactured simple practical furniture during the late eighteenth, nineteenth, and early twentieth centuries. Their religious beliefs prohibited them from incorporating any unnecessary ornamentation or decoration in their handiwork. Like this stool, most of their furniture was simple, delicate, and extremely sturdy.

Making the Parts

Cut the parts to the sizes shown in the Bill of Materials. You can cut all of these from a 1 x 12 x 6′. If you use dimension lumber, let it sit in your shop for several weeks *before* you cut it. This will give it a chance to dry out and adjust to the environment. Dimension lumber is not as well cured as cabinet grade lumber — it has a greal deal more moisture content.

Lay out the arches on the legs and brace with a compass. Cut these shapes on a bandsaw, then sand the sawn edges to remove the saw marks. A drum sander makes short work of this chore.

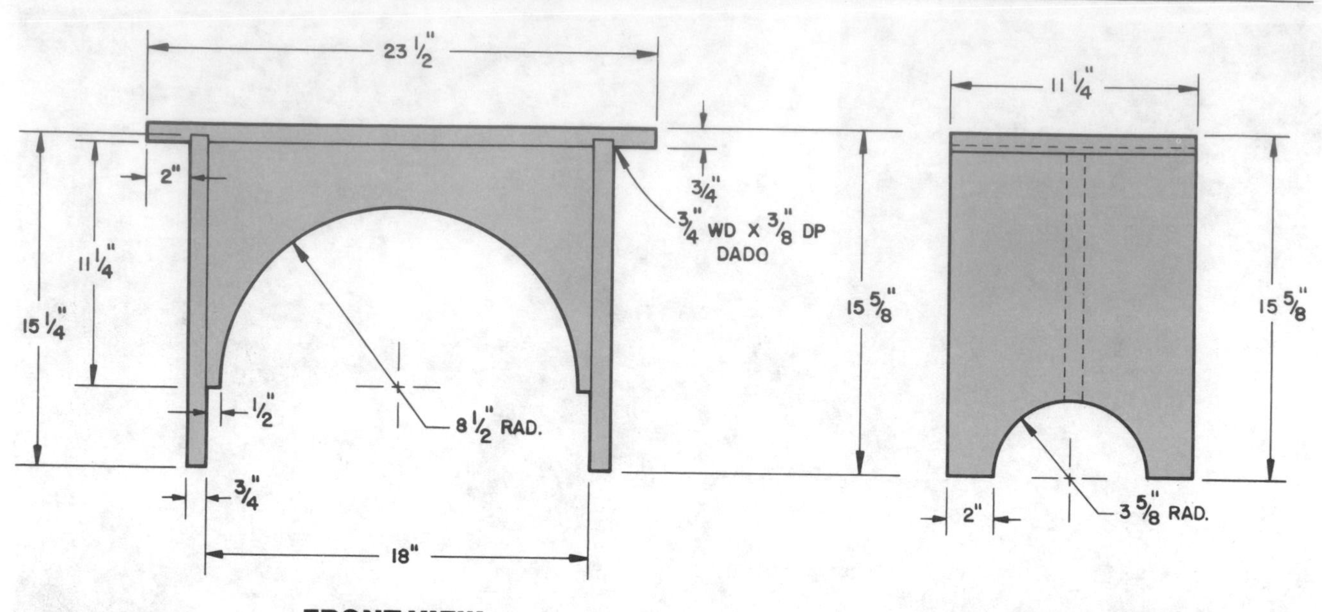

Using a dado cutter or a router, cut ¾″-wide, ⅜″-deep dadoes in the underside of the seat where shown in the *Front View.* If you use a router for this operation, try making the simple routing jig shown here to guide your cut. This jig is nothing more than a large T-square. Use the cross of the "T" to align the jig, then clamp the leg of the "T" — the straightedge — to the stock. Cut the dado with the base of the router riding firmly against the straightedge. (See Figure 1.)

Assembly and Finishing

Finish sand all the parts, then dry assemble them to check the fit. When you're satisfied that they fit properly, assemble them with glue and screws. Counterbore and countersink the screws, then cover the heads with wooden plugs. Sand the plugs flush with the surface of the wood.

Do any necessary touch-up sanding on the completed bench, then apply a finish. Traditionally, a country bench like this would have been finished with milk paint. We used a modern substitute — exterior latex paint, diluted 1:1 with water. Once the paint was dry, we sanded the edges of the seat to simulate wear and give the project an antique look.

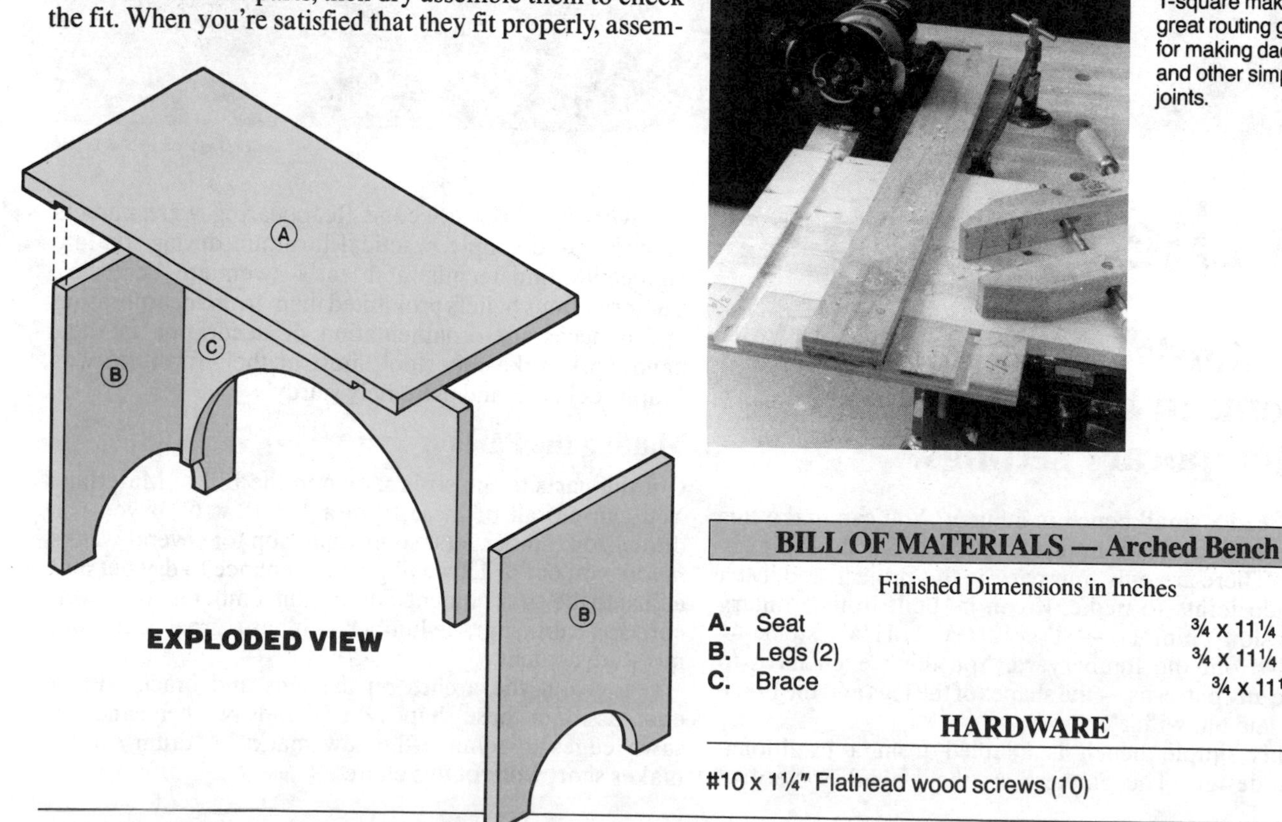

Figure 1. A large T-square makes a great routing guide for making dadoes and other simple joints.

BILL OF MATERIALS — Arched Bench

Finished Dimensions in Inches

A.	Seat	¾ x 11¼ x 23½
B.	Legs (2)	¾ x 11¼ x 15¼
C.	Brace	¾ x 11¼ x 18

HARDWARE

#10 x 1¼″ Flathead wood screws (10)

Router Joinery Jig

Your router is one of the most useful tools in your shop for cutting simple joinery — rabbets, dadoes, grooves, slots, and mortises. All you need (besides your router) to make any one of these joints is a straight bit to cut with and a way to guide the router as it cuts.

◆ The simple T-shaped jig shown here is a guide for the router. It's assembled like an ordinary T-square: Screw the "cross" (short piece) to the leg (long piece), making sure that the edges of both parts are *precisely* 90° from each other. After you attach the parts, mount a 3/4" straight bit in your router and use the jig to cut a dado in a piece of scrap wood. Rout both the workpiece *and* one side of the cross. (This routed dado in the cross serves as an indicator so that you can quickly align the jig on a workpiece.) If you wish, change bits and rout a 1/2"-wide dado on the other side of the cross. You may also wish to make a second jig and rout 3/8"-wide and 1/4"-wide dadoes in the cross.

◆ To use these jigs, first find the dado in the cross that matches the diameter of the bit you have mounted in your router. Press the cross of the "T" against the edge of the workpiece that you want to rout — this will align the leg so that it's square to the edge. Line up the dado in the cross with the marks for the dado, rabbet, groove, etc. that you want to cut. (See Figure A.) Clamp the leg to the workpiece. Cut the joint, keeping the base of the router pressed firmly against the leg. (See Figure B.)

Figure A. Use the dado in the cross to align the jig on the workpiece. The width of the dado must match the diameter of your router bit.

Figure B. Clamp the leg of the jig to the workpiece and use it as a straightedge to guide the router as you cut.

3"
3/4"
27"
3/4"
3"
3/4" WD X 1/2" DP DADO
12 3/4"

EXPLODED VIEW

Courtesy George Effingham.

Bachelor's Chest

A small, tall chest of drawers provides as much storage as larger chests, but requires less space.

Traditionally, a bachelor's chest is a tall chest of small drawers. The width and the depth of the drawers (and the case) are much smaller than ordinary chests of drawers, so that the piece occupies less floor space. But there are more drawers (and the case is taller), so that a bachelor's chest offers almost as much drawer space as an ordinary chest of drawers.

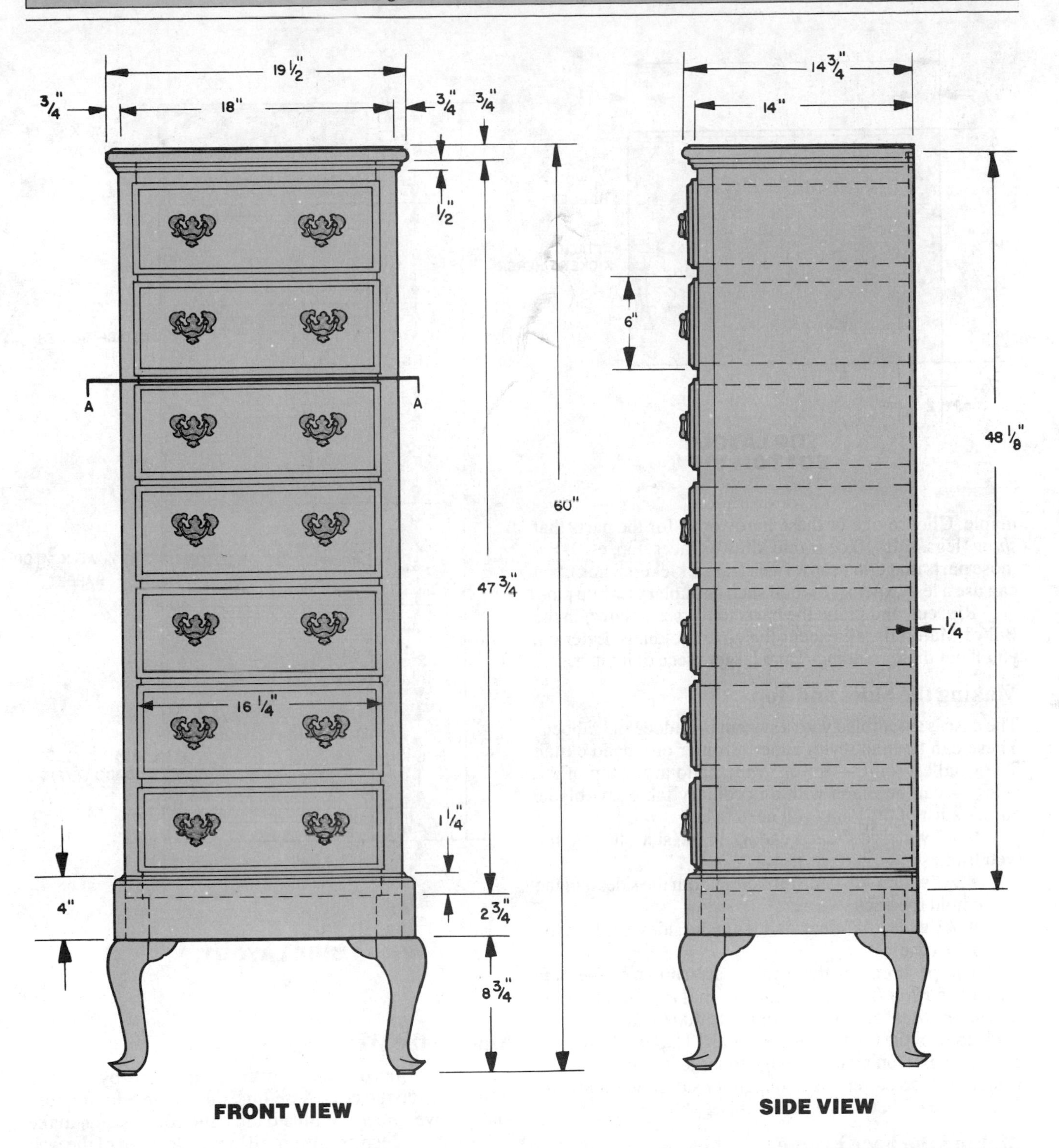

FRONT VIEW

SIDE VIEW

Although it's smaller than most case pieces, this bachelor's chest is built using traditional case construction. Each drawer is supported on a web frame, and these frames are joined to the sides of the case. The case, in turn, sits on a leg-and-rail frame.

As with most case pieces, this is a time-consuming project to make. But it's not difficult. There are no fancy joints to be made, just lots of ordinary dadoes, rabbets, and grooves. You can save some time by *mass-producing* some of these parts and joints. Many of the parts are redundant because there are five identical drawers and web frames, and four identical legs. Carefully plan your work to make as many cuts as you can with each tool setup, and the work will progress much quicker.

Selecting and Preparing the Wood

The chest is designed along classic lines — the cabriole legs, the shaped drawer fronts, and the moldings used to build this piece were all popular with furnituremakers in the eighteenth century. The traditional wood used for classic furniture is mahogany. However, some American craftsmen also used native walnut, cherry, and figured

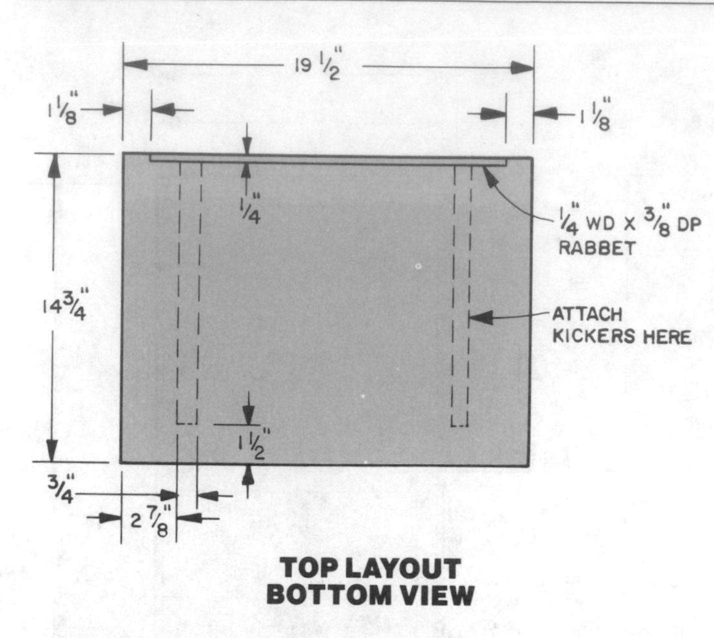

TOP LAYOUT
BOTTOM VIEW

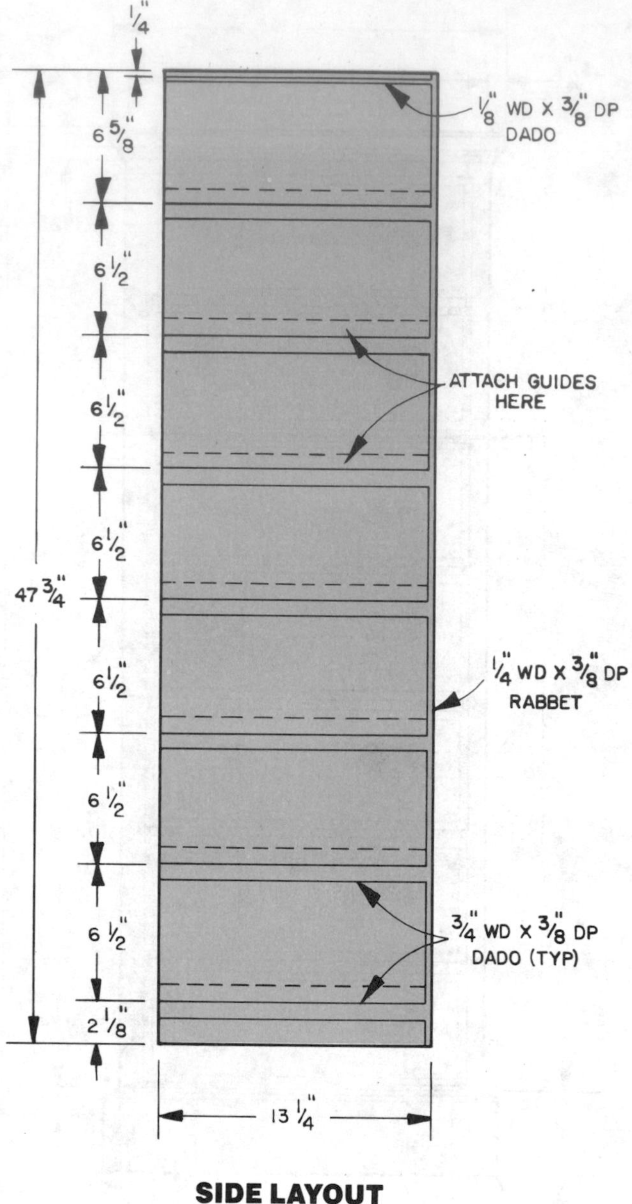

SIDE LAYOUT

maple. Choose one of these hardwoods for the parts that *show* (legs, sides, face frame, drawer faces, top, etc.). For those parts that don't show (web frame, kickers, back), you can use a less expensive wood such as poplar or white pine.

Rip, cut, and plane the parts to the sizes shown in the Bill of Materials, all except the cove moldings. Later on, you'll cut these moldings from larger piece of lumber.

Making the Sides and Top

The case is assembled with a system of dadoes and rabbets. These can be made with either a router or a dado cutter. The smallest joint — the 1/8"-wide dado at the top of the sides — can be made with an ordinary table saw blade. Here's a list of the joints you need to cut:

- 3/4"-wide x 3/8"-deep dadoes in the sides to hold the web frames
- 1/4"-wide x 3/8"-deep rabbets in both the sides and the top to hold the back
- 1/8"-wide x 3/8"-deep dadoes in the sides to attach the top to the case

The positions of these joints are shown in the *Side Layout* and *Top Layout.* Remember that the sides must be *mirror images* of each other. And note that the rabbet in the back edge of the top is "double-blind." That is, it's stopped at both ends. Don't cut it through to the side edges. Stop the router or dado cutter 1 1/8" from either side, and square the ends of the rabbet with a bench chisel.

Making the Face Frame

Join the members of the face frame with dowels. Use a doweling jig to guide your drill when making the stopped dowel holes in the frame members. Glue the parts together, checking that the frame is square as you clamp it together.

Tip ◆ While dowels are a common way to join face frames, they aren't the only way. Traditionally, craftsmen used mortises and tenons before the invention of doweling jigs. Today doweling jigs are being replaced by "biscuit" or plate joinery.

Making the Web Frames

As we mentioned, each drawer is supported by a "web frame" inside the case. Assemble this frame with tongue-and-groove joinery. With a dado cutter or a router, make 1/4"-wide, 3/8"-deep grooves in all the *inside* edges of the web frame rails. (See Figure 1.) Then cut 1/4"-wide, 3/8"-long tenons or "tongues" in the ends of the stiles, using the same tool. (See Figure 2.)

Glue the rails and stiles together to make seven frames. When you clamp up the parts, check that each assembly is square. The completed frames must be square if the drawers are to slide easily in and out of the case. After the glue dries on the rails and stiles, glue the kickers to the underside of the completed frames, as shown on the *Web Frame Layout.* Attach the kickers to just *six* of the seven frames. The bottom web frame does not need kickers.

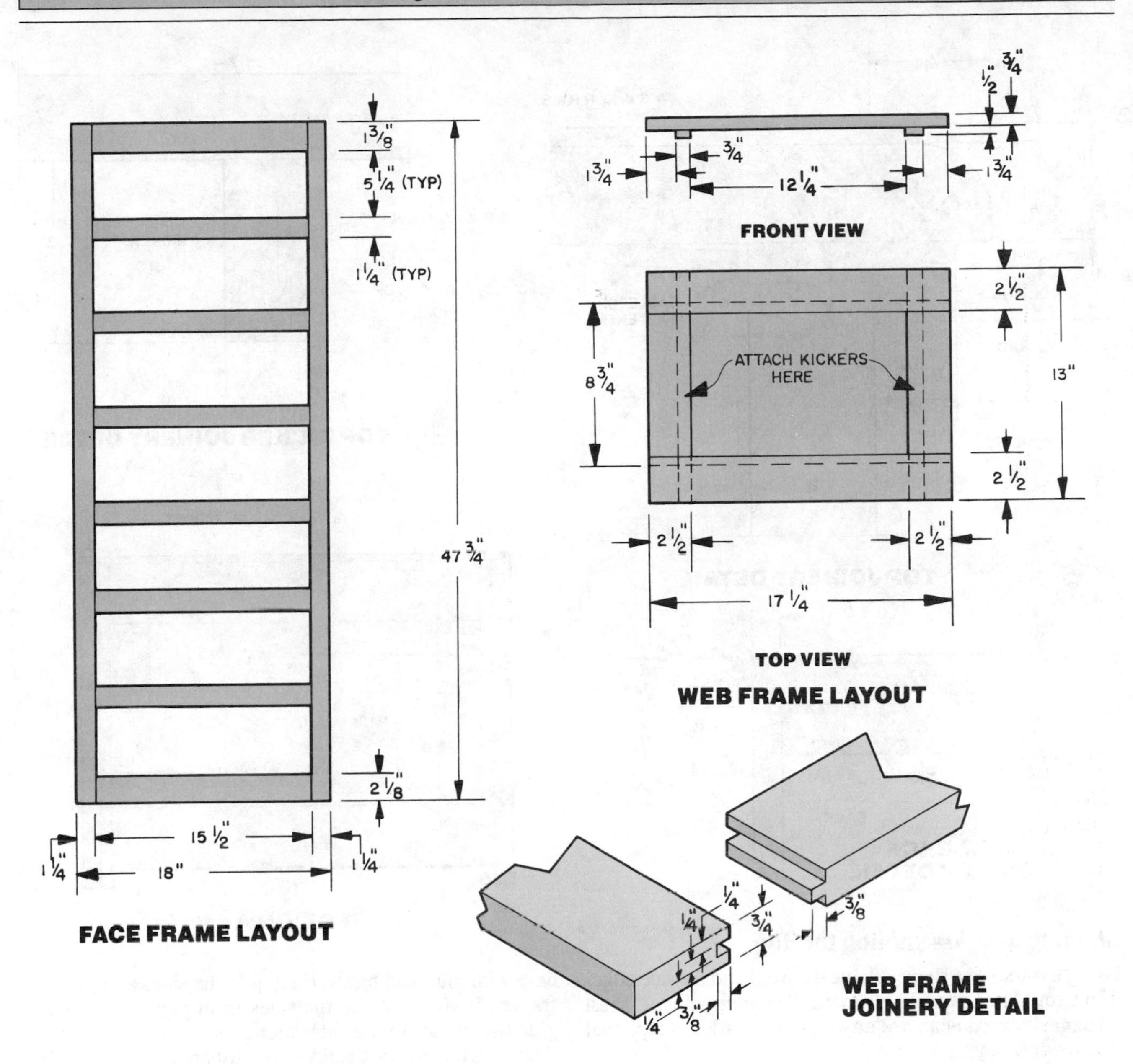

Figure 1. Cut ¼"-wide, ⅜"-deep grooves along one edge of the web frame rails.

Figure 2. Make matching tongues, ¼" wide and ⅜" long, in the ends of the web frame stiles.

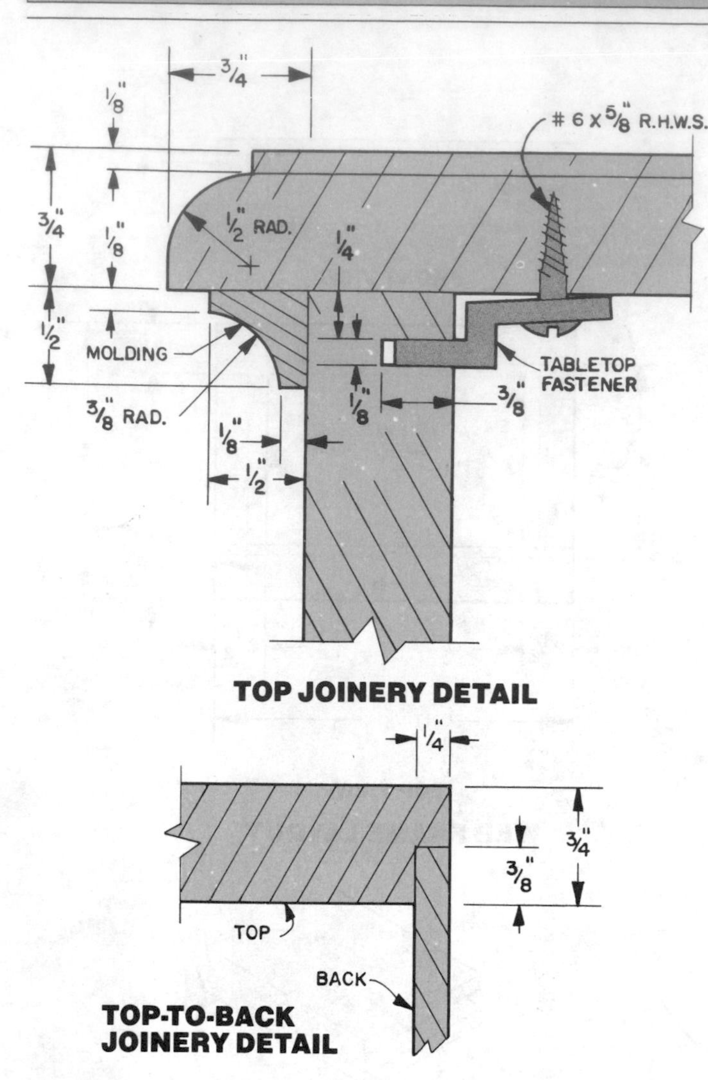

TOP JOINERY DETAIL

TOP-TO-BACK JOINERY DETAIL

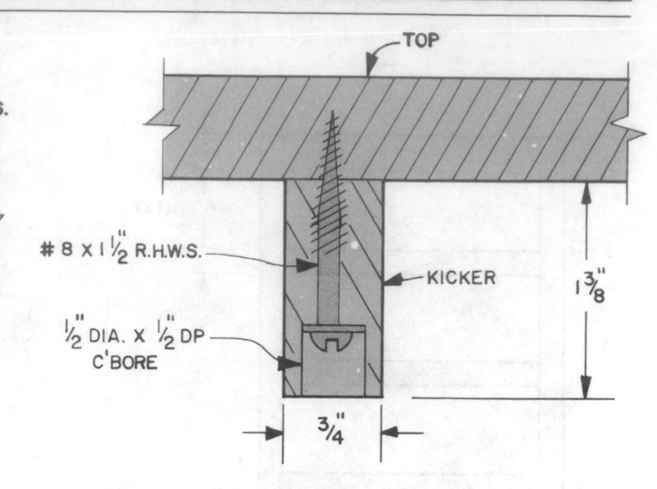

TOP KICKER JOINERY DETAIL

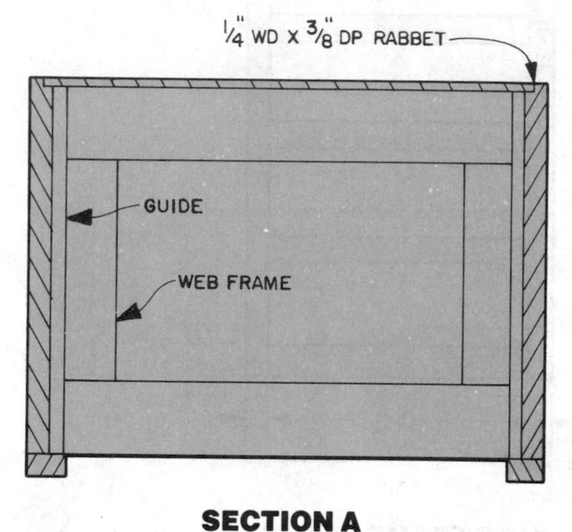

SECTION A

Shaping and Assembling the Top

Using a router or a shaper, shape the front and the side edges of the top. The shape shown in the *Top Joinery Detail* is just a suggestion; you can use any type of classical shape that suits your fancy.

Drill pilot holes and counterbores in the bottom edge of the top kickers, as shown in the *Top Kicker Joinery Detail*. The pilot holes should be *slightly* larger than the shanks of the screws. This will allow the top to expand and contract with changes in temperature and humidity. Secure the kickers to the underside of the top with roundhead wood screws. *Do not* glue the kickers to the top.

Assembling the Case

It's best to completely assemble the case *before* you make the drawers. That way, you can fit the drawers to the case. To get ready to assemble the case, finish sand all the parts. Smooth the web frame, but you don't need to finish sand it. As you sand, be careful not to round over any edges or corners that adjoin other parts when the project is put together.

Dry assemble the case without glue to check the fit of the parts. Use band clamps to hold the parts together temporarily. When you're satisfied with the fit, reassemble the case with glue and brads. First, join the sides and the web frames. If you've made the sides from plywood, you can glue the frames to the sides along the entire length of the dadoes. If the sides are solid wood, just apply glue to the first 1"–2" of the dadoes (nearest the front edge). This will allow the sides to expand and contract.

Tip ◆ To reinforce the dado joints that join the web frames to the sides, drive #10 x 1¼" flathead wood screws from *inside* the case, so that they won't show on the outside. Angle the screws, as if you were "toenailing" the parts together with screws instead of nails. Drive the screws from inside and *underneath* the bottom, counter, and web frame, and inside and *above* the top. One more consideration: If the sides are made of solid wood, reinforce the web frame near the front edge *only* — where it's glued to the sides. (See Figure 3.)

As you clamp up this assembly, make sure that all the parts are square to each other. To keep them square while the glue cures, tack the back in place with a few brads. *Do not* drive the brads home. Leave the heads showing so that you can easily remove them.

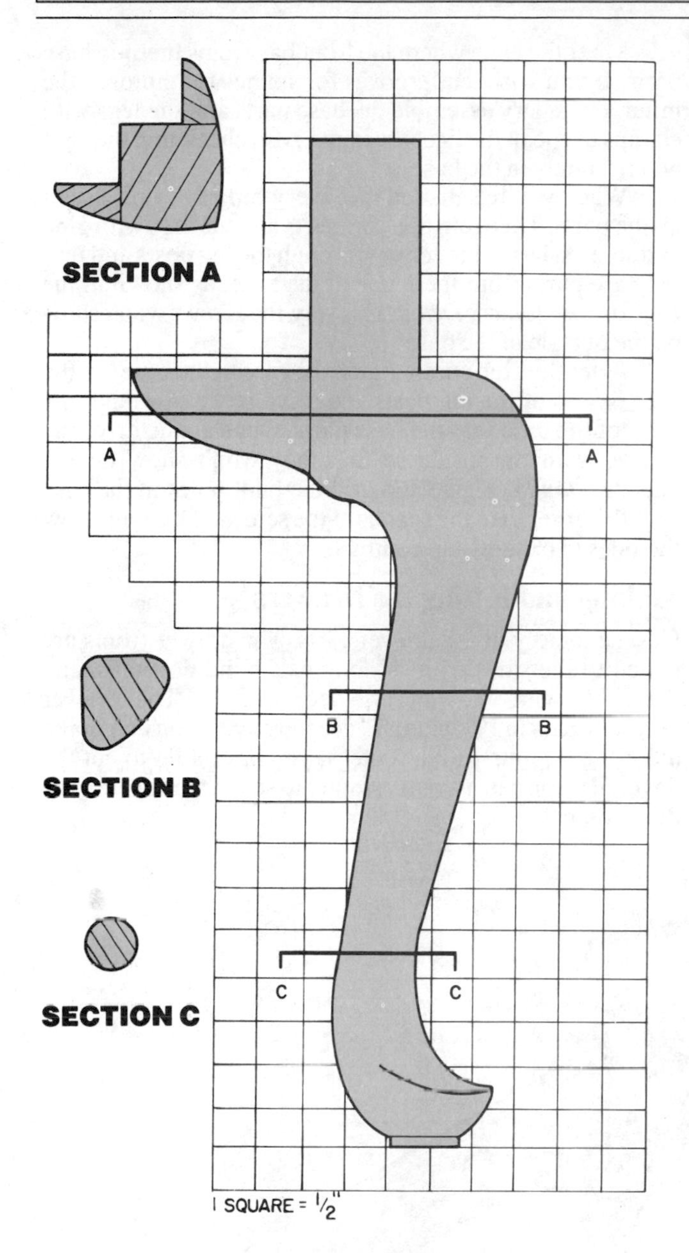

LEG PATTERN

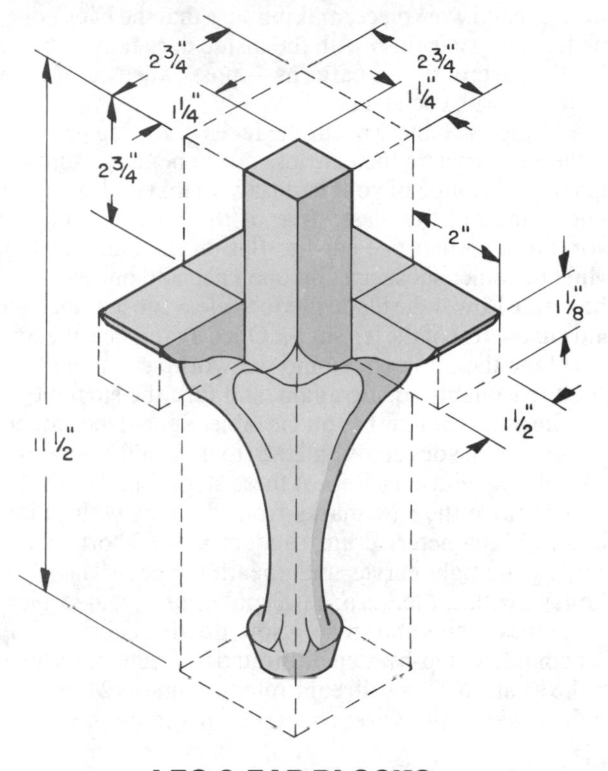

LEG & EAR BLOCKS ASSEMBLY DETAIL

After the glue cures, remove the clamps and attach the face frame with glue. You may reinforce the frame-to-case joints with hidden splines or "biscuits", but it isn't necessary. The stiles and the sides, as well as the rails and horizontal parts all meet long grain to long grain, and the grain direction is parallel. There are no end grain joints or opposing grains, so a glue joint should be adequate.

When the glue on the face frame cures, remove the back so that you can attach the top more easily. Secure the top to the sides with tabletop fasteners, as shown in the *Top Joinery Detail.* Screw these fasteners to the underside of the top so that the flange on each fastener hooks into the 1/8"-wide dado in the side.

Tack the drawer guides in place with brads. *Don't* use glue. The grain direction of the drawer glides is perpendicular to that of the sides. The wire brads will bend slightly as the sides expand and contract. But if you glue the guides in place, the guides will restrict the movement of the sides and the case may eventually warp or split.

Finally, tack the back in place. Drive the nails home this time; you shouldn't need to remove the back again.

Cutting the Cabriole Legs

If you've made cabriole legs for a previous project, then you understand how to make a compound cut on your bandsaw: Cut the design in one face, tape the waste back to the workpiece, and cut the second face. However, these legs aren't quite that simple. Because all the legs have "ears," the process is more involved.

Glue up the leg and ear stock, as shown in the *Leg and Ear Blocks Assembly Detail.* Let the glue cure for at least 24 hours, then trace the leg and ear patterns on the two *inside*

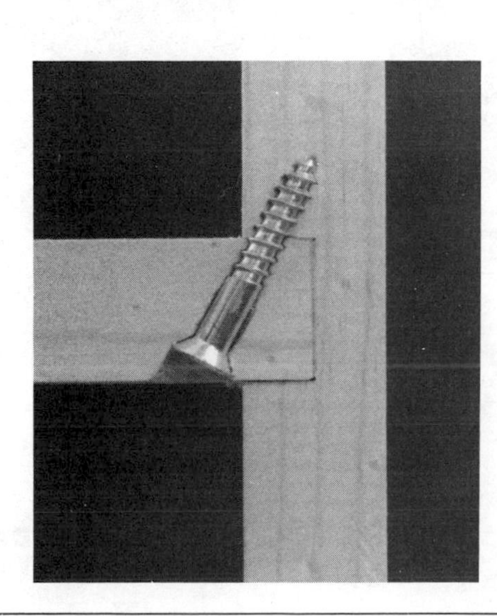

Figure 3. To secure the web frames to the sides, drive flathead wood screws at an angle, up through the frames and into the sides from *inside* the case. Using this method, the screws won't be visible from the outside.

faces of each workpiece, making sure that the back edge of the leg pattern is flush with the inside corner. Also be sure that the parts of the leg patterns — posts, knees, ankles, feet — line up with each other.

Using the bandsaw, cut the faces of the leg post down to the knee (where the cabriole curve begins). Adjust the upper blade guide of your bandsaw so that it clears the ear block, and cut the waste free of the posts. Position the workpiece so that one ear lies flat on the bandsaw table, while the other sticks up. Cut one knee and one ear, saving the scrap. Lower the blade guide to clear the leg stock only, and cut the rest of the leg shape. Once again, save the scrap.

Tape the scrap back onto the workpiece to make the stock reasonably square again, and turn the stock 90°, so that the other ear now lies on the table. Repeat the sequence of cuts. When you remove all the stock, you'll have a rough cabriole leg with ears. Repeat these steps for all of the legs.

Remove the saw marks from the legs with sanders. Small (1″-diameter) drum sanders make short work of sanding the tight curves underneath the ears. Then sculpt the legs with a file, rasp, saw, spokeshave, and sander to round the corners and create a soft, flowing cabriole shape. For complete step-by-step illustrated instructions on how to make a cabriole leg with ears, refer to Figures 2 through 12 in the *Queen Anne Tables* chapter earlier in this book.

Making the Base

Shape the top edge of the front bases and side base parts. The shape shown in the *Base Profile* is just a suggestion; you can use any classical shape that suits your fancy.

Miter the ends where the front base joins the side base parts. If you wish, cut grooves for splines to reinforce the miter joints. Dry assemble the base parts and the legs with clamps to check the fit of the joints. Also check that the case will fit snugly in the base.

When you're satisfied that everything fits, finish sand all the parts. Then join the base parts and the legs with glue and screws. Drive the screws through the leg posts and into the base parts from the *inside* of the base, as shown in the *Leg-to-Base Joinery Detail.* This way, the screws won't show on the outside of the base.

After the glue cures, attach the case to the base. Sit the case on top of the leg posts and drive screws through the sides of the case into the base parts. Once again, drive the screws from the inside so that they won't show on the outside. *Don't* use glue and drill the pilot holes in the case slightly larger than the shanks of the screws. This will allow the sides to expand and contract.

Making and Fitting the Drawers

Cut the joinery in the drawer parts. The drawer fronts are joined to the sides with 3/8″-long half-blind dovetails, and the back with 3/4″-wide, 3/8″-deep dadoes. The drawer bottom floats in 1/4″-wide, 3/8″ deep grooves. You can make all of these joints with a router if you have a jig to cut the dovetails. You can also use a router to shape the edges of the drawer faces.

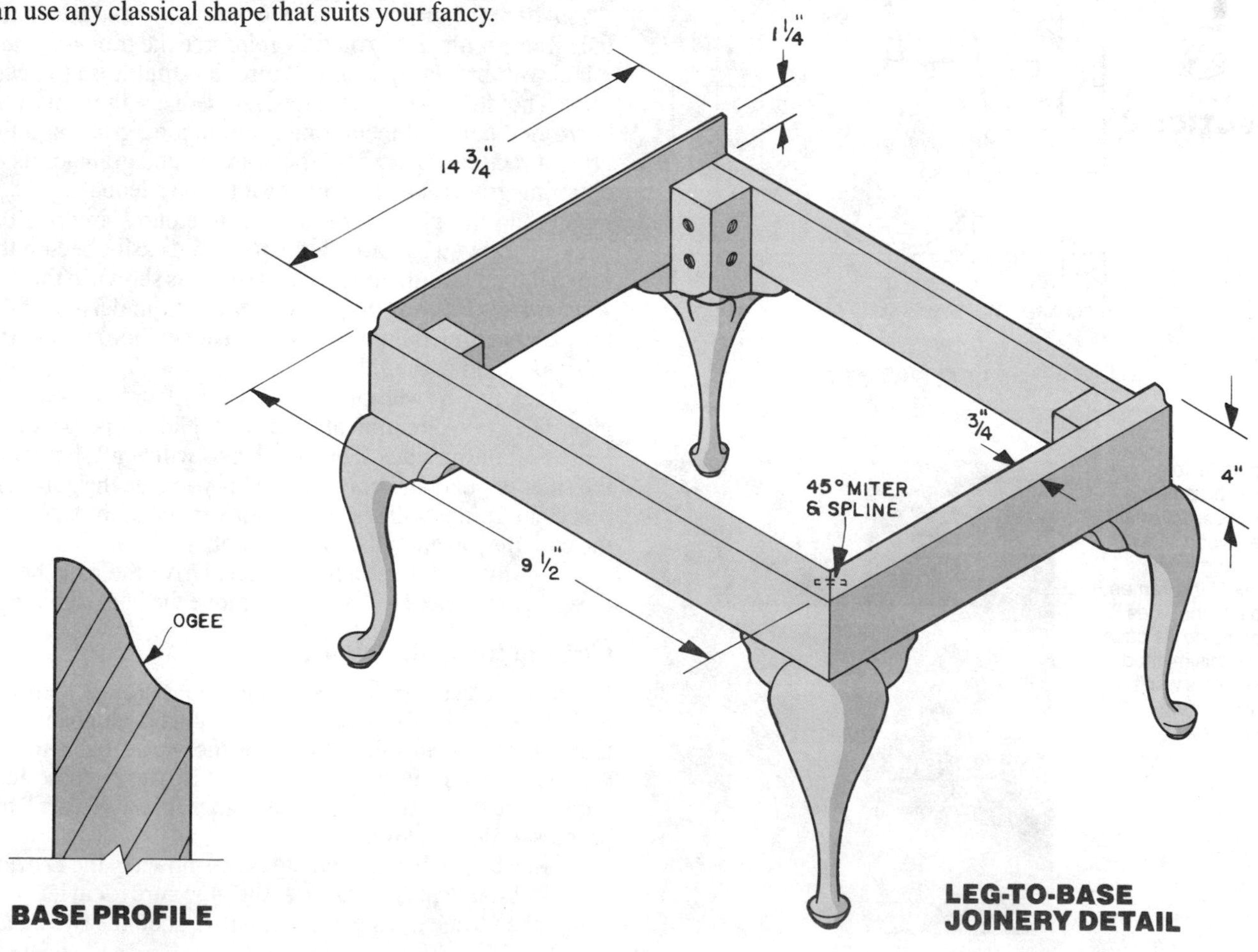

Finish sand the drawer faces. Dry assemble the drawers to check the fit of the parts. Also check the fit of the drawers in the case. If everything fits properly, reassemble the parts with glue. Do not glue the drawer bottoms in the grooves; just let them float. Be sure the drawers are square when you clamp them together; otherwise, they may not work properly. After the glue cures, install the pulls and fit the drawers in the case.

Tip ◆ Rub the bottom edges of the assembled drawer with paraffin wax to help it slide smoothly in and out of the case.

Making and Attaching the Molding

Select a board 4″ wide or wider, and plane it to ½″-thick. Cut a ⅜″-radius cove in one edge of the board, using a router or a shaper. Rip the cove shape from the edge of the board, creating a ½″-thick, ½″-wide molding.

Caution: *Do not* try to cut a molding shape in a slender or narrow piece. The wood may splinter or come apart in your hands. This is why you cut the shape in a wide board and *then* rip the slender molding from it.

Cut and miter the molding to fit around the sides and the front of the case, just under the top. You can glue the front molding in place, but attach the side pieces with brads. The reason for this is the same as for the drawer guides that you nailed to the inside of the case: The grain of the molding is perpendicular to the grain of the sides. The wire brads will bend slightly as the wood expands and contracts, but the glue would restrict the movement.

Finishing Up

Remove the drawers from the case and the pulls from the drawers. Do any necessary touch-up sanding, then apply a finish to the case and the drawer faces. Be sure to apply as many coats of finish to the inside of the case as you do to the outside. If the finish is uneven, one side of a board may absorb moisture faster than the other side. This will eventually cause the board to warp and the case may be distorted. After the finish dries, re-install the drawers and hardware.

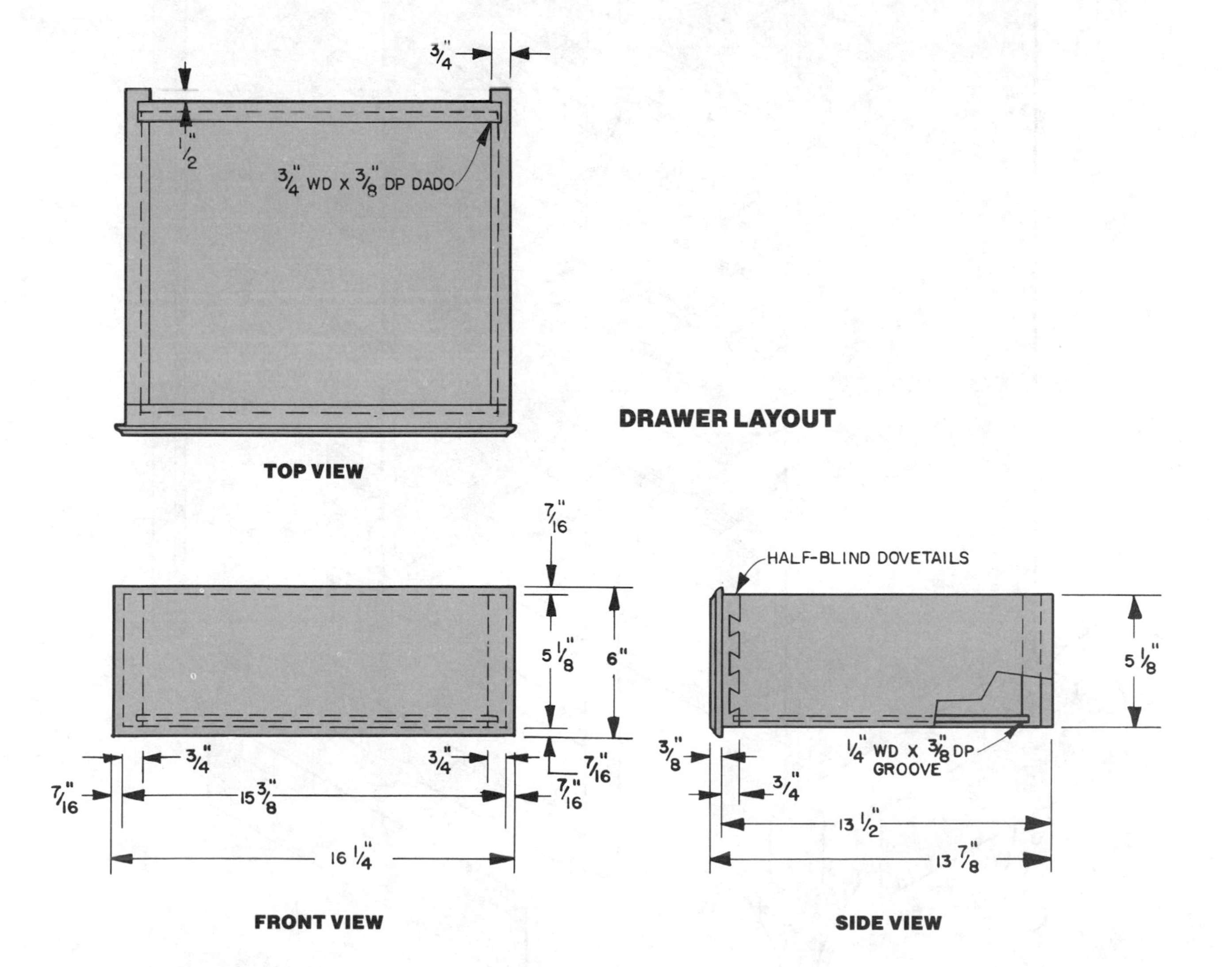

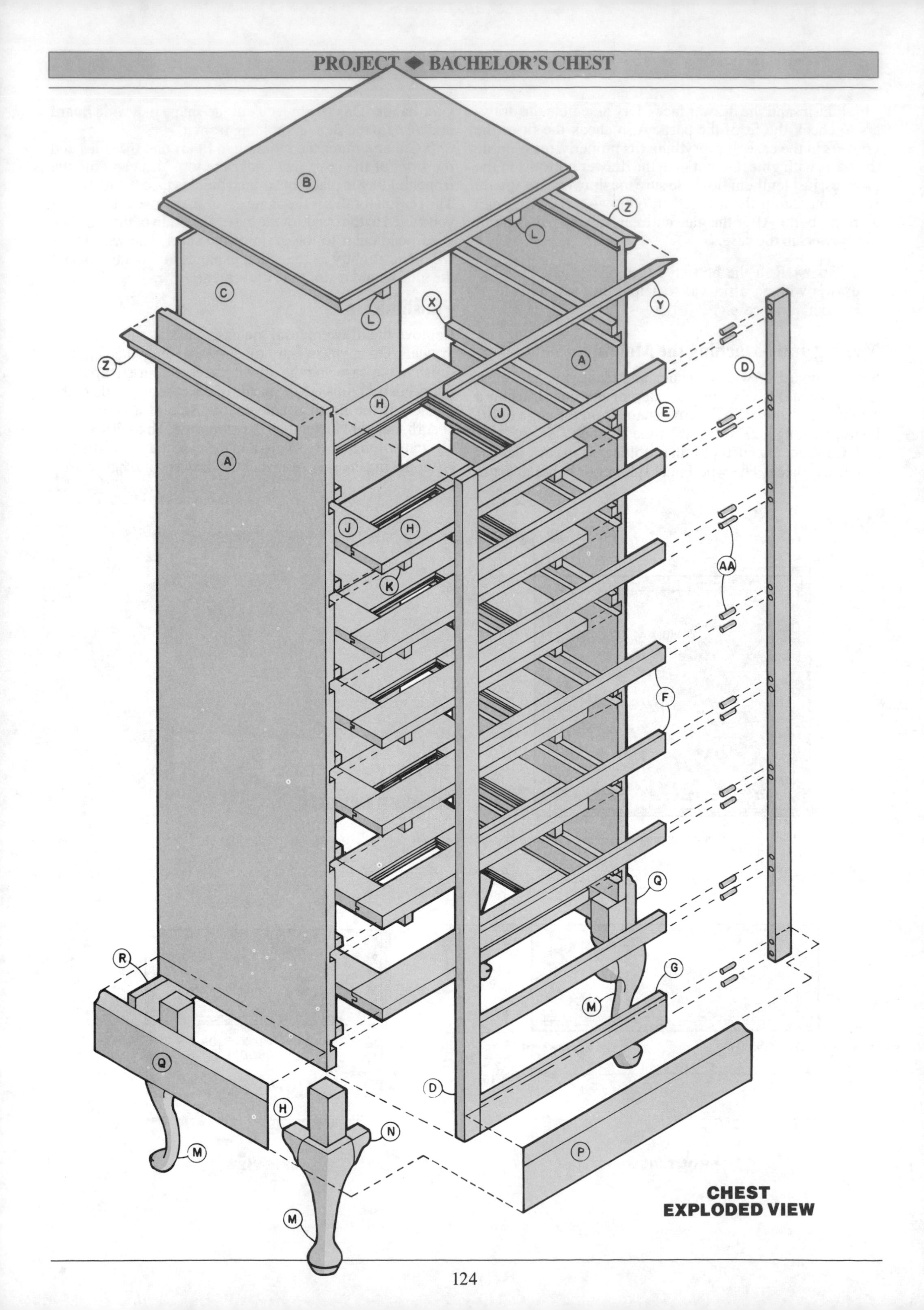

CHEST EXPLODED VIEW

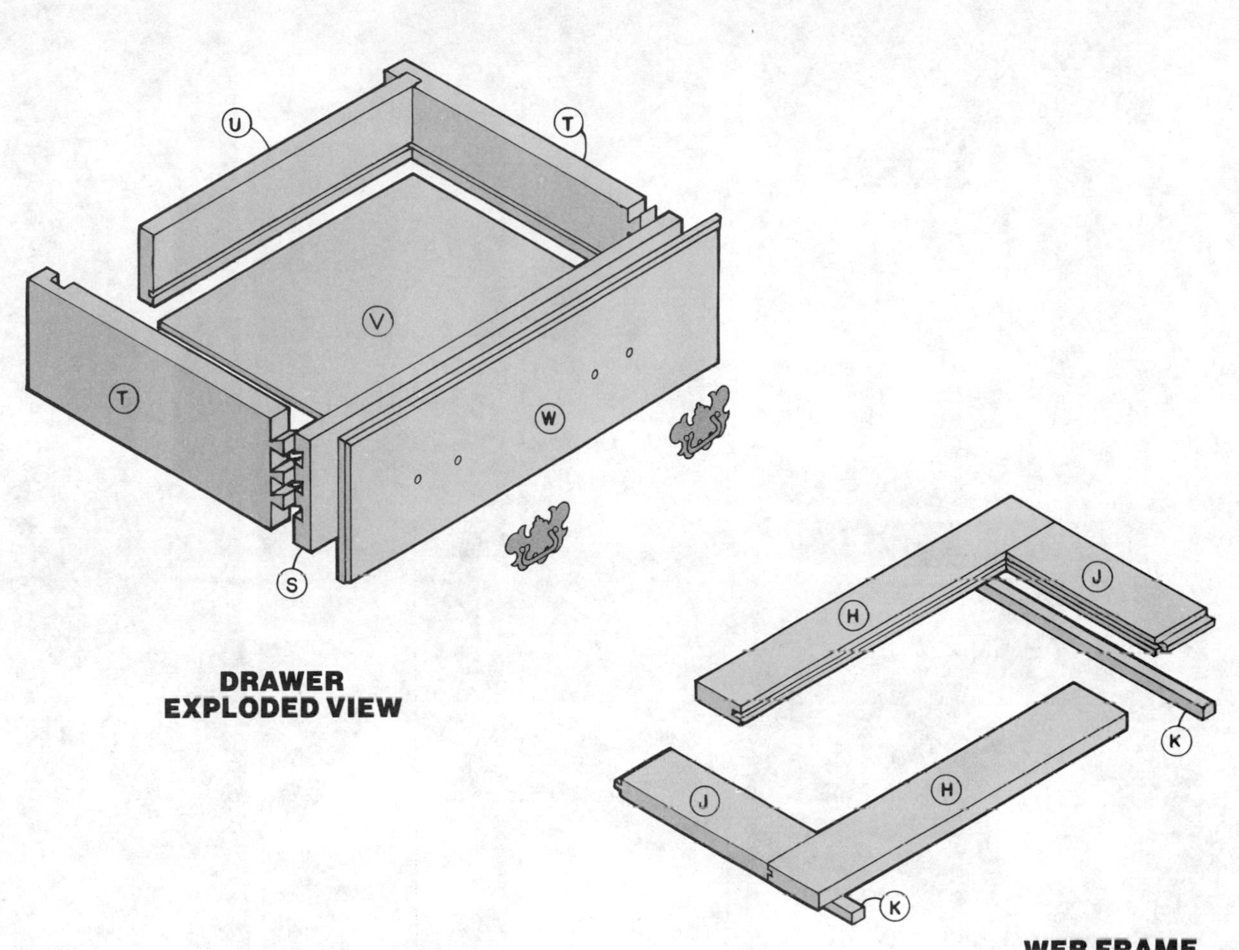

DRAWER EXPLODED VIEW

WEB FRAME EXPLODED VIEW

BILL OF MATERIALS — Bachelor's Chest

Finished Dimensions in Inches

	Part	Dimensions
A.	Sides (2)	¾ x 13¼ x 47¾
B.	Top	¾ x 14¾ x 19½
C.	Back	¼ x 17¼ x 48⅛
D.	Face frame stiles (2)	¾ x 1¼ x 47¾
E.	Face frame top rail	¾ x 1⅜ x 15½
F.	Face frame middle rails (6)	¾ x 1¼ x 15½
G.	Face frame bottom rail	¾ x 2⅛ x 15½
H.	Web frame rails (14)	¾ x 2½ x 17¼
J.	Web frame stiles (14)	¾ x 2½ x 8¾
K.	Kickers (12)	½ x ¾ x 13
L.	Top kickers (2)	¾ x 1⅜ x 13
M.	Legs (4)	2¾ x 2¾ x 11½
N.	Ears (8)	1⅛ x 1½ x 2
P.	Base front	¾ x 4 x 19½
Q.	Base sides (2)	¾ x 4 x 14¾
R.	Base back	¾ x 2¾ x 18
S.	Drawer fronts (7)	¾ x 5⅛ x 15⅜
T.	Drawer sides (14)	¾ x 5⅛ x 13⅛*
U.	Drawer backs (7)	¾ x 5⅛ x 14⅝
V.	Drawer bottoms (7)	¼ x 12¼* x 14⅝
W.	Drawer faces (7)	⅜ x 6 x 16¼
X.	Drawer guides (14)	½ x ¾ x 13
Y.	Front cove molding	½ x ½ x 19
Z	Side cove molding	½ x ½ x 14½
AA.	Dowels (32)	¼ dia. x 2

** These dimensions may change slightly, depending on your router jig or the type of joinery you use to attach the drawer fronts to the drawer sides.*

HARDWARE

Drawer pulls and mounting screws (14)
Tabletop fasteners (8)
#6 x ⅝″ Roundhead wood screws (8)
#8 x 1½″ Roundhead wood screws and washers (4)
#10 x 1¼″ Flathead wood screws (20–24)
#12 x 1¾″ Flathead wood screws (16)
1″ Brads (¼ lb.)

Designed by Nick Engler, built by Chris Walendzak.

Storage Rack and Room Divider

One project does the work of two!

Do you have a large room that you'd like to break up into smaller living and work areas? After you break the room up, will you need to create storage spaces for the individual areas? This project will perform both functions. It's a room divider *and* a storage rack.

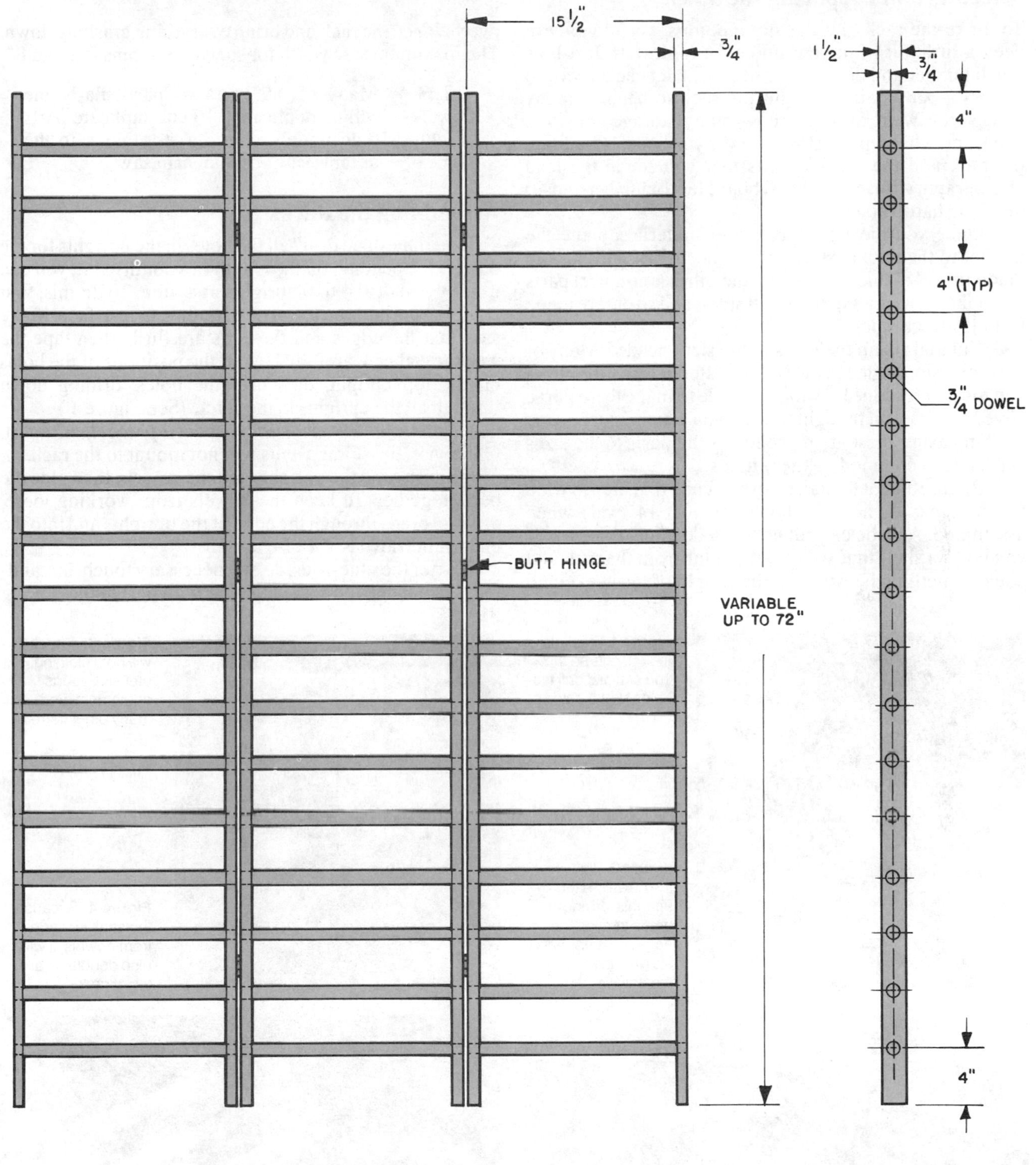

The rack is made and used in a similar manner to a dressing screen. There are two or more panels, each panel hinged to the one beside it. To stand the rack in place, arrange the panels in a zig-zag pattern so that they all support each other.

The panels are constructed like small ladders, but with more rungs. From these rungs you can hang several different storage units — shelves, bins, and hooks. You can even use the rungs themselves as storage for quilts, towels, tablecloths, and other linens. As you hang things on the rack, the open spaces between the rungs begin to fill in. This helps create the illusion of privacy on both sides of the rack, and makes the project an effective room divider as well as a versatile storage system.

Selecting and Preparing the Stock

To make the rack and the storage units, you're going to need a little bit of lumber and a *lot* of dowels. Just how much lumber and dowels you need will depend on several factors — how tall you want the rack to be, how many panels you want to make, how many storage units you need, and what type of storage units you need. In building the rack and the storage units that you see in the lead photograph, we used about 30 board feet of lumber and 40 48″-long hardwood dowels.

Once you have gathered your materials, plane the lumber to the thicknesses that you need. The uprights are made from ¾″-thick stock. All the other non-dowel parts — hooks, shelving supports, bin sides, and so on, are made from ½″-thick stock.

Cut and rip all the parts to the sizes needed. Many of the dimensions listed in the Bill of Materials are variable — you must determine how long or wide to make these parts. Give some careful thought to what you want to store on the rack; measure these items, then cut the parts to the sizes needed to accommodate these items.

Be careful not to make storage units that are too wide for the racks — no unit should be over 14″ wide when assembled. Also be careful not to make them too deep. If you build a shelf that sticks out too far from the rack and place something heavy on it, the weight of the item could overbalance the rack and bring everything crashing down. The maximum safe width for shelves and bins is about 8″.

Tip ◆ Many of the parts — particularly the dowels — will be duplicates. To cut duplicate parts quickly and accurately, clamp a stop block to the fence of your table saw or radial arm saw.

Assembling the Racks

To save time, "pad drill" all the holes in the uprights for the dowels. Depending on the length of your drill bit, you can usually pad drill 4 to 6 uprights at a time. To do this, first stack the uprights on top of one another, face to face. Make sure that the edges and the ends are flush, then tape the stack together. Carefully lay out the positions of the holes on the top upright, then drill the holes, drilling down through all the uprights in the stack. (See Figure 1.)

Note: The dowels *must* be spaced *precisely* 4″ apart. Otherwise, the storage units will not mount to the rack.

Finish sand the uprights and the dowels, then glue the parts together. To keep the dowels from working loose, drive 1″ brads through the edge of the uprights and into the ends of the dowels. (See Figure 2.)

After the glue dries, do any necessary touch-up sanding. Then hinge the racks together with butt hinges.

Figure 1. Stack up the uprights so that you can pad drill the holes for the dowels.

Figure 3. A hook will hold clothing, utensils, sports equipment, and many other items.

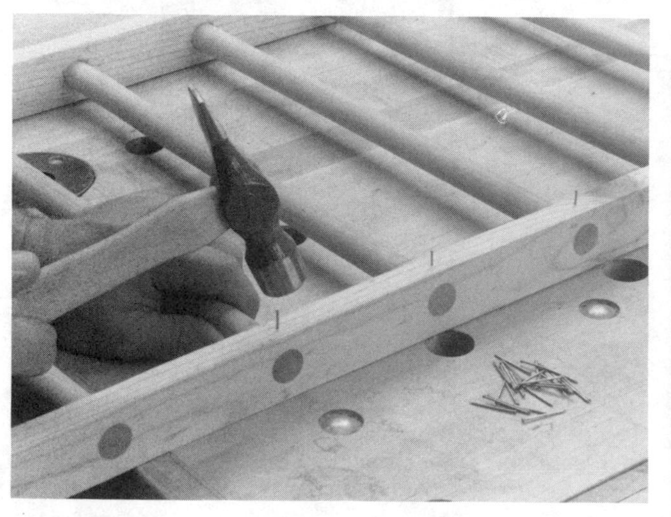

Figure 2. Pin the dowels in the uprights, driving brads through the edge of the uprights and into the ends of the dowels.

Figure 4. Because the shelf is made from dowels, it will also double as a towel rack.

Assembling the Storage Units

We show four different types of storage units in this chapter. (See Figures 3, 4, 5, and 6.) Each of them is built in a different manner.

Tip ◆ As you cut out the parts for each storage unit, pay careful attention to the grain direction, as marked on the working drawings. The grain must run in the proper direction to keep the holders from breaking or splitting.

Hooks — Enlarge the *Hook Layout* and trace it onto a thin piece of hardboard to make a template. Cut out the template with a bandsaw or scroll saw. Sand the sawn edges to remove any saw marks. Use the template to trace the shape of the hook onto the stock, then cut out the hook. Repeat, making as many hooks as you need.

As designed, two areas of the hook shape are weak, and are in danger of breaking. To reinforce these areas, drive 4d finishing nails into the edge of the hook, where shown in the *Hook Layout.* Using your hand-held drill, spin the nails into the wood as far as you can. (See Figure 7.) Then remove the head of the nail from the drill chuck, and hammer the nail the rest of the way into the wood. (See Figure 8.) This combination of spinning and hammering will seat the nail securely without splitting the thin stock.

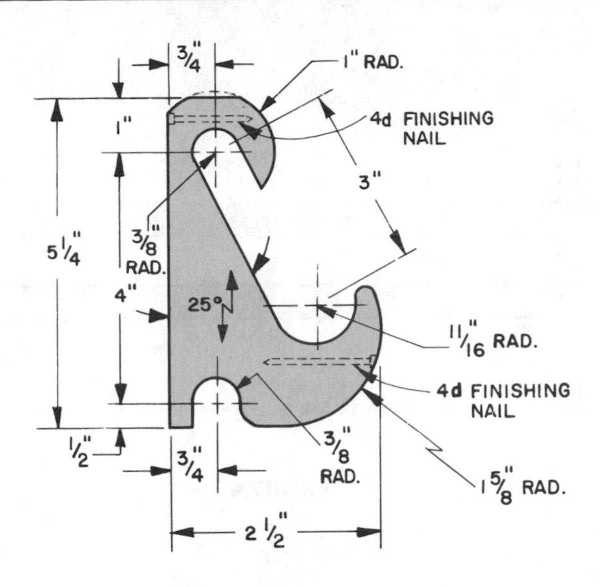

HOOK LAYOUT

After you have reinforced the areas on the hook that require it, sand the sawn edges to remove the saw marks. Finish sand all the surfaces of the hook.

Figure 5. A shallow bin will hold small items such as spices, condiments, collectables, and so on.

Figure 6. The deep bin will hold larger, heavier objects than the shallow bin.

Figure 7. Certain parts of the hooks, shelving supports, and bin holders must be reinforced with finishing nails. To keep the thin wood from splitting, use a hand drill to spin the nails most of the way into the stock...

Figure 8. ...then remove the drill and hammer the nails home.

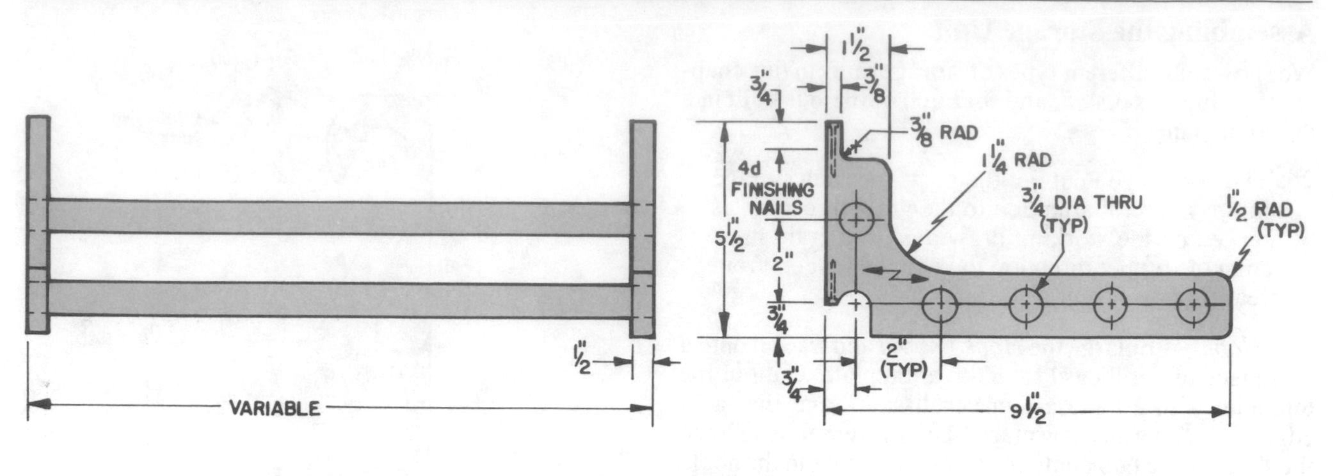

Shelves — Enlarge the *Shelf/Side View* to make a template, then use the template to trace the shape of the shelf support onto the stock. Cut out as many shelf supports as you need. Drill ¾″-diameter holes through the supports and reinforce the weak areas of the supports with 4d finishing nails. The positions of the holes and the nails are shown in the drawings.

Cut the dowels that you need to make the shelves — 5 dowels per shelf. The length of these dowels is variable; they can be as long as you want to make them up to 14″. If you cut them longer than that, the shelf won't fit on the rack.

Finish sand the dowels and the supports, then glue the dowels to the supports. Keep the dowels in place with brads, driving the brads through the edge of the supports and into the ends of the dowels — the same way you pinned the dowels in place in the racks. When the glue dries, do any necessary touch-up sanding.

Tip ◆ You can make a simple variation on this shelf by substituting a solid board for the four bottom dowels. Nail and glue the board between the supports. This will give you a solid shelf.

Shallow and Deep Bins — Both the shallow and the deep bins are built in exactly the same manner. The only difference is in the "holders." The shallow bin attaches to two dowels in the racks and the deep bin hooks to three.

Make a template for the holder and the shapes of the sides. Trace these shapes on the stock, and cut them out. Remember each pair of holders/sides must be *exactly* the same. Reinforce the weak areas of the holders with 4d nails, where shown on the *Holder Layout, Shallow Bin/Side View,* and *Deep Bin/Side View.*

Finish sand all the parts of the bins. Assemble the sides/holders, front, back, and bottom with glue and 1″ brads. After the glue dries, do any necessary touch-up sanding.

Tip ◆ To save time and work, you can "pad saw" up to eight hooks, shelving supports, or bin holders on your bandsaw. Stack up the pieces and hold the stack together with masking tape, just as you did when you pad drilled the uprights. (See Figure 9.)

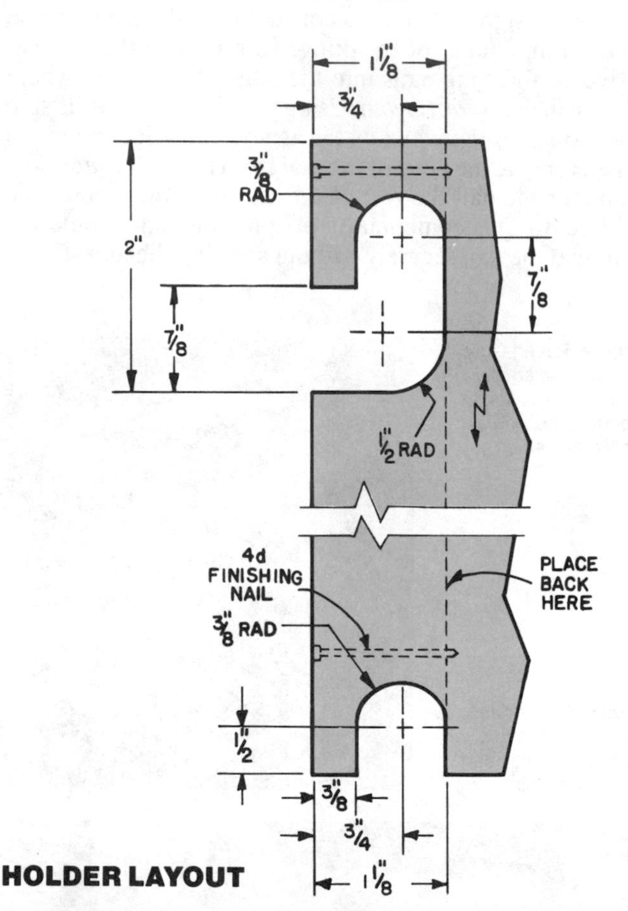

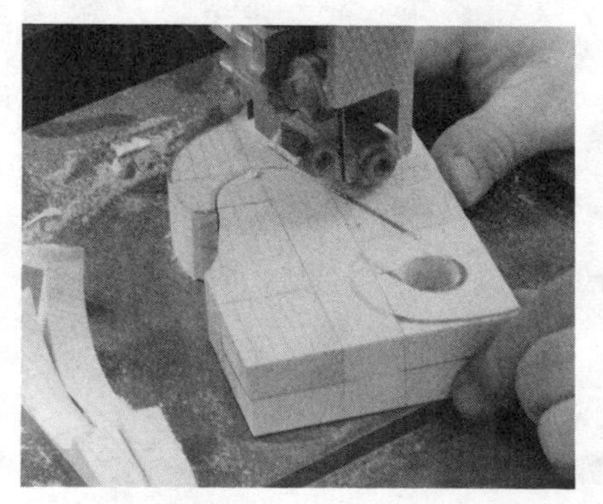

Figure 9. You can make several hooks, shelving supports, or bin holders by pad sawing the shapes on a bandsaw.

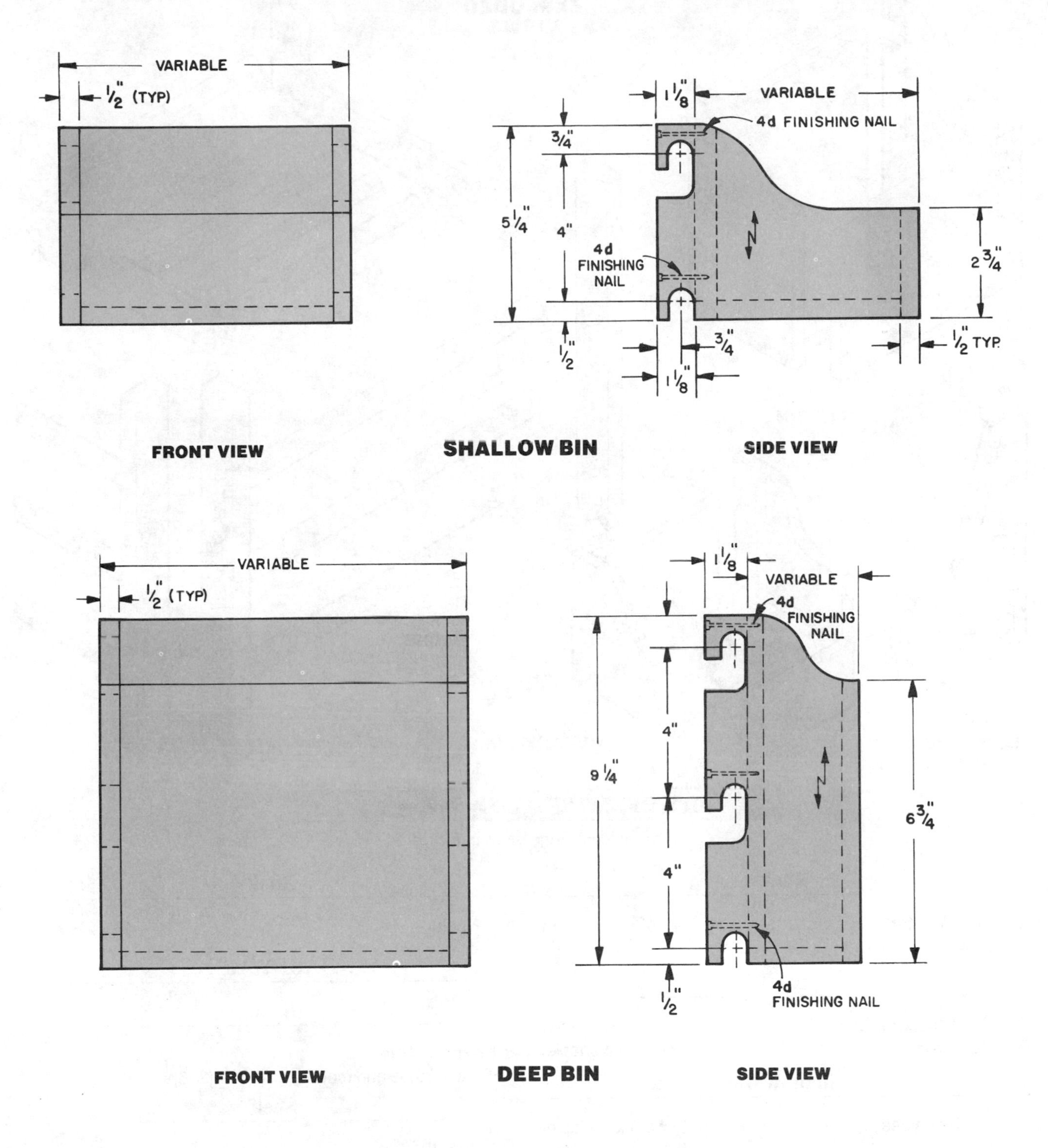

Finishing Up

When you've completed the rack and the storage units, tack the panels of the rack apart, removing the hinges. Select a finish for the completed project. We recommend you avoid "building" finishes — finishes that build up or coat the wood, such as varnish and polyurethane. These may interfere with the various holders, making it harder to get the hooks, shelves, and bins on and off the rack.

Instead, use a penetrating finish such as Danish oil, linseed oil, or tung oil. These soak into the wood without building up on the surface. If you want a bit of color, you can also paint the rack with latex paint, diluted 1:1 with water. This thinned latex paint will act like a stain. It will soak into the wood, coloring it without building up overmuch on the surface.

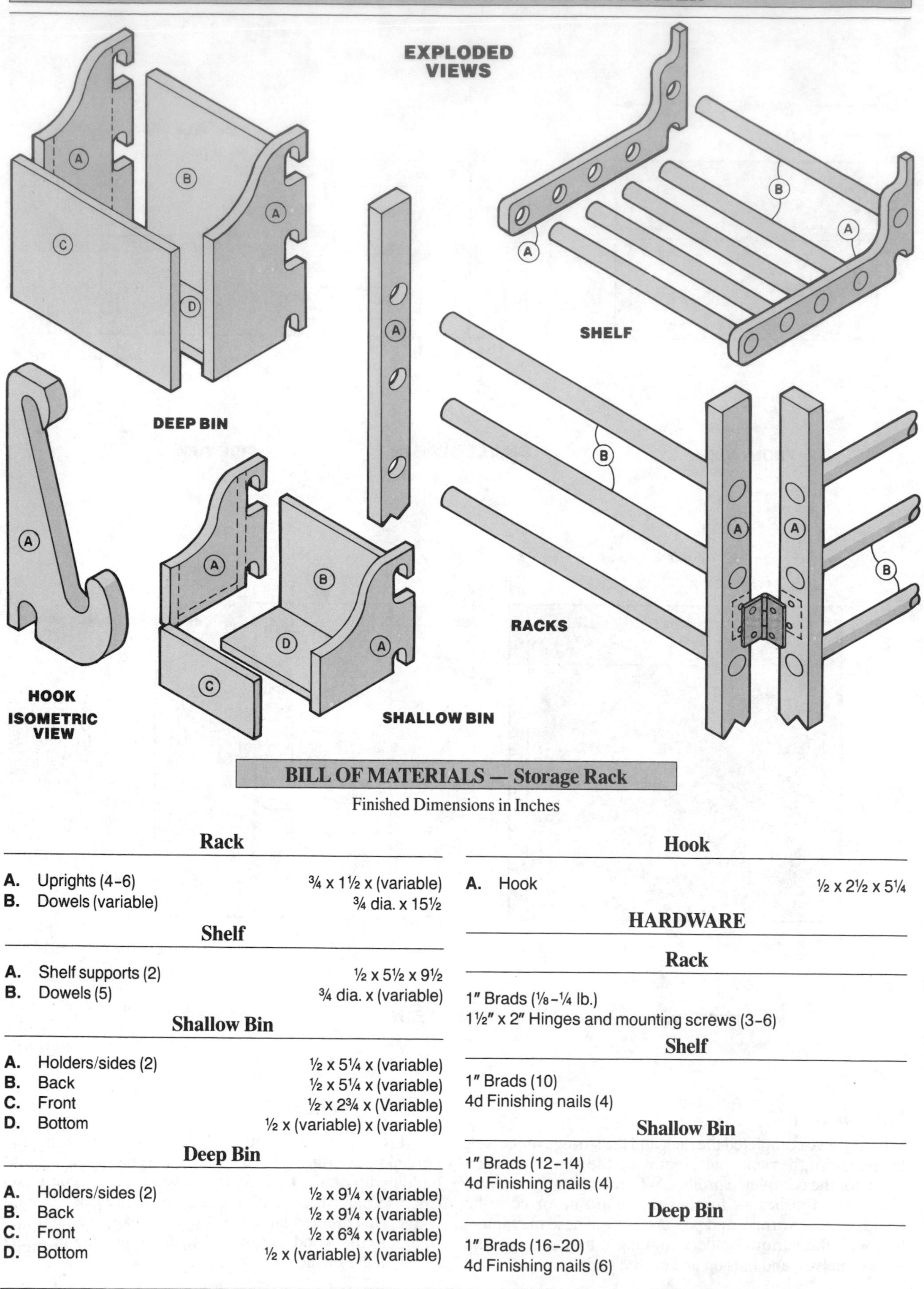

BILL OF MATERIALS — Storage Rack

Finished Dimensions in Inches

Rack

A.	Uprights (4-6)	¾ x 1½ x (variable)
B.	Dowels (variable)	¾ dia. x 15½

Shelf

A.	Shelf supports (2)	½ x 5½ x 9½
B.	Dowels (5)	¾ dia. x (variable)

Shallow Bin

A.	Holders/sides (2)	½ x 5¼ x (variable)
B.	Back	½ x 5¼ x (variable)
C.	Front	½ x 2¾ x (Variable)
D.	Bottom	½ x (variable) x (variable)

Deep Bin

A.	Holders/sides (2)	½ x 9¼ x (variable)
B.	Back	½ x 9¼ x (variable)
C.	Front	½ x 6¾ x (variable)
D.	Bottom	½ x (variable) x (variable)

Hook

A.	Hook	½ x 2½ x 5¼

HARDWARE

Rack

1″ Brads (⅛-¼ lb.)
1½″ x 2″ Hinges and mounting screws (3-6)

Shelf

1″ Brads (10)
4d Finishing nails (4)

Shallow Bin

1″ Brads (12-14)
4d Finishing nails (4)

Deep Bin

1″ Brads (16-20)
4d Finishing nails (6)

Designed and built by Larry Callahan.

Hidden-Wire Audio Rack

This ingenious rack holds your audio equipment and conceals the wiring.

Shelving systems and cabinets that are designed to hold electronic components often give short shrift to the *wires.* There may be a few large holes in the backboard so that you can thread the cords out behind the unit, but that's all. As a result of this oversight, the back of your entertainment centers and audio racks often become an incomprehensible tangle of power cords, patch cords, speaker wires, and antenna wires.

Furthermore, if you have just one nearby power outlet, you can't safely plug all the dangling power cords into this single receptacle. Instead, you have to run extension cords from other outlets. This only adds to the confusion.

Larry Callahan's ingenious design for his audio rack changes all that. Larry is an electronics expert and a music lover from West Milton, Ohio. He has built several racks for friends and family that have *false backs* and hidden compartments to conceal all the various cords and wires. Each rack also has a *power strip* with a built-in circuit-breaker mounted inside the hidden compartment, so that all the power cords can be plugged into a single location. The only wires that extend from the back are a single power cord and a few speaker wires.

Selecting and Preparing the Stock

To make this rack, you'll need several different types of materials. The top, sides, bottom, shelves, doors, and false back are made from cabinet-grade plywood. You'll need one 4′ x 8′ sheet of 1/4″ plywood, and one-and-one-half sheets of 3/4″ plywood. You'll also need some solid wood to trim the edges of this plywood — 4/4 stock planed down to 3/4″ thick. Finally, you'll need 8/4 stock, some of it planed down to 1 7/8″ thick to make the corner posts, and the rest of it cut to 1″-square strips to trim the top.

Select solid wood and plywood that matches. Birch and oak are the most readily available — you can easily find cabinet-grade birch and oak plywood at most building supply centers. Any lumberyard that deals in hardwoods should have a good supply of solid birch and oak. Other species of wood will be harder to get. You'll have to special-order walnut, cherry, and mahogany plywood, even though you can find the solid wood at the lumberyard. In a pinch, you can build the entire project from solid wood.

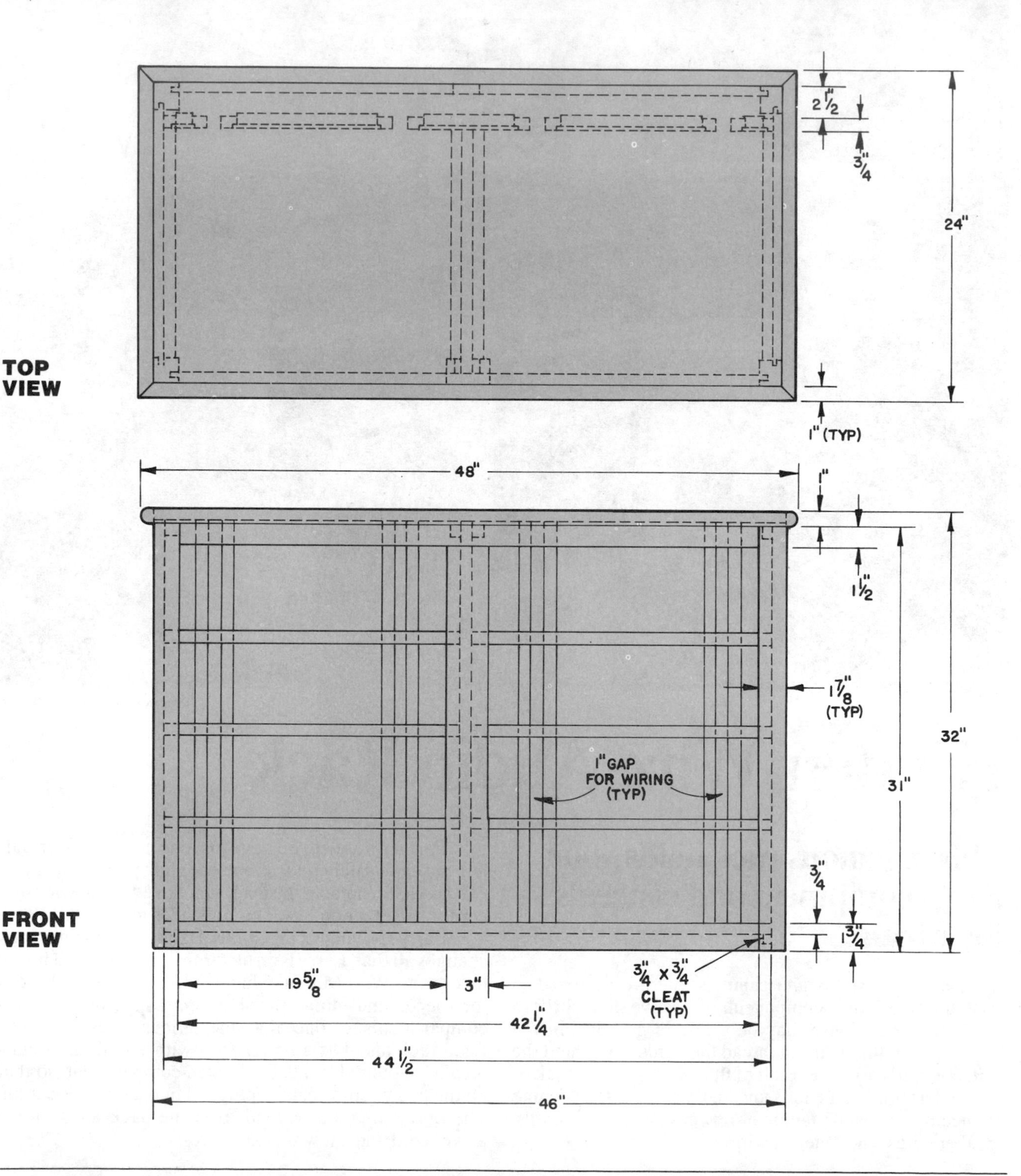

Once you've selected and purchased the wood, cut and rip the parts to the sizes shown in the Bill of Materials. However, *don't* cut the door panels or any of the trim parts to size just yet. Wait until you've assembled the case to make the door panels, so that you can fit the doors to the cabinet. And wait until you've cut the joinery on the plywood parts to make the trim. Depending on how accurately you cut the joinery, you may have to adjust the dimensions of the trim slightly.

Cutting the Joinery

While there are a lot of joints in this project, many of them are repeats. You can use the same power tool setups to cut several different joints in different parts. So as long as you're organized, it shouldn't take you too long to make the joints.

Start by making the joints in the plywood parts. Most of these are best cut with a router. Here's a list:

- ½"-wide x ¼"-deep dadoes in the sides and divider to hold the shelving standards
- ¼"-wide x ⅜"-deep rabbets on all four edges of the top
- ¼"-wide x ⅜"-deep rabbets on the front and back edges of the bottom
- ¼"-wide x ⅜"-deep rabbets on the front edges of the shelves
- ¼"-wide x ¼"-long tenons on all four edges of the sides

Carefully measure the plywood parts after you cut the joints and adjust the dimensions of the trim accordingly. Cut them to size, all except the top trim and the door trim. Don't cut these trim parts to length until you're ready to miter the ends.

Cut the joinery in the solid wood parts:

- ⅜"-wide x ¼"-deep grooves along the inside edges of the top trim parts
- ⅜"-wide x ¼"-deep grooves along the inside faces of the shelf trim
- ⅜"-wide x ¼"-deep grooves along the inside faces of the bottom rails
- ¼"-wide x ¼"-deep grooves along the faces of the corner posts that join the sides
- ¼"-wide x ¼"-deep *blind* grooves in the faces of the corner posts that join the rails
- ¼"-wide x ¼"-deep grooves along the inside edges of the side trim
- ¼"-wide x ¼"-deep grooves along the inside edges of the door trim
- ¼"-wide x ¼"-long tenons on the ends of the side trim
- ¼"-wide x ¼"-deep rabbets along the inside edges of the false back trim

Most of these joints are fairly easy to make, but the blind grooves in the posts require some special care. You can make them with a hand-held router, but it's much easier to use an overarm router or a router table, if you have them.

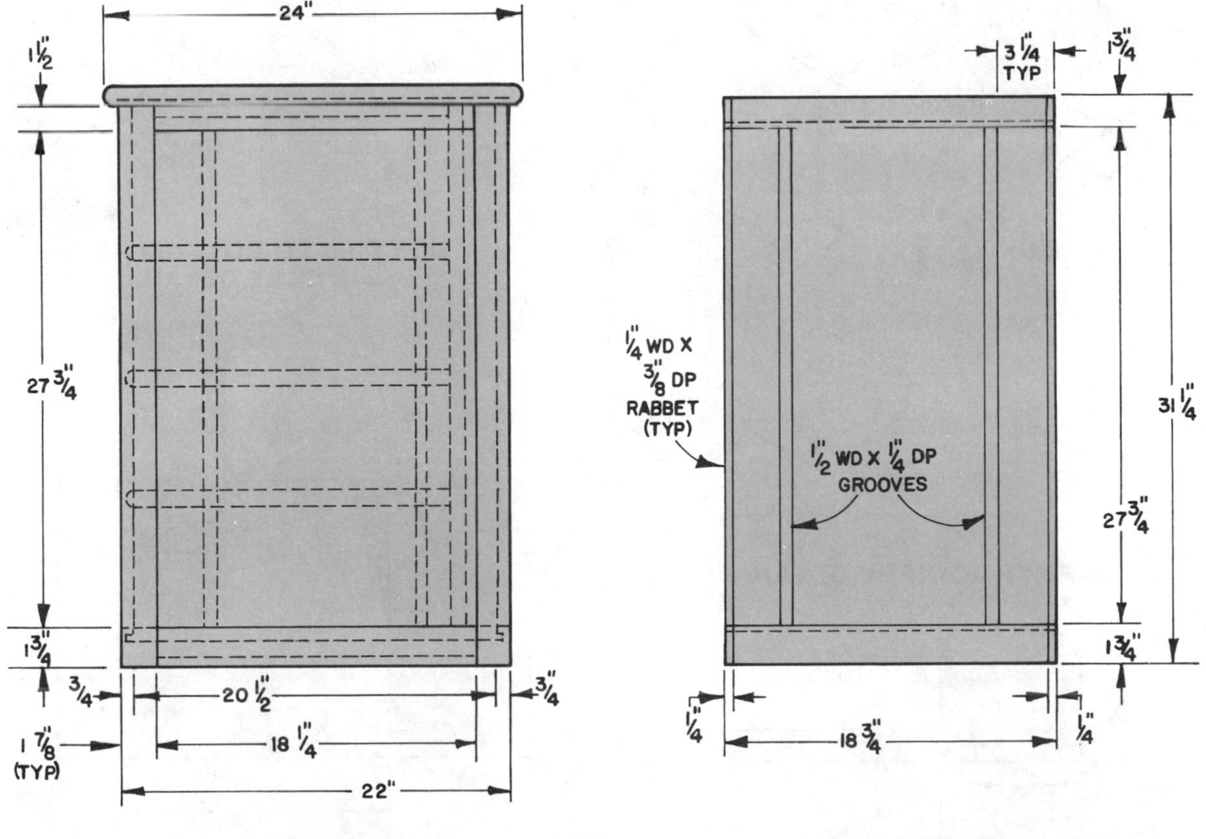

SIDE VIEW

SIDE & SIDE TRIM LAYOUT

Figure 1. Make the blind grooves in the legs with either a router table or a router arm, if you have one. Attach stops to the fence to stop the cut.

Use a fence to guide the wood and a stop block to stop the cut when it reaches the proper length. (See Figure 1.)

There are just a few odd joints to finish up: Miter the ends of the top trim to fit the top. Round the bottom edges of the tenons of the rails, so that they fit the blind grooves. Also, drill dowel holes to join the middle posts and the rails. Countersink pilot holes for flathead screws in the cleats. And while you're at the drill press, make the 1 1/8"-diameter holes in the back middle rail for the power cords.

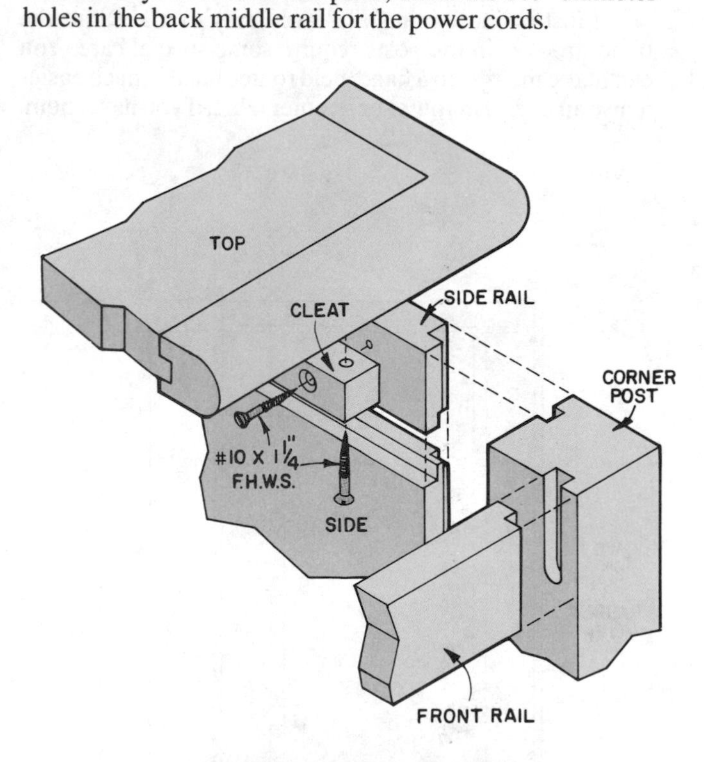

CORNER JOINERY DETAIL

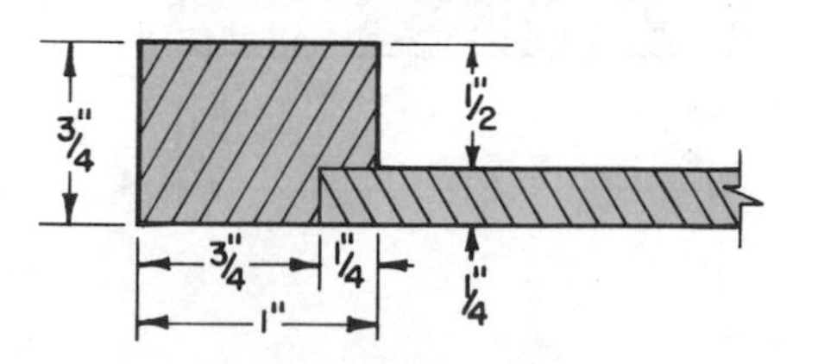

FALSE BACK JOINERY DETAIL

Rounding the Edges

To give the completed project a soft, contemporary look, many of the edges are rounded. Some of these have to be rounded before you assemble the parts; others can wait till after assembly. At this time, round the edges of the top trim, shelf trim, and the outside corners of the corner posts.

Note: This step is optional. If you prefer a harder look, you may leave the corners sharp. For a look somewhere in between hard and soft, just "break" the edges with a hand plane.

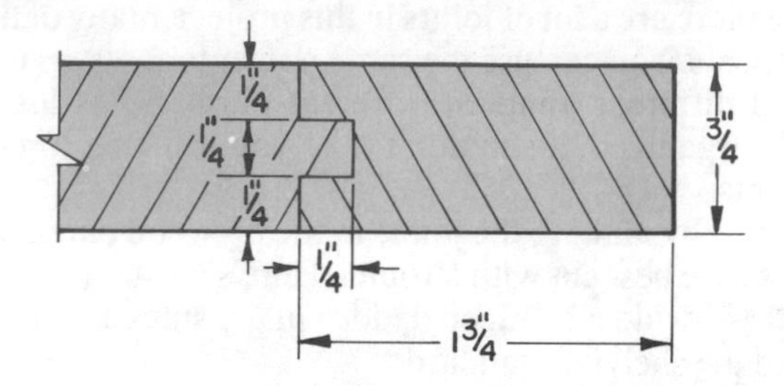

SIDE TRIM JOINERY DETAIL

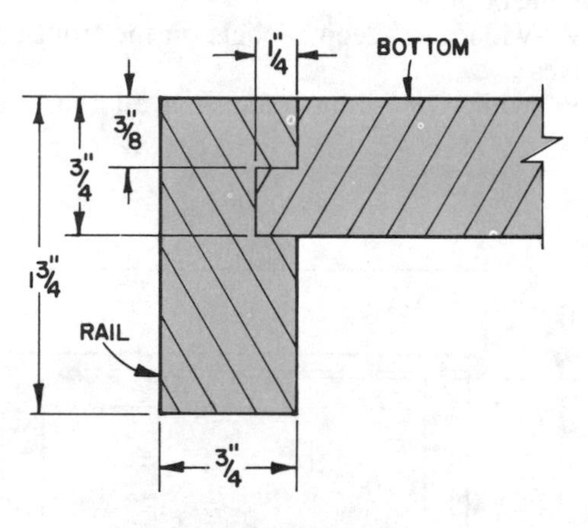

BOTTOM-TO-BOTTOM RAIL JOINERY DETAIL

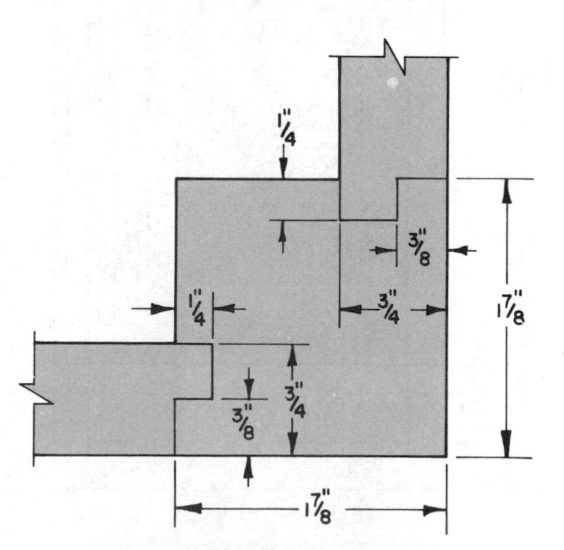

CORNER POST JOINERY DETAIL

Assembling the Trim to the Plywood Parts

Lightly sand all the parts you have made so far to remove the mill marks. Don't finish-sand them yet; that will come after you've partially assembled the pieces.

Dry assemble the parts, checking the fit of the joints. If necessary, do a little touch-up work with hand chisels to get the parts to fit precisely. Then glue together the following parts:

- The top trim to the top
- The side trim to the sides
- The middle posts to the rails and the rails to the corner posts
- The false back trim to the false back panels
- The shelf trim to the shelves
- The middle post sides and spacers to the divider

As you glue these parts up, be very careful that the parts remain square to each other. This is an especially important concern when gluing the rails to the corner posts. If these parts aren't square, then the case won't go together properly.

Wipe off any excess glue with a *very* wet rag — wet enough to completely dissolve the glue so that it doesn't remain in the pores of the wood. This will raise the grain slightly, but you'll never notice it after you finish sand the assemblies. If you let the excess glue dry on the wood, you run the risk of gouging the plywood veneers when you scrape the glue off.

3/4"
1"
1/4"
3/8"
1"
ROUND OVER

TOP TRIM & SHELF TRIM JOINERY DETAIL

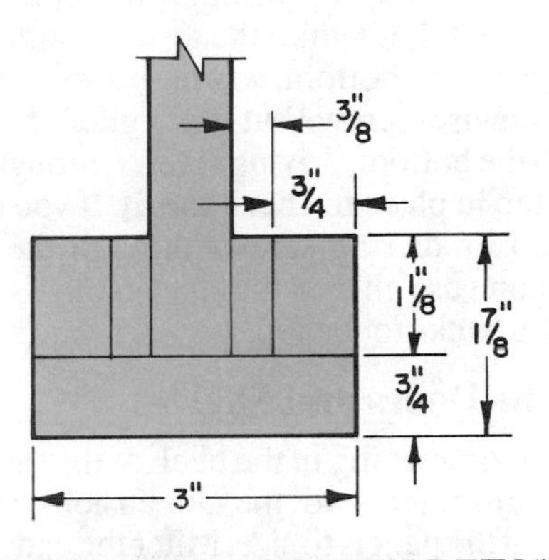

CENTER POST JOINERY DETAIL

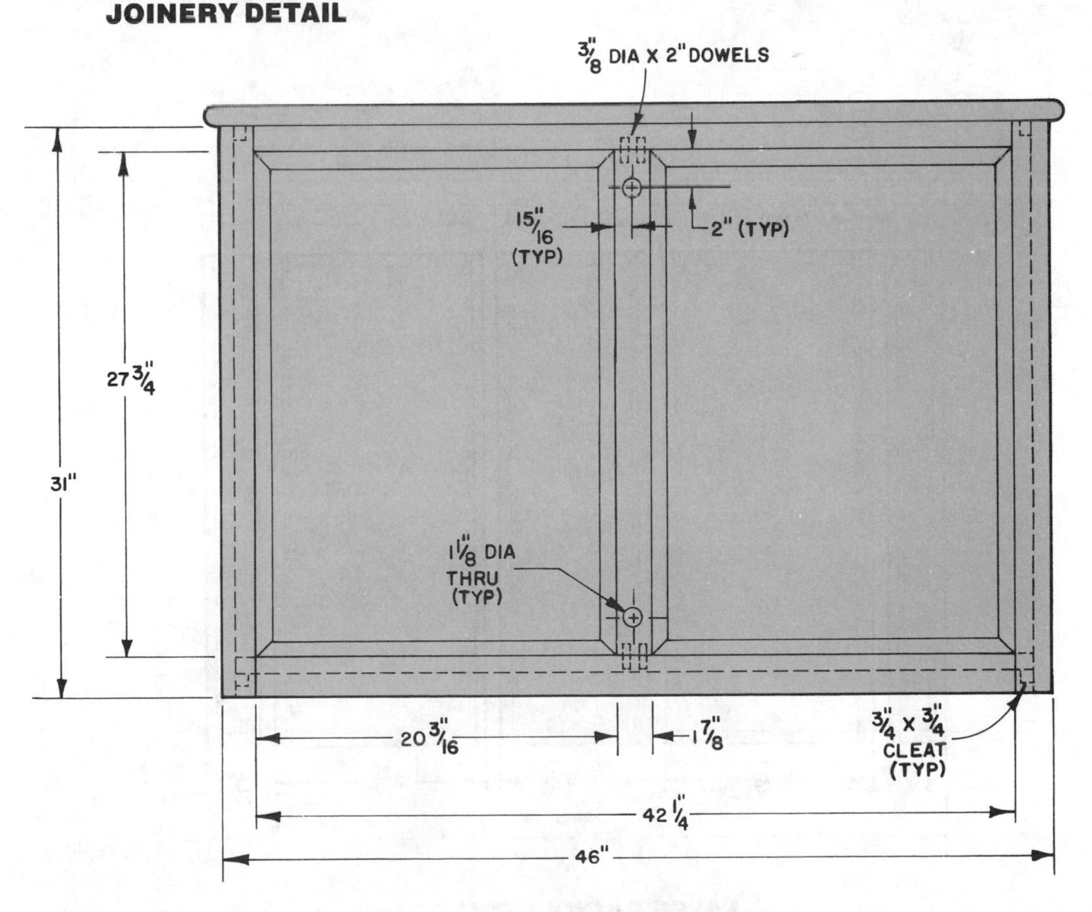

BACK VIEW

Assembling the Case

Finish sand all the parts and assemblies. Be very careful not to sand the plywood too much. You don't want to sand away the veneer. Attach the shelving standards to the side assemblies and divider assembly with screws.

Dry assemble the bottom, side assemblies, front assembly, and back assembly to check the fit. If you're satisfied with the way these parts go together, glue them up. Check that the case is square before you clamp up the parts. While the glue is drying on the case, glue the false back cleats to false back assemblies, flush with the top and bottom edge.

When the glue dries on the case, remove the clamps. Glue the divider in place, and reinforce the glue joints by driving flathead screws up through the bottom into the divider. Screw (but don't glue) the top and bottom cleats to the sides, divider, and bottom, where shown in the working drawings. Likewise, screw (but don't glue) the false back assemblies to the bottom, driving screws through the cleats.

Put the top in place to check the fit. If you're satisfied, secure the top by driving screws through the top cleats. Once again, don't use glue on the cleat joint. Also, screw the top of the false backs to the top.

Figure 2. Magnetic Tutch-Latches® open the doors when you push on them and eliminate the need for door pulls. Without the pulls, you can put the audio rack flush against a wall.

Installing the Doors and Shelves

Measure the door opening in the back of the case. If necessary, make adjustments to the dimensions of the door panels, then cut the panels to size. Miter the ends of the door trim and glue it to the door panels.

Tip ◆ Some woodworkers prefer to make their door slightly oversize, then plane down the edges. This way, they can get a perfect fit.

Mortise the door and the corner posts for the butt hinges, then hang the doors in the opening. To keep the doors closed, install magnetic Tutch-Latches® near the bottom inside corner of each door. (See Figure 2.)

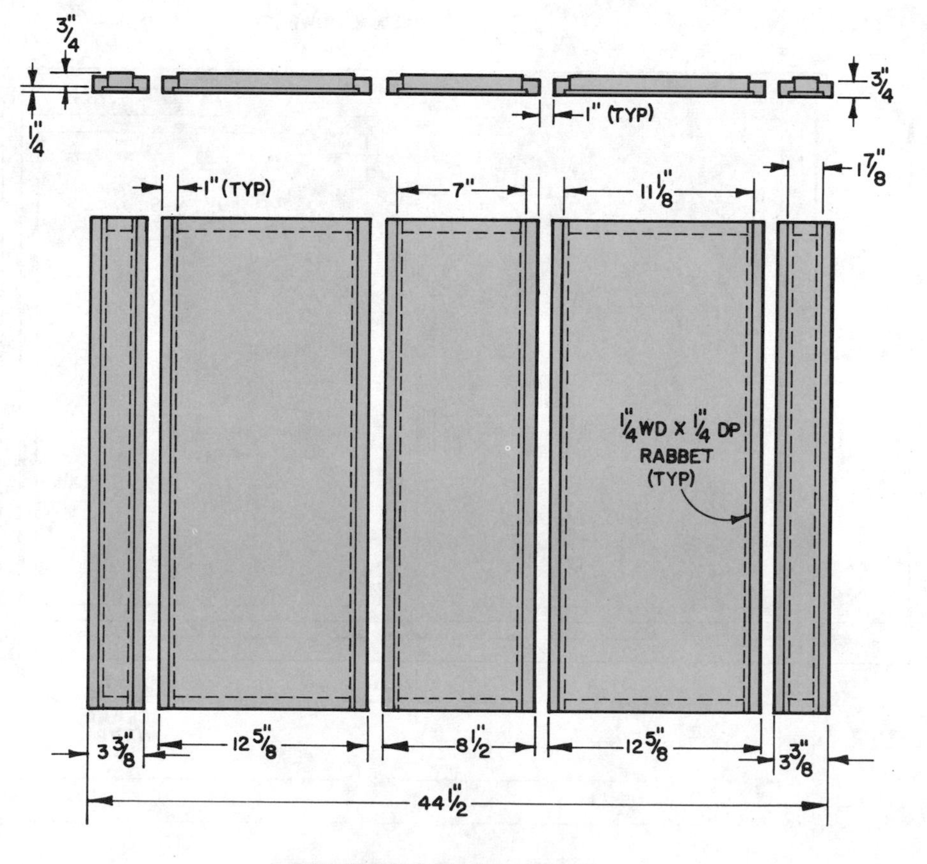

FALSE BACK LAYOUT

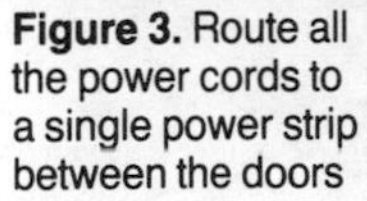

Figure 3. Route all the power cords to a single power strip between the doors and the false back. Then you only have to plug a single cord into an outlet.

Once the doors are in place, check the inside measurements of the case to see how the shelves will fit. If necessary, adjust the dimensions of the shelves and trim them down to size. With a bandsaw or a backsaw, cut the notches in the front corners of each shelf as shown in the *Shelf Layout.* Install clips in the shelving standards to hold the shelves, then lay the shelves in place on top of these clips.

Finishing Up

Once you've completely assembled and fitted all the parts, remove the shelves, doors, and all the hardware from the completed case. If you wish, round the inside edges of the front opening to further soften the appearance of the piece. Do any necessary touch-up sanding, and apply a finish.

When the finish dries, turn the case over and install inside glides in the bottoms of the corner posts. (If you want to make this piece movable, you could install casters instead.) Then re-install the doors and shelves.

Finally, mount a power strip inside the case, between the doors and the false back. (See Figure 3.) Make sure this power strip is rated for sufficient amperage to handle all the electronic equipment you plan to put in the completed rack. Also, make sure the power strip has a built-in breaker. When you arrange the equipment in the rack, run the cord in between the gaps in the false back and plug them into the strip. Run the cord from the strip out of one of the holes in the rails and plug it into a wall outlet.

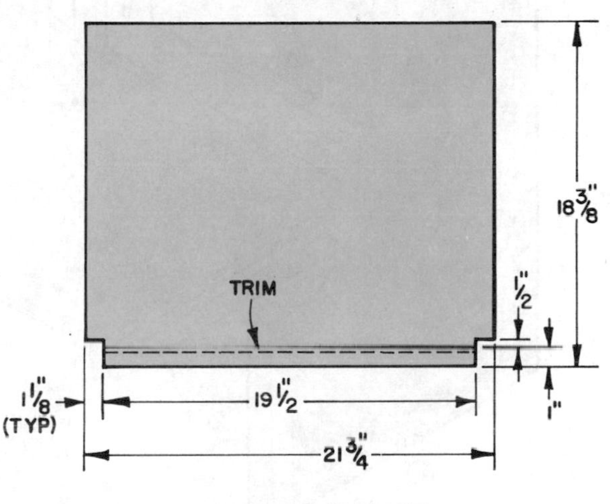

SHELF LAYOUT

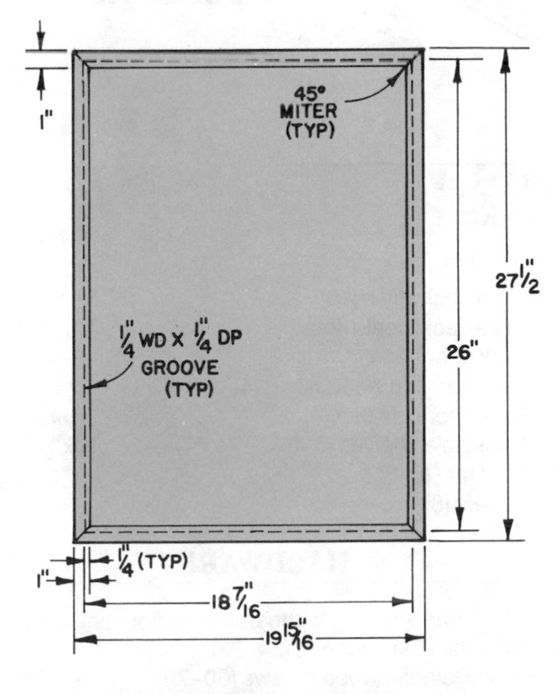

BACK DOOR LAYOUT

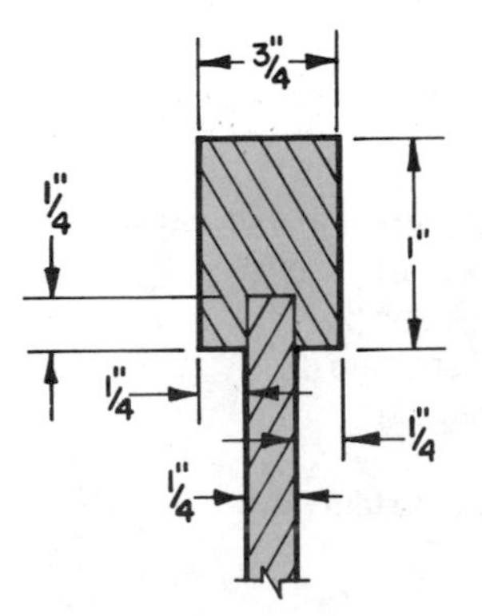

DOOR JOINERY DETAIL

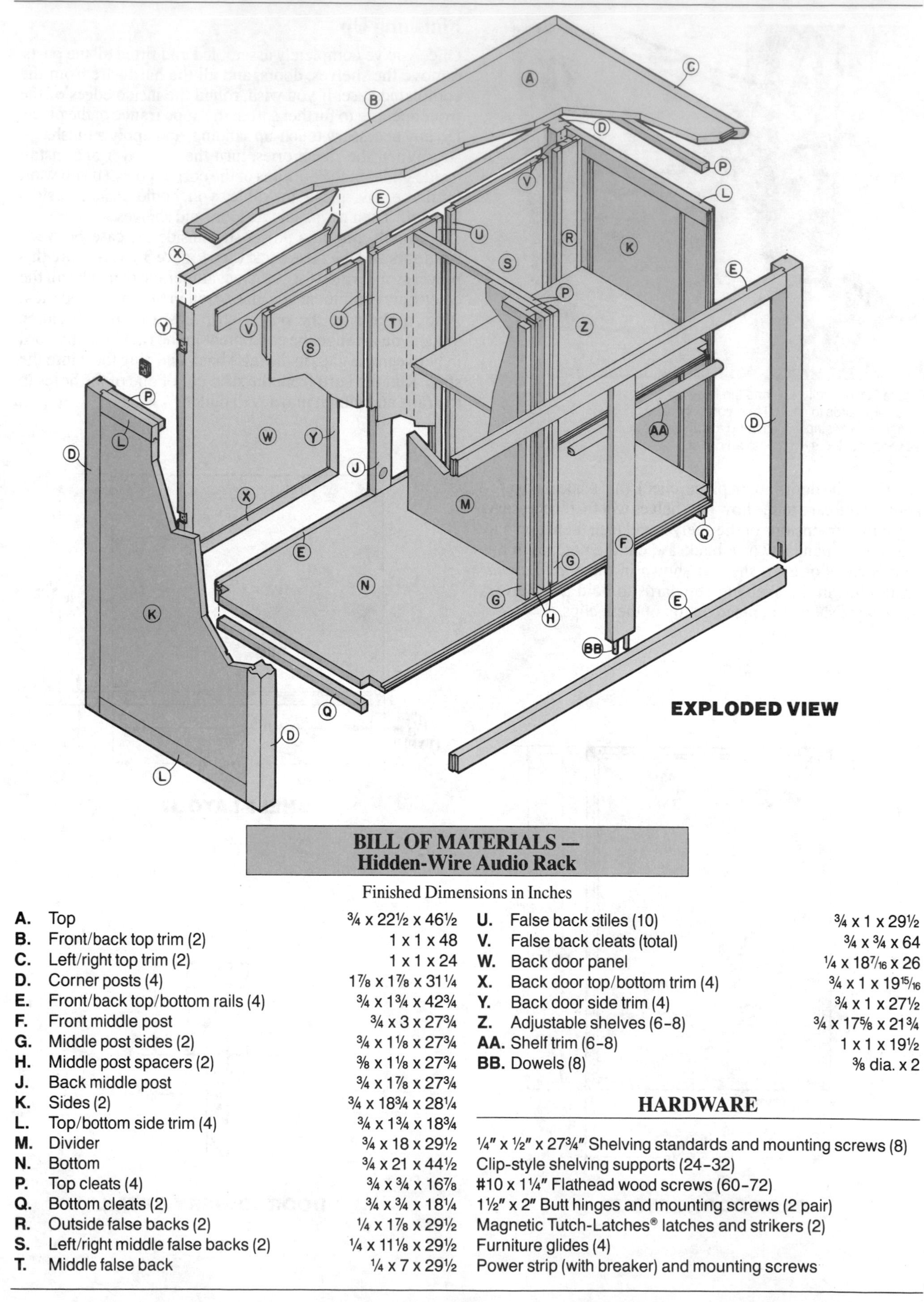

BILL OF MATERIALS — Hidden-Wire Audio Rack

Finished Dimensions in Inches

Part	Description	Dimensions
A.	Top	¾ x 22½ x 46½
B.	Front/back top trim (2)	1 x 1 x 48
C.	Left/right top trim (2)	1 x 1 x 24
D.	Corner posts (4)	1⅞ x 1⅞ x 31¼
E.	Front/back top/bottom rails (4)	¾ x 1¾ x 42¾
F.	Front middle post	¾ x 3 x 27¾
G.	Middle post sides (2)	¾ x 1⅛ x 27¾
H.	Middle post spacers (2)	⅜ x 1⅛ x 27¾
J.	Back middle post	¾ x 1⅞ x 27¾
K.	Sides (2)	¾ x 18¾ x 28¼
L.	Top/bottom side trim (4)	¾ x 1¾ x 18¾
M.	Divider	¾ x 18 x 29½
N.	Bottom	¾ x 21 x 44½
P.	Top cleats (4)	¾ x ¾ x 16⅞
Q.	Bottom cleats (2)	¾ x ¾ x 18¼
R.	Outside false backs (2)	¼ x 1⅞ x 29½
S.	Left/right middle false backs (2)	¼ x 11⅛ x 29½
T.	Middle false back	¼ x 7 x 29½
U.	False back stiles (10)	¾ x 1 x 29½
V.	False back cleats (total)	¾ x ¾ x 64
W.	Back door panel	¼ x 18 7/16 x 26
X.	Back door top/bottom trim (4)	¾ x 1 x 19 15/16
Y.	Back door side trim (4)	¾ x 1 x 27½
Z.	Adjustable shelves (6–8)	¾ x 17⅝ x 21¾
AA.	Shelf trim (6–8)	1 x 1 x 19½
BB.	Dowels (8)	⅜ dia. x 2

HARDWARE

¼″ x ½″ x 27¾″ Shelving standards and mounting screws (8)
Clip-style shelving supports (24–32)
#10 x 1¼″ Flathead wood screws (60–72)
1½″ x 2″ Butt hinges and mounting screws (2 pair)
Magnetic Tutch-Latches® latches and strikers (2)
Furniture glides (4)
Power strip (with breaker) and mounting screws

Designed and built by David T. Smith.

Tilt-Top Occasional Table

This country-style tilt-top table looks just as pretty with the top up or down.

Do you find yourself short of table space now and then, during large family gatherings and other special occasions? You can solve that problem with this handsome, traditional "occasional" table. The table is so called because it's only used occasionally as a table.

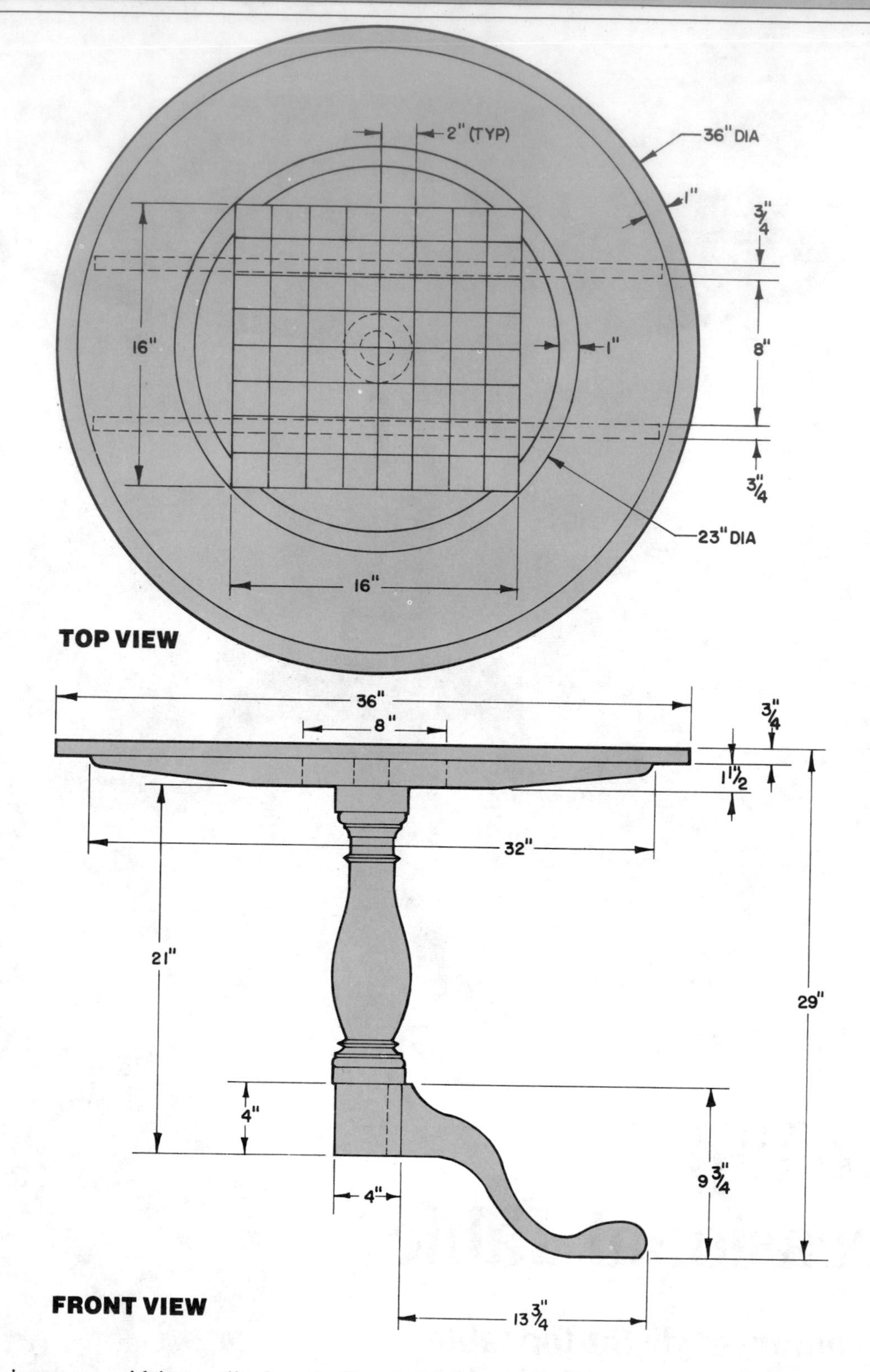

Most of the time it's in storage, with its top tilted vertically, sitting flat against a wall.

Because these tables spend so much of their time with the top vertical, the tops were often gaily painted. This helped provide decoration, turning an otherwise utilitarian piece of furniture into a bit of folk art. These paintings could be anything from "grain" paintings (paint applied to imitate fancy wooden veneers and inlays) to an actual scene or portrait. This particular table was painted with a bright checkerboard pattern, so that it could be used occasionally as a gaming table, as well as for eating and serving.

Despite its antique appearance, this table is a contemporary interpretation of an historical piece. It was built at the Workshops of David T. Smith, near Morrow, Ohio. David, and the craftsmen who work with him, specialize in making "museum-quality" reproductions of old country furniture. Except for the date, this table is indistinguishable from a valuable antique.

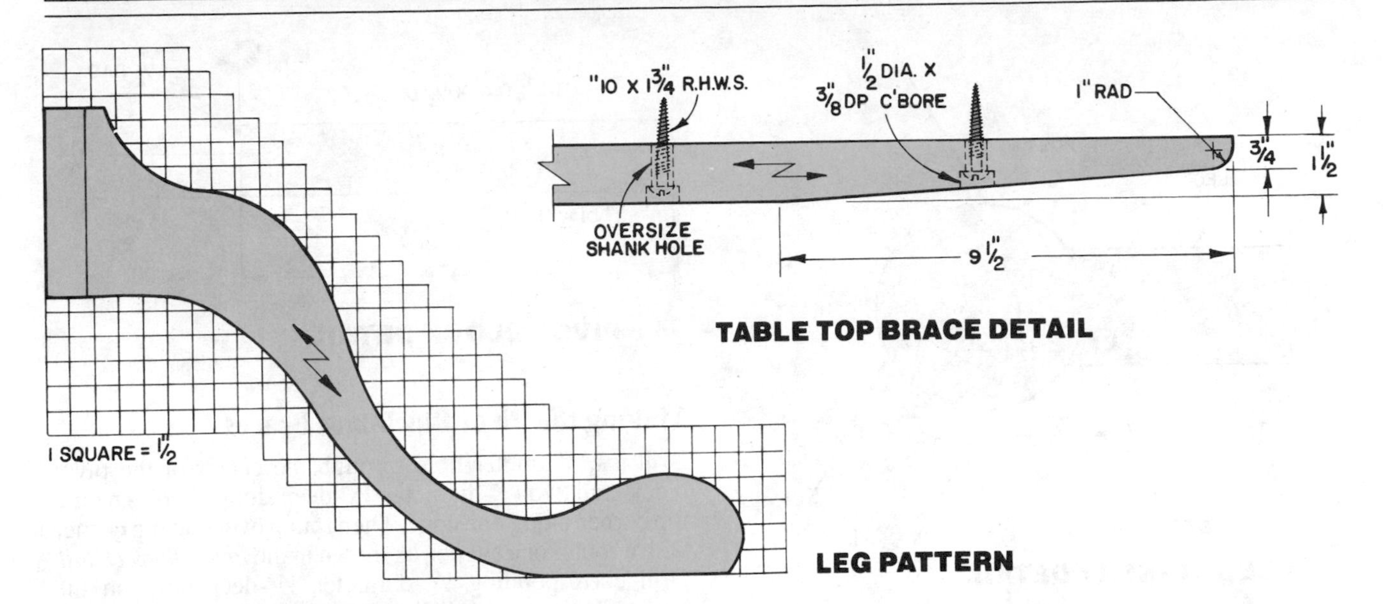

Choosing and Preparing the Stock

When selecting the lumber for this project, look for clear, straight grains especially for the legs. Burls and knots can be very attractive, but they may weaken this particular piece. If the wood grains in the legs are not straight, the legs may break at the ankles.

The stock for the top and the post may have some figuring. But be wary of using boards for the top that may warp or cup when the weather changes. The top is only lightly braced, and it could give you trouble later on, long after you've finished the project. Bring the lumber into the shop and let it sit for several weeks until it gets acclimated to an indoor environment. Then inspect any individual boards for cups and warps. If you find any, set the defective board aside and use another.

> **Tip ◆** If you can find it, use quarter-sawn or rift-sawn lumber for the top. This particular type of lumber is more stable and less prone to cupping than plain-sawn lumber.

Cut and rip the braces, wedges, and the pivot block to the size shown in the Bill of Materials. Make the other parts slightly oversize. Glue up the pieces for the top, positioning the boards so that the end grains (growth rings) all curve in the same direction, *towards* the top surface. This way, if the top warps, it will bow up in the center, where the braces are thickest and strongest. Unless the warp is very pronounced, the braces should be strong enough at this point to keep the top flat.

Enlarge the *Leg Pattern,* make a template, and lay out the shape of the legs on the stock *before* you cut the stock to size. Pay careful attention to the grain direction in the legs, as shown in the pattern. The grain running through the ankle should be as long as possible.

Cutting the Parts to Shape

Lay out the shapes of the top and the braces, as shown in the *Top View* and *Table Top Brace Detail.* Using a bandsaw, cut these shapes from the stock. Then sand the sawn edges of the top and braces to remove the saw marks.

There's no sense in sanding the legs until you have completely shaped them. You'll do this later, after you have cut the joinery.

> **Tip ◆** When sanding the table, take care to preserve a "fair" curve — that is, an even curve with no flat spots. Keep the sander moving, and be careful not to sand any one place too much.

Joining the Legs and the Post

The legs are joined to the post with sliding dovetails. Because of the dimensions of the parts involved, you can't make these *entirely* by machine, using ordinary home workshop tools. They will require some hand work. But the joints aren't particularly difficult to make if you work carefully.

Make the dovetail tenons on the ends of the legs first. Carefully mark the shapes of the tenons on the *bottom* surface of each leg. Also mark a piece of 2″-thick scrap — you want to cut an extra tenon in this scrap to use as a template when you carve the slots. Cut the faces of the tenons on a table saw. Tilt the blade at 10° and position the rip fence to guide the stock. Cut one side of a leg, then turn the stock around and cut the other side. (See Figure 1.) Repeat for all the legs and the scrap.

Figure 1. Cut the faces of the dovetail tenons with your table saw. Tilt the blade (or the table) at 10°.

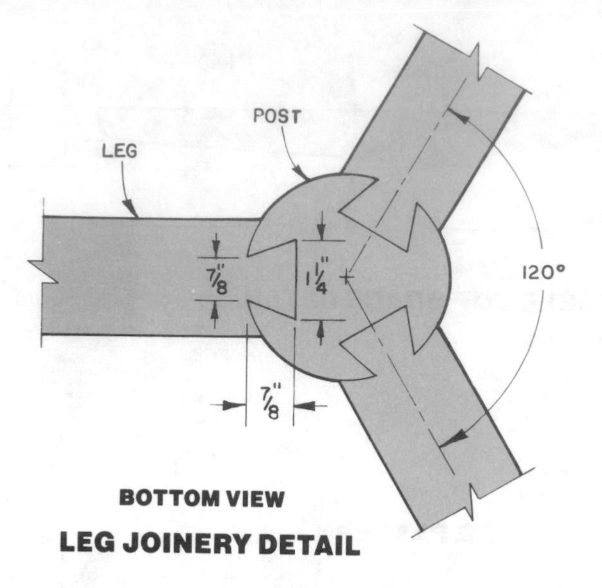

LEG JOINERY DETAIL

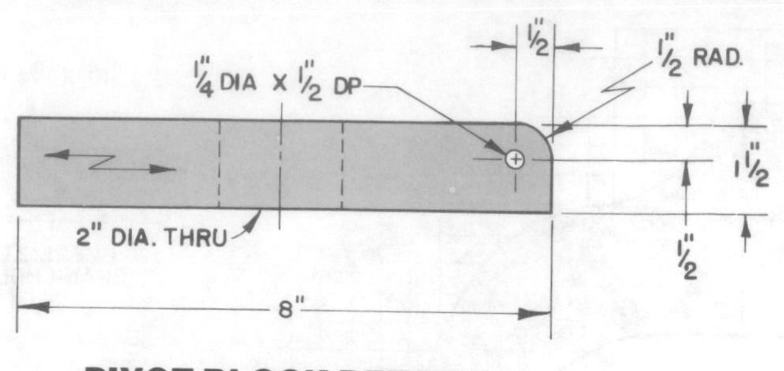

PIVOT BLOCK DETAIL

Cut the waste free from the tenons on a bandsaw. (See Figure 2.) To keep the legs and the scrap stable while you saw them, clamp them in a wooden hand screw. Remember, the shoulder of the tenon must follow the same curved contour as the surface of the post.

Turn the post stock to a 4″-diameter cylinder, then turn 4″ of the bottom end down to 3⅝″ in diameter. Lightly sand this portion of the post. Do *not* turn any other shapes in the post at this time. These shouldn't be turned until *after* you've cut the joinery. Otherwise, you may damage some of the portions of the turning.

Carefully mark the location of the dovetail slots on the bottom of the post, as shown in the *Leg Joinery Detail/ Bottom View.* Mount the post in a V-jig, and remove as much waste from the slots as possible by drilling a series of ⅞″-diameter, ⅞″-deep stopped holes down the center of the slots. A Forstner bit works best for this procedure. (See Figure 3.)

Carefully remove the remainder of the waste from the slots with a sharp bench chisel. Check your progress every so often with the tenon you cut in the scrap. (See Figure 4.) Be careful not to pare away too much stock — the tenon should fit snug.

Making the Pivot Block and Braces

Drill a 2″-diameter hole through the center of the pivot block, and two ¼″-diameter, ½″-deep stopped holes near a top corner, along one edge. Then round over that top corner with a router or a shaper, as shown in the *Pivot Block Detail.* Drill corresponding ¼″-diameter, ½″-deep holes in the braces. These holes will be used to hinge the top to the post.

Also, drill holes in the edges of the braces for the screws that you will use to mount the braces to the top. Each brace should have four holes, evenly spaced along the length. Counterbore each hole to hide the heads of the screw. Then drill the shank holes slightly oversize — ¼″ in diameter for #10 screws. These oversize holes will allow the top to expand and contract with changes in humidity and temperature.

Completing the Shapes of the Legs and Post

Using a drawknife or a spokeshave, carefully round over the top edge of the legs. (See Figure 5.) Pare the stock in the middle of each leg so that the ankle tapers down to 1″ wide, then flares out again at the foot to 2″ wide. This is shown in the *Leg Detail/End View* drawing. Fine-shape the legs with double-cut files. When you're finished, the feet should appear slightly bulbous.

Put the post back on the lathe and complete the turning, as shown in the *Post Layout.* Carefully turn the round tenon on the top of the post to *exactly* 2″ in diameter. Then finish-sand the turning on the lathe. *Do not* sand the round tenon on the top of the post, or the last 4″ on the bottom of the post. If you do, you'll change the diameters slightly. The legs and the pivot block may not fit.

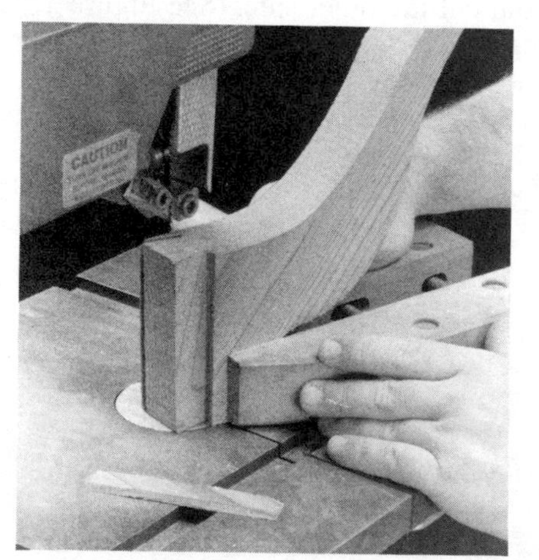

Figure 2. Remove the waste from either side of the tenons with a bandsaw. Clamp the legs in wood screws to hold them upright.

Figure 3. Drill a series of holes to remove as much waste as possible from the dovetail slots.

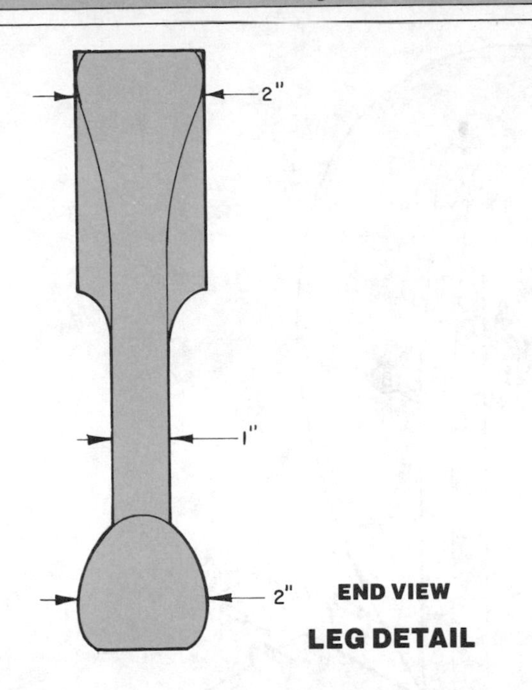

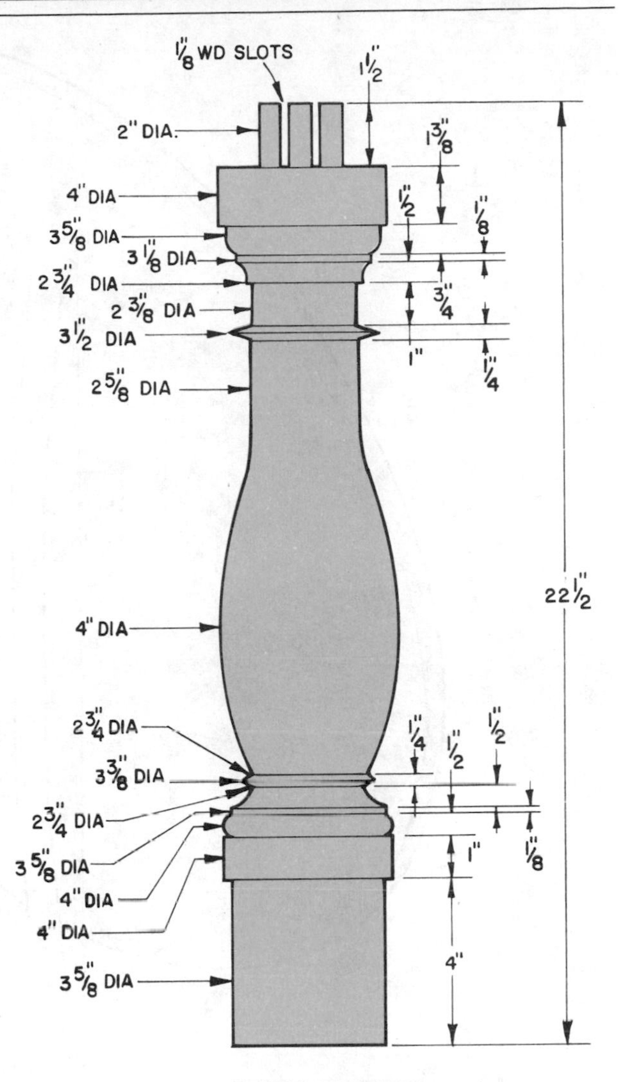

After you remove the post from the lathe, cut two slots in the round tenon. Later on, you'll drive wedges into these slots to secure the pivot block to the post.

Assembling the Table

Install the striker plate for the catch in the pivot block. Insert the metal pins in the stopped holes, and put the braces in place on either side of the block. Using toothpicks, space the braces about 1/16" away from the pivot block so that they won't rub. Clamp this assembly to the underside of the table top.

Secure the braces to the table top with roundhead wood screws. *Do not* glue the braces in place. Then install the catch, screwing it to the underside of the top, just opposite the striker plate. Check the action of the block and the latch.

With the table top still upside down, glue the post to the pivot block. Release the catch, tilt the post, and drive the wedges into the slots in the round tenon. Raise the post so that it's upright again and glue the legs in their slots.

Let the glue cure completely, then remove the braces and all the hardware. Do any necessary touch-up sanding on the completed table and apply a finish. Be careful to apply as many coats to the underside of the table top as you do to the top side. This will ensure that both surfaces will "breathe" evenly, losing and gaining moisture at an even rate. This, in turn, will help keep the top from warping. When the finish dries, rub it out and reassemble the table.

Figure 4. Remove the remainder of the waste with a bench chisel. Make a tenon in a piece of scrap and use it as a template to check your progress as you carve out the slots.

Figure 5. Shape the legs with a drawknife or a spokeshave, tapering them at the ankle so that the foot appears bulbous.

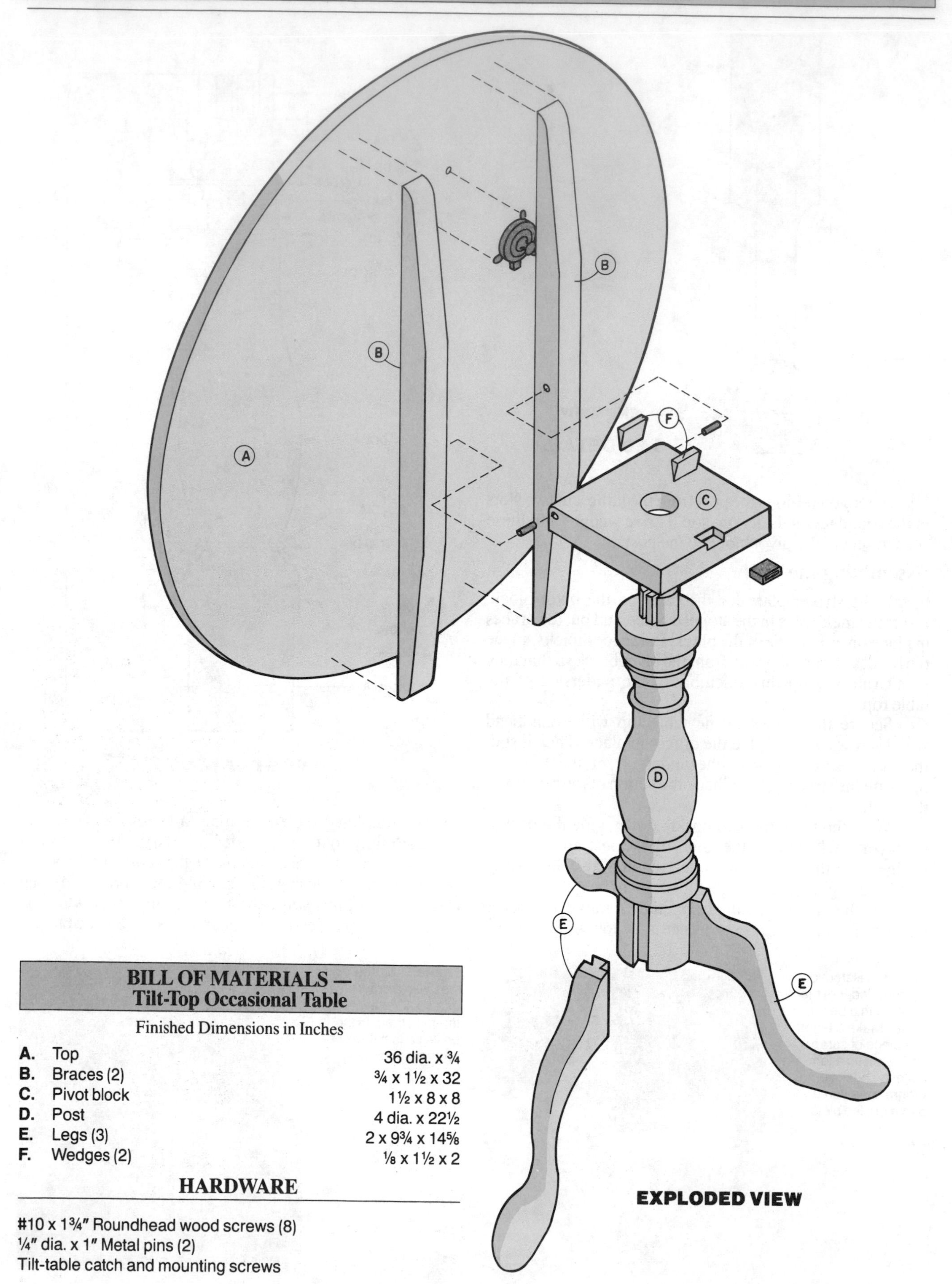

BILL OF MATERIALS — Tilt-Top Occasional Table

Finished Dimensions in Inches

	Part	Dimensions
A.	Top	36 dia. x ¾
B.	Braces (2)	¾ x 1½ x 32
C.	Pivot block	1½ x 8 x 8
D.	Post	4 dia. x 22½
E.	Legs (3)	2 x 9¾ x 14⅝
F.	Wedges (2)	⅛ x 1½ x 2

HARDWARE

#10 x 1¾″ Roundhead wood screws (8)
¼″ dia. x 1″ Metal pins (2)
Tilt-table catch and mounting screws

Designed and built by Phil Baird.

Contemporary Canopy Bed

It's attractive; it's practical; it can be built easily from inexpensive lumber — sweet dreams for woodworkers!

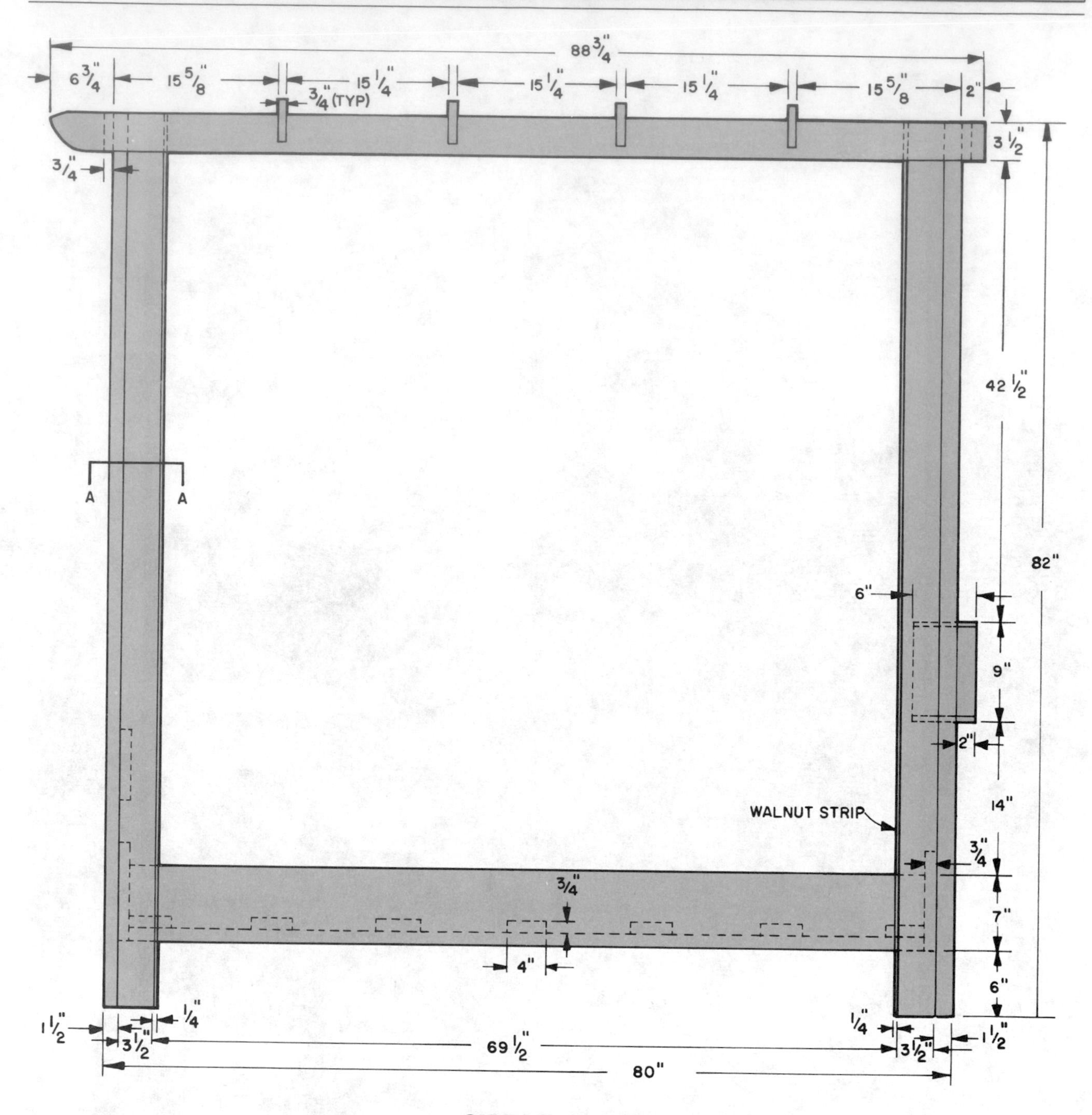

SIDE VIEW

There is beauty in simplicity.

The full-size bed frame that you see here was built from standard dimension lumber. There is no fancy joinery; in fact, most of the parts are assembled with butt joints and wood screws. The only other joints are notches and rabbets — four rabbets join the parts of the headboard shelving unit; eight notches join the canopy slats to the canopy frame. But despite the inexpensive materials and simple construction, the bed frame is sturdy and attractive.

Phil Baird, who designed the bed frame, specializes in inexpensive, simple projects. He teaches woodworking to junior high school students, and he is constantly thinking of simple projects that his students might attempt. He has to use inexpensive materials — he doesn't have the budget for cabinet-grade lumber. But he still wants the projects to be practical and attractive. Otherwise, the kids won't want to build them.

The bed frame is, Phil points out, somewhat larger and more complex than the projects he ordinarily builds in the classroom. But it still reflects his mind-set as a craftsman. You can build this project in a few class periods. If you use your imagination, there's a lot of beauty that you can create from simplicity.

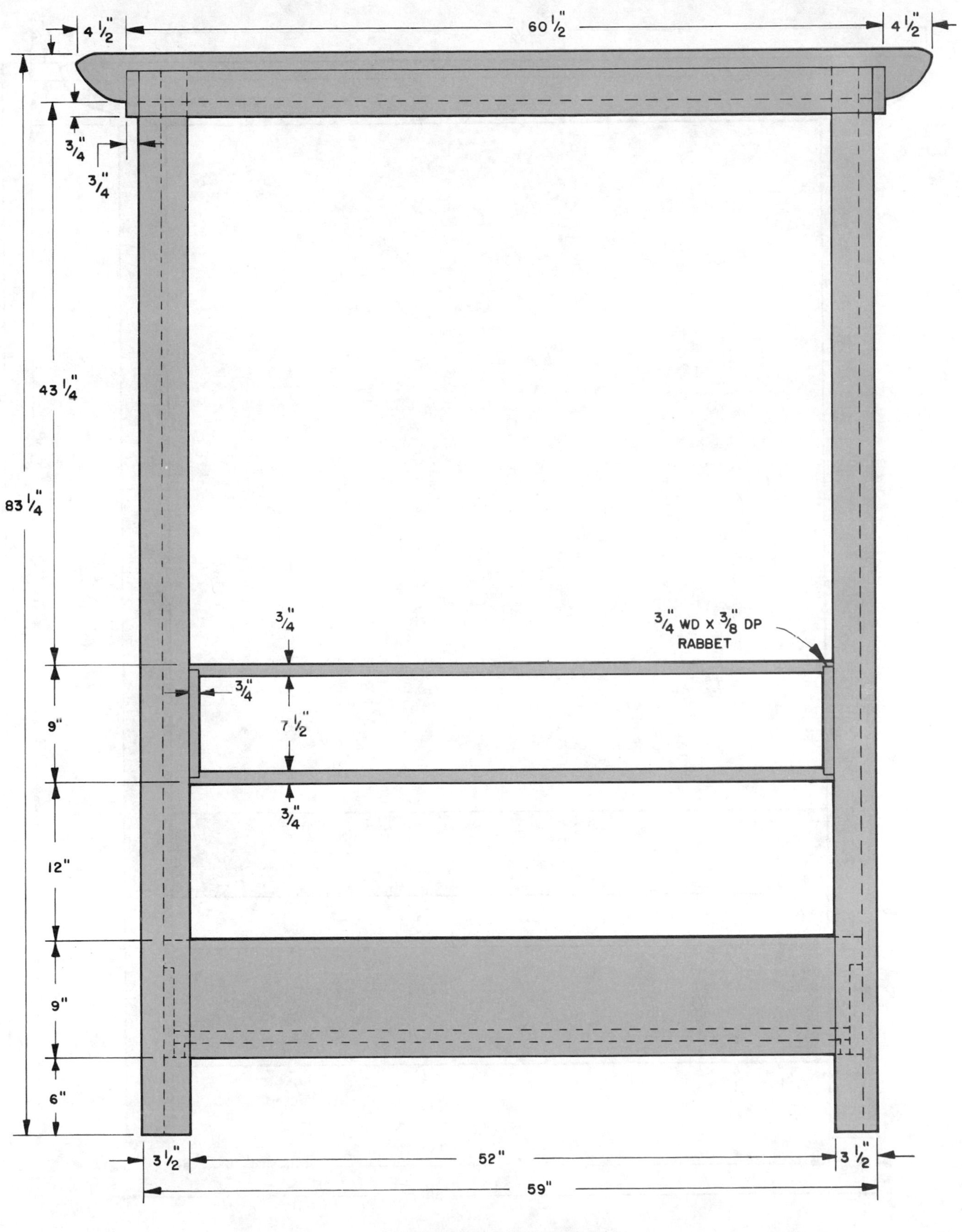

HEADBOARD/END VIEW

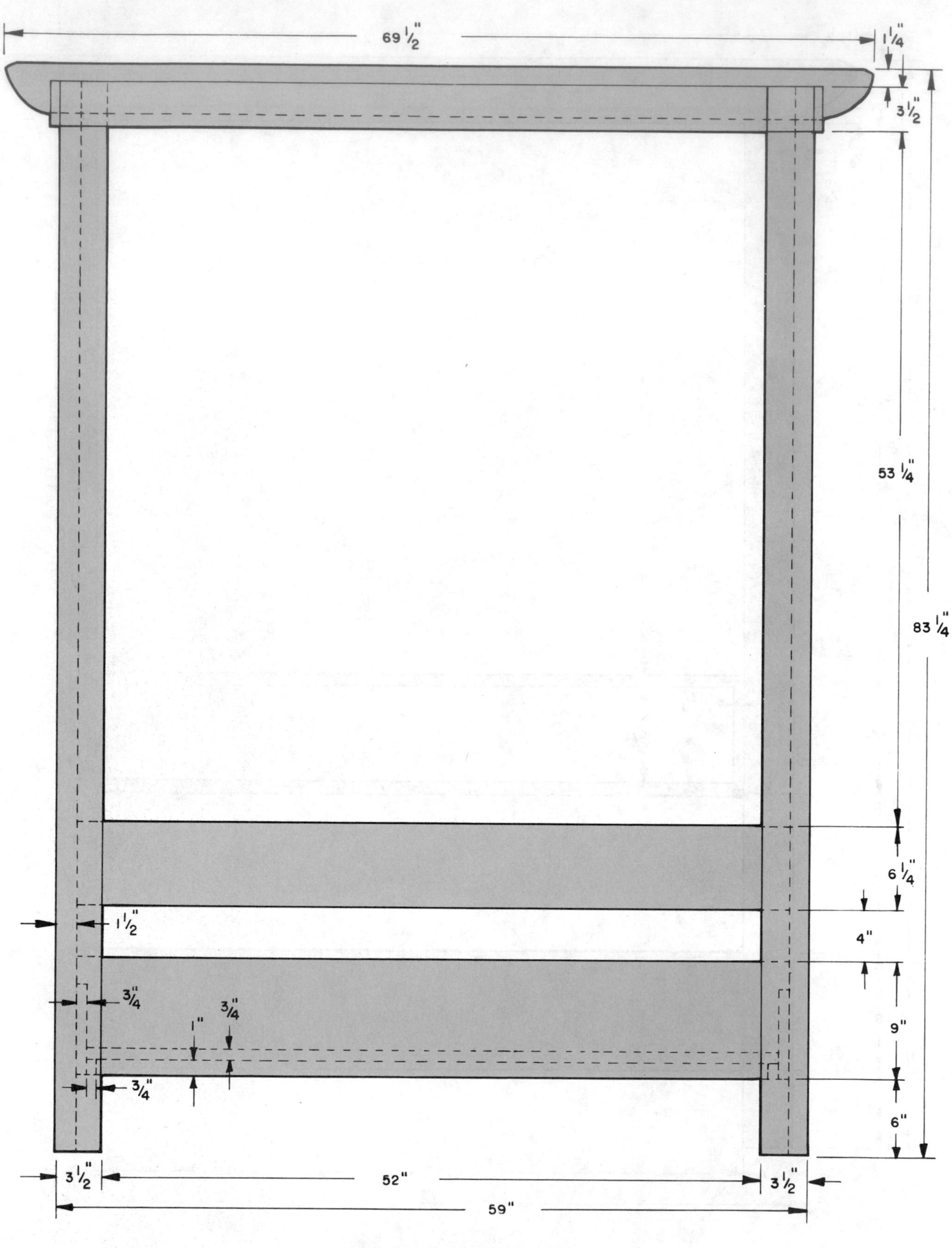

FOOTBOARD/END VIEW

Adjusting the Dimensions

As shown in the working drawing, the bed frame is designed to hold a standard full-size mattress and box springs. However, the dimensions of the frame can be easily adjusted to fit other sizes of mattresses and springs. Simply change the length of the *horizontal* parts (slats, stretchers, shelves, rails) to the dimensions you need. Allow an extra ½″ side-to-side and head-to-foot to make room for sheets and covers.

Here's a list of standard bedding sizes:

Twin: 39″ x 75″
Full: 54″ x 75″
Queen: 60″ x 80″
King: 78″ x 80″

Preparing the Materials

As we mentioned, you can build this bed *almost* entirely from dimension lumber, with the exception of three parts — two essential, and one not so essential. The essential parts are the bed rails and ledgers. These must be made from a hardwood, such as oak, maple, or birch (Phil used birch), so that they will support the weight of the mattress and springs. The non-essential parts are the accent strips. Phil made these from a dark wood — walnut — so that they would contrast with the lighter yellow pine. You could also use mahogany or cherry. Or, you could stain strips of ordinary pine dark, then attach them to the bed posts. You could also eliminate the strips altogether — they are not essential to the design.

The dimension lumber is not essential to the design, either. If you wish, you can build this project entirely from cabinet-grade woods. You may want to use a dark-colored wood for most of the parts and a light-colored wood for the accent strip — just the opposite of what Phil did. It's up to you.

If you do use dimension lumber, there are several precautions that you should take. First of all, purchase *clear* stock, not construction-grade. This is more expensive than the lower grades, but it's also stronger and has less tendency to warp or twist.

Secondly, remember that this stock is not cured as thoroughly as cabinet-grade lumber. It may have twice to three times the moisture content. To compensate for this, stack the lumber in your garage or covered patio and let it sit for two to three months. Then bring it into your shop and let it sit another two to three weeks *before* you start building. This will give the lumber a chance to dry out, then adjust itself to the temperature and humidity indoors.

When you're satisfied that the lumber has cured long enough, cut and rip all the parts to the sizes shown in the Bill of Materials.

Cutting the Joinery

There are only two joints to cut — rabbets and notches. Make the rabbets in the shelves first, using a dado cutter or a router. If you have neither of these, you can also cut rabbets with an ordinary table saw blade. Set the blade height so that it cuts just ⅜″ deep, then pass the stock over the blade several times, removing just a little bit of stock with each pass. (See Figure 1.)

Make the notches in the canopy slats with a handsaw and a chisel. Carefully mark the notches on the stock, then saw each side of each notch. Remove the waste with the chisel. (See Figures 2 and 3.)

Cutting the Shapes

Enlarge the pattern for the ends of the canopy slats and trace it on the stock. Cut the shapes with a sabre saw, then sand away the saw marks. These shapes, by the way, are just suggestions. You can alter them to suit your own taste — or leave the ends square, if you prefer.

Figure 2. To make the notches in the canopy slats, first cut the sides of each notch with a handsaw.

Figure 1. To cut a rabbet with a table saw, pass the board over the blade several times until you have cut the joint to the desired width.

Figure 3. Then remove the waste with a bench chisel.

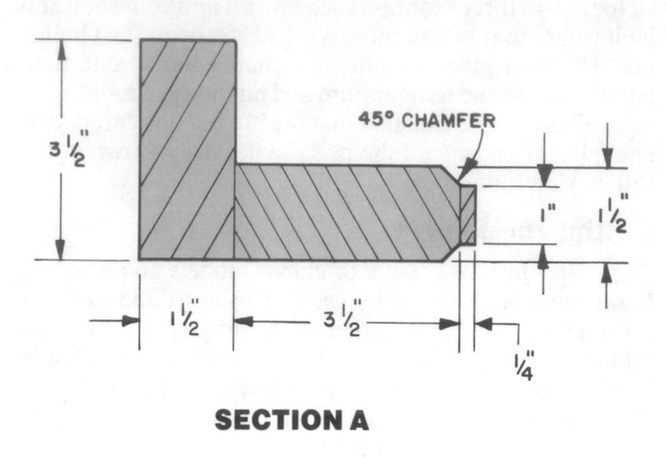

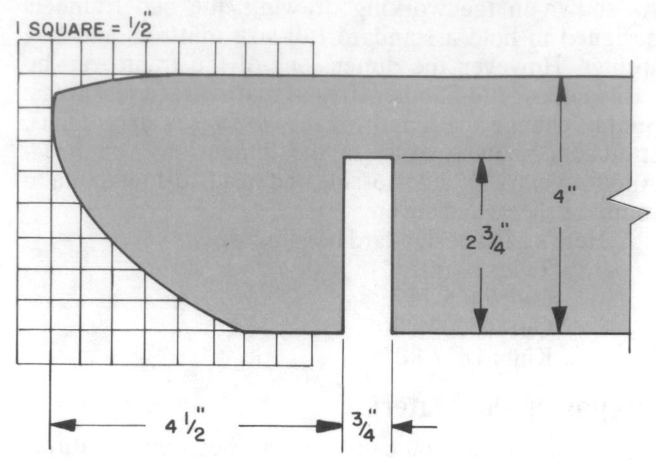

CANOPY SLAT DETAIL AND PATTERN

Using a bench plane or a jointer, chamfer the corners of the bed posts where you will attach the accent strip, as shown in *Section A.* Be careful not to cut the chamfers too wide — otherwise, the strips won't fit.

Tip ◆ Draw pencil lines on the bed post stock to indicate the limits of the chamfer. When you plane or joint the chamfer, don't cut past the pencil lines. (See Figure 4.)

Assembling the Bed Frame

Finish sand all the parts, with the exception of the bed slats and the ledger — these don't need to be sanded. As you sand, be careful not to round over any corners or edges that will join to other parts.

Figure 4. Mark the bed post stock so that you don't cut the chamfers too wide.

Glue up the L-shaped bed posts. Also, glue the accent strips to the posts where shown in *Section A.* Wipe away any excess glue with a wet rag. When the glue cures, sand the glue joints to make sure that the outside surfaces are flush and even.

Also, glue up the bed rails and ledgers. These parts also make an L-shaped assembly. Finally, glue up the headboard shelves unit. Reinforce the glue joints with flathead wood screws. Countersink and counterbore the screws, then cover the heads with wooden plugs. Sand the plugs flush with the surface of the wood.

With *screws only* (no glue), assemble the bed frame parts to make a headboard and a footboard. Screw together two bed post assemblies, the shelving unit assembly, a canopy stretcher, and a bottom stretcher to make the headboard. Assemble two bed posts, the footboard stretcher, a canopy stretcher, and the bottom stretcher to make the footboard. Always drive the screws from the *inside* surfaces of the assemblies, then cover the screw heads with wooden plugs so that they won't be noticed when the bed frame is completely assembled.

Find a helper for the final assembly. These headboard and footboard assemblies are too large to handle safely on your own. Using screws (but no glue), attach the headboard to the footboard with the bed rails and canopy rails. Once again, drive the screws from the inside. But this time, *don't* cover the heads. You want to be able to remove the screws should you ever need to move the bed. Lay the canopy slats and the bed slats in place, but don't attach them with glue or screws. Gravity will keep them in place.

Finishing Up

Disassemble the bed frame, removing the slats and detaching the headboard, footboard, and rails. Do any necessary touch-up sanding, then apply a finish to all the parts with the exception of the bed slats. Since these will never be seen once the mattress is in place, it's not necessary to finish them.

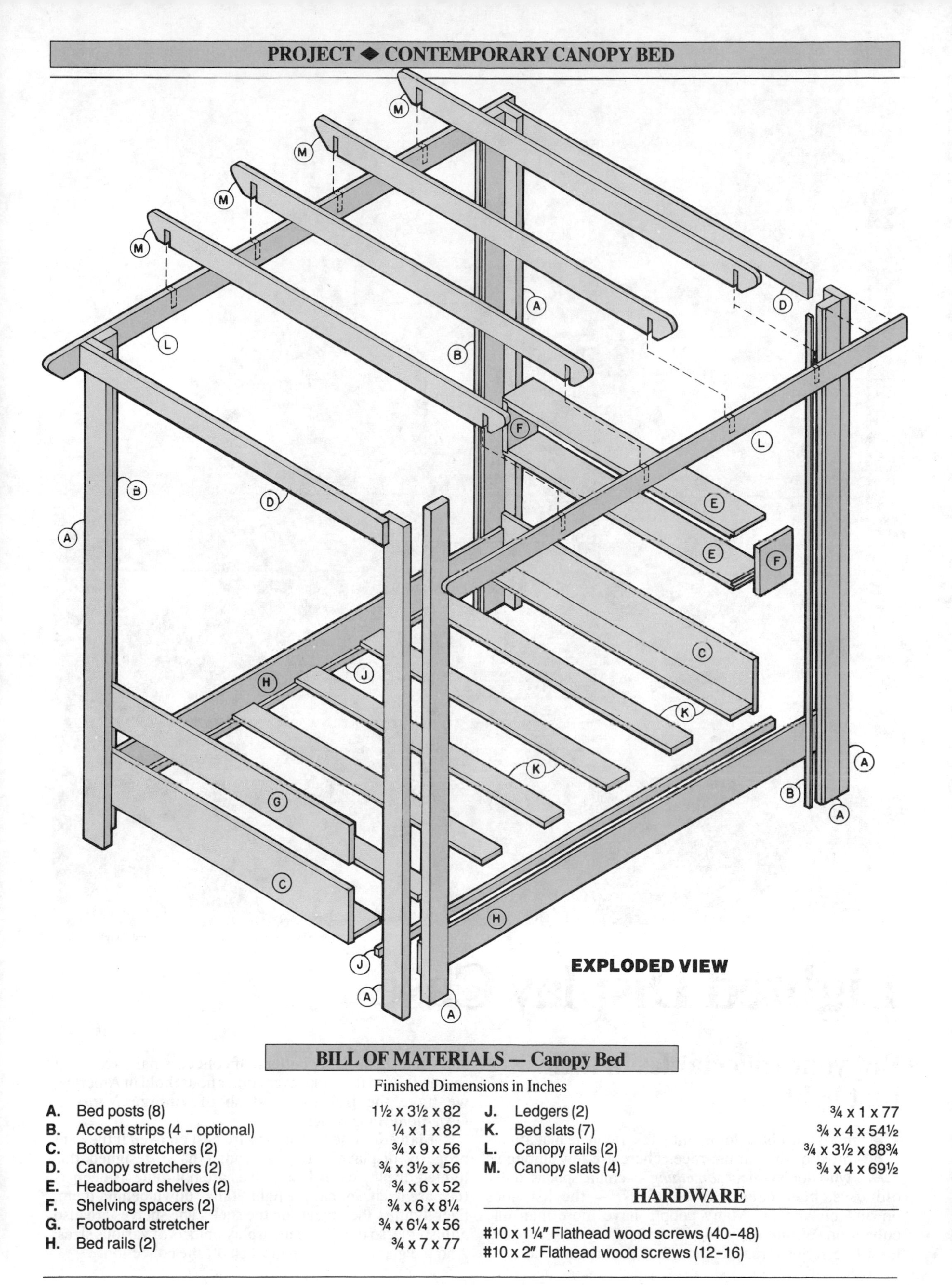

BILL OF MATERIALS — Canopy Bed

Finished Dimensions in Inches

	Part	Dimensions
A.	Bed posts (8)	1½ x 3½ x 82
B.	Accent strips (4 - optional)	¼ x 1 x 82
C.	Bottom stretchers (2)	¾ x 9 x 56
D.	Canopy stretchers (2)	¾ x 3½ x 56
E.	Headboard shelves (2)	¾ x 6 x 52
F.	Shelving spacers (2)	¾ x 6 x 8¼
G.	Footboard stretcher	¾ x 6¼ x 56
H.	Bed rails (2)	¾ x 7 x 77
J.	Ledgers (2)	¾ x 1 x 77
K.	Bed slats (7)	¾ x 4 x 54½
L.	Canopy rails (2)	¾ x 3½ x 88¾
M.	Canopy slats (4)	¾ x 4 x 69½

HARDWARE

#10 x 1¼″ Flathead wood screws (40–48)
#10 x 2″ Flathead wood screws (12–16)

Designed by Nick Engler. Built by Nick Engler and Chris Walendzak.

Lighted Display Case

Put your collectables in their best light.

There must be a dominant pack-rat gene that affects most of the human race. There are few among us who don't collect *something* — china, spoons, dolls, old toys, beer cans, carved birds — the list goes on and on and on. Many people have more than one collection. Within the walls of my own home there are at least five serious treasure-hoards. I accumulate old tools and wind-up toys. My better half collects small boxes and seashells. And then, like every other household in America, we have the traditional stash of vintage *National Geographic* magazines.

Many of these collections are best enjoyed if they are properly displayed. To that end, I have designed this lighted display case. The shelves are not quite as deep as the case itself, so that the light "falls" down behind them, backlighting the objects on the shelf. The shelves are also adjustable, so that you can display objects of various sizes. And the glass doors keep the dust off the collection.

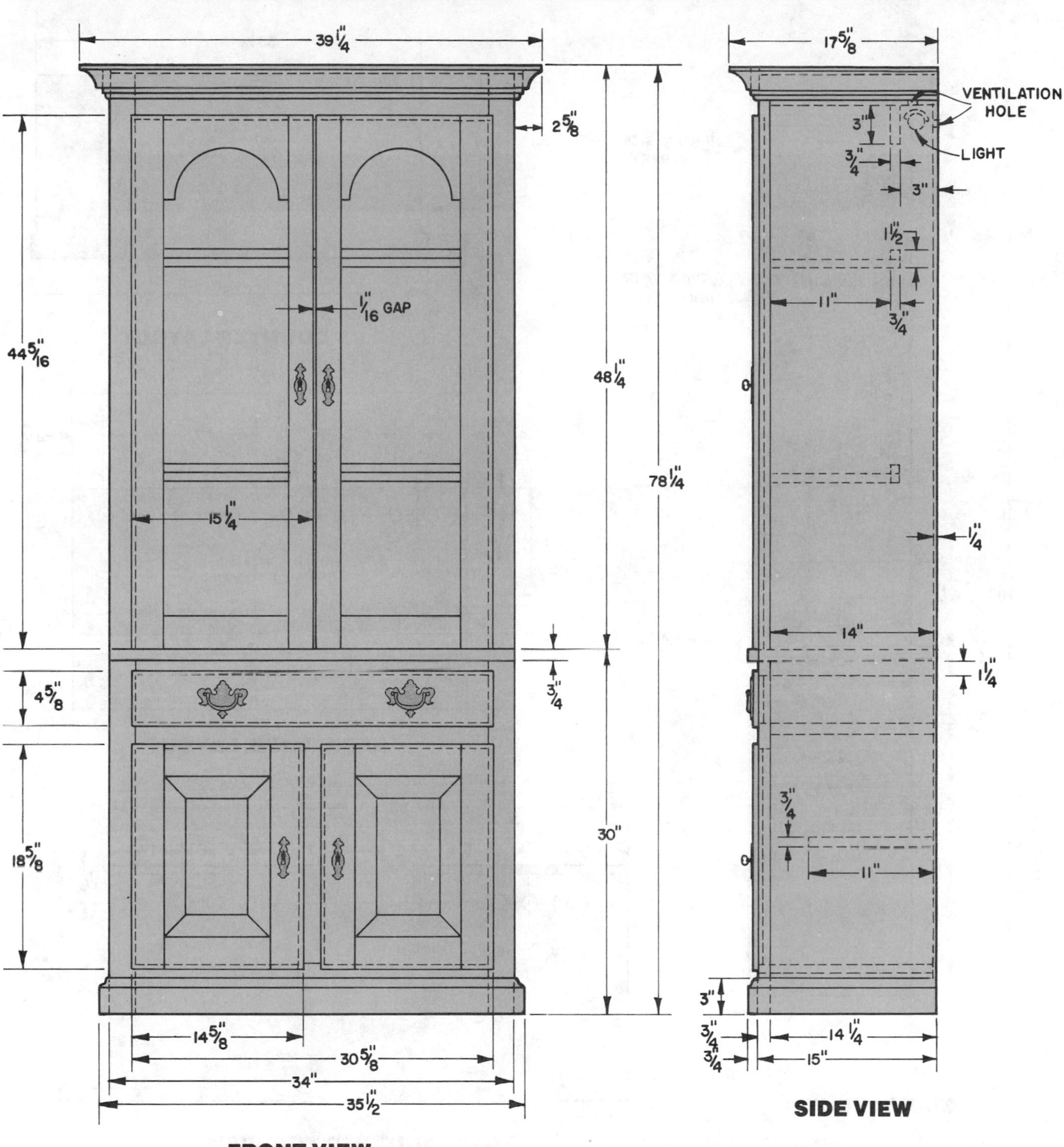

FRONT VIEW

Below waist level, the display case turns into an enclosed cabinet. This is because objects that are displayed near the floor are harder to inspect and appreciate than those displayed at eye level. Besides, many collectors appreciate having closed space to keep those portions of their collection that they don't want to display. Model-makers, for example, frequently have unfinished models, as well as glue, tools, and materials that they would rather store out of sight. You may also want to keep another, completely unrelated collection in the cabinet space.

Selecting and Preparing the Stock

Use cabinet-grade lumber and plywood for the parts that show, such as the sides, shelves, and back. Make those that don't show, such as the web frame pieces, from utility wood and plywood. You can cut down on some of the solid cabinet-grade lumber you need by substituting ¾" cabinet-grade plywood for the larger pieces — the sides, top, bottom, counter, and shelves. Edge the front of the counter and shelves with strips of solid wood to hide the plies. Once you have gathered the parts you need, cut and rip all the parts to size.

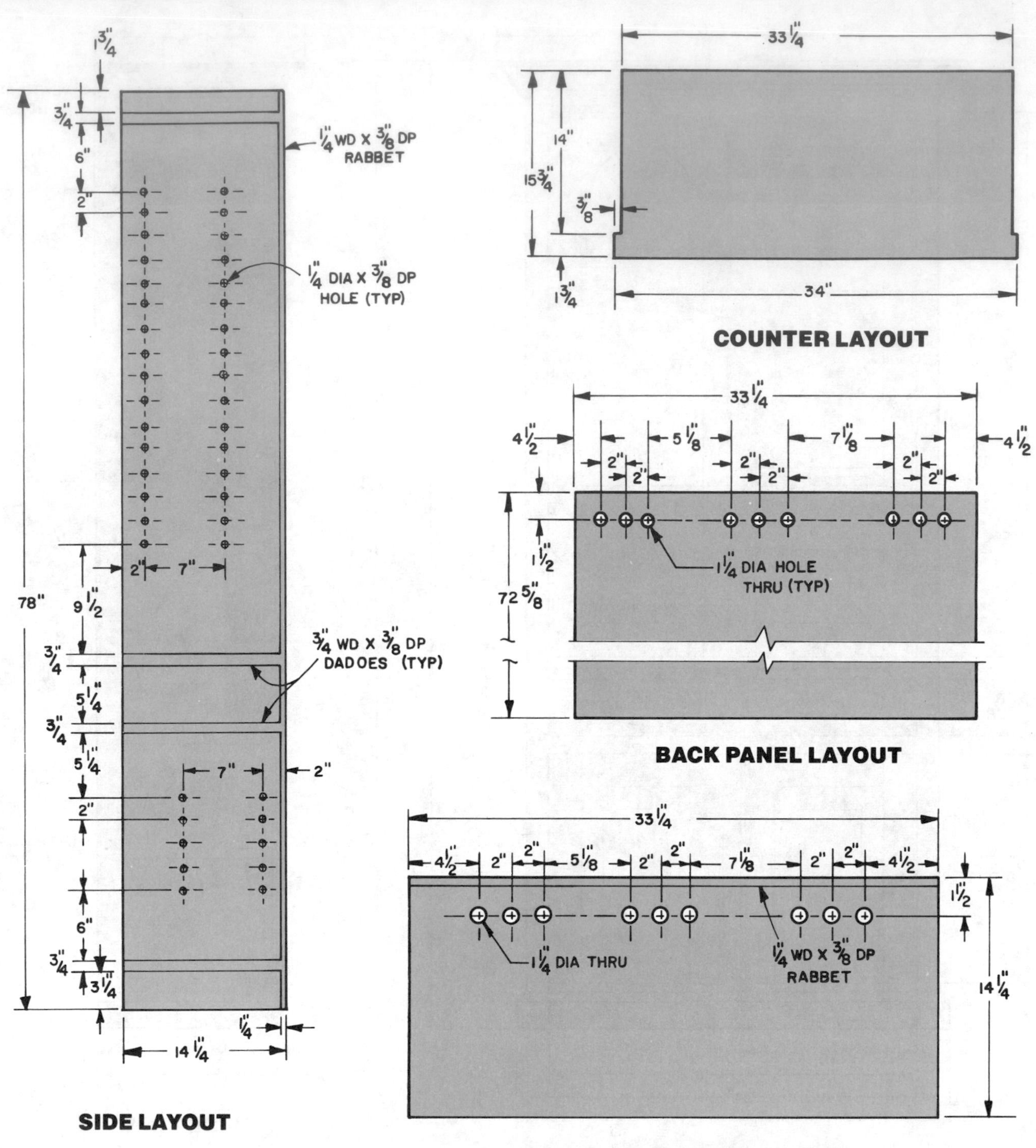

Important Note: You should make *all* the larger parts from plywood or *all* from solid wood. Don't mix plywood and solid wood. The case won't be able to expand and contract properly.

Cutting the Case Joinery

The parts of the case are joined with a system of dadoes and rabbets. With a router, make 3/8"-wide, 3/8"-deep rabbets in the back edges of the sides and the top. Then rout 3/4"-wide, 3/8"-deep dadoes in the sides. Make each dado or rabbet in several passes, cutting 1/8" deeper with each pass.

Tip ◆ To make sure that both sides are routed exactly the same, clamp them front edge to front edge so that you can rout two dadoes at once — one in each piece. Lay a straightedge across *both* pieces to guide the router, and secure the straightedge to the sides.

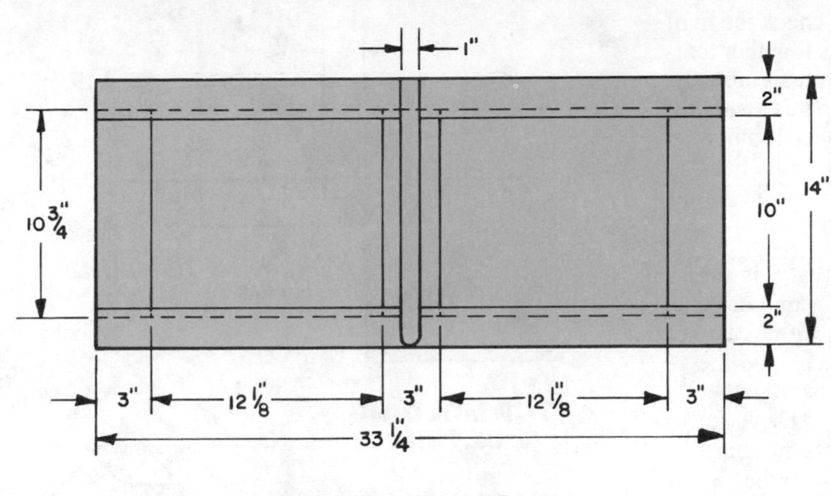

WEB FRAME LAYOUT

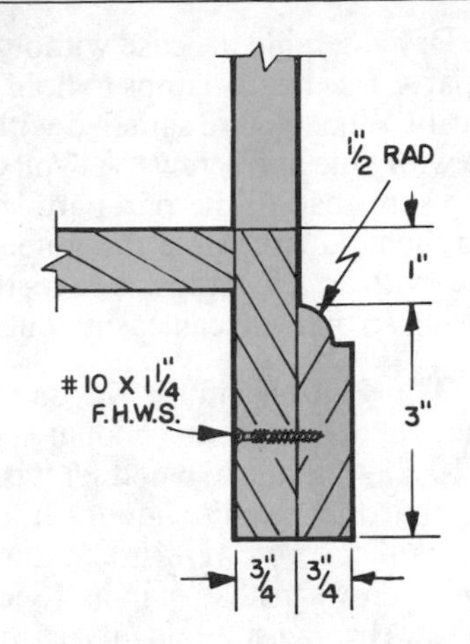

BOTTOM MOLDING DETAIL

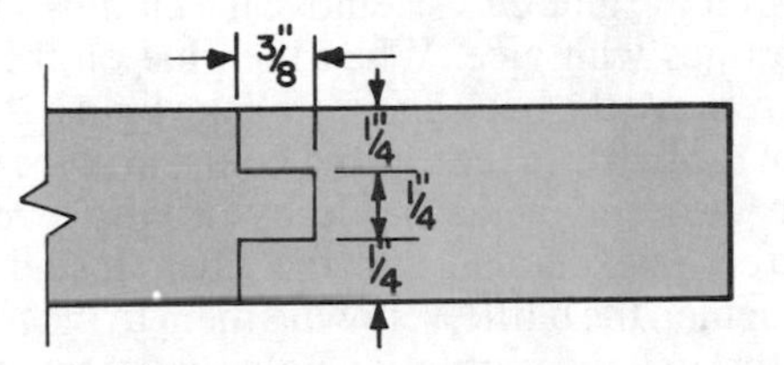

WEB FRAME JOINERY DETAIL

The counter — the middle fixed shelf in the case — must be notched to fit correctly. Cut these notches with a bandsaw or a hand saw, as shown in the *Counter Layout.*

Drilling the Holes

Drill stopped holes, 1/4" in diameter and 3/8" deep, in both sides, as shown in the *Side Layout.* These will hold pin-style shelving supports. The supports, in turn, will hold the adjustable shelves in the upper and lower sections of the case.

Cut ventilation holes through the top and the back, where shown in the *Top Layout* and *Back Panel Layout.* These ventilation holes help to dissipate the heat from the cabinet lights, and prevent the heat from scorching the wood or causing it to warp.

Making the Frames

The drawer is supported by a web frame. The frame is held together with tongue-and-groove joinery. Using a dado cutter or a router, make 1/4"-wide, 3/8"-deep grooves in all the *inside* edges of the web frame rails. Then cut 1/4"-wide, 3/8"-long tenons or "tongues" in the ends of the stiles. Glue the rails and stiles together, making sure that the frame is square.

After the glue dries on the rails and stiles, round the front edge of the drawer guide, as shown on the *Web Frame Layout.* Attach the drawer guide to the *top* surface of the frame, centered on the middle stile.

To make the face frames, join the members with dowels. Use a doweling jig to guide your drill when making the stopped dowel holes in the frame members. Glue the parts together, checking that the frames are square as you clamp them together.

Assembling the Case

Completely assemble the case *before* you make the doors and drawer. That way, you can fit the doors and drawer to the case. But before you assemble the case, finish sand all the case parts. As you sand, be careful not to round over any edges or corners that adjoin other parts when the project is put together.

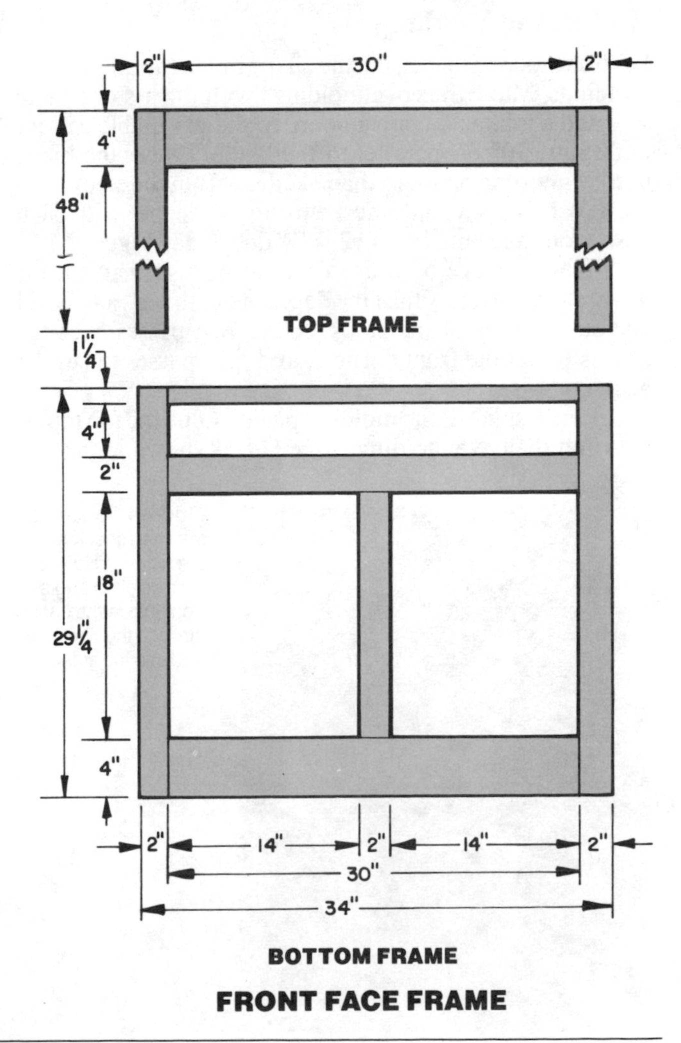

FRONT FACE FRAME

Dry assemble the case without glue to check the fit of the parts. Use band clamps to hold the parts together temporarily. When you're satisfied with the fit, reassemble the case with glue and screws. As you clamp up this assembly, make sure that all the parts are square to each other. To keep them square while the glue cures, tack the back in place with a few brads. Leave the heads of the brads showing so that you can easily remove them.

Tip ◆ To reinforce the dado joints that join the sides to the top, bottom, counter, and web frame, drive #10 x 1¼" flathead wood screws from *inside* the case, so that they won't show on the outside. Angle the screws, as if you were "toenailing" the parts together with screws instead of nails. (See Figure 1.) Drive the screws from inside and *underneath* the bottom, counter, and web frame, and from inside and *above* the top.

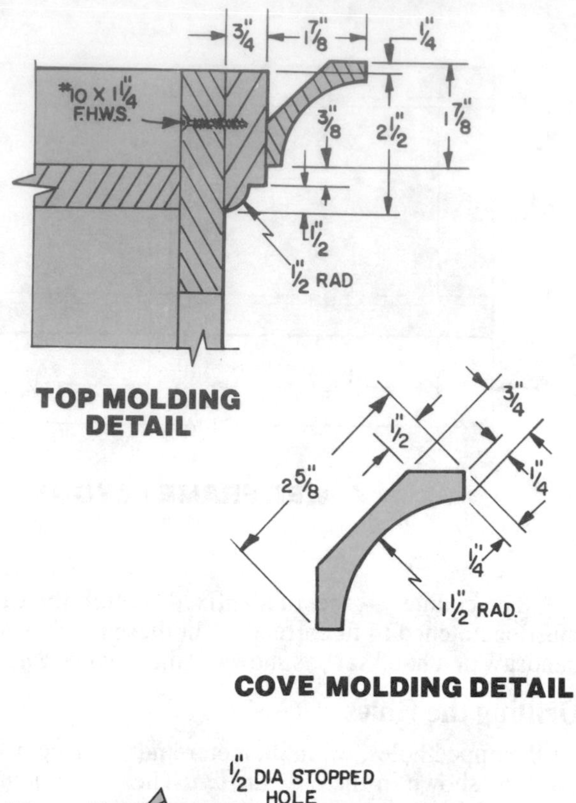

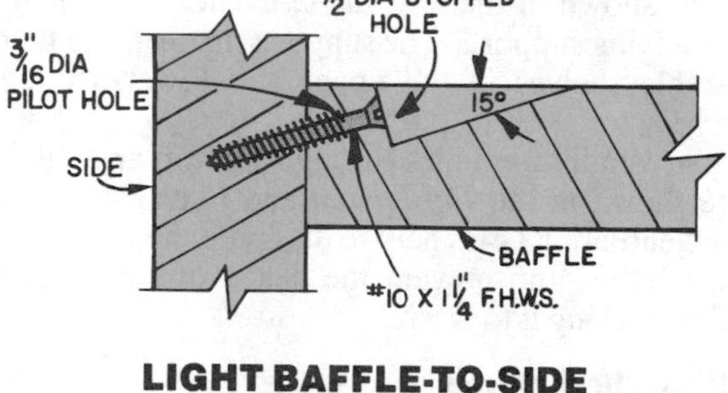

After the glue cures, remove the clamps and attach the face frames with glue. When the glue on the face frame cures, remove the back and install the light baffle. Glue the edge of the baffle to the top and hold it in place with screws. Secure the ends of the baffle by driving screws through the screw pockets and into the sides. Install the cabinet lights behind the baffle, screwing them to the top. Insert the cords through the ventilation holes in the top, then replace the back.

Adding the Molding

With a router or shaper, cut the shape of the top and bottom moldings. Make the cove moldings with the aid of a table saw and a jointer. Clamp a board to the worktable of your table saw, 30° off parallel to the blade. Lower the blade until it's cutting no more than ⅛" deep. Run the stock over the saw blade several times, cutting ⅛" deeper with each pass. Continue until the cove is ½" deep. (See Figure 2.)

Tilt the fence of your jointer to 45°, so that it leans toward the knives. Adjust the depth of cut to 5/32", and bevel all four corners of the stock. Make *two* passes over the knives to cut the front corners, and *four* passes to cut the back corners.

Finish sand all the molding pieces. Glue the top moldings and the cove moldings together, as shown in the *Top Molding Detail.* Cut the moldings to size, mitering the ends where the pieces meet. Attach them to the case with glue and screws.

Figure 1. To secure the fixed shelves to the sides, drive screws at an angle from inside the case, through the shelves, and into the sides.

Figure 2. To make the cove molding, pass the stock over a saw blade at an angle to the blade. Make several passes, cutting ⅛" deeper with each pass.

Making the Drawer and Doors

Cut the joinery in the drawer parts. Assemble the front to the sides with ⅜"-long half-blind dovetails, and the back to the sides with ¾"-wide, ⅜"-deep dadoes. The drawer bottom floats in ¼"-wide, ⅜"-deep grooves. You can make all of these joints with a router, if you have a jig to cut the dovetails. Also, round over the edges of the drawer face, and notch the bottom edge of the back, as shown in the *Drawer Back Layout.*

Dry assemble the drawer to check the fit of the parts. Also check the fit of the drawer in the case. If both fits are good, reassemble the parts with glue. Do not glue the bottom in the grooves; just let it float. After the glue cures, install the pulls and fit the drawer in the case.

To make the doors, cut ¼"-wide, 1"-long tenons in the ends of the rails, and slot mortises in the inside edges of the door stiles. With a bandsaw, cut an arch in the top door rails. Assemble the door frames with glue and, once again, check that the assemblies are square as you clamp them together.

When the glue cures, rout the back of the frames, making ⅜"-wide, ⅜"-deep rabbets all around the inside edges. Also, make rabbets in *all* the outside edges of the bottom doors and *two* outside edges of the top doors, where shown in the drawings. Square the corners of the *inside* rabbets with a chisel. Rout out the stock behind the arches in the top doors, so that you can use rectangular panes of glass in these doors. (See Figure 3.) Round over the front of the *outside* edges with a router, to match the drawer face.

Figure 3. Remove extra stock from the back of the arches in the top doors so that you can fit the doors with rectangular panes of glass.

Cut raised panels for the bottom doors. Mount the panels in the frames, securing them with small metal turn-buttons. Do not glue the panels in place, just let them float in the rabbets. Also, don't install the glass in the top doors just yet.

Check the fit of the doors in the case. If they fit to your satisfaction, mount them to the case with semi-concealed offset hinges. Depending on the make of these hinges, you may have to mortise them in the back of the doors. Also install the pulls and catches.

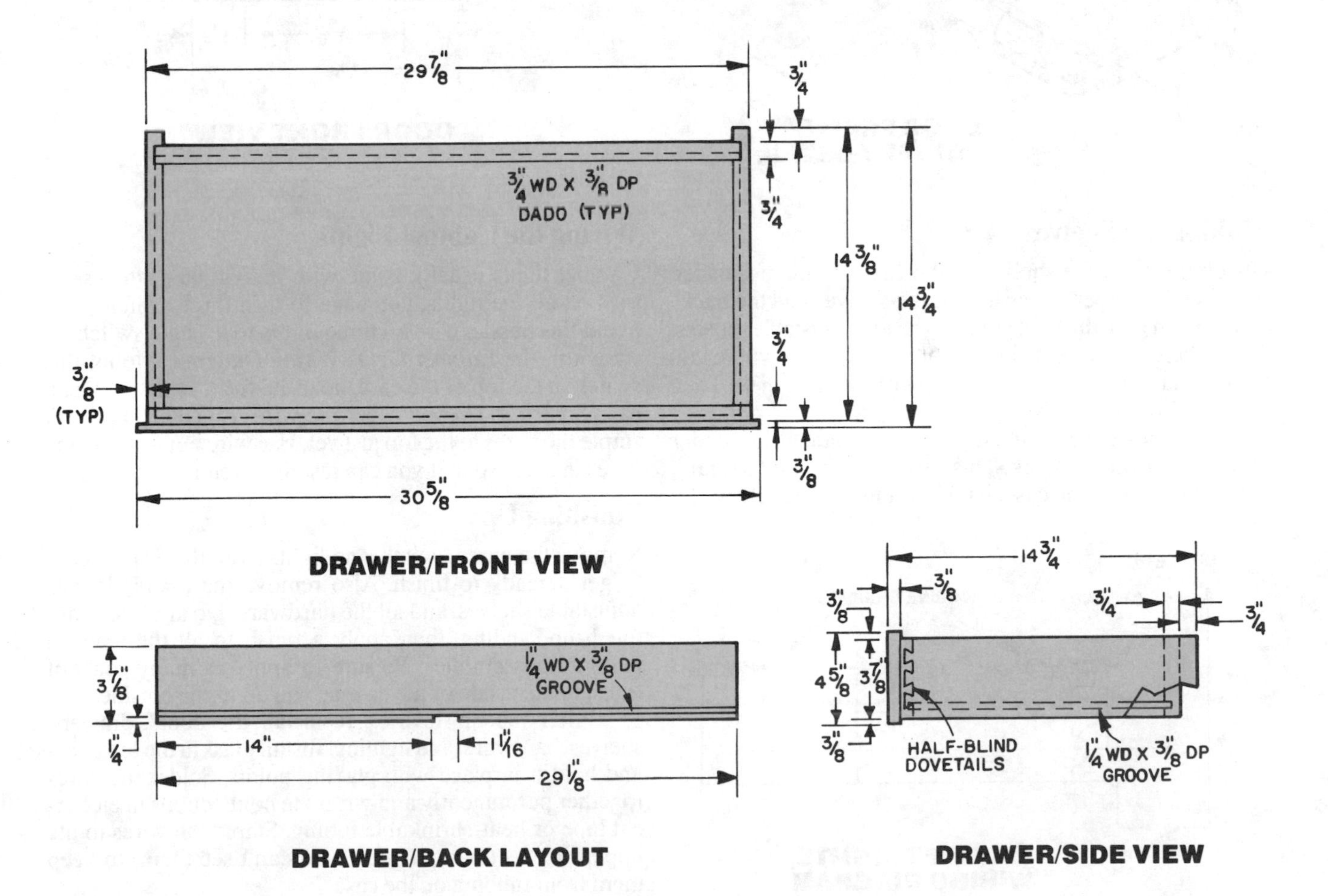

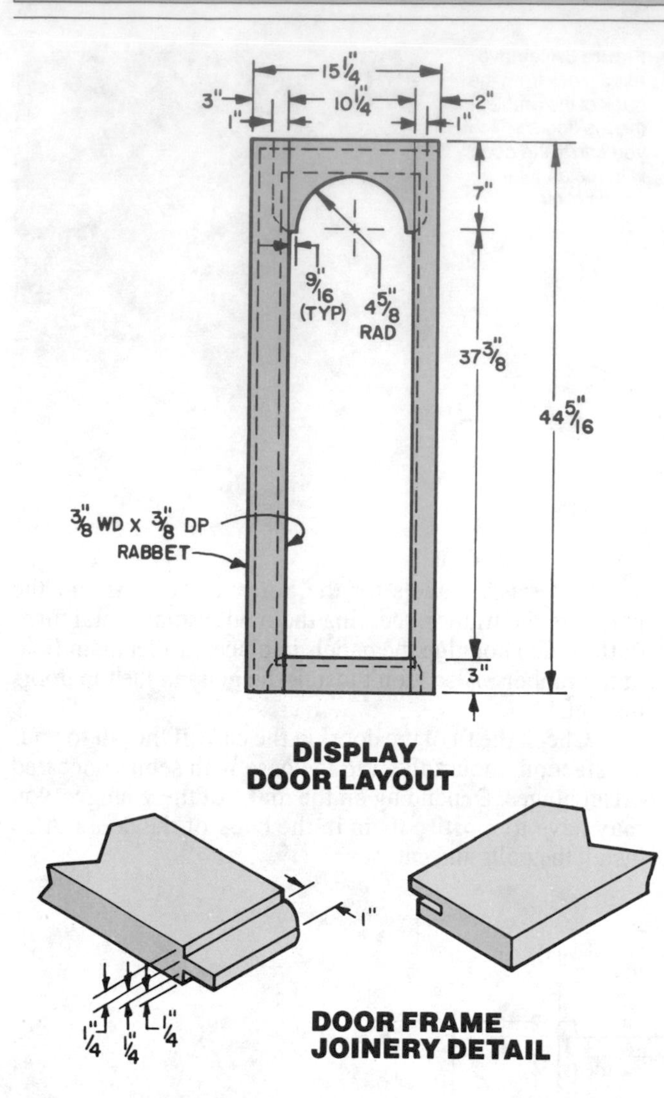

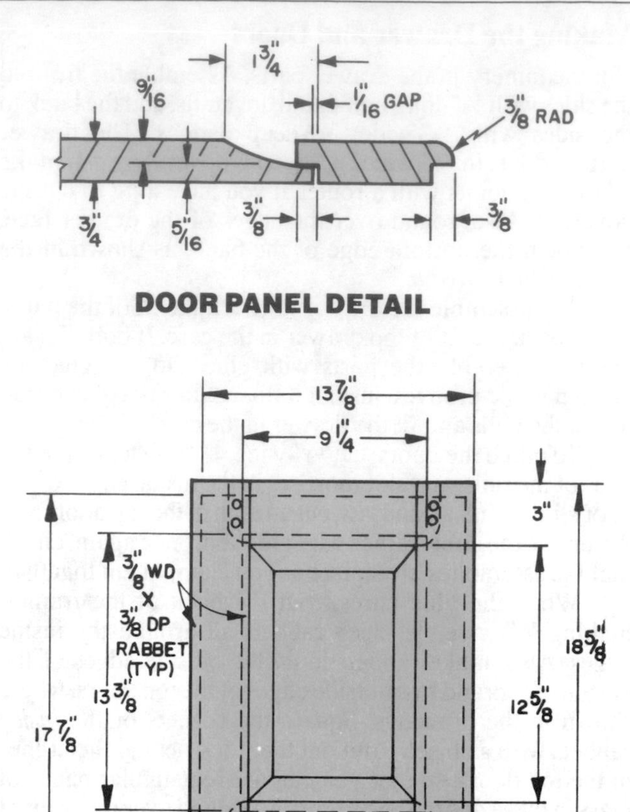

Making the Shelves

Check the fit of the shelves in the case. If you're satisfied that they fit properly, finish sand the shelves and the back-stops. Then glue the backstops to the top adjustable shelves. Place shelving supports in the holes in the sides where you want to hang the shelf — four supports to each shelf. Then lay the adjustable shelves in place.

The back edges of the top shelves should be just under two inches from the back. This will allow the light to "fall" down the back of the case, backlighting all the shelves.

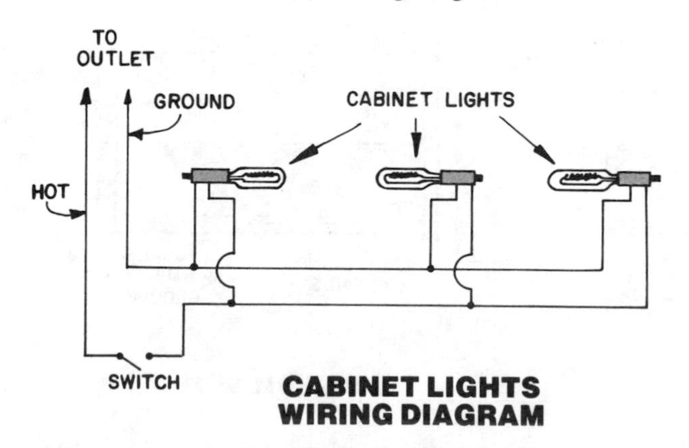

Wiring the Cabinet Lights

Cabinet lights usually come with individual switches. To turn on all the lights, you have to turn three switches. To avoid this hassle, wire all three lights to a single switch, as shown in the *Cabinet Lights Wiring Diagram.* Mount this switch in the top of the case, near the front so that you can easily reach it. *Do not* solder the wires together, and don't staple the wires to the top just yet. Use wire nuts and lay the wires in place so that you can test the circuit.

Finishing Up

Remove the wires, switch, and lights from the display case to get it ready to finish. Also remove the doors, drawer, adjustable shelves, and all the hardware. Do any necessary touch-up sanding, then apply a finish to all the wooden parts and assemblies. Be sure to apply as many coats of finish to the inside of the case as you do to the outside.

After the finish dries, re-install the doors, drawers, shelves, hardware, and lighting. Install glass in the top doors and hold it in place with glazing points. Solder the wires together permanently and wrap the connections in electrical tape or heat-shrinkable tubing. Staple the wires to the upper face of the top (where you can't see them) to keep them from rubbing on the case.

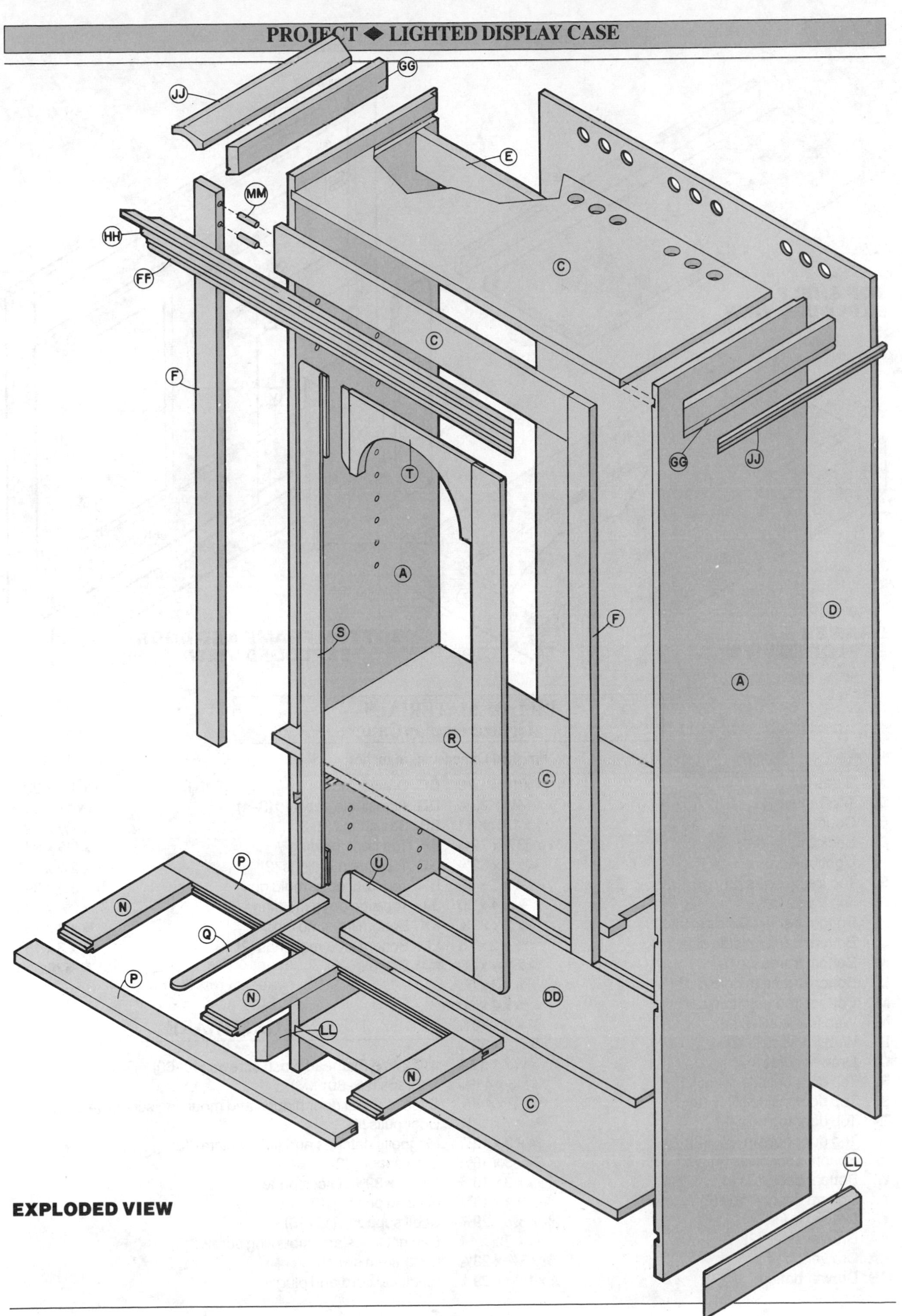
JJ
GG
MM
HH
FF
E
C
C
F
T
A
S
R
C
F
D
A
GG
JJ
P
N
Q
U
P
N
DD
LL
N
C
LL
EXPLODED VIEW

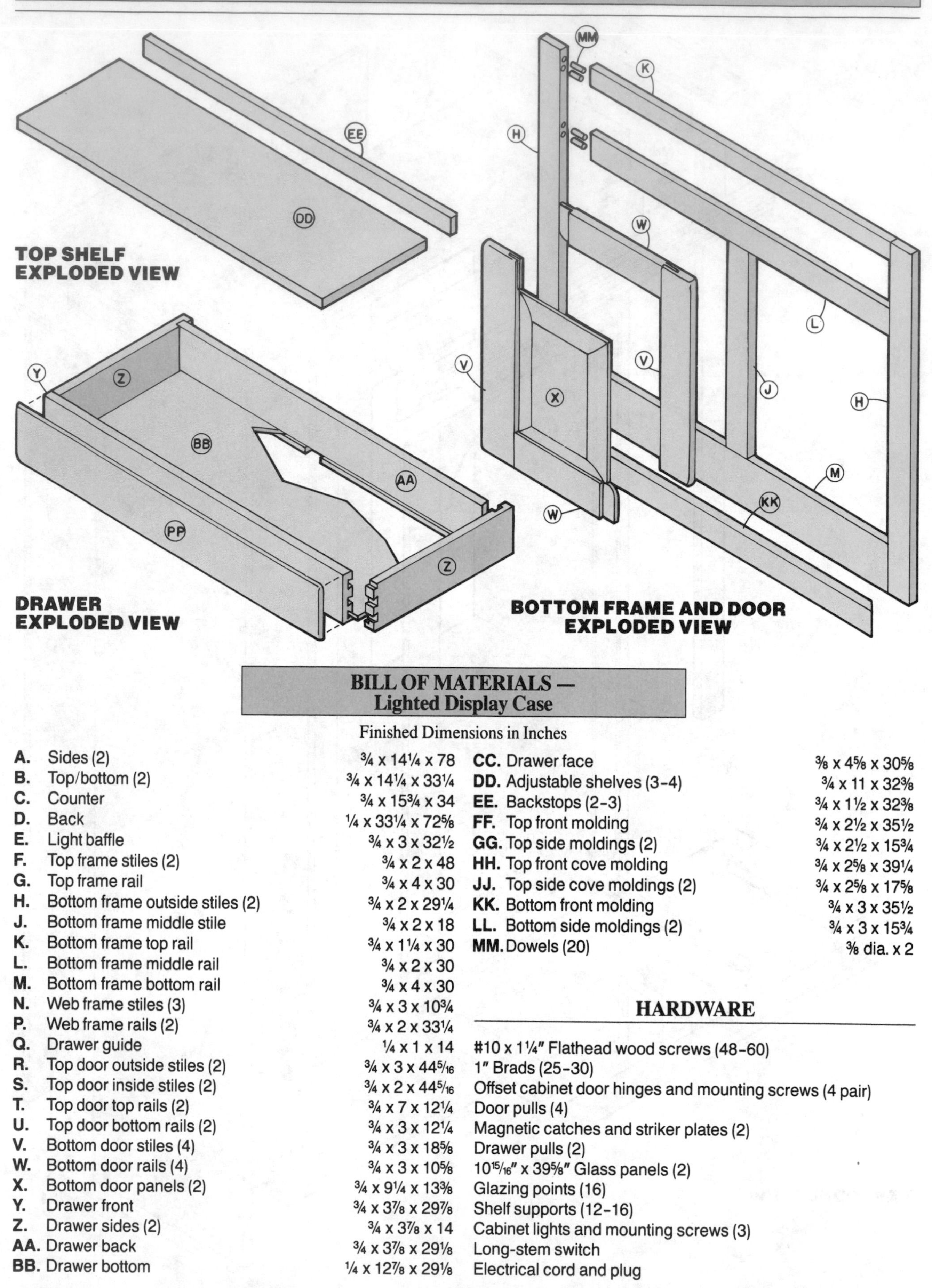

BILL OF MATERIALS — Lighted Display Case

Finished Dimensions in Inches

Part	Dimensions
A. Sides (2)	¾ x 14¼ x 78
B. Top/bottom (2)	¾ x 14¼ x 33¼
C. Counter	¾ x 15¾ x 34
D. Back	¼ x 33¼ x 72⅝
E. Light baffle	¾ x 3 x 32½
F. Top frame stiles (2)	¾ x 2 x 48
G. Top frame rail	¾ x 4 x 30
H. Bottom frame outside stiles (2)	¾ x 2 x 29¼
J. Bottom frame middle stile	¾ x 2 x 18
K. Bottom frame top rail	¾ x 1¼ x 30
L. Bottom frame middle rail	¾ x 2 x 30
M. Bottom frame bottom rail	¾ x 4 x 30
N. Web frame stiles (3)	¾ x 3 x 10¾
P. Web frame rails (2)	¾ x 2 x 33¼
Q. Drawer guide	¼ x 1 x 14
R. Top door outside stiles (2)	¾ x 3 x 44 5/16
S. Top door inside stiles (2)	¾ x 2 x 44 5/16
T. Top door top rails (2)	¾ x 7 x 12¼
U. Top door bottom rails (2)	¾ x 3 x 12¼
V. Bottom door stiles (4)	¾ x 3 x 18⅝
W. Bottom door rails (4)	¾ x 3 x 10⅝
X. Bottom door panels (2)	¾ x 9¼ x 13⅜
Y. Drawer front	¾ x 3⅞ x 29⅞
Z. Drawer sides (2)	¾ x 3⅞ x 14
AA. Drawer back	¾ x 3⅞ x 29⅛
BB. Drawer bottom	¼ x 12⅞ x 29⅛
CC. Drawer face	⅜ x 4⅝ x 30⅝
DD. Adjustable shelves (3–4)	¾ x 11 x 32⅜
EE. Backstops (2–3)	¾ x 1½ x 32⅜
FF. Top front molding	¾ x 2½ x 35½
GG. Top side moldings (2)	¾ x 2½ x 15¾
HH. Top front cove molding	¾ x 2⅝ x 39¼
JJ. Top side cove moldings (2)	¾ x 2⅝ x 17⅝
KK. Bottom front molding	¾ x 3 x 35½
LL. Bottom side moldings (2)	¾ x 3 x 15¾
MM. Dowels (20)	⅜ dia. x 2

HARDWARE

#10 x 1¼″ Flathead wood screws (48–60)
1″ Brads (25–30)
Offset cabinet door hinges and mounting screws (4 pair)
Door pulls (4)
Magnetic catches and striker plates (2)
Drawer pulls (2)
10 15/16″ x 39⅝″ Glass panels (2)
Glazing points (16)
Shelf supports (12–16)
Cabinet lights and mounting screws (3)
Long-stem switch
Electrical cord and plug

TECHNIQUES

Text by Nick Engler.

Resawing

There's a fine art to making thin boards out of thick ones.

Resawing is the art of slicing large boards into smaller ones. And it is an art — any woodworker who has done a lot of resawing will testify to that. To resaw a board — and do a good job of it — you have to know your machine intimately and develop a "feel" for the wood. This blend of knowledge and skill is what elevates this simple technique to an art.

It's a useful art, well worth the time it takes to learn it. Most woodworking projects call for several different thicknesses of stock, while lumberyards usually only sell 4/4 (1″ thick) and 8/4 (2″ thick) cabinet-grade woods. It takes forever to work 4/4 lumber down to ¼″ thick on a small planer. Resawing saves an enormous amount of time. It also saves wood. You can get two, possibly three ¼″-thick boards from a single 4/4 board.

The Best Tool for the Job

The art of resawing — and the tools needed to do it — have developed over hundreds of years. Medieval "joyners" used a primitive rip saw. (I'm told that the average joyner could resaw about four boards in his lifetime — five, if he started young.) In the late eighteenth century, European cabinetmakers developed the "veneer" saw to resaw expensive, imported mahogany lumber. Then, in the mid-nineteenth century, toolmakers developed the first bandsaws. This saw was tailor-made for resawing. The kerf of the bandsaw blade was narrow (so there was little waste), and the action of the tool kept the wood pressed against the table. For over a hundred years, the bandsaw has remained the best tool for the job.

But even though nothing does it better, resawing "pushes the envelope" of the bandsaw. Often times, when you resaw a board, you're sawing through as much wood as the tool was meant to handle. On most homeshop bandsaws, the depth-of-cut is 6″ — a little less than the typical width of a board in the hardwood bins of your local lumberyard. Cutting through the width of a hardwood board puts enormous demands on every part of the machine — the frame, the guides, the blade, and the motor.

Figure 1. Before you resaw, check that the "cutting length" — the portion of the blade between the guides — is perfectly square to the bandsaw table.

Figure 2. Here's an example of what a little vibration can do to the quality of your cut. The motor pulley that came with my bandsaw had a bad wobble that caused the blade to vibrate. I resawed the left half of this board using the wobbly pulley, and the right half using a better pulley that I bought as a replacement.

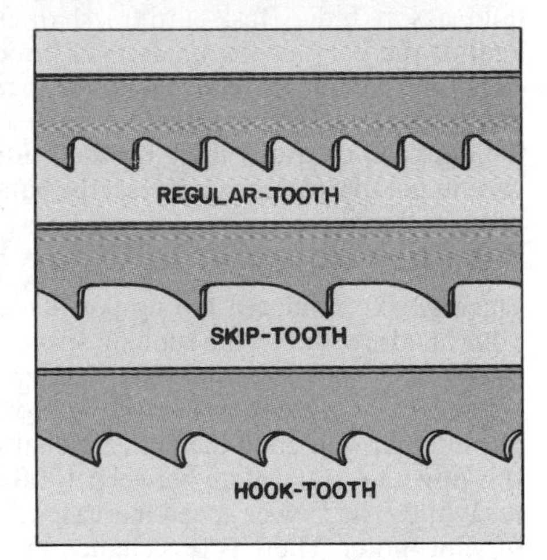

Figure 3. There are three types of woodcutting bandsaw blades, as these are classified according to the type of teeth on the blade — (1) regular or raker tooth, (2) skip tooth, and (3) hook tooth.

Because of this, if there is *anything* out of whack on your bandsaw, the effects will be magnified when you're resawing. If the best tool for the job is to be an adequate tool for the job, all the parts have to be properly aligned, adjusted, and balanced to work in harmony.

Back to the Basics

To understand how the parts of your bandsaw work together — and what could go wrong when they don't — we need to review a few basics. Let's start with a definition: The bandsaw is a thin, continuous blade, running under tension between two or more wheels. A frame supports the wheels and the blade, while a table supports the work and keeps it at the proper angle to the blade.

Since the blade is thin, it can be distorted or deflected easily. Feed the work too quickly or turn it too abruptly, and the blade will bend or twist. To keep the blade running true, most bandsaws have two sets of blade guides and thrust bearings, above and below the table. These support the blade from three directions. The bearings back up the blade and keep it from bending when you feed the stock. The guides rub against the sides and keep it from twisting.

If any of these parts are poorly aligned or adjusted, the quality of the cut will suffer. The thicker the stock, the greater the effect of the misalignment or maladjustment. When cutting thin stock, you may be able to live with a bandsaw that's seriously out of whack. You may not even know it *is* out of whack — the problems may not be discernible. But they will become all too apparent when you try to resaw. So, before beginning a resawing operation, *take the time to check your saw.* If necessary, realign or readjust the blade tracking, blade tension, angle of the table to the blade (It must be precisely square. See Figure 1.), relationship of the upper and lower blade guides (they must be in line), position of the thrust bearings, and the position of the blade guides.

All of these things should be discussed in-depth in your owner's manual. There's no sense in giving them more than a mention here. But there is one common problem that you won't find in your manual — *vibration.* No manufacturer likes to admit that their machine vibrates, but they all do. And this vibration can affect the quality of the cut as much or more than anything else on the checklist.

Vibration is the cumulative effect of all the tiny problems with all the moving parts on the bandsaw. It starts at the motor and travels up the pulleys, belt, and the wheels to the blade itself. The blade picks up the vibrations of the machine and slaps back and forth in the kerf, the teeth scraping one face of the cut and then the other. If the vibration is too great, this will produce a "washboard" effect — the cut will be rough and uneven. (See Figure 2.)

Many things add to the problem of vibration. Motors are sometimes out of balance, pulleys wobble, belts may not be formed properly, wheels can be out of round. If you suspect one or more of these may be causing your bandsaw to vibrate excessively, track down the problem and fix it.

Choosing and Using a Blade

Once you're certain that your bandsaw is running smoothly, the next step in resawing is to choose an appropriate blade. There's no way to over-emphasize the importance of this. As surprising as it may sound, choosing a good blade is more important than choosing a good bandsaw. Traditionally, the best choice for resawing is the widest blade your bandsaw will handle, with as few "teeth per inch" as you can find. For most homeshop bandsaws, this is a ½"-wide blade, with 3 to 4 teeth per inch.

In addition to the number of teeth, you must also select the *type* of teeth on the blade. There are three choices — regular or raker, skip-tooth, and hook-tooth. (See Figure 3.) Ordinary wood-cutting bandsaw blades have raker teeth. The teeth are close together with a minimum set to produce a fairly smooth cut. They cut well in thin stock, but there isn't enough "chip clearance" between the teeth to cut thick stock. The gullets fill up quickly with sawdust, and the resulting friction generates a lot of heat. The wood burns and pitch loads up on the blade. As you might imagine, raker teeth are not well-suited for resawing.

Skip-tooth blades (sometimes called "buttressed" blades) have only half as many teeth as a same-size raker blade. There is more room for chip clearance between the teeth, and consequently the blades cut well in thick stock. Many experienced woodworkers prefer these for resawing, although the advantages over hook-teeth are debatable.

Hook-tooth blades have more teeth than the skip-tooth variety, but fewer than the ordinary raker. The gullets are fairly deep, so there is adequate chip clearance for cutting thick stock. The tooth design makes the blade cut aggressively — the stock almost feeds itself. You don't have to pay quite so much attention to the feed pressure, and this frees you to concentrate on tracking the cut. There is a hidden danger, however. Because the cut is aggressive, you may feed the stock too fast without knowing it. This may cause the motor to bog down or the blade to cup.

Once you select a blade for resawing, you may want to "tune" it slightly so that it runs as smoothly as possible. Some blades — especially new ones — have a slight "tick" when they're running. This is usually caused by a bad weld. Either the weld is slightly misaligned, or it hasn't been properly ground. In either case, it will affect the quality of the cut. It may also cause the blade to break prematurely if you don't eliminate the tick.

Unless the weld has been badly botched, you can smooth out this tick by "stoning" the blade while it's running. Turn on the machine and let it get up to speed, then hold a soft India (fast cutting) sharpening stone *lightly* against the back of the blade. You'll feel the weld bump each time it comes around. Continue to feed the stone very gently until you feel the bump disappear. After you stone the back, do the same thing on each side of the blade. Be careful not to stone the teeth, just the band.

Adjusting the Speed

Once you've mounted the proper blade for resawing on your bandsaw, adjust the running speed of the blade. (This may not be possible on some machines.) The standard speed for a homeshop bandsaw is approximately 3000 feet per minute (fpm), and the conventional wisdom is to slow this down to somewhere between 1000 and 1500 fpm for resawing. The slower speed increases the effective torque of your motor. There is less chance that the machine will bog down while cutting through thick stock. The slower speed also reduces the friction of the blade in the cut. Since the blade does not get quite so hot, it stays sharp longer, doesn't load up with pitch quite so fast, and there is less chance that it will burn the wood.

But, as I said, this is just the conventional wisdom. In experimenting with different blade/speed combinations, I found that the bandsaw leaves a smoother cut on the resawn board if you run it at the standard 3000 fpm or even *slightly* higher. The blade has to be sharp, and you have to resist the temptation to feed the stock too quickly. As long as you keep the feed rate slow, there are more cuts per inch and the normal washboarding evens out. Each tooth takes a smaller bite, carrying away fewer chips, so the temperature of the blade stays within limits.

By the way, if you don't know the speed of your saw, it's easy enough to figure out. Divide the diameter, in inches, of the motor pulley (MP) by the diameter of the bandsaw pulley (BP) to get the pulley ratio. Multiply this ratio times the rpm of the motor (RPM) and the circumference of the bandsaw drive wheel. (The circumference is the diameter of the wheel (DW) times *pi* (3.1416).) Since the answer is in inches, divide by 12 to get feet per minute. Here's the equation:

$$\frac{MP}{BP} \times RPM \times DW \times \frac{3.1416}{12} = FPM$$

Preparing the Stock

Once you've adjusted the speed, square two adjacent sides of the boards that you want to resaw. *This is important!* Since the table is square to the blade, the stock must sit square on the table. The stock must also have a flat side to help you guide it past the blade. To square the stock, first run it through your planer to smooth one face. Then joint an adjacent edge, keeping the smooth face pressed against the jointer fence. When you resaw, rest the jointed edge on the table and keep the smooth face flat against the bandsaw pivot or fence — whatever you're using to help guide the wood.

Final Preparations

Adjust the upper blade guide so that it's just ⅛" to ¼" above the upper edge of the wood. This, too, is very important. The closer together the blade guides, the less chance there will be that the blade will distort in the cut. Also, any exposed blade is a safety hazard.

Finally, gather up the safety tools you'll need — a push stick or a push shoe, a featherboard, a saw stand, safety glasses, and a dust mask. The push stick or push shoe will help you finish the cut, keeping your fingers out of harm's way. Most woodworkers use a push stick, but I prefer the shoe — the pressure from the sole of the shoe helps keep the stock flat against the pivot or fence. When resawing with a fence, I use a thick featherboard for the same reason.

If you're resawing long stock without shop help, you'll need a saw stand — maybe two, one for infeed and one for outfeed. These support the portions of the stock that hang over the sides of the table. You'll also need safety glasses and a dust mask because, as you're about to find out, resawing kicks up a *lot* of sawdust. If you have a dust port on your bandsaw, hook this up to a shop vacuum or dust collector.

Resawing Techniques

Now you're ready to resaw. There are three different techniques, depending on what you use to guide the stock past the blade — free-hand, pivot, and fence.

Free-hand resawing — Because of the design of the bandsaw, it's possible to resaw free-hand, with nothing to guide the stock. As I said earlier, the motion of the blade keeps the stock against the table; there's no danger of it kicking back or falling over. As long as the bottom edge of the stock is jointed flat and you can follow a line with a blade, you'll get good results.

Practically, however, it's easier to be accurate if you use *something* to guide the stock and help keep it upright.

When resawing free-hand, I employ a piece of 2 x 4 as a guide block. Any old scrap of wood will do, as long as it's been cut off at 90° and will fit comfortably in one hand.

Once you've located a suitable guide block, scribe the upper edge of the board to be resawn with a marking gauge, marking the cuts you want to make. (See Figure 4.) After marking the stock, grasp the guide block in one hand and the board in the other. Hold the block down against the table to one side of the blade, and press the planed side of the board up against it. Slowly feed the stock into the blade, turning both the board *and* the guide block as needed to keep the blade following the cutline. Keep the board against the guide block all through the cut. (See Figure 5.) Feed the last few inches with the aid of a push stick or push block.

Obviously, this technique does not work well for large boards. The stock has to be small enough for you to safely and competently handle with one hand. But it's a useful method to know when you need just a little bit of thinned-out stock, and don't want to take the time to set up a pivot or a fence. If the stock is narrow enough, you don't even have to change blades.

Pivot resawing — If you'd rather have both hands free to guide the wood when you resaw small stock, you can use a fixed pivot instead of a guide block. This pivot is clamped to the table on one side of the blade. The distance from the blade to the pivot determines the width of the cut.

You'll have to make the pivot; it's not available as a bandsaw accessory. The edge of this pivot should be *pointed,* not round, to provide a true "pivot point." When the wood pivots against a rounded edge, it moves sideways in relation to the blade. This movement is very slight, but it's enough to distort the blade. Any such distortion will detract from the quality of the cut. A pointed pivot eliminates most of this movement. When you mount the pivot on your machine, the point should be dead-even with the teeth of the blade, as you look at the bandsaw from the side. (See Figure 6.)

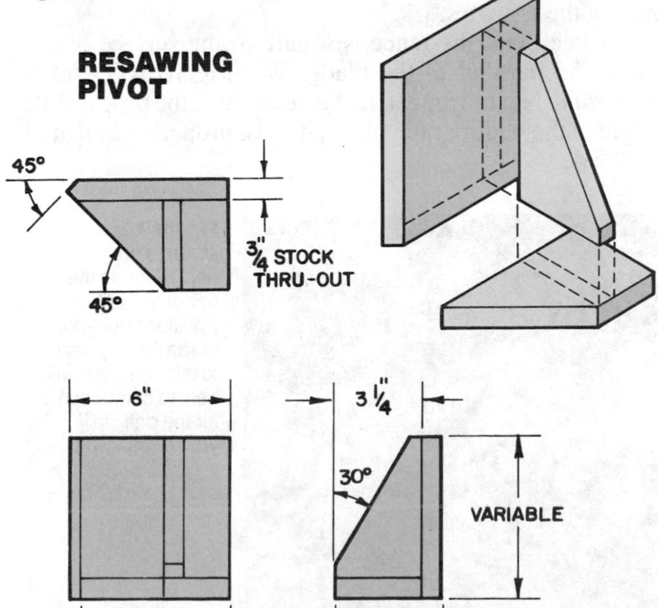

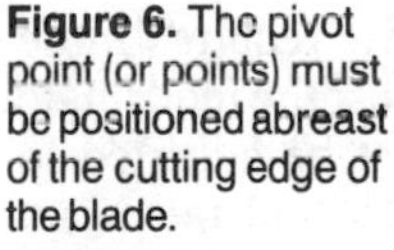
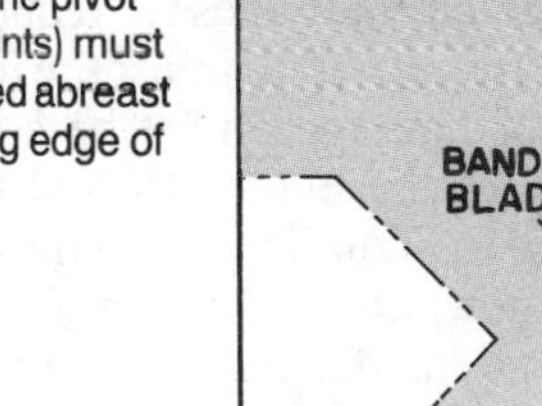

Once you've positioned the pivot and clamped it to the table, proceed in much the same manner as you would with a free-hand cut. Mark the cutting line on the top edge of the stock, and feed the stock into the blade. Make the blade follow the cutline by turning the stock slightly (adjusting the feed angle) as needed, but always keep the smooth side of the stock firmly against the pivot. (See Figure 7.)

Figure 4. Use a marking gauge to mark the cutlines on the upper edge of the board. I do this even when I resaw with a fence. The cutlines help me monitor the "drift" of the blade as it cuts.

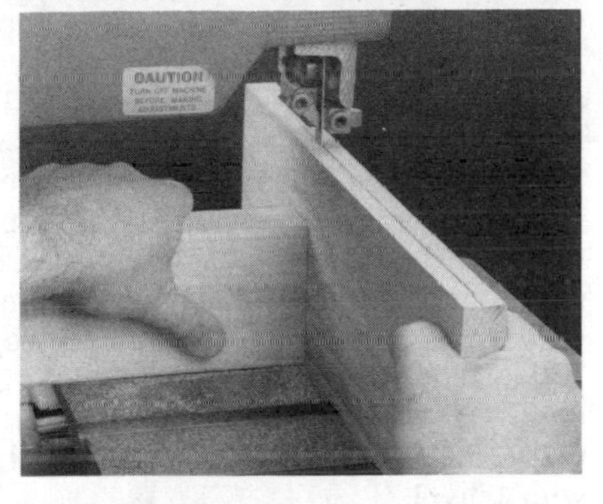

Figure 5. When resawing free-hand, use a large scrap of wood as a guide block. One end of this scrap must be cut off at 90°. This helps to keep the wood square to the table.

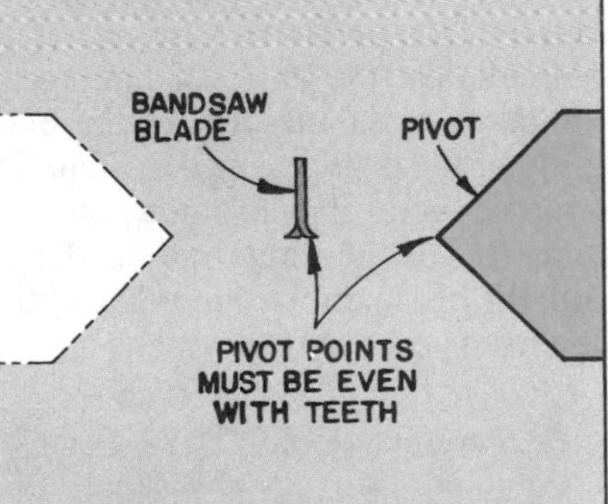

Figure 6. The pivot point (or points) must be positioned abreast of the cutting edge of the blade.

Figure 7. Clamp the pivot securely to the bandsaw table. The distance between the pivot and the blade determines the width of the cut. When you cut, keep the smooth (planed) face of the stock against the pivot.

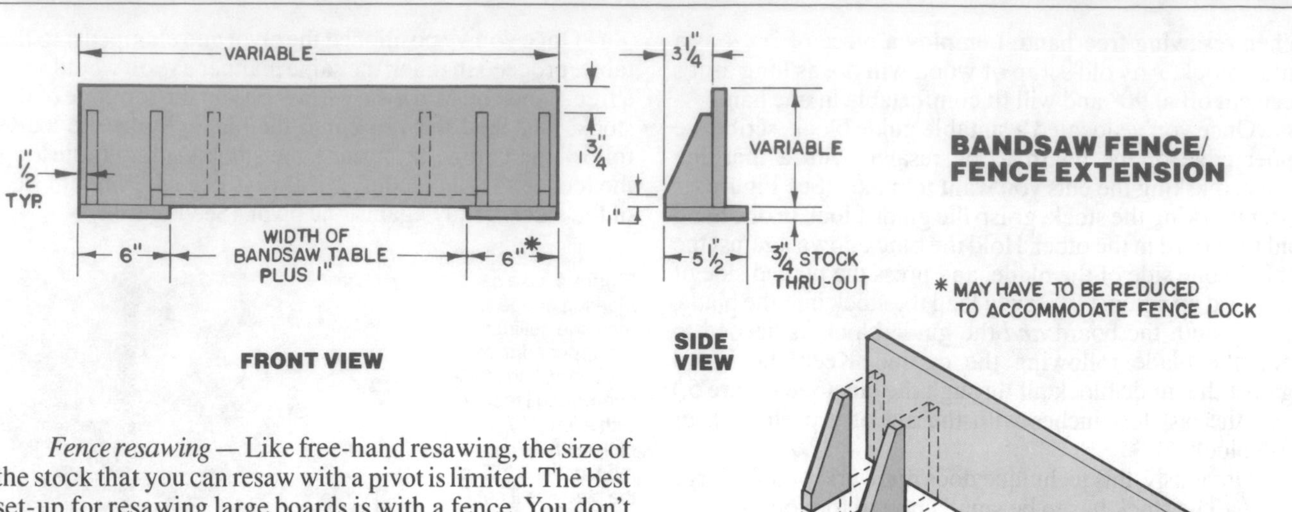

Fence resawing — Like free-hand resawing, the size of the stock that you can resaw with a pivot is limited. The best set-up for resawing large boards is with a fence. You don't need to maneuver the stock at all, just keep it flat against the fence and feed it into the blade.

Like the pivot, you'll have to make the fence. Most manufacturers don't offer bandsaw fences. This fence or fence extension should be longer than the bandsaw table is wide. A long fence provides better support for the stock. You may also want to add "ledges" on the bottom edge of the fence where it overhangs the table. These provide additional support and make it easier to control long boards.

Finally, the fence or fence extension should be somewhat shorter than the width of the stock that you want to resaw, so that you can properly adjust the height of the upper blade guide. You may want to make several fences for various sizes of stock. I've made two, 3"- and 4½"-high. The 3" fence provides adequate support for resawing stock up to 4½" wide, and the 4½" fence works well for stock up to 6" wide. Anything narrower than 3", I resaw free-hand or with a pivot.

Positioning the fence on the bandsaw requires more care than the pivot. Because you can't adjust the feed angle of the stock, the angle of the fence must be adjusted to compensate for the drift of the blade. To find the exact angle of the drift, scribe a straight line down the edge of a scrap of wood that's somewhat longer than your table is wide. Resaw the scrap free-hand, adjusting the feed angle until the blade tracks the cutline with only minimal correction from you. Stop the saw and clamp the scrap to the table. (See Figure 8.) The angle of the scrap on the table — probably a few degrees off parallel with the width of the blade — is the angle you should use to set your fence.

Draw a line on your table with a soft-lead pencil, using the scrap as a straightedge. Position your bandsaw fence parallel to this line. (See Figure 9.) Like the pivot, the distance from the blade to the fence determines the thickness of the resawn stock.

Check that the fence is square to the surface of the table and parallel to the blade. (See Figure 10.) *This is important!* Not only must the fence be set at the proper drift angle to the width of the blade, it must properly aligned to the blade.

Figure 8. Before you can resaw with a fence, you must first find the "drift" of your blade. Scribe a straight line down the middle of a long scrap, and saw the line. As you cut, adjust the feed angle until the blade tracks the cutline accurately. Stop cutting and clamp the scrap to the table.

Figure 9. Use the scrap to draw a pencil line on the bandsaw table. Position your shop-made fence parallel to this line. This will help to compensate for the drift while you're resawing.

Cut a small "test piece" off the end of the board you want to resaw, about 12″ long. (You don't want to start right in, cutting an 8′-long board, without first checking your setup.) Scribe a line along the top edge. The line isn't necessary, of course; you're not going to follow a cutline as you do with free-hand or pivot resawing. But the line will help you monitor whether or not the blade is drifting in the cut. Resaw the test piece, keeping the smooth or planed face firmly against the fence.

As you cut, look and listen for problems. Does the machine bog down easily? Is there excessive chatter? Does the blade wander back and forth? Does it pull to one side? After you finish the cut, inspect the test piece for more problems. Is the cut the proper width? Is the thickness even across the width of the board? Is there excessive wash-boarding? Most of these problems can be easily corrected by checking the alignment and adjustment of your machine. When you're satisfied with the results of your test cuts, start resawing the good stuff. (See Figure 11.)

A Few Notes on Cupping and Blade Tension

One particularly common problem — cupping — needs a bit more of an explanation. Cupping is when blade bows in the wood, cutting a curve through the thickness of the stock. (See Figure 12.) This can be caused by many different things — too much feed pressure, a dull blade, a blade that's too flimsy for the job. But the most common cause is not enough blade tension. This may surprise and worry you, particularly if you've already adjusted the tension to the recommended setting on the scale. Can you safely adjust the tension higher? Yes, as long as the blade and the weld are in good condition.

Blade tension is not an absolute. You don't necessarily want to run a particular blade at a particular tension all the time. Some cutting jobs may progress better with the blade tensioned higher than normal, and resawing is one of those jobs. Most blades will withstand higher tensions than recommended with no damage. But how high can you go — safely?

I talked to an engineer who designs woodworking tools, and he recommended that I use this method: Mount the blade and crank up the tension to the recommended setting on the scale. Cut a test piece and, if you're not satisfied with the result, give the tension knob an extra turn or two. Stop when you get a good, smooth cut with no cupping.

By the way, whenever you adjust the tension you should have the wheel covers closed or secured. If the blade should break — whether because of a bad weld or too much tension — you want something solid between you and the teeth. Also, don't adjust the tension so high that it collapses the tension spring (that is, the coils must not close completely). When the coils are open, this spring provides a "shock absorber" to dampen the vibrations of the machine. Once the coils of the spring have collapsed, minor problems with your bandsaw quickly become major ones. Both the blade and the machine may be over-stressed.

Finally, don't use flat washers or a piece of pipe as spacers to shore up the spring. Contrary to a popular bit of woodworking mythology, this does *not* raise the tension. All it does is make it easier to collapse the tension spring.

Figure 10. The fence or the fence extension must be parallel to the cutting length of the blade. If the blade is square to the table, then the fence should also be square. Note the ledges on either side of the fence. These provide additional support for the stock on the infeed and outfeed sides of the table.

Parting Thoughts

As you can see, there is more to resawing than the woodworking books and owner's manuals may have led you to believe. But it's a useful technique, one that will save you a good deal of time and money — and lumber.

Better yet, everything that I've told you about resawing *translates.* That is to say, there are many other applications for all this knowledge; it isn't just bandsaw trivia. Exploring resawing in depth is an education in bandsaw design and operation. This, in turn, helps you to use the tool to your best advantage.

Figure 11. Keep the stock pressed firmly against the fence as you feed it. Besides a fence, you may need a few other shop aids when you resaw. The featherboard helps keep the stock flat against the fence, and the saw stand helps to support long boards.

Figure 12. One of the most common resawing problems is "cupping" — the blade bows in the stock. Usually, this problem can be cured by increasing the blade tension. The piece of wormy chestnut on the left was cut with the tension too low. The piece on the right was cut after the tension had been readjusted.

Text by Jim McCann.

Duplication Carving

Need to make exact copies of intricate parts for a project? Here's how to do it the easy way.

Every now and then, you come across a woodworking project with not one, but *several* intricately-shaped parts. The "Queen Anne Tables" at the beginning of this book is one such project. To make the complete set — coffee table, corner table, and end table — you need to make twelve cabriole legs. Each cabriole must be chiseled, filed, and sanded to give it smooth flowing contours.

What's more, these shapes are all duplicates of each other. The four short cabriole legs on the coffee table are the same, and so are the eight long cabrioles on the corner table and end table. You'd think that there would be some tool to easily duplicate the shapes without having to make each one over again from scratch. Well, there is — your router.

Actually, you need a little more than your router. You also need a special attachment for the router called, simply, a "duplicator." Several different companies make duplicators and offer them at different prices, from just over a hundred dollars on up to a thousand or more. The one shown here — a "Dupli-Carver" — is typical of many of the duplicators that you'll find near the low end, price-wise. It's reasonably sturdy and accurate, and it can be adapted to duplicate long, large shapes like cabriole legs.

How It Works

The duplicator "traces" a three-dimensional shape and cuts it in wood. The shape is traced with a "stylus" and cut with a router. First, you mount a bit in the router that has exactly the same profile as the stylus. (There are several different sizes and shapes of styli and matching bits for tracing both rough and fine details.) Then you move the stylus across the solid shape. The stylus moves the router in exactly the same way, so that it duplicates the shape in a block of wood.

Duplicating a spindle shape, such as a cabriole leg, isn't quite that simple; but the same principle applies. However, in additional to moving the stylus, you must also rotate the legs. Both the pattern leg (the "shape") and the duplicated leg must rotate in unison. Several of the duplicator manufacturers make special accessories to do this. The accessory for the Dupli-Carver is called, as you might have guessed, the "Spindle-Carver."

Mounting the Pattern Leg and the Blank

The first thing you need to duplicate a shape such as a cabriole leg is a cabriole leg. So you're going to have to make one by hand. This will become your "pattern leg." The others will be exact copies of it, so take your time while making it. Do not sand this leg yet, just shape it with a file.

Tip ◆ The duplicator makes a good rotating vise for holding the leg stock while you shape it.

Drill a hole dead-center in the bottom of the feet of the leg blanks, so that you can mount them on the duplicating machine. When you rough out the cabriole shapes of the blanks on the bandsaw, cut all the curves except the ears ⅛" *oversize.* You may want to make oversize templates for marking the cabriole shapes on these leg blanks. The extra stock will make up for any inconsistencies in size or shape from blank to blank.

Depending on the shape of the leg, you may also have to make an adaptor to hold the blank on the machine. I did when I duplicated the cabriole legs for the Queen Anne tables — the working drawings for this adaptor are shown in Figure 1. In fact, you'll have to make two adaptors — one for the pattern and one for the blank. They must be exactly alike. To make them so, stack the adaptor blanks together, then pad drill and pad saw the holes and circular shapes.

Mount the adaptor stock on the baseplate with sheet metal screws. Fit the pattern leg and a leg blank to them. (See Figure 2.) If the recesses are slightly large, wedge the legs in place so that the *inside* surfaces of the legs are tight against the adaptor. (See Figure 3.)

Figure 2. Mount the adaptor to the spindle plate of the duplicator with sheet metal screws.

Figure 3. If the recesses in the adaptor are too large, wedge the legs securely.

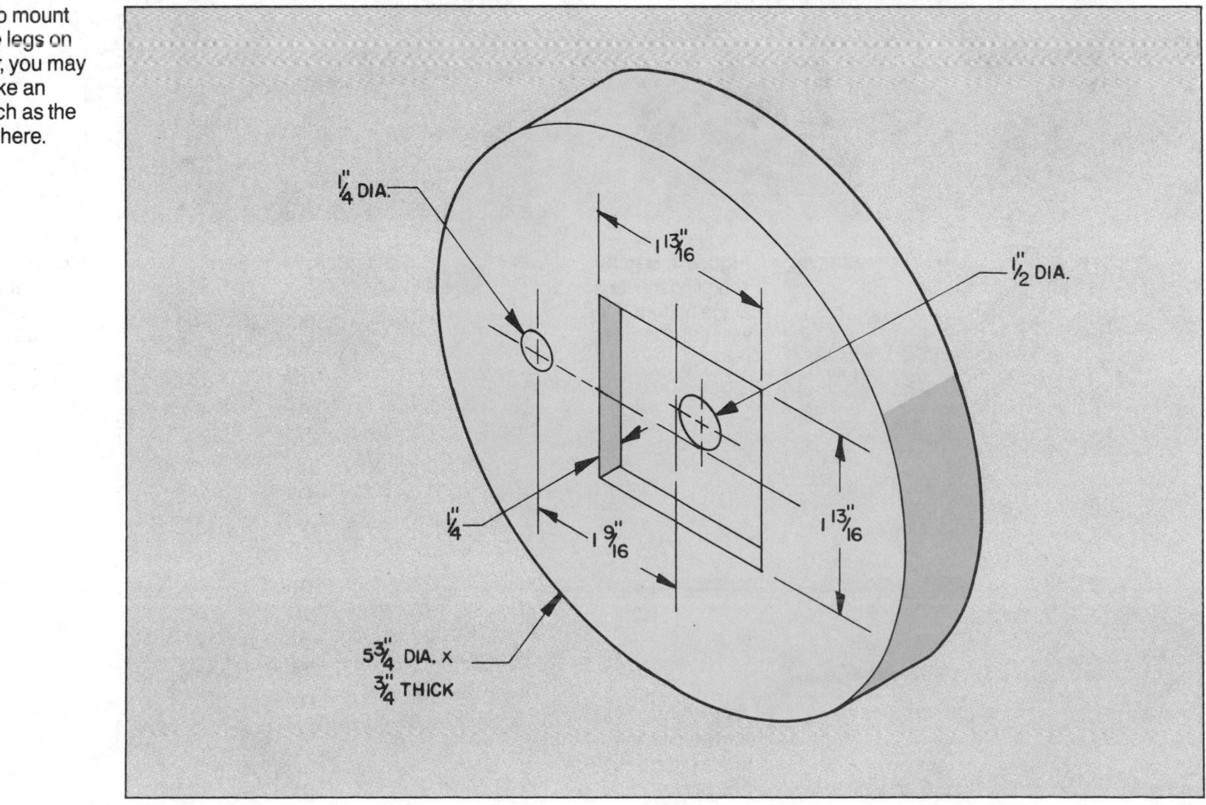

Figure 1. To mount the cabriole legs on a duplicator, you may have to make an adaptor, such as the one shown here.

Rotate the leg and the blank so that you can access the surfaces you want to duplicate with the duplicator — I prefer to start with the outside corner facing up. Be sure that you can easily reach the bottom of the foot with both the bit and the stylus. Lock the parts in place so that they won't rotate.

Carefully align the bottom of the foot on the pattern leg with the bottom of the foot on the leg blank. You can do this by simply resting the stylus on the bottom of the pattern leg and adjusting the machine until both the stylus and the router bit touch the bottom of their respective feet. This adjustment has to be checked from time to time, and readjusted every time you mount a new leg blank.

Carving the Cabriole Shape

During the actual duplication or sculpting, the router bit will remove varying amounts of stock, depending on how big a bite you tell it to take with the stylus. When you only have to remove small amounts of stock — that is, make shallow cuts — you can hold the stylus directly against the surface of the pattern leg. But when cutting large amounts of stock — when forming the foot, for example — you must carve the wood away in stages. Hold the stylus slightly above the surface of the leg and make several passes, cutting deeper with each pass. Finish the cut when the stylus is resting on the surface of the leg.

If you have a variable speed router, use slower speeds for removing large amounts of stock. The router will be easier to control. Always move the stylus so that the router bit cuts *against* the direction of rotation. This is especially important when you are cutting with the side of the bit. This will help keep the router from digging gouges in the wood or from "climbing" the stock, out of control.

Begin sculpting the legs at the bottom. Sculpt the bottom and the front of the foot. (See Figure 4.) This is one of those times when you will be cutting with the side of the bit, so remember the direction of rotation and watch how you move the stylus. The round bit will leave a concave edge where the bottom of the foot and the foot pad meet. You can clean this up with a file later.

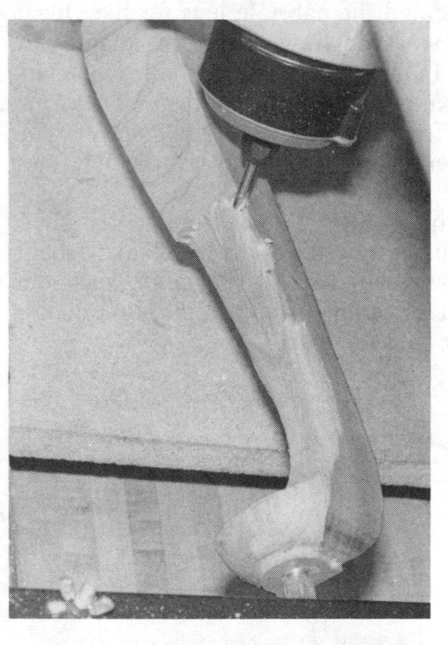

Figure 6. Sculpt the shin, as far as you can comfortably reach.

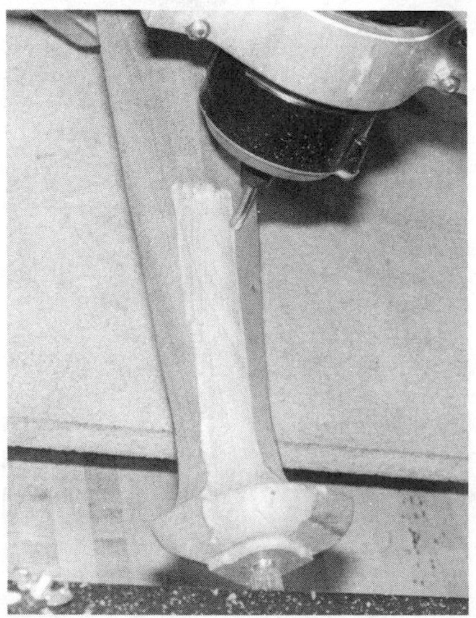

Figure 4. Begin sculpting the legs at the bottom. Start with the bottom of the foot.

Figure 5. Then move up to the ankle and the toe.

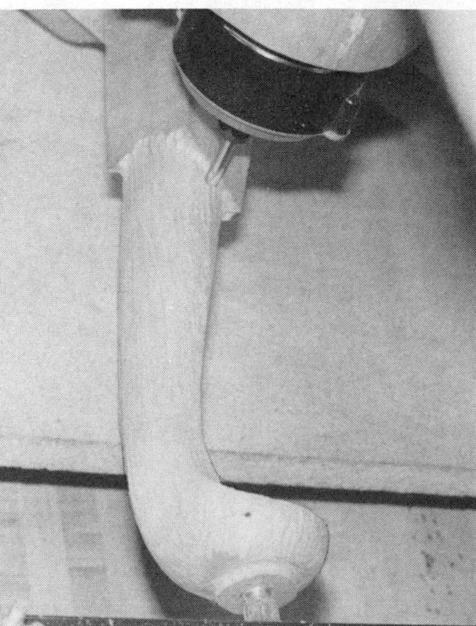

Figure 7. After you finish with a surface, turn the pattern and the leg blank 90° counterclockwise and begin all over again.

Now move the leg to sculpt the top front of the foot. Remember to work from left to right, moving the bit from the ankle to the toe. This will help you to control the cuts. (See Figure 5.) Complete this portion of the leg by working on up over the shin as far as you can reach, comfortably. (See Figure 6.) Go back over the area that you just sculpted and clean up the surfaces, trying to make them as smooth as possible.

Rotate the pattern and the blank 90° counterclockwise and lock them in place. Sculpt the bottom left side of the foot and the lower leg, using the same procedures as you used on the front. (See Figure 7.) Repeat this for the back of the leg and the right side. Turn the pattern and the blank just 90° each time.

Once you have formed the lower section, reposition yourself so that you can comfortably reach the upper parts of the leg. Adjust the position of the pattern and the blank so that the outside corners are facing up, and lock them in place. Sculpt the top and front side of the knee and the upper leg. (See Figure 8.) Once again, use the same procedures to remove stock from this portion of the leg as you did to remove stock from the lower section. Each time you finish a side, rotate the leg 90° counterclockwise and begin a new surface. (See Figure 9.) Then repeat the entire procedure for all the leg blanks.

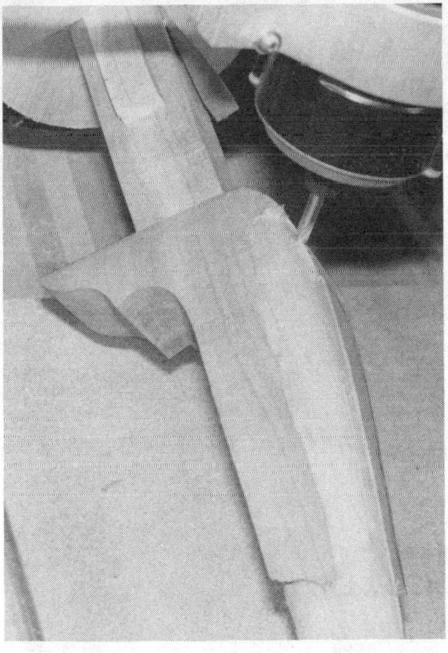

Figure 8. After you've done all four sides of the lower leg, switch to the upper section. Start with the top outside corner of the knee.

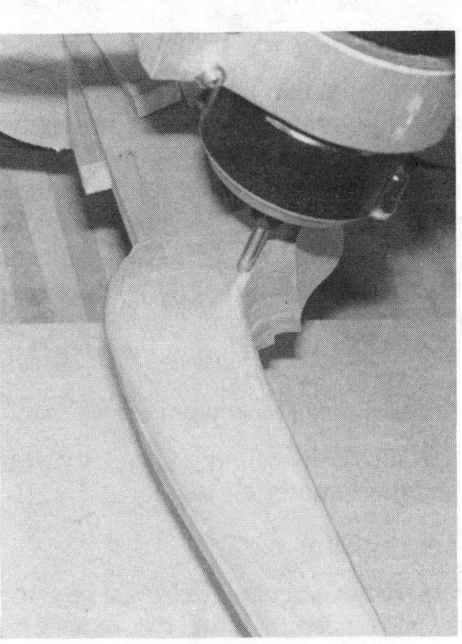

Figure 9. Once again, as you finish a surface, rotate the pattern and the leg blank. Always rotate in the same direction.

Smoothing the Duplicated Legs

Once you have sculpted all the legs, they will need to be smoothed, detailed, and sanded. Leave the pattern leg mounted in the duplicator for reference, and begin smoothing the middle sections of the leg blank with double-cut files and rasps. (See Figure 10.) I used a half-round (Bastard) file, flat file, cabinetmakers rasp, and rat-tail file for various parts of the leg. Stop removing stock just as soon as the mill marks from the router disappear. This will keep the cabriole shape consistent from leg to leg.

Use a light touch to avoid gouging the wood, especially when working with rasps. If you wish, use several layers of masking tape to protect areas of the legs (such as the posts) that you don't want to accidentally damage with the files.

Sand the leg while the blank is still mounted in the duplicator. As I mentioned, these machines make excellent vises for holding the cabriole legs while you work on them.

Parting Thoughts

These instructions pertain specifically to cabriole legs, but the procedures are essentially the same for any shape. Duplicators are not only useful for making duplicate legs, but many other wooden parts — signs, intricate moldings, ball-and-claw feet, finials, carved chair seats and chair backs. The list is endless.

They also have other applications besides making new furniture, particularly in repair and restoration. If you have a cracked leg on an antique rocker, you can use the old, ruined part as a pattern to create a new, precise duplicate. Restore broken gun stocks in the same way. Or replace missing architectural moldings in old houses. Again, the list is endless. The duplicator is an extremely versatile tool, one that extends the woodworking capabilities of your router more than I have room to tell here.

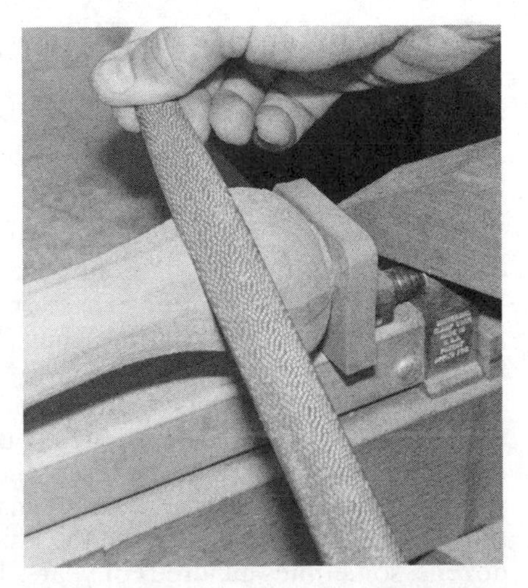

Figure 10. After sculpting the cabriole shape with the router, remove the millmarks with files and rasps.

The author thanks Wood-Mizer Products of Indianapolis, Indiana, for their help in preparing this article.

Text by Nick Engler.

Weaving Chair Seats

Here are two traditional methods for covering the seats of country chairs.

The seats of "turner's chairs," such as the weaver's chair earlier in this book, are frequently woven onto the chair frame. These seats are, in fact, an important *structural* part of the chair. Without them, the frame would soon fall apart.

The woven seat acts like a huge band clamp. Each time you sit in the seat, the weight of your body tightens the clamp, drawing the frame together. The parts of the chair actually flex *less* while you're sitting in it than many other types of chairs, and this keeps the chair serviceable for dozens, sometimes hundreds of years. That's why it is not unusual to find two-hundred-year-old turner's chairs in antique shops throughout New England.

Materials

Chair seats can be woven from a variety of materials — rush, cloth tape, wooden splints, leather strips, cane, rope, even twisted paper! We don't have time to cover all these materials in this chapter, but we will show you how to work with two of the most long-lasting and attractive materials — cloth tape and rush. These materials can be purchased from several different mail-order sources. Here are two:

The Connecticut Cane and Reed Company
P.O. Box 1276
Manchester, CT 06040

Shaker Workshops
P.O. Box 1028
Concord, MA 01742

If you live in or near a large city, you may also be able to find these materials locally at a crafts shop.

Terminology

Before we can explain to you how to weave either tape or rush, we need to define two new terms — warp and woof.

All weaving is composed of warps and woofs. On a chair, the *warps* are the strands of rush, tape, or whatever that go front to back. The *woofs* are the strands that go side to side. (See Figure 1.) The warps and the woofs are intertwined — sometimes under, sometimes over — creating a *weave* or pattern. You can make different patterns by changing the manner in which the strands travel over and under each other.

Weaving a Rush Seat

Of the two materials, rush is by far the most ancient. Quite possibly, the first turner's chairs were covered with rush seats.

The "rush" we use today, however, is quite different from traditional rush. Traditionally, the rush leaves were twisted into long cords as they were being woven onto the chair frames — you made the cord at the same time that you made the chair seat. Today, the rush cord comes pretwisted. And if you untwist it, you'll likely find that it isn't rush at all. It's either fiber cord or brown paper, the same type of paper used to make grocery bags.

This fiber/paper cord comes in several different sizes, from 2/32" in diameter up to 6/32". Most beginners find it easier to work with 5/32"- or 6/32"-diameter cord. You can also buy the cord in 2-pound and 10-pound coils. As a beginner, you'll find the 2-pound coils easier to work with. You can save some money by purchasing the 10-pound coils, but you'll have to spend the time unwinding the cord, cutting it, and re-rolling it into 2-pound coils before you can use it. A 2-pound coil is *usually* sufficient to weave a single chair, but this will depend on the dimensions of the chair seat and how tight you weave it. Best buy a little extra for each chair.

In addition to the cord, you'll also need:

- 30-40 tacks and a tack hammer, to attach the cord to the chair frame
- Masking tape, to splice lengths of cord together
- Cotton batting, to "pad" the chair seat as you weave it
- A pail of water, to wet the cord before you work with it
- A combination square to check your work
- Scissors, needlenose pliers, a spring clamp, a pencil, and a short length of scrap wood

Begin your rush seat by "filling in the corners." Turner's chair frames are, more often than not, trapezoid-shaped when you look at them from the top. The warp and the woof are perpendicular (square) to each other. When you impose a square on top of this trapezoid, it leaves two "corners" on either side of the chair. (See Figure 2.) These must be filled in with short lengths of cord. Using the square, find the corners and mark them on the front chair rail. (See Figure 3.)

Cut a short length of cord from the coil, a little longer than the front rail. Wet it in the water — wet fiber cord is easier to work with. Tack one end to the left side chair rail, near the front rail. Bring the cord forward, *over* the front rail, back *over* itself, and *over* the side rail. (See Figure 4.) This is the basic weaving technique for rush. Every time you come to a corner, go over, over, and over.

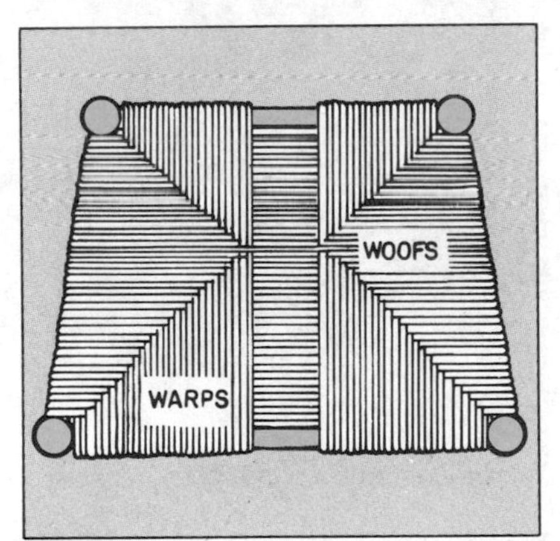

Figure 1. In a chair seat weave, the *warps* are the strands that go front to back. The *woofs* go side to side.

Figure 2. When you impose a square on an ordinary frame chair seat, there will be two "corners" on either side.

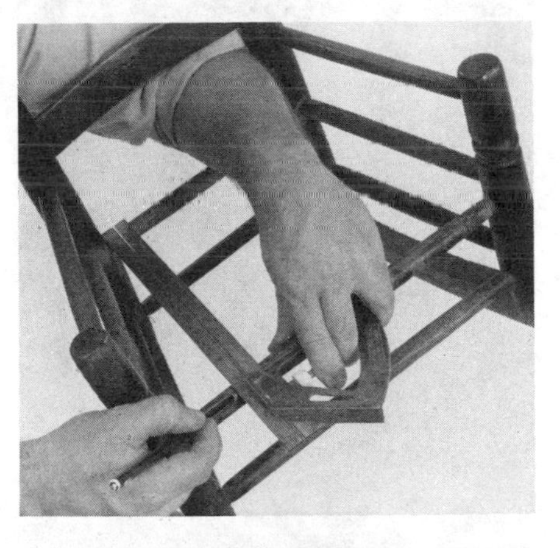

Figure 3. Mark the base of these corners on the front rail with a pencil.

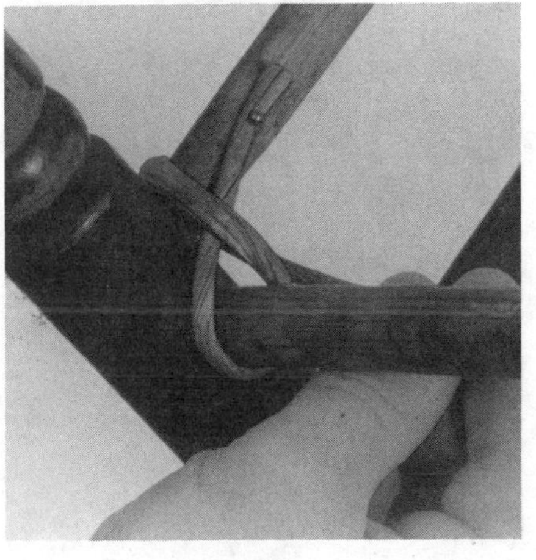

Figure 4. When you come to a post, weave the rush *over* the rail, back *over* the rush, then *over* the second rail.

Bring the cord sideways, go over the right side rail, back over the cord itself, then over the front rail. Tack the cord to the right side rail, near the front rail, and cut off any excess. (See Figure 5.) Then repeat the process over and over, each time cutting the cord a little longer and tacking it to the side rails a little further back from the front rail. Every third or fourth cord, check your work with the combination square. (See Figure 6.) *This is very important!* The warps must be perpendicular to the front rail, and the woofs must be parallel to the front rail. If they aren't, there will be holes or gaps in your pattern when you finish the seat.

Tip ◆ The secret to keeping the warps and the woofs square is knowing when to pull the cord tight. Put tension on the cord as you bring it over the chair rail on the first "over" in each set of three "overs". Don't pull it as tight when you bring it back over itself, then over the other rail. This takes some practice.

If the warps and the woofs are out of square, there are several ways to bring them back into the proper alignment. If the angle is *acute* and the warp takes up too much space on the front rail, place the wooden scrap against the last warp and tap it back toward a corner. (See Figure 7.) If the angle is *obtuse* and the warp takes up too little space on the front rail, place the scrap on top of all the warps and tap it with the hammer. This will mash the cord, spreading the warps out along the rail. Sometimes you need to hit the warps pretty hard to get them to spread out. You may want to dispense with the scrap and use a nylon or rawhide mallet so that you can pound on them directly.

If the hammer doesn't do the job, you'll have to resort to the needlenose pliers to correct your work. To spread out the warps, carefully un-twist the cords where they loop over the rail. This will flatten them so that they take up more space. If the warps need to be compressed, twist the cords tighter.

As you work, stuff cotton batting in between the rush to pad the seat. The weave creates small pockets between the cords at the corners. Every third or fourth warp-and-woof, fill these pockets with batting. (See Figure 8.) Be careful not to overstuff the pockets. Put in just enough batting to help hold the cords taut.

As you work, you'll have to tack the ends of the cords further and further back on the side rails. When you reach the back rail, you will have filled in the corners completely. At this point, you can start a *continuous* four-post weave. Cut a length of cord ten to twenty feet long off the coil — not so long that it's difficult to work with. Wet the cord and tack one end to the left side rail, as near to the back rail as possible. Weave the front left corner, the front right corner,

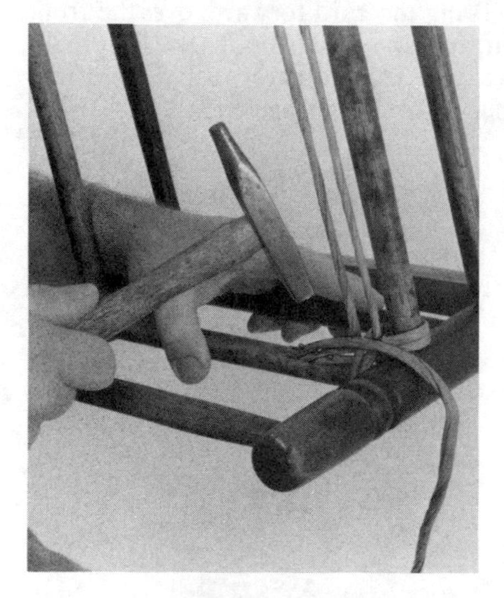

Figure 5. As you're filling in the corners, tack the ends of the fiber cord to the side rails.

Figure 6. Every few rows, check your work with a combination square to make sure the warps and woofs are perpendicular.

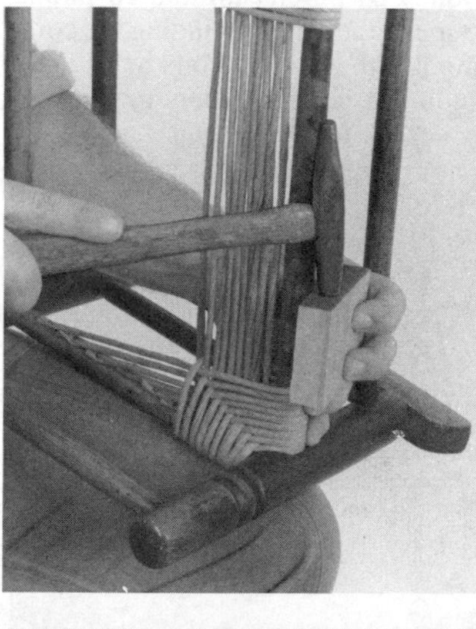

Figure 7. If the warps and woofs are out-of-square, you can tap them into place with a hammer and a scrap of wood.

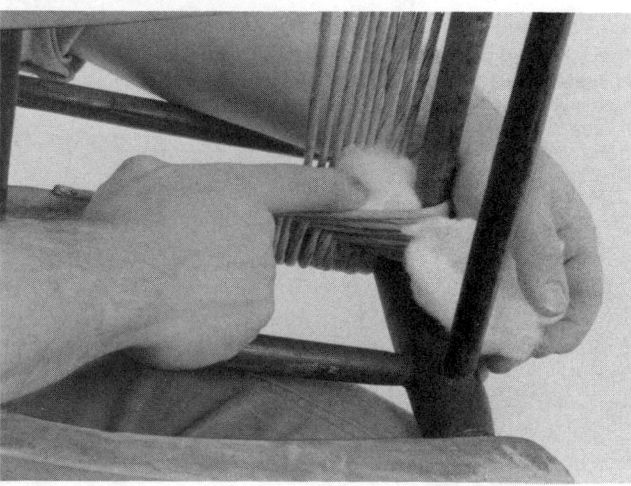

Figure 8. As you weave, stuff the "pockets" in the rush with cotton batting.

the back right corner, and the back left corner, proceeding around the corners of the chair in a counterclockwise direction. (See Figure 9.)

Tip ◆ Left-handed people may find it easier to weave in a *clockwise* direction.

Continue weaving corner after corner. Stop every third or fourth revolution to check your work for squareness and to stuff the pockets with batting. Also check that the weaving proceeds evenly out from the corners, along each rail. You don't want to completely cover one side rail before you've covered the other.

Keep the cord damp — but not too wet — and keep your hands clean so that the cord doesn't get dirty. When you come to the end of a length of cord, splice another length to it. Untwist the tail end of the old length and the leading end of the new one, then twist the ends together. Wrap the splice with masking tape to make sure that it holds. (See Figure 10.) Be careful to make these splices where they won't show — *between* the weaves that are building out from the corners. This way, they will eventually be covered by the weaves and no one will ever see them.

On most chairs, the weaves will probably cover the side rails before they completely cover the front and back rails. When you get to this point, begin weaving *warps only,* front to back. Cut an extra-long length of cord before you start this portion of the chair weave, enough to finish the chair. There will be no way to hide the splices if you have to join the cords during the front-to-back weave.

Weave the cord *over* the front rail, up through the center of the woofs — there should be a slight opening here — *over* the back rail, then up through the center again. (See Figure 11.) Once again, notice that the pattern is all *over.* Keep this in mind all through your weave. Every time you come to a rail, take the cord *over* it.

Completely cover the front and back rails, filling in the middle of the weave. Finish by tacking the end of the cord to the bottom side of the back rail, where it won't show too much. (See Figure 12.) Some rush weavers prefer to tie the end of the cord to an adjacent warp on the bottom side of the chair, using string or twine. If you tie off the last warp, use twine that blends with the cord.

Wait for the rush to dry completely before using the chair. If you wish, you can also apply a finish. The fiber cord will take a stain, if you want to make it darker. Traditionally, rush is finished with either a thin shellac or a mixture of linseed oil and turpentine to help protect the chair seat. But you can use most anything, as long as you thin it sufficiently so that it soaks into the fiber cord and doesn't build up on the surface.

Figure 9. After you fill in the corners, begin a continuous four-post weave, working counterclockwise around the chair frame.

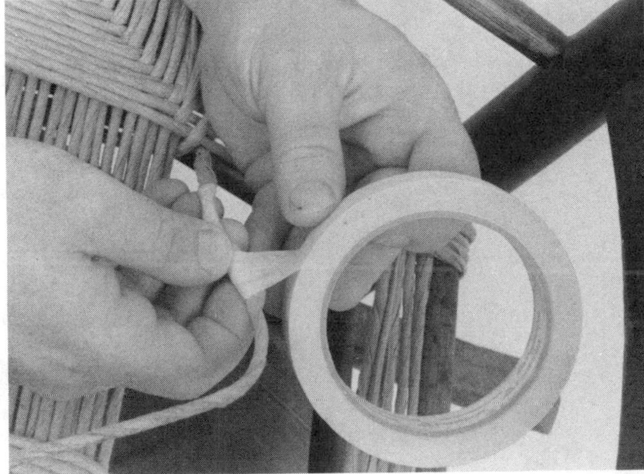

Figure 10. When you come to the end of a length of cord, splice a new length onto it with masking tape.

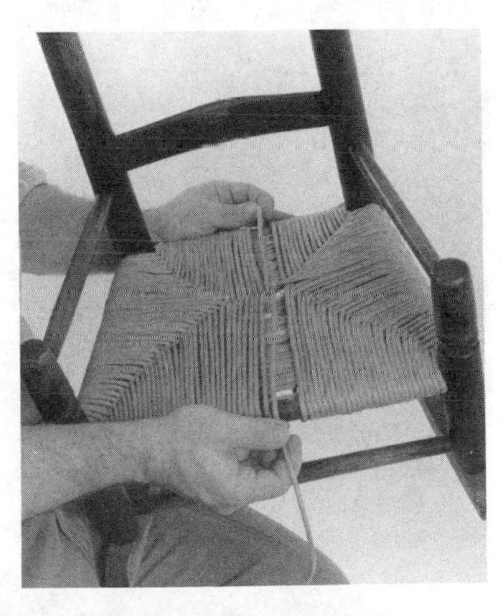

Figure 11. After you completely cover the side rails, begin a front-to-back weave to fill in the middle of the seat.

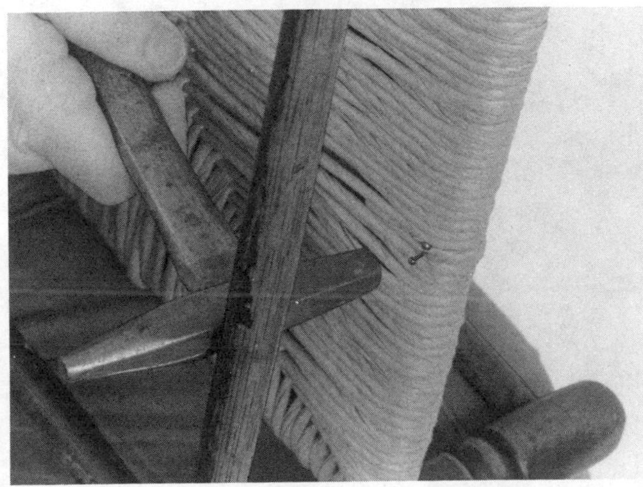

Figure 12. Tack the very end of the cord to the bottom side of the back rail, where it won't be seen.

Weaving Cloth Tape

Cloth tape chair seats first appeared on turner's chairs in the early nineteenth century. At first, cloth seats were fairly rare. But the Shakers — an industrious religious society renowned for their craftsmanship — began to weave seats of tape or "listing" on the chairs that they sold to the general public. Because of their comfort and durability, these chairs became enormously popular. The Shakers sold thousands upon thousands of their chairs all over America, and by the twentieth century, cloth seats were as common as rush.

Cloth tape comes in two common widths — 1″ and ⅝″. 1″-wide tape is the most popular, especially if you're weaving a simple checkerboard pattern. More complex patterns, such as the herringbone, are best woven from ⅝″-wide tape. The tape also comes in an enormous variety of colors. Most seat weavers prefer to mix two colors, using one color for the warp and the other for the woof.

You purchase the tape by the yard — it usually comes in 5-yard and 10-yard rolls. You *normally* need 30 yards of 1″-wide tape to cover a single chair seat — 15 yards of one color and 15 of another.

In addition to the tape, you'll also need:

- 20-24 tacks and a tack hammer to secure the tape to the chair frame
- A needle and thread to splice the tape
- A 1″-thick pad of foam rubber to pad the seat
- Scissors, to cut and trim the tape
- A metal spoon, to help even out the weave

Begin by weaving the warp (front-to-back). If you're using two colors of tape, use the *darker* color for the warp. Since the warp covers the front rail, this will show dirt less than a lighter color. Mark the front rail so that you know where the "corners" are, just as you would do if you were weaving a rush seat. Tack the end of a 10-yard roll of cloth tape to the left side rail, near the back rail. (See Figure 13.) Stretch the warp tape under the back rail, then bring it forward and over the front rail, backward and under the back rail again. (See Figure 14.) Do *not* attempt to fill in the corners. Leave these open; you'll fill them in later. Continue wrapping the warp onto the frame until you've covered the back rail, then tack the warp tape to the right side rail and cut it off.

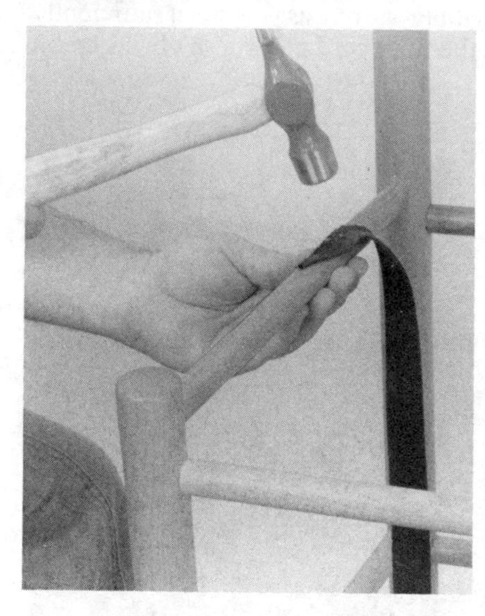

Figure 13. To begin the warp, tack the end of the cloth tape to the left side rail.

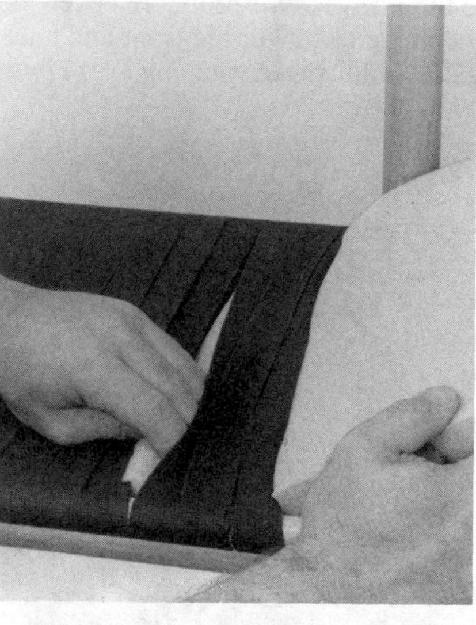

Figure 15. Stuff the cavity between the top and bottom warps with a foam rubber pad.

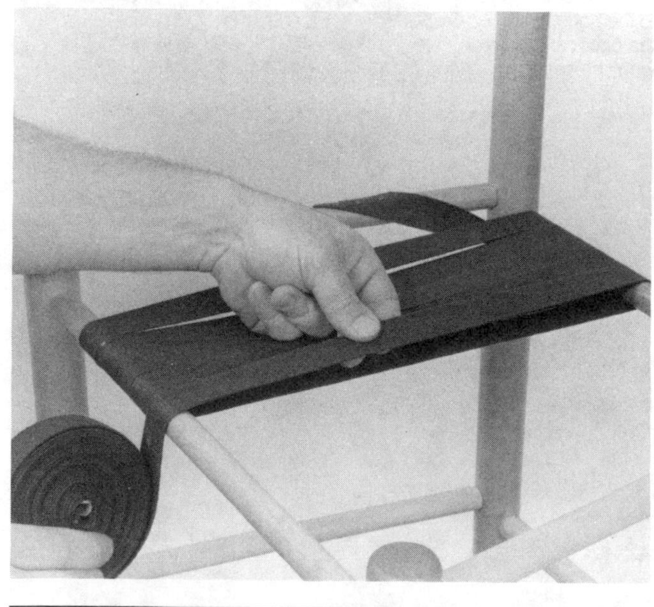

Figure 14. Wrap the warp tape over the back and front rails until you have completely covered the back rail. Leave the corners on either side open.

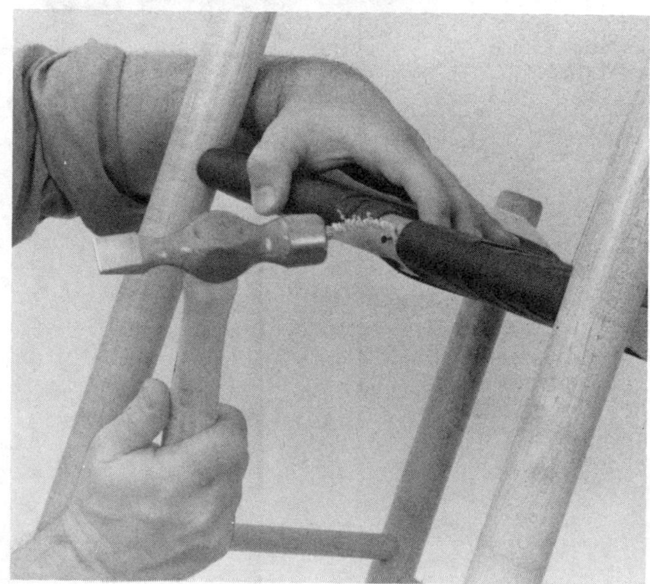

Figure 16. Temporarily, pull the warps aside and tack the beginning end of the woof tape to the back rail.

The top and bottom warps will have a large pocket between them. Stuff this pocket with a 1″-thick foam pad, cut to the shape of the seat. (See Figure 15.) Carefully work the pad in between the tape until it completely fills the space between the rails.

Insert the end of a 10-yard woof roll into the space between the warps, near the back rail. Temporarily, spread the warps on the back rail apart and tack the woof tape to it. (See Figure 16.) Bring the woof tape under the left side rail and begin weaving it over and under the top warp tapes. How you weave the woofs in and out of the warps will determine the pattern of the weave. If you weave over one and under one, alternating at the beginning of each new warp row, then you will make a simple checkerboard pattern. If you weave over two and under two, skipping one at the beginning of each new row, you can make a herringbone pattern. (See Figure 17.)

Continue weaving the woofs, pulling the entire roll over and under the warps, slowly unrolling it as you go. (See Figure 18.) The pattern that you weave on the bottom of the chair should be exactly the same as what you weave on the top. Every two or three rows, stop weaving and "comb" the woof tapes with your fingers, evening them out so that the warps and the woofs are square to one another. (See Figure 19.)

As your weaving draws closer to the front rail, you will probably have to splice a 5-yard woof roll to the end of the 10-yard roll. Overlap the ends of the rolls and sew them together with a needle and thread. (See Figure 20.) Make this splice on a *bottom* woof, beneath the chair seat where it won't show.

As you finish up the woofs, the weaving will become tighter and tighter. During the last few rows, you won't be able to work with a roll; you'll have to unroll the woof tape and pull the whole length through the warps. You'll also find it increasingly hard to comb with your fingers. Instead, use the handle of a spoon to help even out the weave. (See Figure 21.)

When you finish the woofs, tack the tape to the underside of the front rail and cut it off. (See Figure 22.) Then fill in the corners with a short length of warp tape, so that you completely cover the front rail. Weave the short warp tapes

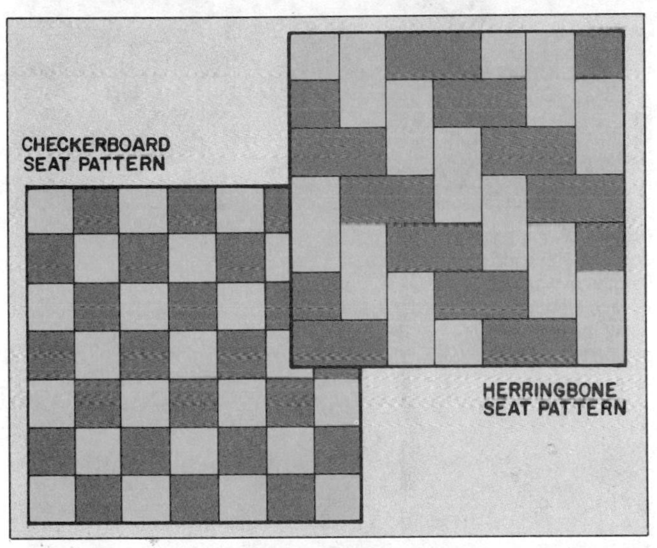

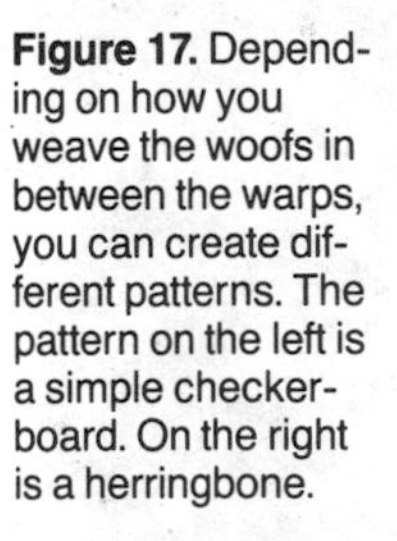

Figure 17. Depending on how you weave the woofs in between the warps, you can create different patterns. The pattern on the left is a simple checkerboard. On the right is a herringbone.

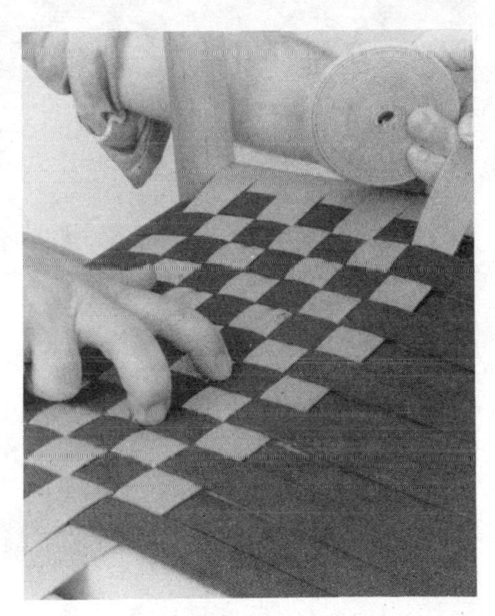

Figure 19. Every few rows, stop and comb the woof tapes with your fingers to make the woofs square to the warps.

Figure 18. Push the woof roll over and under the warps, slowly unrolling the tape as you go.

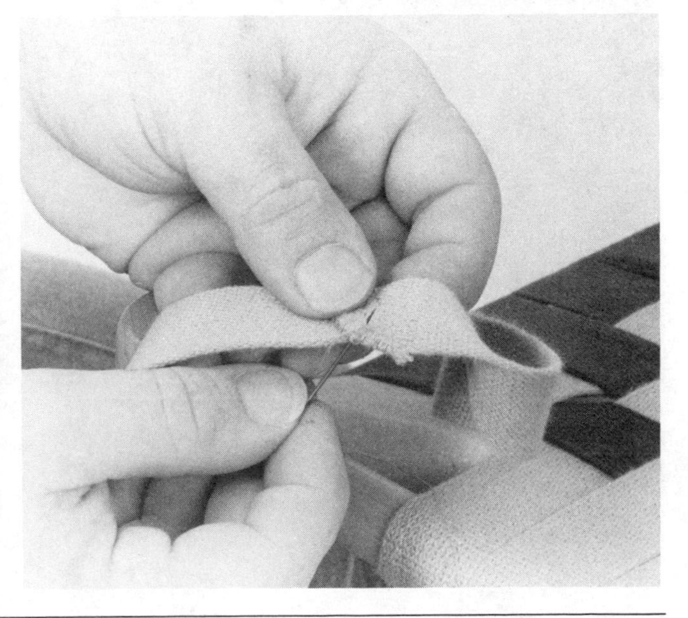

Figure 20. To splice two rolls of tape, overlap the ends and sew them together.

over and under the woofs, following the same pattern that began earlier. (See Figure 23.) If you have trouble weaving the tapes in and out, use the spoon to help pry the woofs apart where you need to insert the warps. When you've covered the front rail, temporarily spread the woof tapes apart and tack the ends of the short warps to the side rails. (See Figure 24.) When you put the woofs back in place, you won't be able to see where you've attached the warps.

After you finish the weave, give the whole seat a thorough going over with the handle of the spoon. Make sure that the weave is even and all the warps and woofs are square. Also make sure that you can't see any of the places where you tacked the tapes to the rails. If necessary, trim any loose threads that may be hanging out between the tapes — but be careful not to cut the tapes themselves! Finally, sit on the finished seat. Bounce up and down a couple of times. This will help to even out the tension in the tapes.

The author thanks K.C. Parkinson of the Connecticut Cane and Reed Company for his invaluable help in preparing this chapter.

Figure 21. As the weaving gets tighter and tighter, use the handle of a spoon to help even out the weave and square up the woofs and the warps.

Figure 23. Fill in the corners with short lengths of warp tape. Weave them in and out of the woofs, completing the pattern.

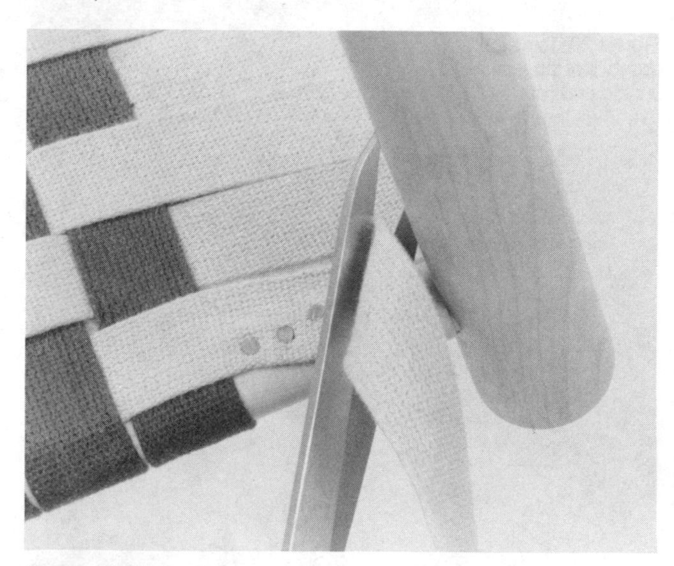

Figure 22. When you've completely covered the side rails, tack the end of the woof tape to the underside of the front rail.

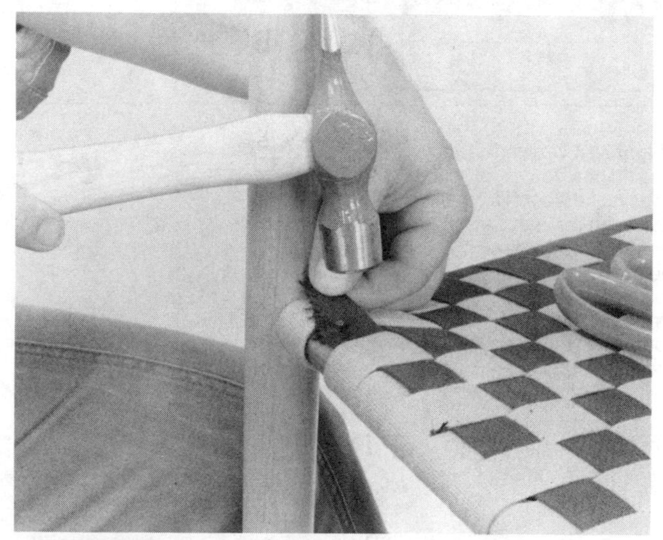

Figure 24. Temporarily spread the woof tapes apart and tack the ends of the short warp tapes to the side rails.

Text by David Wakefield.

Drying Your Own Lumber

Invest a little time and save bundles when you buy lumber.

Unfortunately for woodworkers, wood costs money. There are ways to beat the high cost of lumber, however. You just have to do a little looking around.

The easiest way to save money on wood is to do what the furniture companies do — buy in quantity. If you live in an area where there are hardwood forests, there will probably be a hardwood distributor nearby where you can order lumber. However, you'll have to buy somewhere in the neighborhood of 500-1000 board feet to get the best prices. Even if you had the cash to buy ten year's worth of lumber, where would you put it?

Buying from a Sawmill

The other way to get hardwood economically is to go directly to the sawmill. In many states, if you write to the Department of Natural Resources, they will send you a book with all the registered sawmills in the state, listed by county. This book will also tell you the number of board feet that each sawmill cuts per year (which will give you a good idea of the size of the operation), and the services available: planing, resawing, kiln-drying, and so on.

If you live in a rural wooded area, as I do, there will probably be three small unlisted sawmills for every large one listed. Look around. Check the phone book. Sometimes these mills will be sawing mostly railroad ties and have stacks of 4/4 board left over. They may sell these cheap to get rid of them. Also, many railroad tie and pallet sawmills will know enough to set aside cabinet-grade walnut and cherry logs, but won't have the established market to sell the lumber at top prices. You may be able to get some real bargains.

Kiln-drying — Pros and Cons

You may have found a sawmill that will supply you with green lumber, and you're considering having it kiln-dried. (The sawyer should be able to put you in touch with kiln operators in the vicinity.) If that's the case, you'll want to know a few things about kiln-drying.

The main advantage of kiln-drying is that it's fast. Air-drying wood takes at least a year. In a kiln, however, green wood can be dried in as little as two weeks. Although most kilns will dry only their own wood, you may find one that will dry your lumber. This could enable you to get started working in a matter of weeks.

The other advantage to kiln-drying is that it takes the moisture content a bit lower than air-drying because it drives out the 'bound water' — water held inside the cell walls. This process, however, makes wood 'thirsty'. Kiln-dried lumber will have a tendency to take on moisture in your shop unless the ends of the boards are painted and you store your lumber in a very dry area, such as a loft or attic.

Be careful that the storage area isn't *too* hot, though, or the ends of the boards may check. There is still some moisture present in kiln-dried lumber (about 7%), and excessive heat will drive this out too quickly. However, if you have to choose between a hot storage area or a wet one, take the heat. Changes in humidity are far more destructive to wood than changes in temperature. If the only space you have available for wood storage is damp, install a dehumidifier to keep it dry.

There are three distinct disadvantages to kiln-drying. First, kiln-dried lumber tends to be more brittle. Some woodworkers use air-dried wood exclusively because it has a lively resilience that is lost in kiln-drying. Secondly, drying wood too quickly can cause surface checking and/or case hardening. This is especially common with oak. (See Figure 1.) And finally, the color may be changed slightly. Walnut is a prime example. When walnut is kiln-dried, it's usually steamed. The steam disperses the tannins responsible for the dark colors evenly throughout the rest of the wood. The dark and light areas (heartwood and sapwood) blend together. This process makes more of the wood into high-grade lumber, since sapwood is worth less than heartwood, but it washes out the depth and intensity of the color. A piece of air-dried walnut often has a rich purple cast to it which is lost in the steaming process.

Figure 1. If the moisture is removed from a board too quickly, it will form surface checks. This is sometimes called 'case hardening'.

Air-drying — Pros and Cons

The main advantage to air-drying lumber is that you can do it yourself for free. Once you've built a drying rack, your only cost is for transportation from the sawmill. And you'll find that the price of green lumber at the sawmill is substantially lower than dried lumber from the kiln or the distributor. In some cases, it may be several dollars per board foot lower. This will vary quite a bit, depending on the type of wood and the area of the country, but the savings will be attractive in any case.

There are three disadvantages to air-drying lumber. The first is that it requires space. Five hundred board feet of lumber will make a stack 4′ wide by 8′ long by 2½′ tall. The second disadvantage is that it takes time. Generally speaking, it takes a year to dry a 4/4 (1″ thick) board, 2¼ years for an 8/4 board, and four to five years for a 12/4 board.

The third disadvantage is that air-drying doesn't remove as much moisture from the wood as kiln-drying, and the wood is less stable. However, if you carefully design and build your projects to allow for the movement of the wood, this shouldn't be a problem.

Tip ◆ The old masters had to work with air-dried wood exclusively — there were no kilns. They controlled the tendency of the wood to expand and contract by finishing both the inside *and* outside of their completed pieces. They were also careful to apply just as many coats of finish to the inside as the outside. This way, the wood "breathed" the moisture in and out *evenly* on all sides of the boards as the humidity changed. The boards expanded and contracted at the same rate on all sides, and there was little tendency for the wood to warp or twist.

How to Air-Dry Your Own Lumber

The most important factor in air-drying is the air circulation. Although the basement may seem to be the perfect place to dry your wood, the opposite is probably true. Usually, the air in a basement is stagnant and humid. There is little circulation to remove the humidity. More often than not, green lumber stored in a basement will mildew and rot, rather than dry.

An attic, on the other hand, is usually too hot, and will dry the wood too quickly. As I said before, this results in surface checking. The wood on the outside of the board dries faster than the inside. As it dries, it shrinks and cracks develop.

The best place to dry wood, believe it or not, is outside. Look for a spot that gets a breeze and isn't exposed to a lot of direct sunlight. This will allow the wood to dry at a slow, even rate. You can build a simple drying rack, as shown in Figure 2. Make sure this rack is well off the ground and perfectly flat. Do not put the cross supports more than two feet apart or the boards will sag as they dry.

Once you've built the drying rack, you're ready to stack the lumber. To allow proper air circulation between each board, you'll need to put 'stickers' (small sticks) in between the rows to ensure proper air circulation. I use commercial furring strips for stickers, but any dry wood will do. The stickers should be as long as the width of the

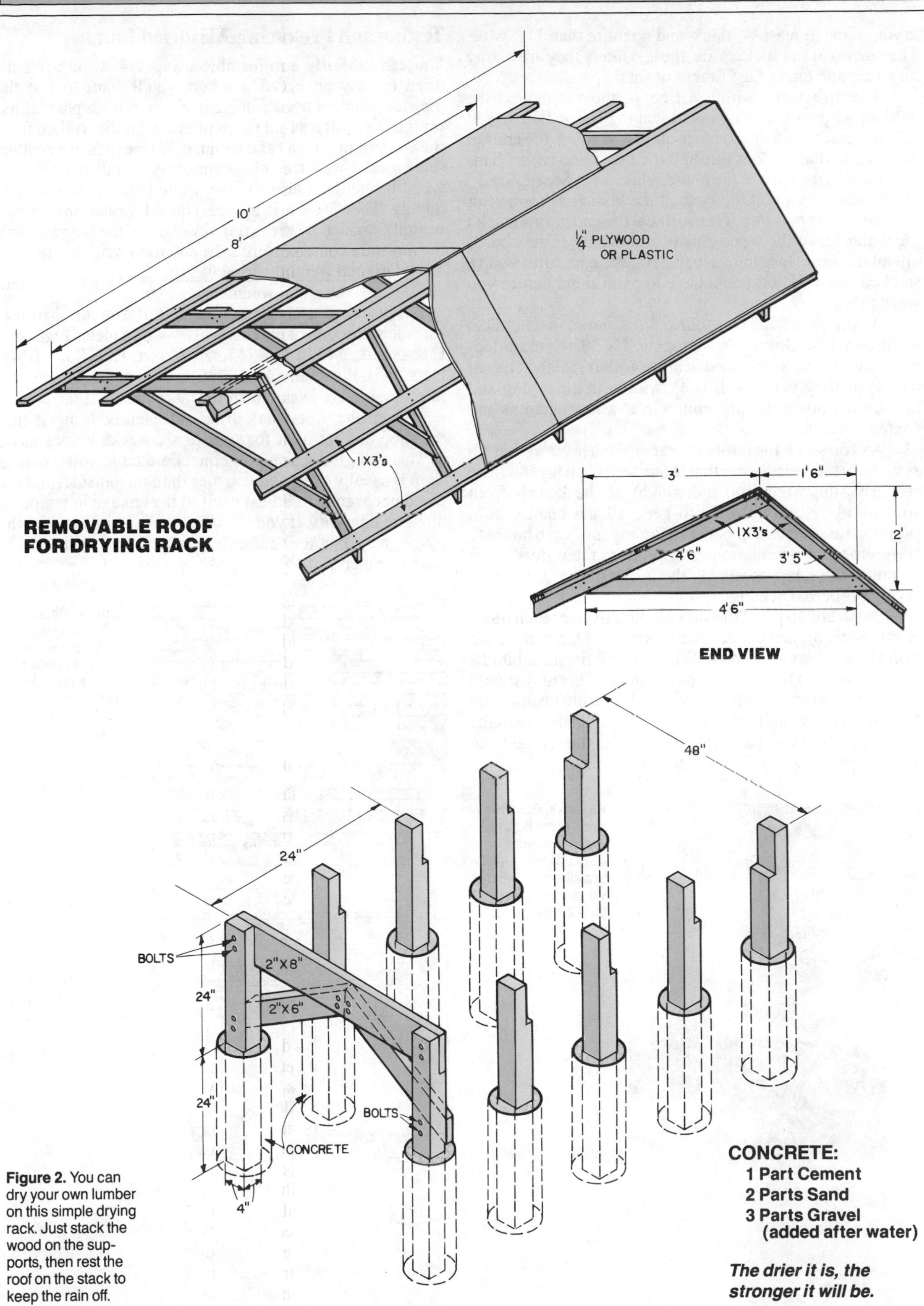

Figure 2. You can dry your own lumber on this simple drying rack. Just stack the wood on the supports, then rest the roof on the stack to keep the rain off.

drying rack, at least ¾″ thick, and no more than 1½″ wide. The narrower the stickers are, the less likely they are to trap moisture and encourage fungus or rot.

The structures within a tree — the xylem and the phloem — pass water up and down the trunk. Because of this, water leaves a board more quickly through the ends of the boards than it does through the faces and edges. This can result in the ends of the boards checking. (See Figure 3.) To prevent this, paint the ends of the boards as soon after they are cut as possible. This will seal the end grains and let the water leave the wood slowly and evenly. If the boards are all the same length, you can paint the ends after you've stacked them. If not, you'll have to paint them before you stack them.

A note on sealing end grains: The Chapman Chemical Company, P.O. Box 9158, Memphis, TN 38109, manufactures a wax emulsion called Sealtite #60 to seal the ends of boards as they dry. It will work with both air-drying and kiln-drying processes, and comes in a variety of colors and container sizes.

As you stack the lumber, arrange each layer so that it's as wide as the layer beneath it. That way, each layer will be properly supported, and the weight of the boards from above and below will help to keep all the boards from cupping. Leave space in between the edges of each board to allow for air circulation. Positioning them too close together will keep boards on the inside of the stack from drying properly. (See Figure 4.)

Be careful to place the stickers directly over each other, in line with the supports. (See Figure 5.) Don't stack the wood more than 4′–5′ thick. When you've finished, build a simple roof and lay it on top of the stack. This roof should have plenty of overhang, to keep the rain from dripping on the stack. If you can't build your rack in the shade, paint the roof with aluminum paint. This will reflect the sunlight and prevent the stack from getting too hot.

Figure 3. Paint the ends of the boards to prevent them from checking. If left unpainted, the ends will dry out faster than the rest of the board.

Testing and Preparing Air-dried Lumber

You can be fairly comfortable using 4/4 wood after it's dried for a year. For 8/4 wood, you'll want to test the moisture content before using it. There is a simple method for this. Saw off a small piece of green lumber (taken from the *inside* of the stack) and weigh it. An inexpensive postage scale works well for this purpose. Now put the piece of wood in the oven at 350° for a few hours to dry it thoroughly. Then weigh it again. The difference in the two weights, divided by the original weight of the wood, equals the moisture content. Here's the equation written out:

$$\frac{\text{Original weight - dried weight}}{\text{Original weight}} = \text{\% Moisture content}$$

A note on measuring moisture content: You can also measure moisture content the easy way — with a meter. Lignomat U.S.A. Ltd., 14345 N.E. Morris Court, P.O. Box 30145, Dept. B-H, Portland, OR 97230, makes several models of moisture meters. Write them for more information.

Once the wood has dried sufficiently, bring it into the shop and let it sit for four to six weeks before using it. This will give it time to get acclimated to your shop. A shop is usually drier and warmer than the outside, and the wood needs time to adjust itself to the change in temperature and humidity. If you cut into the wood right away, the pieces may change shape before you get a chance to assemble them.

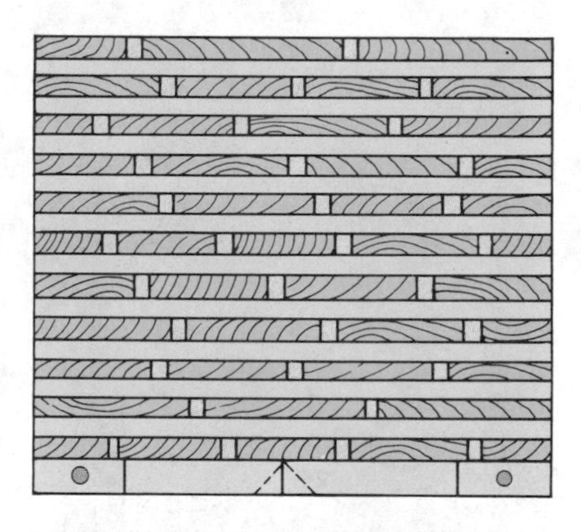

Figure 4. When you stack your green wood, don't stack the boards edge to edge. Leave a space in between each board so that the air can circulate freely.

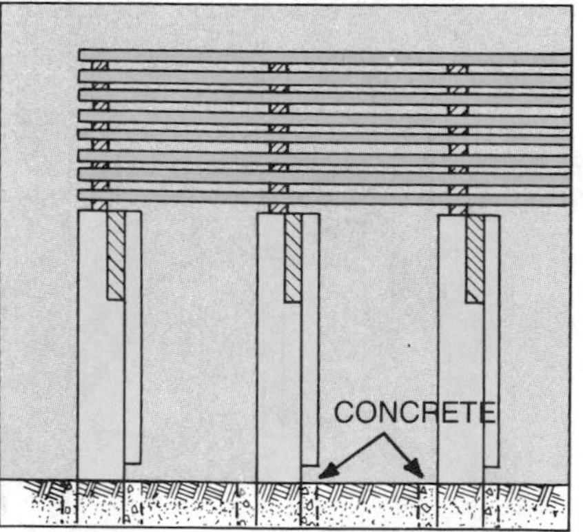

Figure 5. If you're careless about where you place the stickers, many of the boards will dry with a bad warp or bend. The stickers must be carefully placed one above the next, directly over the supports.